A Christmas Treasury

A CHRISTMAS TREASURY

EDITED BY JACK NEWCOMBE

THE VIKING PRESS ✳ NEW YORK

LIBRARY OF CONGRESS CATALOGING IN PUBLICATION DATA
Main entry under title:
A Christmas treasury.
   1. Christmas—Literary collections. I. Newcombe,
Jack.
PN6071.C6C57   808.8′33   81-50583
ISBN 0-670-22110-4   AACR2

Printed in the United States of America
Set in CRT Garamond

Pages 473–74 constitute an extension of the copyright page.

Grateful acknowledgment is made to the following for permission to reprint copyrighted material:

Audubon and George Plimpton: "Tsi-Lick! Goes the Henslow's" (retitled: "The Christmas Bird Count"), by George Plimpton. From *Audubon*, November 1973, Vol. 75, No. 6. Copyright © 1973 by George Plimpton.

The Estate of J. M. Barrie and Hodder & Stoughton: "The Ghost of Christmas Eve," from *My Lady Nicotine* by J. M. Barrie, 1913.

Curtis Brown Ltd. and A. P. Watt Ltd.: "The Christmas That Almost Wasn't," by Ogden Nash. Copyright © 1957 by Ogden Nash, published by Little, Brown and Company.

The Caxton Printers, Ltd.: "Of Argonauts and Holly Wreaths," from *Christmas on the American Frontier 1800–1900* by John E. Baur. Published in 1961 by The Caxton Printers, Ltd., Caldwell, Idaho.

Chatto and Windus Ltd., Mrs. Laura Huxley, and Harper & Row, Publishers, Inc.: "New-Fashioned Christmas," from *The Olive Tree and Other Essays* by Aldous Huxley. Copyright 1937 by Aldous Huxley; renewed © 1965 by Laura A. Huxley.

Mrs. Robert P. Tristram Coffin: "Christmas in Maine," by Robert P. Tristram Coffin. Copyright 1935, 1941 by Robert P. Tristram Coffin.

Delacorte Press/Seymour Lawrence: A Christmas Story, by Katherine Anne Porter, illustrated by Ben Shahn. Text copyright 1946, © 1967 by Katherine Anne Porter. Illustrations copyright © 1967 by Ben Shahn.

J. M. Dent & Sons Ltd.: "The White Road," by E. F. Bozman. From *Ghost Stories* Selected and Introduced by John Hampden, An Everyman's Library Edition.

For Laura, Scott, Tod, and Polly

The Gospel. St. Luke ii. i.

And it came to pass in those days, that there went out a decree from Cæsar Augustus, that all the world should be taxed. (And this taxing was first made when Cyrenius was governor of Syria.) And all went to be taxed, every one into his own city. And Joseph also went up from Galilee, out of the city of Nazareth, into Judæa, unto the city of David, which is called Bethlehem; (because he was of the house and lineage of David:) to be taxed with Mary his espoused wife, being great with child. And so it was, that, while they were there, the days were accomplished that she should be delivered. And she brought forth her firstborn son, and wrapped him in swaddling clothes, and laid him in a manger; because there was no room for them in the inn. And there were in the same country shepherds abiding in the field, keeping watch over their flock by night. And, lo, the angel of the Lord came upon them, and the glory of the Lord shone round about them: and they were sore afraid. And the angel said unto them, Fear not: for, behold, I bring you good tidings of great joy, which shall be to all people. For unto you is born this day in the city of David a Saviour, which is Christ the Lord. And this shall be a sign unto you; Ye shall find the babe wrapped in swaddling clothes, lying in a manger. And suddenly there was with the angel a multitude of the heavenly host praising God, and saying, Glory to God in the highest, and on earth peace, good will toward men.

The Gospel. St. Matthew ii. 1.

When Jesus was born in Bethlehem of Judæa, in the days of Herod the king, behold, there came wise men from the east to Jerusalem, saying, Where is he that is born King of the Jews? for we have seen his star in the east, and are come to worship him. When Herod the king had heard these things, he was troubled, and all Jerusalem with him. And when he had gathered all the chief priests and scribes of the people together, he demanded of them where Christ should be born. And they said unto him, In Bethlehem of Judæa: for thus it is written by the prophet, And thou Bethlehem, in the land of Juda, art not the least among the princes of Juda: for out of thee shall come a Governor, that shall rule my people Israel. Then Herod, when he had privily called the wise men, enquired of them diligently what time the star appeared. And he sent them to Bethlehem, and said, Go and search diligently for the young child; and when ye have found him, bring me word again, that I may come and worship him also. When they had heard the king, they departed; and, lo, the star, which they saw in the east, went before them, till it came and stood over where the young child was. When they saw the star, they rejoiced with exceeding great joy. And when they were come into the house, they saw the young child with Mary his mother, and fell down, and worshipped him: and when they had opened their treasures, they presented unto him gifts; gold, and frankincense, and myrrh. And being warned of God in a dream that they should not return to Herod, they departed into their own country another way.

CONTENTS

＊　x　＊

INTRODUCTION

The Christmas legend was such a large part of my growing up in Vermont that the celebration and its ideal surroundings have become inseparable in my mind. There were times, I am sure, when I couldn't imagine Christmas existing far beyond the high banks of snow that lined the streets of my hometown. The stories I first listened to and those I later read only strengthened the impression that Christmas was meant to take place where I lived so easily, with the long season's expectations, sights, sounds; the increased reminders of good and evil; the mandatory churchgoing; the seeking of harmony among family and friends; the belief in small miracles and in the spirits released through the pages of Dickens.

There was always snow in Vermont—except for one frightening year—and it wasn't until I finally left home that I realized Christmas might thrive without it, that it could take place in the imagination, one properly stoked by memories and the rereading of a favorite book or Christmas story. The images have traveled long distances with me, to holidays spent in Britain, Europe, California, New York, Washington, and once in Bethlehem, Pennsylvania.

When I was young we listened to stories about Christmas, read about Christmas, waited with anticipation for the gift book that was always there under the tree. Oh, of course, we sang about Christmas and in school participated in verse-speaking choirs on Christmas themes. But it was through the story reading that we supported the fantasy of a season especially made for those of us lucky enough to be young, and not too poor, in Vermont.

The narrow, hard-packed paths we followed to and from school were the Great North Road of Dickens where "it snowed and snowed, and still it snowed and never left off snowing." And when we passed the stark chapel spire on College Hill the winter night-wind did have "a dismal trick of wandering round and round a building of that sort, and moaning as it goes; and of trying, with its unseen hand, the windows and doors and seeking out some crevices by which to enter." It didn't matter that the chapel bell tolled somnolently whatever the season. "They were old Chimes, trust me. Centuries ago, these bells had been baptized by bishops; so many centuries ago, that the register of their baptism was lost long, long before the memory of man, and no one knew their names."

When, reluctantly, we headed home from the sliding hill or the playground skating rink, provoked by the rapid nightfall of late December, we surely felt kinship with Kenneth Grahame's Rat and Mole as they walked into the small village on "soft feet over a thin fall of powdery snow" where "little was visible but squares of a dusky orange-red on either side of the street, where the firelight or lamplight of each cottage overflowed through the casements into the dark world without. Most of the low latticed windows were innocent of blinds, and to the lookers-in from outside, the inmates, gathered round the tea-table, absorbed in handiwork, or talking with laughter and gesture, had each that happy grace . . . which goes with perfect unconsciousness of observation."

Approaching our homes, sleds bouncing lightly behind us or skates laced together and slung over our shoulders, we looked eagerly into familiar windows for the signs of the season: the box of tree lights waiting to be tested, mysterious and brown-wrapped packages freshly arrived by mail, the last touches being made on the wreath which had grown magnificently from a few backyard evergreens and an old wire coat hanger. Our noses wrinkled with anticipation at the smell of Christmas cookies left out to cool on kitchen counters.

I am not certain when I first became acquainted with the stories of English Christmas in Washington Irving's *Sketch Book,* but there were scenes and even a character or two that withstood the passage of time and fitted suitably into my small landscape. It was then possible to believe in, however momentarily, the words of the old song:

> A man might then behold
> At Christmas, in each hall
> Good fires to curb the cold
> And meat for great and small.
> The neighbors were friendly bidden

And all had welcome true,
The poor from the gates were not chidden
When this old cap was new.

For there was a wealthy man in our town not unlike Irving's Simon Bracebridge, the kindly bachelor and master of revels among children. Each Christmas Eve dozens of us who had enjoyed his generosity through the year (picnics, parties, home movies and travel reels from his wondrous projector) went to his large brick home on the far side of the college campus, lighted our candles, and sang carols. He, too, had "a sparkle of the eye and a voice that was by no means bad." Dressed as splendidly as a squire he came to the door and sang with us before inviting us to share the mounds of candies, cookies, cakes, and fruits waiting inside.

Years later, when I finally did get a chance to experience Christmas in England, I found that the practice of caroling had commercial considerations as strong as the illuminations festooning London's Oxford Street. The sound of approaching voices, the sight of wavering tapers in Chelsea where we lived meant reaching into the Christmas gratuity fund already depleted by the milkman, postman, dustmen, green grocer, butcher. A neighbor described an experience with an enterprising holiday visitor: he answered his front door knocker in the early, already dark, hours of Christmas Eve and found a boy of about eight or nine standing alone at the entrance, wearing a baggy sweater and a football scarf wrapped securely around his neck.

"A shilling for the carolers, sir?" the boy asked.
"Why, yes," the neighbor said. "But where are they?"
"That would be me, sir," came the quick response. And he launched into a high-pitched "Hark, The Herald Angels Sing!"

My neighbor said that he tipped the solo caroler a pound note and the thought of his youthful initiative kept his spirits soaring throughout the holidays.

The boy was, in his own way, following the remunerative footsteps of the eighteenth-century waits who "rude as may be their minstrelsy" break "upon the midwatches of a winter night with the effect of perfect harmony"—as Washington Irving commented.

Thomas Hardy deals sensitively (and sometimes farcically) with the tradition in the early chapters of *Under the Greenwood Tree,* the story of the ecclesiastical bandsmen. Hardy had originally called the novel, published in 1872, "The Mellstock Quire." In a preface to a new edition written a quarter-century later, he lamented the passing of these small orchestral groups.

> They usually received so little payment for their performances that their efforts were really a labour of love ... the gratuities received yearly by the musicians were somewhat as follows: From the manor-house ten shillings and a supper; from the vicar ten shillings; from the farmers five shillings each; from each cottage-household one shilling; amounting altogether to not more than ten shillings a head annually— just enough, as an old executant told me, to pay for their fiddlestrings, repairs, rosin and music paper (which they mostly ruled themselves).

I am pleased to include Thomas Hardy's dedicated church musicians in this collection of writings about Christmas. The chapters from his second and most ebullient novel are reminders that the best of "Christmas literature" was the result not of the author's intentional effort to write of the season's myths and sentimental traditions but of the use of the holiday to serve appropriately the fictional narrative. In Melville's *Moby-Dick* the *Pequod* sets sail from Nantucket on Christmas Day, with Captain Ahab "invisibly enshrined within his cabin." For Ishmael the beginning of the perilous voyage on a day which quickly turned to darkness in the wintry Atlantic provoked thoughts of the paradox of Christmas on shipboard where one could expect only a "poke in the rear or a kick in the ass."

In Willa Cather's "December Night," an episode in *Death Comes for the Archbishop,* the recurring doubts of Father Latour about his mission in the heathen surroundings of old Santa Fe are removed by the clandestine visit to the empty Roman church by a Mexican woman slave as the Novena of Christmas approaches. Although a selection from an essay by Henry Thoreau does not mention Christmas, the reader can draw from it the rewards of reflection and solitude that can be attained during this change of season.

If you ask friends and strangers for "best-remembered" stories about Christmas you are not apt to hear the names of Melville, Cather, or Hardy, but those of Charles Dickens, the father of Christmas storytellers, Washington Irving, and, perhaps, O. Henry. The stories they remember listening to when they were below reading age were those of Beatrix Potter, Hans Christian Andersen, Mary Mapes Dodge, the famous verse that Clement Moore first wrote for his own children in 1822. Included here are several of those favorites that are as secure among the tales read aloud at Christmas as is the appearance of the angel at the summit of the traditionally adorned Christmas tree.

Dickens, writing profusely about Christmas and reciting his popular works before audiences in England and America, became the author who seemed to embody the very spirit of the season. "Who can be insensible to the outpourings of good feeling, and the honest interchange of affectionate attachment, which abound in this season of the year?" Dickens wrote in *Sketches by Boz* in 1836.

> A Christmas family-party! We know of nothing in nature more delightful! There seems a magic in the very name of Christmas.... Kindly hearts that have yearned towards each other, but have been withheld by false notions of pride and self-dignity, are again reunited, and all is kindness and benevolence! Would that Christmas lasted the whole year through (as it ought), and that the prejudices and passions which deform our better nature, were never called into action among those to whom they should ever be strangers!

Dickens was an ideal narrator for a time when the ceremonies of Christmas, many of German origin and only recently imported, were expanding among the middle and even lower classes in England and America. Queen Victoria set the grand scale for family gathering, gift giving, the spreading of monarchial bounty. During her reign Christmas was declared an official day of rest, an act that at last recognized the right of the working class to celebrate the occasion. It came some years after Dickens had touched the sentiments of the English middle classes with his 1843 fable of greed and goodwill, *A Christmas Carol,* which became the most famous of Dickens's Christmas books, although both *The Chimes* and *The Cricket on the Hearth,* also written in the 1840s, were nearly as popular at the time.

The Pickwick Papers, published when Dickens was in his early twenties, provides the description of the ultimate in Christmas merriment, the Pickwickian celebration at Mr. Wardle's Manor Farm, Dingley Dell. Yet at the beginning of the chapter the young Dickens reminds the reader of the distance between the recollection and the event itself, and of how Christmastime has the trick of awakening dormant sympathies. "Happy, happy Christmas, that can win us back to the delusions of our childish days," he cautions, taking a stand on the far side of sentimentality.

He then takes us aboard the Muggleton coach, crowded with Mr. Pickwick, his friends, their gifts of codfish and barrels of oysters, on the quintessential journey to Christmas. It is the stuff that legend, etching, greeting cards are made of: the confident, sure-handed coachman; the response in darkened villages to the sound of horse hoof and wheel-rim on uneven cobblestones; Mr. Pickwick and friend Mr. Tupman hurrying in their greatcoats to ascend the coach after popping out at a country-town inn for a warming glass of ale. And the Christmas remembered at Dingley Dell is bright with dancing, eating, and drinking, kissing under the mistletoe, a joining of family, guests, and servants for the traditional storytelling.

Some twenty years after *The Pickwick Papers,* Dickens, as editor of *Household Words,* was obligated to provide "Christmas stories" for the enlarged, holiday issues of the magazine. The stories did not necessarily have Christmas themes, but I have chosen the first part of one, "The Holly-Tree," which sets an austere holiday scene at a remote inn during a splendid Dickensian snowfall. It becomes an appealing parody by a master of Christmastime entertainment.

The Dickens influence on Christmas writing continued for generations after his death in 1870, but neither subsequent authors' enjoyment of the holidays nor their ability to express it seemed to approach his. Yet modern writers have, with a made-for-Christmas offering, been able to reach a far wider readership than any attracted to their more serious work. Dylan Thomas's nostalgic, fanciful *A Child's Christmas in Wales,* which developed from a broadcast he did for the BBC in 1945, has been read by countless people who are unfamiliar with his lyrical poetry. Truman Capote's sentimental return to a rural Alabama childhood in *A Christmas Memory* has probably made a deep impression on more readers than his artful early writing in *Breakfast at Tiffany's* or his later reportage.

As Victorian adherence to custom began to disappear from Christmas texts—easy prey to a more aggressive commercialism—humor and satire had their brief, popular place. American magazine and newspaper readers could look forward to a seasonal pouring from Christopher Morley, Damon Runyon, Franklin P. Adams, H. L. Mencken, Frank Sullivan, James Thurber. Cartoonists and writers of humor of the pretelevision era of the 1930s and early forties, following the sure satirical paths set long ago by William Makepeace Thackeray and Sir Max Beerbohm, among others, eagerly took on the ceremonies of the season. They made it more tolerable, often more joyous, for readers. If it is harder now to encounter examples of wit, or passable attempts at humor, in words written for and about the season, it is easily argued that there is little enough of it at all times of the year. Yesterday's anticipated irony and spoof have been replaced by today's unvarying recipes for coping ("How to Avoid Christmas Blahs"; "You, Too, Can Stop Hating Christmas") and for home baking, home decorating, and home gift making.

Before most of us were even aware of it, the cadences of Christmas verse and Christmas carol were gliding lightly through our heads. Clement Moore's verse made childhood memorizing easy; soft, hymnal syllables hung in the air until they became the everyday sounds we heard in the weeks that stretched before Christmas. Although the merry rhymesters have pretty much carried the day on volume alone, serious poets for centuries have responded to the religious origins as well as the succeeding follies of Christmas.

John Milton's "On the Morning of Christ's Nativity," which appeared just months following his degree from Christ's College, Cambridge, in 1629, is of major attraction for scholars. As a hymn of rejoicing for the "Heaven-born child," it remains for the rest of us as beautiful as any in the English language. Alfred, Lord Tennyson's thoughts of his dead friend, Arthur Hallam, and of the conflict he felt between faith and doubt, are heightened at Christmastime through several sections of "In Memoriam." Read the spare lines of Thomas Hardy's "The Oxen" and share the impact of the old folk-belief that cattle do drop to their knees at midnight, Christmas Eve, just as the animals responded in the stable at Bethlehem. Perhaps the most stunning lines since the New Testament on the birth of Christ are those of the sixteenth-century poet Robert Southwell in "The Burning Babe." It stays a shining reminder that poems of Christmas, written by the notable and the obscure, may bring a sense of discovery or the warmth of reacquaintance.

These contents, prose and verse, provide no particular tracing of the development of Christmas customs, no review of the variety of ethnic and religious expressions of the season or of the biblical telling of the miraculous vision and the adoration of the Magi. There are selections that suggest the evolution of the most popular mythical figure of childhood, St. Nicholas, a.k.a. Santa Claus. I have included several recollections of regional Christmas celebrations in the United States, some dating back to the country's early development, which indicate how enthusiastically Continental and English customs were adapted. There are examples of writers' preoccupation with the symbol of the Christmas tree, its stand in folklore, and its strong visibility today. Also, the Christmas feast has a pleasant continuity in writings about holidays in Victorian banquet halls, in mountain homes in northern Georgia, in small towns in Iowa, and in a black farming community in Virginia. For me these particular choices have this in common: they bring a surge of well-being, a touch of the "magic" Dickens felt, a wish to share the emotions and to raise a glass with the chorus of "Adeste Fideles" sung on a crystal-cold midnight.

A collection of Christmas writing should have no more predetermined shape than that of the evergreen just shaken free of its seller's twine. It should offer surprises, a few personal gaps and idiosyncrasies, the fullness one hoped for, and familiarity enough to engage one's memory of Christmases past. It should also furnish reading pleasure that will spread through the seasons.

JACK NEWCOMBE

THE FIR TREE

HANS CHRISTIAN ANDERSEN

Out in the forest stood a pretty little Fir Tree. It had a good place; it could have sunlight, air there was in plenty, and all around grew many larger comrades—pines as well as firs. But the little Fir Tree wished ardently to become greater. It did not care for the warm sun and the fresh air; it took no notice of the peasant children, who went about talking together when they had come out to look for strawberries and raspberries. Often they came with a whole potful, or had strung berries on a straw. Then they would sit down by the little Fir Tree and say, "How pretty and small that one is!" and the Tree did not like to hear that at all.

"Oh, if I were only as great a tree as the others!" sighed the little Fir. "Then I would spread my branches far around, and look out from my crown into the wide world. The birds would then build nests in my boughs, and when the wind blew, I could nod just as grandly as the others yonder."

He took no pleasure in the sunshine, in the birds, and in the red clouds that went sailing over him morning and evening. When it was winter and the snow lay all around, white and sparkling, a hare would often come jumping along, and spring right over the little Fir. Oh! this made him so angry. But two winters went by, and when the third came, the little Tree had grown so tall that the hare was obliged to run around it.

"Oh! to grow, to grow, and become old; that's the only fine thing in the world," thought the Tree.

In the autumn, woodcutters always came and felled a few of the largest trees; that was done this year too. And the little Fir Tree, which was now quite well grown, shuddered with fear, for the great stately trees fell to the ground with a crash, and their branches were cut off, so that the trees looked quite naked, long, and slender—they could hardly be recognized. But then they were laid upon wagons, and horses dragged them away out of the wood. Where were they going? What destiny awaited them?

In the spring, when the Swallows and the Stork came, the Tree asked them, "Do you know where they were taken? Did you not meet them?"

The Swallows knew nothing about it, but the Stork looked thoughtful, nodded his head, and said, "Yes, I think so. I met many new ships when I flew out of Egypt; on the ships were stately masts. I fancy that these were the trees. They smelt like fir. I can assure you they're stately—very stately."

"Oh, that I were only big enough to go over the sea! What kind of thing is this sea, and how does it look?"

"It would take too long to explain all that," said the Stork, and he went away.

"Rejoice in thy youth," said the Sunbeams. "Rejoice in thy fresh growth, and in the young life that is within thee."

And the wind kissed the Tree, and the dew wept tears upon it; but the Fir Tree did not understand that.

When Christmas time approached, quite young trees were felled, sometimes trees which were neither so old nor so large as this Fir Tree that never rested but always wanted to go away. These young trees, which were almost the most beautiful, kept all their branches; they were put upon wagons, and horses dragged them away out of the wood.

"Where are they all going?" asked the Fir Tree. "They are not greater than I—indeed one of them was much smaller. Why do they keep all their branches? Whither are they taken?"

"We know that! We know that!" chirped the Sparrows. "Yonder in the town we looked in at the windows. We know where they go. Oh! they are dressed up in the greatest pomp and splendor that can be imagined. We have looked in at the windows, and have perceived that they are planted in the middle of the warm room, and adorned with the most beautiful things—gilt apples, honey cakes, playthings, and many hundreds of candles."

"And then?" asked the Fir Tree, and trembled through all its branches. "And then? What happens then?"

"Why, we have not seen anything more," said the Sparrows. "But it was incomparable."

"Perhaps I may be destined to tread this glorious path one day!" cried the Fir Tree rejoicingly. "That is even better than travelling across the sea. How painfully I long for it! If it were only Christmas now! Now I am great and grown-up, like the rest who were led away last year. Oh, if I were only on the carriage! If I were only in the warm room, among all the pomp and splendor! And then? Yes, then something even better will come, something far more charming, or else why should they adorn me so? There must be something grander, something greater still to come, but what? Oh! I'm suffering, I'm longing! I don't know, myself, what is the matter with me!"

"Rejoice in us," said Air and Sunshine. "Rejoice in thy fresh youth here in the woodland."

But the Fir Tree did not rejoice at all, but it grew and grew. Winter and summer it stood there, green, dark green. The people who saw it said, "That's a handsome tree!" and at Christmas time it was felled before any one of the others. The axe cut deep into its marrow, and the tree fell to the ground with a sigh. It felt a pain, a sensation of faintness, and could not think at all of happiness, for it was sad at parting from its home, from the place where it had grown up. It knew that it should never again see the dear old companions, the little bushes and flowers all around—perhaps not even the birds. The parting was not at all agreeable.

The Tree only came to itself when it was unloaded in a yard, with the other trees, and heard a man say, "This one is perfect; we only want this one!"

Now two servants came, in gay liveries, and carried the Fir Tree into a large, beautiful saloon. All around the walls hung pictures, and by the great stove stood large Chinese vases with lions on the covers. There were rocking chairs, silken sofas, great tables covered with picture books, and toys worth a hundred times a hundred dollars—at least the children said so. And the Fir Tree was put into a great tub filled with sand; but no one could see that it was a tub, for it was hung round with green cloth, and stood on a large, many-colored carpet. Oh, how the Tree trembled! What was to happen now? The servants and the young ladies, also, decked it out. On one branch they hung little nets cut out of colored paper—every net was filled with sweetmeats; golden apples and walnuts hung down as if they grew there; and more than a hundred little candles, red, white, and blue, were fastened to the different boughs. Dolls that looked exactly like real people—the Tree had never seen such before—swung upon the foliage, and high on the summit of the Tree was fixed a tinsel star. It was splendid, particularly splendid.

"This evening," said all, "this evening it will shine."

"Oh," thought the Tree, "that it were evening already! Oh, that the lights may be soon lit up! When may that be done? I wonder if trees will come out of the forest to look at me? Will the Sparrows fly against the panes? Shall I grow fast here, and stand adorned in summer and winter?"

Yes, he did not guess badly. But he had a complete backache from mere longing, and the backache is just as bad for a tree as the headache for a person.

At last the candles were lighted. What a brilliance, what splendor! The Tree trembled so in all its branches that one of the candles set fire to a green twig, and it was scorched.

"Heaven preserve us!" cried the young ladies, and they hastily put the fire out.

Now the Tree might not even tremble. Oh, that was terrible! It was so afraid of setting fire to some of its ornaments, and it was quite bewildered with all the brilliance. And now the folding doors were thrown open, and a number of children rushed in as if they would have overturned the whole Tree; the older people followed more deliberately. The little ones stood quite silent, but only for a minute; then they shouted till the room rang.

They danced gleefully round the Tree, and one present after another was plucked from it.

"What are they about?" thought the Tree. "What's going to be done?"

And the candles burned down to the twigs, and as they burned down they were extinguished, and then the children received permission to plunder the Tree. Oh! they rushed in upon it, so that every branch cracked again. If the Tree had not been fastened by the top and by the golden star to the ceiling, it would have fallen down.

The children danced about with their pretty toys. No one looked at the Tree except one old man, who came up and peeped among the branches, but only to see if a fig or an apple had not been forgotten.

"A story! A story!" shouted the children, and they drew a little fat man toward the Tree, and he sat down just beneath it—"for then we shall be in the green wood," said he, "and the tree may have the advantage of listening to my tale. But I can only tell one. Will you hear the story of Ivede-Avede, or of Klumpey-Dumpey, who fell downstairs, and still was raised up to honor and married the Princess?"

"Ivede-Avede!" cried some. "Klumpey-Dumpey!" cried others. And there was a great crying and shouting. Only the Fir Tree was quite silent, and thought, "Shall I not be in it? Shall I have nothing to do in it?" But he had been in the evening's amusement, and had done what was required of him.

And the fat man told about Klumpey-Dumpey, who fell downstairs, and yet was raised to honor and married the Princess. And the children clapped their hands, and cried, "Tell another! Tell another!" for they wanted to hear about Ivede-Avede. But they only got the story of Klumpey-Dumpey. The Fir Tree stood quite silent and thoughtful; never had the birds in the wood told such a story as that. Klumpey-Dumpey fell downstairs, and yet came to honor and married the Princess!

"Yes, so it happens in the world!" thought the Fir Tree, and believed it must be true, because that was such a nice man who had told it. "Well, who can know? Perhaps I shall fall downstairs too, and marry a Princess!" And it looked forward with pleasure to being adorned again, the next evening, with candles and toys, gold and fruit. "Tomorrow I shall not tremble," it thought. "I will rejoice in all my splendor. Tomorrow I shall hear the story of Klumpey-Dumpey again and, perhaps, that of Ivede-Avede too." And the Tree stood all night, quiet and thoughtful.

In the morning the servants and the chambermaid came in.

"Now my splendor will begin afresh," thought the Tree. But they dragged him out of the room, and upstairs to the garret, and here they put him in a dark corner where no daylight shone.

"What's the meaning of this?" thought the Tree. "What am I to do here? What is to happen?"

And he leaned against the wall, and thought and thought. And he had time enough, for days and nights went by and nobody came up; and when at length someone came, it was only to put some great boxes in a corner. Now the Tree stood quite hidden away, and the supposition was that it was quite forgotten.

"Now it's winter outside," thought the Tree. "The earth is hard and covered with snow, and people cannot plant me. Therefore I suppose I'm to be sheltered here until spring comes. How considerate that is! How good people are! If it were only not so dark here, and so terribly solitary—not even a little hare! That was pretty out there in the wood, when the snow lay thick and the hare sprang past; yes, even when he jumped over me—but then I did not like it. It is terribly lonely up here!"

"Piep! Piep!" said a little Mouse, and crept forward. And then came another little one. They smelt at the Fir Tree, and then slipped among the branches.

"It's horribly cold," said the two little Mice, "or else it would be comfortable here. Don't you think so, you old Fir Tree?"

"I'm not old at all," said the Fir Tree. "There are many much older than I."

"Where do you come from?" asked the Mice. "And what do you know?" They were dreadfully inquisitive. "Tell us about the most beautiful spot on earth. Have you been there? Have you been in the storeroom, where the cheeses lie on the shelves and hams hang from the ceiling, where one dances on tallow candles, and goes in thin and comes out fat?"

"I don't know that!" replied the Tree. "But I know the wood, where the sun shines and where the birds sing."

And then it told all about its youth. The little Mice had never heard anything of the kind; and they listened and said, "What a number of things you have seen! How happy you must have been!"

"I?" said the Fir Tree, and it thought about what it had told. "Yes, those were really quite happy times." But then he told of the Christmas Eve, when he had been hung with sweetmeats and candles.

"Oh!" said the little Mice, "how happy you have been, you old Fir Tree!"

"I'm not old at all," said the Tree. "I only came out of the wood this winter. I'm only rather backward in my growth."

"What splendid stories you can tell!" said the little Mice.

And the next night they came with four other little Mice, to hear what the Tree had to relate. And the more it said, the more clearly did it remember everything, and thought, "Those were quite merry days! But they may come again. Klumpey-Dumpey fell downstairs, and yet he married the Princess. Perhaps I may marry a Princess too!" And then the Fir Tree thought of a pretty little Birch Tree that grew out in the forest. For the Fir Tree, that Birch was a real Princess.

"Who's Klumpey-Dumpey?" asked the little Mice.

And then the Fir Tree told the whole story. It could remember every single word, and the little Mice were ready to leap to the very top of the tree with pleasure. Next night a great many more Mice came, and on Sunday even two Rats appeared. But these thought the story was not pretty, and the little Mice were sorry for that, for now they also did not like it so much as before.

"Do you only know one story?" asked the Rats.

"Only that one," replied the Tree. "I heard it on the happiest evening of my life; I did not think then how happy I was."

"It's a very miserable story. Don't you know any about bacon and tallow candles—a storeroom story?"

"No," said the Tree.

"Then we'd rather not hear you," said the Rats. And they went back to their own people. The little Mice at last stayed away also, and then the Tree sighed and said, "It was very nice when they sat around me, the merry little Mice, and listened when I spoke to them. Now that's past too. But I shall remember to be pleased when they take me out."

But when did that happen? Why, it was one morning that people came and rummaged in the garret. The boxes were put away, and the Tree brought out. They certainly threw him rather roughly on the floor, but a servant dragged him away at once to the stairs, where the daylight shone.

"Now life is beginning again!" thought the Tree.

It felt the fresh air and the first sunbeams, and now it was out in the courtyard. Everything passed so quickly that the Tree quite forgot to look at itself, there was so much to look at all round. The courtyard was close to a garden, and here everything was blooming. The roses hung fresh and fragrant over the little paling, the linden trees were in blossom, and the Swallows cried, "Quinze-wit! Quinze-wit! My husband's come!" But it was not the Fir Tree that they meant.

"Now I shall live!" said the Tree rejoicingly, and spread its branches far out. But, alas! they were all withered and yellow, and the Tree lay in the corner among nettles and weeds. The tinsel star was still upon it, and shone in the bright sunshine.

In the courtyard were playing a couple of the merry children who had danced round the Tree at Christmas time, and had rejoiced over it. One of the youngest ran up and tore off the golden star.

"Look what is sticking to the ugly old fir tree," said the child, and he trod upon the branches till they cracked again under his boots.

And the Tree looked at all the blooming flowers and the splendor of the garden, and then looked at itself, and wished it had remained in the dark corner of the garret. It thought of its fresh youth in the wood, of the merry Christmas Eve, and of the little Mice which had listened so pleasantly to the story of Klumpey-Dumpey.

"Past! past!" said the old Tree. "Had I but rejoiced when I could have done so! Past! past!"

And the servant came and chopped the Tree into little pieces; a whole bundle lay there. It blazed brightly under the great brewing copper, and it sighed deeply, and each sigh was like a little shot. And the children who were at play there ran up and seated themselves at the fire, looked into it, and cried, "Puff! Puff!" But at each explosion, which was a deep sigh, the tree thought of a summer day in the woods, or of a winter night there, when the stars beamed; he thought of Christmas Eve and of Klumpey-Dumpey, the only story he had ever heard or knew how to tell. And then the Tree was burned.

The boys played in the garden, and the youngest had on his breast a golden star, which the Tree had worn on its happiest evening. Now that was past, and the Tree's life was past, and the story is past too: Past! past!—and that's the way with all stories.

SAINT STEPHEN WAS A CLERK

ANONYMOUS

Saint Stephen was a clerk
  In King Herod's hall,
And servèd him of bread and cloth
  As ever king befall.

Stephen out of kitchen came,
  With boar's head on hand,
He saw a star was fair and bright
  Over Bethlehem stand.

He cast adown the boar's head
  And went into the hall:
"I forsake thee, King Herod,
  And thy workès all.

"I forsake thee, King Herod,
  And thy workès all;
There is a child in Bethlehem born
  Is better than we all."

"What aileth thee, Stephen?
  What is thee befall?
Lacketh thee either meat or drink
  In King Herod's hall?"

"Lacketh me neither meat nor drink
    In King Herod's hall;
There is a child in Bethlehem born
    Is better than we all."

"What aileth thee, Stephen?
    Art thou wode[1] or ginnest to breed?[2]
Lacketh thee either gold or fee[3]
    Or any rich weed?"

"Lacketh me neither gold nor fee,
    Ne none rich weed;
There is a child in Bethlehem born
    Shall helpen us at our need."

"That is all so sooth, Stephen,
    All so sooth, I-wis,[4]
As this capon crowè shall
    That lieth here in my dish."

That word was not so soon said,
    That word in that hall,
The capon crew *Christus natus est*
    Among the lordès all.

"Riseth up, my tormentors,
    By two and all by one,
And leadeth Stephen out of this town,
    And stoneth him with stone."

Tooken they Stephen
    And stoned him in the way,
And therefore in his even
    On Christès own day.

[1] Mad.
[2] Become (mad).
[3] Material wealth.
[4] *Gewiss,* certainly.

I Saw Three Ships

ANONYMOUS

I

As I sat under a sycamore tree,
/ A sycamore tree, a sycamore tree,
I looked me out upon the sea
On Christ's Sunday at morn.

II

I saw three ships a-sailing there,
/ A-sailing there, a-sailing there,
Jesus, Mary and Joseph they bare
On Christ's Sunday at morn.

III

Joseph did whistle and Mary did sing,
/ Mary did sing, Mary did sing,
And all the bells on earth did ring
For joy our Lord was born.

IV

O they sail'd in to Bethlehem!
/ To Bethlehem, to Bethlehem;
Saint Michael was the sterèsman,
Saint John sate in the horn.

V

And all the bells on earth did ring
/ On earth did ring, on earth did ring:
Welcome be thou Heaven's King,
On Christ's Sunday at morn!

THE CAT ON THE DOVREFELL

PETER CHRISTEN ASBJÖRNSEN and JÖRGEN MOE

from EAST OF THE SUN AND WEST OF THE MOON

Once on a time there was a man up in Finnmark who had caught a great white bear, which he was going to take to the King of Denmark. Now, it so fell out, that he came to the *Dovrefell* just about Christmas Eve, and there he turned into a cottage where a man lived, whose name was Halvor, and asked the man if he could get house-room there for his bear and himself.

"Heaven never help me, if what I say isn't true!" said the man; "but we can't give anyone house-room just now, for every Christmas Eve such a pack of *Trolls* come down upon us, that we are forced to flit, and haven't so much as a house over our own heads, to say nothing of lending one to anyone else."

"Oh?" said the man, "if that's all, you can very well lend me your house; my bear can lie under the stove yonder, and I can sleep in the side-room."

Well, he begged so hard, that at last he got leave to stay there; so the people of the house flitted out, and before they went, everything was got ready for the *Trolls;* the tables were laid, and there was rice porridge, and fish boiled in lye, and sausages, and all else that was good, just as for any other grand feast.

So, when everything was ready, down came the *Trolls*. Some were great, and some were small; some had long tails, and some had no tails at all; some, too, had long, long noses; and they ate and drank, and tasted everything. Just then one of the little *Trolls* caught sight of the white bear, who lay under the stove; so he took a piece of sausage and stuck it on a fork, and went and poked it up against the bear's nose, screaming out:

"Pussy, will you have some sausage?"

Then the white bear rose up and growled, and hunted the whole pack of them out of doors, both great and small.

Next year Halvar was out in the wood, on the afternoon of Christmas Eve, cutting wood before the holidays, for he thought the *Trolls* would come again; and just as he was hard at work, he heard a voice in the wood calling out:

"Halvor! Halvor!"

"Well," said Halvor, "here I am."

"Have you got your big cat with you still?"

"Yes, that I have," said Halvor; "she's lying at home under the stove, and what's more, she has now got seven kittens, far bigger and fiercer than she is herself."

"Oh, then, we'll never come to see you again," bawled out the *Troll* away in the wood, and he kept his word; for since that time the *Trolls* have never eaten their Christmas brose with Halvor on the *Dovrefell*.

THE GHOST OF CHRISTMAS EVE

J. M. BARRIE

A few years ago, as some may remember, a startling ghost paper appeared in the monthly organ of the Society for Haunting Houses. The writer guaranteed the truth of his statement, and even gave the name of the Yorkshire manor-house in which the affair took place. The article and the discussion to which it gave rise agitated me a good deal, and I consulted Pettigrew about the advisability of clearing up the mystery. The writer wrote that he "distinctly saw his arm pass through the apparition and come out at the other side," and indeed I still remember his saying so next morning. He had a scared face, but I had presence of mind to continue eating my rolls and marmalade as if my briar had nothing to do with the miraculous affair.

Seeing that he made a "paper" of it, I suppose he is justified in touching up the incidental details. He says, for instance, that we were told the story of the ghost which is said to haunt the house, just before going to bed. As far as I remember, it was only mentioned at luncheon, and then sceptically. Instead of there being snow falling outside and an eerie wind wailing through the skeleton trees, the night was still and muggy. Lastly, I did not know, until the journal reached my hands, that he was put into the room known as the Haunted Chamber, nor that in that room the fire is noted for casting weird shadows upon the walls. This, however, may be so. The legend of the manor-house ghost he tells precisely as it is known to me. The tragedy dates back to the time of Charles I, and is led up to by a pathetic love-story, which I need not give. Suffice it that for seven days and nights the old steward had been anxiously awaiting the return of his young master and mistress from their honeymoon. On Christmas Eve, after he had gone to bed, there was a great clanging of the doorbell. Flinging on a dressing-gown, he hastened downstairs. According to the story, a number of servants watched him, and saw by the light of his candle that his face was an ashy white. He took off the chains of the door, unbolted it, and pulled it open. What he saw no human being knows; but it must have been something awful, for without a cry the old steward fell dead in the hall. Perhaps the strangest part of the story is this: that the shadow of a burly man, holding a pistol in his hand, entered by the open door, stepped over the steward's body, and gliding up the stairs, disappeared, no one could say where. Such is the legend. I shall not tell the many ingenious explanations of it that have been offered. Every Christmas Eve, however, the silent scene is said to be gone through again; and tradition declares that no person lives for twelve months at whom the ghostly intruder points his pistol.

On Christmas Day the gentleman who tells the tale in the scientific journal created some sensation at the breakfast-table by solemnly asserting that he had seen the ghost. Most of the men present scouted his story, which may be condensed into a few words. He had retired to his bedroom at a fairly early hour, and as he opened the door his candle-light was blown out. He tried to get a light from the fire, but it was too low, and eventually he went to bed in the semi-darkness. He was wakened—he did not know at what hour—by the clanging of a bell. He sat up in bed, and the ghost-story came in a rush to his mind. His fire was dead, and the room was consequently dark; yet by and by he knew, though he heard no sound, that his door had opened. He cried out, "Who is that?" but got no answer. By an effort he jumped up and went to the door, which was ajar. His bedroom was on the first floor, and looking up the stairs he could see nothing. He felt a cold sensation at his heart, however, when he looked the other way. Going slowly and without a sound down the stairs, was an old man in a dressing-gown. He carried a candle. From the top of the stairs only part of the hall is visible, but as the apparition disappeared the watcher had the courage to go down a few steps after him. At first nothing was to be seen, for the candle-light had vanished. A dim light, however, entered by the long narrow windows which flank the hall-door, and after a moment the onlooker could see that the hall was empty. He was marvelling at this sudden disappearance of the steward, when, to his horror, he saw a body fall upon the hall-floor within a few feet of the door. The watcher cannot say whether he cried out, nor how long he stood there trembling. He came to himself with a start as he realized that something was coming up the stairs. Fear prevented his taking flight, and in a moment the thing was at his side. Then he saw indistinctly that it was not the figure he had seen descend. He saw a younger man in a heavy overcoat, but with no hat on his head. He wore on his face a look of extravagant triumph. The guest boldly put out his hand towards the figure. To his amazement his arm went through it. The ghost paused for a moment and looked behind it. It was then the watcher realized that it carried a pistol in its right hand. He was by this time in a highly strung condition, and he stood trembling lest the pistol should be pointed at him. The apparition, however, rapidly glided up the stairs and was soon lost to sight. Such are the main facts of the story; none of which I contradicted at the time.

I cannot say absolutely that I can clear up this mystery; but my suspicions are confirmed by a good deal of circumstantial evidence. This will not be understood unless I explain my strange infirmity. Wherever I went I used to be troubled with a presentiment that I had left my pipe behind. Often even at the dinner-table, I paused in the middle of a sentence as if stricken with sudden pain. Then my hand went down to my pocket. Sometimes, even after I felt my pipe, I had a conviction that it was stopped, and only by a desperate effort did I keep myself from producing it and blowing down it. I distinctly remember once dreaming three nights in succession that I was on the Scotch express without it. More than once, I know, I have wandered in my sleep, looking for it in all sorts of places, and after I went to bed I generally jumped out, just to make sure of it. My strong belief, then, is that I was the ghost seen by the writer of the paper. I fancy that I rose in my sleep, lighted a candle and wandered down to the hall to feel if my pipe was safe in my coat, which was hanging there. The light had gone out when I was in the hall. Probably the body seen to fall on the hall floor was some other coat which I had flung there to get more easily at my own. I cannot account for the bell; but perhaps the gentleman in the Haunted Chamber dreamt that part of the affair. I had put on the overcoat before reascending; indeed, I may say that next morning I was surprised to find it on a chair in my bedroom, also to notice that there were several long streaks of candle-grease on my dressing-gown. I conclude that the pistol, which gave my face such a look of triumph, was my briar, which I found in the morning beneath my pillow. The strangest thing of all, perhaps, is that when I awoke there was a smell of tobacco-smoke in the bedroom.

OF ARGONAUTS AND HOLLY WREATHS

JOHN BAUR

from CHRISTMAS ON THE AMERICAN FRONTIER

I n southern California, little touched even in the 1850s by the events occurring in the Mother Lode country, Christmas was celebrated in the old Spanish ways. Farther north, at San Jose, Chester S. Lyman mentioned a Christmas Eve religious service conducted by a "Methodist exhorter recently from Oregon," but few people were present at the meeting. Lyman gave his workmen a holiday along with an extra dinner including pies.

The miners, however, celebrated their holiday and recent strikes up in the diggings. Francis D. Clark, a young fellow who had arrived in California in 1847 and had set out on November 1 from Monterey with three Mexican *carretas* and six yoke of oxen, participated in a "Christmas jollification" with a party of youths in their log cabin called "Independence Hall." On the banks of the Mokelumne, filled with adventurous spirit, camaraderie, and a disregard of both danger and trivia, these young men characterized on that holiday the thousands of Americans who were manning the gold rush and winning a frontier. Of his companions, Clark wrote:

> What cared we if whisky was $20 a bottle, flour $2 a pound, one pound can of oysters one ounce [of gold], fresh beef one dollar a pound, salt fish two dollars, &c., &c? Were not the banks paying out gold *on demand* upon *personal applications?* Oh what happy days those were when after a hard

day's work we returned to our domicile to partake of the feast the "Cook of the Mess" had awaiting us. 'Tis true we had no luxuries, but we possessed robust health and an excellent appetite, and our sleep was as sound on the pine boughs which formed our mattress as ever enjoyed since on a mattress of softer material.

The most appropriate present one could have sent home from California that golden Christmas was what James Clyman enclosed to his friend, Hiram J. Ross, in a letter dated that day: "Enclosed you will find a small specimen of gold. It is found in all shapes and sizes up to twenty pounds in weight."

Possibly the most thoroughly recorded Yuletide merrymaking in early Western history took place in the golden days of '49. Aware that they were making history, scores and even hundreds of Argonauts preserved their doings in diaries, letters, and accounts to the press. Several diggers stumbled on good luck that day. From Georgetown, Charles T. Blake wrote his partners that "we took out fifty-nine dollars in about six hours, bailing about ¾ of the time!!!! The washing of the dirt is generally the least part of the work in Canon digging."

On the Trinity River, William Kelly, a man of education and the rare ability to observe keenly and to write fluently, characterized a typical Forty-niner's holiday. That fabulous personage, so often stereotyped in dress, conversation, and deeds by fiction writers, according to Kelly observed Christmas "if not with a devotional reverence, at least by an abstinence from all labour on that day, which, from earliest childhood at home, we are taught to look forward to with a rapturous eagerness." Kelly and his fellows secured a loin of grizzly bear meat, some six bottles of wine, and two pounds of raisins, which,

together with the contents of our own larder and cellar, furnished us such a dinner as dwellers in the mountains are rarely enabled to enjoy, each member of the mess undertaking that portion of the preparation he was best prepared to deal with; one agreeing to bake, another to roast the venison, another to boil the bacon, one gentleman taking in charge the manufacture of short and sweet bread, a second choosing for his department the pies, made from preserved apples; but Captain S——r's was the *chef-d'oeuvre* of the feast, being a plum-pudding, made ship-shape, not to be excelled in composition, which he launched into a liquid so truly exquisite and congenial, as to leave one in doubt whether to prefer the pudding or the sauce. The part assigned to me was to rig a table, and get the Sheffield ware in order, which I managed admirably by means of the front and end boards of the waggon, making shins of willow sticks, that squeeled and bent, not being far enough advanced in years to "groan" under the superincumbent profusion, a purified-waggon-sheet serving the purposes of the cloth; and, if the cutlery was not all to match, it was matchless in its peculiar variety, a sufficiency being secured by supplying the carvers with bowie-knives, and short swords in lieu of their legitimate instruments.

Christmas dawned as glorious as a day in May, greeting the miners dressed in holiday garb.

Every tent was prepared with some hospitable welcome, manufactured specially, and every estrangement was forgotten and forgiven. . . . Our dinner-table was quite a spectacle in its way in the diggings, with its studied instrumental arrangements, its bear meat, venison, and bacon, its apple-pies pleasingly distributed, its Gothic columns of plain and fancy breads, interspersed at becoming intervals, and its Cardigans flanking the whole gastronomical array; the plum-pudding alone being reserved for second course, from the motives of expedition and economy, as waiters were only to be had by express order from the cities. We had two guests, natives of the *ould* country, settlers in Oregon, who were about returning home, as gold mines, it was said, had been discovered on Rogue's River, which runs through their own territory, one of whom brought me, as a present, a noble dog that I often desired to possess, as their vigilance about a tent at night supersedes the trying necessity of keeping guard.

In towns, both those serving and others far removed from the diggings, Christmas received an even better "send-off." San Francisco, a wonder of the new West, had been born almost literally overnight due to the gold rush which it supplied and stimulated. From a little settlement of a few hundred in 1848, the town had grown suddenly into a crowded emporium, a city which had not yet found its soul, but with plenty of backbone and brains to serve it while it sought one. John W. Audubon, son of the Western painter and naturalist, found no merry Christmas in 1849 in "this pandemonium of a city." He exclaimed:

> Not a *lady* to be seen, and the women, poor things, sad and silent, except when drunk or excited. The place full of gamblers, hundreds of them, and men of the lowest types, more blasphemous, and with less regard for God and his commands than all I have ever seen on the Mississippi, [in] New Orleans or Texas. . . . Sunday makes no difference, certainly not Christmas, except for a little more drunkenness, and a little extra effort on the part of the hotel keepers to take in more money.

Yet a man of more faith, and therefore light in the darkness, could see many uplifting prospects for this city of all future and little past. William S. Jewett, an artist, but not necessarily a futile dreamer, had noticed with his keen eye that on this Christmas Day there were already many churches in San Francisco; two of them at least were filled for the holiday, the Episcopal and the Methodist. He himself attended the Episcopal service, finding there a large congregation of most respectable people, who sang the hymns well and in harmony. For the fire-and-brimstone brotherhood, who saw only retribution as the salvation for the sinning community, Christmas Eve of 1849 offered a powerful warning, for on that day one of the town's frequent devastating conflagrations occurred, destroying the Parker House and its plush monte tables.

Although the early fifties witnessed an increasing number of gold seekers' arrivals in California, for these newcomers workdays remained long, holidays few, and luxuries still rare. Christmas was the prime luxury and for many, the only holiday, decked out in hope and holly. It was even more welcome than Steamer Day at San Francisco or mail day in camp. David Rohrer Leeper, who has preserved much of the fleeting era in which he lived, tells us to what lengths miners might go to provide entertainment.

> As a straw of the prevailing flush times it may be mentioned that Seth Kinsman, the noted hunter and antler chair-maker, and myself were tendered fifty dollars each to preside as the *orchestra* for a Christmas ball at Uniontown in 1852. Kinsman's repertoire consisted mainly of an alternation of "The Arkansas Traveler" and "Hell on the Wabash," and mine was

little more varied on pretensions. He responded. My conscience had not yet reached that degree of elasticity.

Sometimes just chatting was the best form of entertainment one could find, and even that might be the most appropriate. For example, although Nelson Kingsley enjoyed the beautiful weather of Christmas, 1850, and unlike many another miner, could rejoice in such rare "eatables" as fried ham, cheese, and oysters, fresh despite a trip all the way from Boston in sealed cans, he doted on good company. That day he got it. At a friend's cabin Kingsley met a Mr. Smith from Connecticut who had arrived in September. This Yankee told his eager hearers, "old timers" of a year or so in California, all the "news" (probably eight months old!) of New England and provided an intellectual meal such as the miners had not experienced in many months. Consequently, to Kingsley he "seemed an old friend, tho' I never before spoke with him. Many a pleasant 'yarn was spun' during the evening which made the time pass away pleasantly."

Other Argonauts, enjoying the best time of the year, found less peaceful ways to make Christmas pass. Chauncey L. Canfield has given us a purportedly true account of one, Alfred T. Jackson, whose diary he published. Whether real or fictionary, the events at Selby Flat were typical of the lively Yuletide mining camp where a prank was refined into high frontier art. According to Jackson's story, the landlord of the Flat's only hotel had boasted for weeks that he would provide his guests with a real turkey dinner, but most Selbyites were skeptical, and, being real Forty-niners, they were willing to back up their opinions with cash bets. Those who were in on the secret and knew that the landlord had arranged a month before for the delivery of a dozen birds from Marysville, took all bets offered. A week before Christmas, the potential dinners arrived, fat and gobbling. The men who had bet on the turkeys wanted to be paid, but since the wager was on a Christmas feast, the stakeholders decided to wait until the meal itself before giving out the money. It seemed a sure thing anyway, so no one objected. Meanwhile, the condemned turkeys were fattened up while the hotel proprietor advertised the "big feed" at two dollars and a half a head. He even promised mince pie for dessert! But then came the shock; two days before Christmas word spread that the turkeys had disappeared. Everyone was upset, and most especially the hotelkeeper. He had no clues as to who the thieves might have been but, like everyone else at Selby Flat, he suspected the "Saleratus Ranch boys," who were usually at the bottom of any deviltry. And so he demanded that their cabin be searched by the deputy sheriff, but that officer had no warrant. As a result, a very plain dinner was served amid such gloom as only the sorrow caused by losing a rich claim could have surpassed. Only one lone mince pie brightened a bit the dreary day at the mining-camp hotel. Not even a Christmas dance livened things enough to make holiday cheer. Finally, unwilling to remain mystified any longer, fifty of the dinner guests went down to the Saleratus Ranch to see how the hands there had dined. To their surprise, they found no turkey thereabouts, only old pork, some beans, and the remains of tasteless boiled beef. After their amazement had sunk in, the turkey-hungry crew began to suspect that some Indian had stolen their promised gobblers. Then the writer, Alfred Jackson, was asked to go to a cabin owned by Jack Ristine and one Carter. There the turkeys were found at last. All those who had bet on there being no turkey dinner at the hotel were in on the plot! They had stolen the birds, taken them down the creek, killed and picked them, thrown the feathers in the fast-running waters, and then six of the culprits helped Ristine and Carter to prepare a really tasty meal. For a chosen few a good supper had resulted. After the last morsel was downed, the diners buried the turkey bones in the bank of the creek—three feet deep. . . .

THE WHITE ROAD

E. F. BOZMAN

"Mild weather for the time of year."

"Yes," I said; "not very seasonable."

I did not even trouble to turn round and look at the stranger who had addressed me. I remember a soft Sussex voice, strong and deep, and I have an impression of someone tall; but I had come in to have a glass of beer by myself and was not in the mood for chance conversation.

It was Christmas Eve, about nine o'clock in the evening, and the public bar at the Swan Inn was crowded. It was the first evening of my holidays and I had walked over from the farmhouse where I was staying with my mother, using the inn as my objective. I had just come down from London, and was in no need of company; on the contrary, I wanted solitude. However, the landlord recognized me from previous visits and passed the time of night.

"Staying down at the farm again?" he asked.

"Yes," I said.

"Well, we're glad to see you, I'm sure. Did you walk over?"

"Yes. I enjoy the walk. That's what I came out for."

"And for the drink?" he suggested.

"Well, it's good beer," I admitted, and paid for a glass for each of us. I felt rather than saw the stranger who had accosted me hovering behind me, but made no attempt to bring him in. I did not see why I should buy him a drink; and I wanted nothing from him.

"It must be pretty well three miles' walk down to where you are," the landlord said. "A tidy step."

"Yes," I said, "a good three. Two or two and a half down to Ingo Bridge, then another mile from where the lane turns off to West Chapter."

"Well, I suppose you know you've missed the last bus down. Must have been gone half an hour. There's only the one in from the Bridge, and that's the lot."

"Yes, I know," I said; "I don't mind."

Just then I heard the noise of the door latch followed by a creak as the door swung open, and half turned to see the tall stranger going out. I caught a glimpse of him before he shut the door behind him.

"Who was that?" I asked the landlord.

"I didn't notice him—he must have been a stranger to me. Funny thing, now you mention it, he didn't buy a drink."

"He seemed to be hanging round me. Cadging, I suppose."

"You get some funny customers at this time of year." The landlord was evidently not interested in the man. "It'll be dark tonight, along that road," he volunteered.

"Yes," I said. We finished our drinks, I said good night, and made my way to the door across the smoke-laden room.

It was pitch dark outside by contrast with the glow of the inn, and as I slammed the well-used wooden door behind me the shaft of light streaming from the parlor window seemed to be my last link with civilization. The air was extraordinarily mild for the time of year. My way lay by a short cut across the church fields which joined the road leading toward the sea; a difficult way to find at night had I not known it well; alternatively, I could have gone a longer way round, starting in the opposite direction, and making three sides of a square in the road which I was eventually to join by the short cut. I knew my ground and decided on the footpath without hesitation. By the time I reached the church fields I realized that the night was not really so dark as it had seemed to be at first, for I could see the black tower and belfry of the church looming against a background of lighter gray, and a glimmer of light in one corner of the church suggested eleventh-hour preparations for the great festival. Clouds were scudding across an unseen moon, full according to the calendar, discernible now only secondarily by a patch of faintly diffused light toward the south; knowing the lay of the land I could imagine the clouds swept away and the moon hanging in its winter glory over the cold English Channel a few miles away. Although the air was temporarily muggy with the presage of rain, there was a deep underlying chill in land and sea, the ingrained coldness of the short days.

The footpath across the fields was narrow and muddy, a single-file track. I stumbled and slithered my way along it until I reached a narrow wooden bridge with two handrails. Here I paused for a moment, looking at the dark swollen stream which was just visible, black and shining, below my feet.

I was now near the point where the path joined the road, and as I paused, my elbows leaning on the rail of the bridge, listening to the far-reaching silence, I heard in the distance the sound of footsteps along the road. In these days of heavy road-traffic this old-fashioned, unmistakable sound is a rarity, and I listened fascinated. The steady distant tread, gradually loudening, began to grow on me, and by the time I had made up my mind to move it was beating a rhythm in my brain. My path now led diagonally up a sloping bank to the road, and I crept up it silently, hearing and thinking of nothing but the approaching footsteps. The thought occurred to me that I must not let the walker catch me up, that something important, something connected with myself yet out of my own control, depended on the success of my efforts, and I began to hurry. I tried to dismiss the idea, but it would not be banished, and as I reached the swing gate leading out to the road the footsteps sounded unexpectedly near. They rang on the road, and I could hardly resist the temptation to run.

I compromised by stepping out briskly, swinging my arms. It was ludicrous, I argued with myself; there was nothing to be afraid of, and my own feet tried to reassure me by dimming the sound behind me. But the pursuing footsteps would not be drowned; they were implacable. I attempted to speed up, without allowing myself to hurry or panic, but I could not shake them off. They were gaining steadily on me, and as their loudness increased tingles of fear began to go down my spine. I could not turn round and look—could not, I realized, because I was afraid to.

The road at this point runs between high hedges and trees which shut out what little light was coming from the sky. Nothing could be seen except the dark shapes of the trees, and an occasional gleam from the black wet surface of the tarred road. There were some outlying farm buildings and barns immediately ahead, but no glimmer of light came from them. The overhanging elms dripped their moisture on me from leafless branches. No traffic was within earshot; the only sound was of footsteps, mine and my pursuer's.

Left right, left right, left right they went behind me. The walker had long legs. Left right, left right—the din increased alarmingly, and I realized that I must run.

"How far now to the bridge?"

A soft voice, almost in my ear, shocked me, and yet released the tension. I sweated suddenly and profusely.

I recognized the voice of the stranger who had addressed me in the

Swan Inn. He had left just before me and must have walked round by the road, I realized, while I had taken the short cut across the fields. I could not immediately disguise my racing heart, but I managed to speak calmly, in a voice which must have sounded weak in contrast with the strong Sussex resonance of the stranger.

"About two miles," I said.

The stranger said nothing more for the moment, but fell into step beside me, as if assuming that we were to walk together. It was not what I wanted, partly because I was ashamed of my panic of a few moments ago, and partly because I had been looking forward to walking the lonely stretch of road ahead by myself. I turned my head, but could see nothing of my companion except his tall dark form, vaguely outlined, and he must have been wearing a long coat which flapped below his knees. I was the next to break the silence.

"When we get past the farm buildings," I said, "and round the next corner we come to a long open stretch. It's a lovely bit of road, a special favorite of mine, absolutely deserted usually. On clear nights or days you can see the sea in the distance."

"There's a little hill about halfway along—by an S bend."

The stranger's remark surprised me. Why had he asked me about the way if he knew the district?

"So you know the road?" I asked querulously, as if I had been deceived.

The stranger muttered, "Years ago," and something else I could not catch. The detail he had remembered was a significant one. The open stretch ahead of us, nearly two miles in length, promised at first sight to run straight for the sea, where it joined the main coast road; but halfway along this section of the road there was a danger spot for speeding motorists, an unexpected S bend over a little mound. Just past the bend, as the road straightened itself out again and went down the far side of the little hill, heading between low hedges for the sea, there was a notable isolated thorn tree standing on the left of the road. Its trunk leaned toward the sea, while the twigs on top of the trunk were all swept in the opposite direction, like a mat of hair, blown by the prevailing wind. From the trunk two stumpy branches sprouted, each with its bunch of twigs held out like hands; these, too, were wind-swept. The trunk was not gnarled and sprang strongly from the ground—no dead post, driven into the earth from above, could have achieved that appearance of strength.

I was about to refer to this tree, which was a particular landmark of mine, when we heard the sound of a distant motor. My companion seemed to be unexpectedly nervous—I could feel his anxiety. The sound increased rapidly, so different a progress from approaching feet, and before we had rounded the sharp corner leading to the open stretch of road a Southdown bus flung itself round the bend and was almost on us. The headlights flooded us, gleaming on the stranger's face, making him look pale as a ghost, and lighting the road immediately in front of us to a brilliant white.

The stranger was so dazzled by the sudden brightness that he cowered into the hedge, shielding his eyes with his hand. In an instant the bus had charged past us and round another corner, taking its lighted interior and its warm passengers with it into the enveloping darkness of the countryside.

I heard my companion murmur: "The white road. The white road." Something in the way he said the words brought a picture of my youth to my eyes, of a time when this same lonely road was white and dusty, with flints, and I could see myself bicycling along it, in imminent danger of punctures, hurrying to the sea. I saw the white road, the white sea road, not the black and tarred contrivance of today, yet the same road with the same trees and banks. It has always been a lovely country road, and it still is.

We left the farm buildings behind us and entered the lonely stretch. It was too dark for us to see a glimmer of the sea ahead or anything behind the low banked hedges on either side. A light rain began to fall, driving in our faces.

"That was the last bus," I said; "we'll meet no more now."

The stranger ignored this remark, and his next words fitted in exactly with what had been in my mind when the bus distracted us.

"There's a thorn tree, isn't there?" he said, "just beside the road round the double corner." He spoke as if he knew the way by heart, yet obviously he did not remember it exactly. He had not even been sure enough of himself to take the short cut by the church fields.

"Yes," I said; "why do you ask?"

"You've noticed it yourself?" he inquired anxiously.

"Yes."

"And it's still there?"

"Yes, of course." I could not for the life of me imagine what he was driving at. Yet even as I spoke the words confidently I found myself in doubt. I remembered my mother saying something about workmen on the lonely road, how they were widening it at the bend and spoiling its appearance. Like me, she had an affection for it. I had passed the spot that very evening on my way to the inn, yet when I came to think of it I could not be sure whether I had seen the tree or not. I had been preoccupied, and had not looked for it specially. But surely I would have noticed, I thought, and said aloud: "At least it was there the last time I passed."

"When was that?" The stranger spoke very directly and forcibly.

I was about to say this very evening, but realizing my uncertainty, said instead: "About this time last year. I was down here for Christmas."

"There's a story told about that tree in these parts," he said.

"Oh," I said; "what do they say about it?"

"They say there was a suicide on that spot. A man from the village." The Sussex burr was soft and confidential.

"What happened?"

"He hanged himself on the tree."

"A man couldn't hang himself on that tree," I said, "it's too small."

"There's a seven-foot clearance from the fork," he said eagerly.

"Oh, well," I said, "it's a sturdy little tree. I've often noticed it, standing there all alone, holding out its branches like hands."

"Yes," he said, "that's right. Like hands. And have you seen the nails? Long and curved. They haven't been cut, any more than the hair. Have you seen the hair?" His voice was strained, and I felt that he must be looking at me. I turned to read his eyes, but it was too dark to see anything but the tall shape and the long coat beside me.

"That tree didn't grow in a day," I said.

"I don't know how old it is." The stranger spoke apologetically. "But it's an old story—maybe twenty, thirty, forty years old. I couldn't be sure."

There was a pause for a few minutes. We must have covered half the mile between the farm and the tree before I spoke again.

"What's behind the story?" I asked. "What do they say?"

"They say there was a woman in it. A dark girl, one of the coast guard's daughters down at Ingo Bridge. He was a married man, you see."

I waited for him to go on. He spoke as if it mattered vitally to him.

"It had been going on a long time, they say. Then one night, one Christmas Eve, he left his home for good and went to the inn, and perhaps he had a drink or two there, though nobody knows that. He had made up his mind to take the girl. She was going to leave a light burning in her window, and he would see it from the distance, you see, when he turned the corner by the tree. That was to be the sign, if it was all right. Well, he left his home for good, to get that girl. But he never got her. His wife got him—by that tree."

"I thought you said it was suicide."

"Ah, yes, that's what they say. But it was his wife that got him."

"You mean she followed him?"

"No, I mean that she got him there."

We walked another two hundred yards before he added: "I mean that he saw her there, in his mind's eye. He couldn't take the girl then. He couldn't, however much he wanted to. He couldn't because he belonged to his wife. That's what I mean when I say his wife got him."

"It's a queer story," I said. "I've never heard it told before."

"Oh, you hear it among the older men. It's common knowledge," he said.

"It's a queer story," I said, "because who told it in the first place? Who was to know what was in the fellow's mind? Who was to know what actually happened?"

"He was dead, wasn't he?" The stranger spoke irritably. "A man doesn't die in these parts without talk about it. A lot of talk."

"But how did he die?" I insisted. "Did he hang himself or was he murdered?"

"He was murdered."

"What the devil do you mean?" I shouted angrily. "Murdered, by a tree?"

The stranger clutched me by the arm. "Have you seen the tree?" he whispered. "Have you seen it standing there year after year, leaning against the southwest wind, with the hair streaming and the hands outstretched, and the long nails growing—?"

I was suddenly aware of the loneliness of the road and of the darkness and desolation of the downs around me and the sea ahead. The stranger's next remark, though spoken in a low voice, seemed to shatter the darkness.

"By God! what's a man to do when a woman pulls at him? A dark girl. And what do men have daughters for, eh? I ask you that. Whose fault is that?" and then, as if brushing aside an imaginary criticism: "If I were to meet that coast guard's daughter down by the bridge tonight I'd tell her . . ."

His voice tailed off and I said nothing. The coast guards' cottages are still down by the bridge, true enough, but the coast guards had been disbanded years ago. Years ago. He must have known that.

We reached the little hill in the road, mounted it, and turned the first half of the S bend. The light rain had ceased and the clouds were thinning. We both of us knew that when we passed the next corner, the other half of the S, we should see the tree.

Just then the clouds broke suddenly and the full moon shone through. It whitened the black road, silvered the gleam of the sea ahead, and illuminated the low banks and hedges with the dark rising downs beyond. We turned the corner and both stared toward the thorn tree.

There was nothing to be seen. No tree. Nothing. The place where the tree stood was blatantly empty, and the moonlight seemed to emphasize the barrenness, showing it up like a sore, focusing the attention. I suppose I had been unconsciously visualizing the tree as I knew it, because I was more than surprised by its absence; I was shocked, profoundly shocked, and the recollection of that absence of tree, that nothingness, is more vivid to me than my memory of the tree itself. The clouds now scudded from the moon, leaving it cold and clear and agonizingly circular in an expanse of sky. In what seemed to be a blaze of light I put my head down and ran.

I ran toward the silver sea along a white road, a ribbon road of memory, and I could believe that the dust rose under my feet and powdered my boots; though with another part of me I knew that I was wearing shoes, not boots, and was pounding down a wet tarred road. In the moonlight that road seemed white and dusty and I pattered along it with the desperate urgency of a small boy who must deliver some message or run some errand of overwhelming yet not-understood importance. I ran and I ran, urgently and desperately, thinking no more of my strange companion, yet in some way intimately associated with him.

Along the white road I ran, past the signpost at the turning to the farm, knowing yet not knowing what I should see. The clouds had gathered again, a dark pillar over the sea, and the blaze of whiteness was already dimming. There was a light in the coast guard's cottage at Ingo Bridge. I headed straight for it but did not reach it, for a woman lay across the road, an elderly woman. She must have dropped her basket as she fell, and her parcels, little objects and toys that she had bought for her grandchildren perhaps, lay scattered around her. She might have been shopping for Christmas, I thought, and had missed the last bus at Ingo Bridge; then she had tried to walk home, but her strength had failed her, and she had fallen in the road.

I ran to her side and raised her head. She was too weak to stand on her feet, and I lifted her in my arms and carried her the few yards to the coast guard's cottage where the light was still burning. For those few steps the road was white and flinty—but then it is so now; it is only a little byroad—and I found myself speaking not to an old woman who had fainted or was dying, but to a young woman. And the words I spoke were not mine but someone else's; the words of the stranger who had accompanied me to the tree. They were framed without my help.

"That was no murder. That was no murder by the tree. I always belonged to you, all along, really. I see it all now."

The woman opened her eyes and there was an expression of love in them. I could not say whether it was I or my stranger who spoke the next words. They were said very gently and comfortably.

"There are things better left unsaid. Better left; you understand."

She nodded and closed her eyes, and then the stranger and the strangeness left me.

I knocked at the door of the cottage. A man opened it, then called to his wife, a gray-haired woman dressed in black, who must have been a beautiful dark girl in her time. I explained what had happened and they took my burden from me and laid her on their horsehair sofa. They knew who she was, of course, for she was from the village.

But I did not know. I could only guess. And as I walked back in the inky blackness of an oncoming rainstorm, back to my corner, then up the lane to the farmhouse where my mother was waiting up for me, I cast round in my mind for a missing fragment of knowledge, something I must know yet could not remember.

I discovered it at last accidentally, while in my mind's eye I could still see the thorn tree, standing there, holding out its branches, its mat of twigs all set toward the northeast, and from the fork a dark form hanging, twisting slowly in a long coat, a thing with a back to its head but no face, a dark thing twisting slowly beside a long white road which stretched in a dusty ribbon to the sea. I discovered the missing fragment of knowledge in the more exact recollection of my mother's remark, made only that very morning. "They are widening the white road at the bend," she had said—we always used to call it the white road between ourselves—"and this evening they are going to cut down that little old thorn tree."

CHRISTMAS EVE

ROBERT BROWNING

from CHRISTMAS EVE

I

Out of the little chapel I burst
  Into the fresh night-air again.
Five minutes full, I waited first
  In the doorway, to escape the rain
That drove in gusts down the common's centre
  At the edge of which the chapel stands,
Before I plucked up heart to enter.
  Heaven knows how many sorts of hands
Reached past me, groping for the latch
Of the inner door that hung on catch
More obstinate the more they fumbled,
  Till, giving way at last with a scold
Of the crazy hinge, in squeezed or tumbled
  One sheep more to the rest in fold,
And left me irresolute, standing sentry
In the sheepfold's lath-and-plaster entry,
Six feet long by three feet wide,
Partitioned off from the vast inside—
  I blocked up half of it at least.
No remedy; the rain kept driving.
  They eyed me much as some wild beast,
That congregation, still arriving,

Some of them by the main road, white
A long way past me into the night,
Skirting the common, then diverging;
Not a few suddenly emerging
From the common's self thro' the paling-gaps,
—They house in the gravel-pits perhaps,
Where the road stops short with its safeguard border
Of lamps, as tired of such disorder;—
But the most turned in yet more abruptly
    From a certain squalid knot of alleys,
Where the town's bad blood once slept corruptly,
    Which now the little chapel rallies
And leads into day again,—its priestliness
Lending itself to hide their beastliness
So cleverly (thanks in part to the mason),
And putting so cheery a whitewashed face on
Those neophytes too much in lack of it,
    That, where you cross the common as I did,
    And meet the party thus presided,
"Mount Zion" with Love-lane at the back of it,
They front you as little disconcerted
As, bound for the hills, her fate averted,
And her wicked people made to mind him,
Lot might have marched with Gomorrah behind him.

II

Well, from the road, the lanes or the common,
In came the flock: the fat weary woman,
Panting and bewildered, down-clapping
    Her umbrella with a mighty report,
Grounded it by me, wry and flapping,
    A wreck of whalebones; then, with snort,
Like a startled horse, at the interloper
(Who humbly knew himself improper,
But could not shrink up small enough)
—Round to the door, and in,—the gruff
Hinge's invariable scold
Making my very blood run cold.
Prompt in the wake of her, up-pattered
On broken clogs, the many-tattered
Little old-faced peaking sister-turned-mother
Of the sickly babe she tried to smother

Somehow up, with its spotted face,
From the cold, on her breast, the one warm place;
She too must stop, wring the poor ends dry
Of a draggled shawl, and add thereby
Her tribute to the door-mat, sopping
Already from my own clothes' dropping,
Which yet she seemed to grudge I should stand on:
 Then, stooping down to take off her pattens,
 She bore them defiantly, in each hand one,
Planted together before her breast
And its babe, as good as a lance in rest.
 Close on her heels, the dingy satins
Of a female something, past me flitted,
 With lips as much too white, as a streak
 Lay far too red on each hollow cheek;
And it seemed the very door-hinge pitied
All that was left of a woman once,
Holding at least its tongue for the nonce.
Then a tall yellow man, like the Penitent Thief,
With his jaw bound up in a handkerchief,
And eyelids screwed together tight,
Led himself in by some inner light.
And, except from him, from each that entered,
 I got the same interrogation—
"What, you the alien, you have ventured
 "To take with us, the elect, your station?
"A carer for none of it, a Gallio!"—
 Thus, plain as print, I read the glance
At a common prey, in each countenance
 As of huntsman giving his hounds the tallyho.
And, when the door's cry drowned their wonder,
 The draught, it always sent in shutting,
Made the flame of the single tallow candle
In the cracked square lantern I stood under,
 Shoot its blue lip at me, rebutting
As it were, the luckless cause of scandal:
I verily fancied the zealous light
(In the chapel's secret, too!) for spite
Would shudder itself clean off the wick,
With the airs of a Saint John's Candlestick.
There was no standing it much longer.
"Good folks," thought I, as resolve grew stronger,

"This way you perform the Grand-Inquisitor
"When the weather sends you a chance visitor?
"You are the men, and wisdom shall die with you,
"And none of the old Seven Churches vie with you!
"But still, despite the pretty perfection
    "To which you carry your trick of exclusiveness,
"And, taking God's word under wise protection,
    "Correct its tendency to diffusiveness,
"And bid one reach it over hot ploughshares,—
    "Still, as I say, though you've found salvation,
"If I should choose to cry, as now, 'Shares!'—
    "See if the best of you bars me my ration!
"I prefer, if you please, for my expounder
"Of the laws of the feast, the feast's own Founder;
"Mine's the same right with your poorest and sickliest
    "Supposing I don the marriage vestiment:
    "So shut your mouth and open your Testament.
"And carve me my portion at your quickliest!"
Accordingly, as a shoemaker's lad
    With wizened face in want of soap,
    And wet apron wound round his waist like a rope,
(After stopping outside, for his cough was bad,
To get the fit over, poor gentle creature,
And so avoid disturbing the preacher)
—Passed in, I sent my elbow spikewise
At the shutting door, and entered likewise,
Received the hinge's accustomed greeting,
    And crossed the threshold's magic pentacle,
    And found myself in full conventicle,
—To wit, in Zion Chapel Meeting,
On the Christmas-Eve of 'Forty-nine,
    Which, calling its flock to their special clover,
    Found all assembled and one sheep over,
Whose lot, as the weather pleased, was mine.

A CHRISTMAS MEMORY

TRUMAN CAPOTE

I magine a morning in late November. A coming of winter morning more than twenty years ago. Consider the kitchen of a spreading old house in a country town. A great black stove is its main feature; but there is also a big round table and a fireplace with two rocking chairs placed in front of it. Just today the fireplace commenced its seasonal roar.

A woman with shorn white hair is standing at the kitchen window. She is wearing tennis shoes and a shapeless gray sweater over a summery calico dress. She is small and sprightly, like a bantam hen; but, due to a long youthful illness, her shoulders are pitifully hunched. Her face is remarkable—not unlike Lincoln's, craggy like that, and tinted by sun and wind; but it is delicate too, finely boned, and her eyes are sherry-colored and timid. "Oh my," she exclaims, her breath smoking the windowpane, "it's fruitcake weather!"

The person to whom she is speaking is myself. I am seven; she is sixty-something. We are cousins, very distant ones, and we have lived together—well, as long as I can remember. Other people inhabit the house, relatives; and though they have power over us, and frequently make us cry, we are not, on the whole, too much aware of them. We are each other's best friend. She calls me Buddy, in memory of a boy who was formerly her best friend. The other Buddy died in the 1880's, when she was still a child. She is still a child.

"I knew it before I got out of bed," she says, turning away from the window with a purposeful excitement in her eyes. "The courthouse bell sounded so cold and clear. And there were no birds singing; they've gone to warmer country, yes indeed. Oh, Buddy, stop stuffing biscuit and fetch our buggy. Help me find my hat. We've thirty cakes to bake."

It's always the same: a morning arrives in November, and my friend, as though officially inaugurating the Christmas time of year that exhilarates her imagination and fuels the blaze of her heart, announces: "It's fruitcake weather! Fetch our buggy. Help me find my hat."

The hat is found, a straw cartwheel corsaged with velvet roses out-of-doors has faded: it once belonged to a more fashionable relative. Together, we guide our buggy, a dilapidated baby carriage, out to the garden and into a grove of pecan trees. The buggy is mine; that is, it was bought for me when I was born. It is made of wicker, rather unraveled, and the wheels wobble like a drunkard's legs. But it is a faithful object; springtimes, we take it to the woods and fill it with flowers, herbs, wild fern for our porch pots; in the summer, we pile it with picnic paraphernalia and sugar-cane fishing poles and roll it down to the edge of a creek; it has its winter uses, too: as a truck for hauling firewood from the yard to the kitchen, as a warm bed for Queenie, our tough little orange and white rat terrier who has survived distemper and two rattlesnake bites. Queenie is trotting beside it now.

Three hours later we are back in the kitchen hulling a heaping buggy-load of windfall pecans. Our backs hurt from gathering them: how hard they were to find (the main crop having been shaken off the trees and sold by the orchard's owners, who are not us) among the concealing leaves, the frosted, deceiving grass. Caarackle! A cheery crunch, scraps of miniature thunder sound as the shells collapse and the golden mound of sweet oily ivory meat mounts in the milk-glass bowl. Queenie begs to taste, and now and again my friend sneaks her a mite, though insisting we deprive ourselves. "We mustn't, Buddy. If we start, we won't stop. And there's scarcely enough as there is. For thirty cakes." The kitchen is growing dark. Dusk turns the window into a mirror: our reflections mingle with the rising moon as we work by the fireside in the firelight. At last, when the moon is quite high, we toss the final hull into the fire and, with joined sighs, watch it catch flame. The buggy is empty, the bowl is brimful.

We eat our supper (cold biscuits, bacon, blackberry jam) and discuss tomorrow. Tomorrow the kind of work I like best begins: buying. Cherries and citron, ginger and vanilla and canned Hawaiian pineapple, rinds and raisins and walnuts and whiskey and oh, so much flour, butter, so many eggs, spices, flavorings: why, we'll need a pony to pull the buggy home.

But before these purchases can be made, there is the question of money. Neither of us has any. Except for skinflint sums persons in the house occasionally provide (a dime is considered very big money); or what we earn ourselves from various activities: holding rummage sales, selling buckets of hand-picked blackberries, jars of homemade jam and apple jelly and peach preserves, rounding up flowers for funerals and weddings. Once we won seventy-ninth prize, five dollars, in a national football contest. Not that we know a fool thing about football. It's just that we enter any contest we hear about: at the moment our hopes are centered on the fifty-thousand-dollar Grand Prize being offered to name a new brand of coffee (we suggested "A.M."; and, after some hesitation, for my friend thought it perhaps sacrilegious, the slogan "A.M.! Amen!"). To tell the truth, our only *really* profitable enterprise was the Fun and Freak Museum we conducted in a back-yard woodshed two summers ago. The Fun was a stereopticon with slide views of Washington and New York lent us by a relative who had been to those places (she was furious when she discovered why we'd borrowed it); the Freak was a three-legged biddy chicken hatched by one of our own hens. Everybody hereabouts wanted to see that biddy: we charged grownups a nickel, kids two cents. And took in a good twenty dollars before the museum shut down due to the decease of the main attraction.

But one way and another we do each year accumulate Christmas savings, a Fruitcake Fund. These moneys we keep hidden in an ancient bead purse under a loose board under the floor under a chamber pot under my friend's bed. The purse is seldom removed from this safe location except to make a deposit, or, as happens every Saturday, a withdrawal; for on Saturdays I am allowed ten cents to go to the picture show. My friend has never been to a picture show, nor does she intend to: "I'd rather hear you tell the story, Buddy. That way I can imagine it more. Besides, a person my age shouldn't squander their eyes. When the Lord comes, let me see Him clear." In addition to never having seen a movie, she has never: eaten in a restaurant, traveled more than five miles from home, received or sent a telegram, read anything except funny papers and the Bible, worn cosmetics, cursed, wished someone harm, told a lie on purpose, let a hungry dog go hungry. Here are a few things she has done, does do: killed with a hoe the biggest rattlesnake ever seen in this county (sixteen rattles), dip snuff (secretly), tame hummingbirds (just try it) till they balance on her finger, tell ghost stories (we both believe in ghosts) so tingling they chill you in July, talk to herself, take walks in the rain, grow the prettiest japonicas in town, know the recipe for every sort of old-time Indian cure, including a magical wart-remover.

Now, with supper finished, we retire to the room in a faraway part of the house where my friend sleeps in a scrap-quilt-covered iron bed painted rose pink, her favorite color. Silently, wallowing in the pleasures of conspiracy, we take the bead purse from its secret place and spill its contents on the scrap quilt. Dollar bills, tightly rolled and green as May buds. Somber fifty-cent pieces, heavy enough to weight a dead man's eyes. Lovely dimes, the liveliest coin, the one that really jingles. Nickels and quarters, worn smooth as creek pebbles. But mostly a hateful heap of bitter-odored pennies. Last summer others in the house contracted to pay us a penny for every twenty-five flies we killed. Oh, the carnage of August: the flies that flew to heaven! Yet it was not work in which we took pride. And, as we sit counting pennies, it is as though we were back tabulating dead flies. Neither of us has a head for figures; we count slowly, lose track, start again. According to her calculations, we have $12.73. According to mine, exactly $13. "I do hope you're wrong, Buddy. We can't mess around with thirteen. The cakes will fall. Or put somebody in the cemetery. Why, I wouldn't dream of getting out of bed on the thirteenth." This is true: she always spends thirteenths in bed. So, to be on the safe side, we subtract a penny and toss it out the window.

Of the ingredients that go into our fruitcakes, whiskey is the most expensive, as well as the hardest to obtain: State laws forbid its sale. But everybody knows you can buy a bottle from Mr. Haha Jones. And the next day, having completed our more prosaic shopping, we set out for Mr. Haha's business address, a "sinful" (to quote public opinion) fish-fry and dancing café down by the river. We've been there before, and on the same errand; but in previous years our dealings have been with Haha's wife, an iodine-dark Indian woman with brassy peroxided hair and a dead-tired disposition. Actually, we've never laid eyes on her husband, though we've heard that he's an Indian too. A giant with razor scars across his cheeks. They call him Haha because he's so gloomy, a man who never laughs. As we approach his café (a large log cabin festooned inside and out with chains of garish-gay naked light bulbs and standing by the river's muddy edge under the shade of river trees where moss drifts through the branches like gray mist) our steps slow down. Even Queenie stops prancing and sticks close by. People have been murdered in Haha's café. Cut to pieces. Hit on the head. There's a case coming up in court next month. Naturally these goings-on happen at night when the colored lights cast crazy patterns and the victrola wails. In the daytime Haha's is shabby and deserted. I knock at the door, Queenie barks, my friend calls: "Mrs. Haha, ma'am? Anyone to home?"

Footsteps. The door opens. Our hearts overturn. It's Mr. Haha Jones himself! And he *is* a giant; he *does* have scars; he *doesn't* smile. No, he glowers at us through Satan-tilted eyes and demands to know: "What you want with Haha?"

For a moment we are too paralyzed to tell. Presently my friend half-finds her voice, a whispery voice at best: "If you please, Mr. Haha, we'd like a quart of your finest whiskey."

His eyes tilt more. Would you believe it? Haha is smiling! Laughing, too. "Which one of you is a drinkin' man?"

"It's for making fruitcakes, Mr. Haha. Cooking."

This sobers him. He frowns. "That's no way to waste good whiskey." Nevertheless, he retreats into the shadowed café and seconds later appears carrying a bottle of daisy-yellow unlabeled liquor. He demonstrates its sparkle in the sunlight and says: "Two dollars."

We pay him with nickels and dimes and pennies. Suddenly, as he jangles the coins in his hand like a fistful of dice, his face softens. "Tell you what," he proposes, pouring the money back into our bead purse, "just send me one of them fruitcakes instead."

"Well," my friend remarks on our way home, "there's a lovely man. We'll put an extra cup of raisins in *his* cake."

The black stove, stoked with coal and firewood, glows like a lighted pumpkin. Eggbeaters whirl, spoons spin round in bowls of butter and sugar, vanilla sweetens the air, ginger spices it; melting, nose-tingling odors saturate the kitchen, suffuse the house, drift out to the world on puffs of chimney smoke. In four days our work is done. Thirty-one cakes, dampened with whiskey, bask on window sills and shelves.

Who are they for?

Friends. Not necessarily neighbor friends: indeed, the larger share is intended for persons we've met maybe once, perhaps not at all. People who've struck our fancy. Like President Roosevelt. Like the Reverend and Mrs. J. C. Lucey, Baptist missionaries to Borneo who lectured here last winter. Or the little knife grinder who comes through town twice a year. Or Abner Packer, the driver of the six o'clock bus from Mobile, who exchanges waves with us every day as he passes in a dust-cloud whoosh. Or the young Wistons, a California couple whose car one afternoon broke down outside the house and who spent a pleasant hour chatting with us on the porch (young Mr. Wiston snapped our picture, the only one we've ever had taken). Is it because my friend is shy with everyone *except* strangers that these strangers, and merest acquaintances, seem to us our truest friends? I think yes. Also, the scrapbooks we keep of thank-you's on White House stationery, time-to-time communications from California and Borneo, the knife grinder's penny post cards, make us feel connected to eventful worlds beyond the kitchen with its view of a sky that stops.

Now a nude December fig branch grates against the window. The kitchen is empty, the cakes are gone; yesterday we carted the last of them

❋　40　❋

to the post office, where the cost of stamps turned our purse inside out. We're broke. That rather depresses me, but my friend insists on celebrating—with two inches of whiskey left in Haha's bottle. Queenie has a spoonful in a bowl of coffee (she likes her coffee chicory-flavored and strong). The rest we divide between a pair of jelly glasses. We're both quite awed at the prospect of drinking straight whiskey; the taste of it brings screwed-up expressions and sour shudders. But by and by we begin to sing, the two of us singing different songs simultaneously. I don't know the words to mine, just: *Come on along, come on along, to the darktown strutters' ball.* But I can dance: that's what I mean to be, a tap-dancer in the movies. My dancing shadow rollicks on the walls; our voices rock the chinaware; we giggle: as if unseen hands were tickling us. Queenie rolls on her back, her paws plow the air, something like a grin stretches her black lips. Inside myself, I feel warm and sparky as those crumbling logs, carefree as the wind in the chimney. My friend waltzes round the stove, the hem of her poor calico skirt pinched between her fingers as though it were a party dress: *Show me the way to go home,* she sings, her tennis shoes squeaking on the floor. *Show me the way to go home.*

Enter: two relatives. Very angry. Potent with eyes that scold, tongues that scald. Listen to what they have to say, the words tumbling together into a wrathful tune: "A child of seven! whiskey on his breath! are you out of your mind? feeding a child of seven! must be loony! road to ruination! remember Cousin Kate? Uncle Charlie? Uncle Charlie's brother-in-law? shame! scandal! humiliation! kneel, pray, beg the Lord!"

Queenie sneaks under the stove. My friend gazes at her shoes, her chin quivers, she lifts her skirt and blows her nose and runs to her room. Long after the town has gone to sleep and the house is silent except for the chimings of clocks and the sputter of fading fires, she is weeping into a pillow already as wet as a widow's handkerchief.

"Don't cry," I say, sitting at the bottom of her bed and shivering despite my flannel nightgown that smells of last winter's cough syrup, "don't cry," I beg, teasing her toes, tickling her feet, "you're too old for that."

"It's because," she hiccups, "I *am* too old. Old and funny."

"Not funny. Fun. More fun than anybody. Listen. If you don't stop crying you'll be so tired tomorrow we can't go cut a tree."

She straightens up. Queenie jumps on the bed (where Queenie is not allowed) to lick her cheeks. "I know where we'll find real pretty trees, Buddy. And holly, too. With berries big as your eyes. It's way off in the woods. Farther than we've ever been. Papa used to bring us Christmas trees from there: carry them on his shoulder. That's fifty years ago. Well, now: I can't wait for morning."

Morning. Frozen rime lusters the grass; the sun, round as an orange and orange as hot-weather moons, balances on the horizon, burnishes the silvered winter woods. A wild turkey calls. A renegade hog grunts in the undergrowth. Soon, by the edge of knee-deep, rapid-running water, we have to abandon the buggy. Queenie wades the stream first, paddles across barking complaints at the swiftness of the current, the pneumonia-making coldness of it. We follow, holding our shoes and equipment (a hatchet, a burlap sack) above our heads. A mile more: of chastising thorns, burs and briers that catch at our clothes; of rusty pine needles brilliant with gaudy fungus and molted feathers. Here, there, a flash, a flutter, an ecstasy of shrillings remind us that not all the birds have flown south. Always, the path unwinds through lemony sun pools and pitch-black vine tunnels. Another creek to cross: a disturbed armada of speckled trout froths the water round us, and frogs the size of plates practice belly flops; beaver workmen are building a dam. On the farther shore, Queenie shakes herself and trembles. My friend shivers, too: not with cold but enthusiasm. One of her hat's ragged roses sheds a petal as she lifts her head and inhales the pine-heavy air. "We're almost there; can you smell it, Buddy?" she says, as though we were approaching an ocean.

And, indeed, it is a kind of ocean. Scented acres of holiday trees, prickly-leafed holly. Red berries shiny as Chinese bells: black crows swoop upon them screaming. Having stuffed our burlap sacks with enough greenery and crimson to garland a dozen windows, we set about choosing a tree. "It should be," muses my friend, "twice as tall as a boy. So a boy can't steal the star." The one we pick is twice as tall as me. A brave handsome brute that survives thirty hatchet strokes before it keels with a creaking rending cry. Lugging it like a kill, we commence the long trek out. Every few yards we abandon the struggle, sit down and pant. But we have the strength of triumphant huntsmen; that and the tree's virile, icy perfume revive us, goad us on. Many compliments accompany our sunset return along the red clay road to town; but my friend is sly and noncommittal when passers-by praise the treasure perched in our buggy: what a fine tree and where did it come from? "Yonderways," she murmurs vaguely. Once a car stops and the rich mill owner's lazy wife leans out and whines: "Giveya two-bits cash for that ol tree." Ordinarily my friend is afraid of saying no; but on this occasion she promptly shakes her head: "We wouldn't take a dollar." The mill owner's wife persists. "A dollar, my foot! Fifty cents. That's my last offer. Goodness, woman, you can get another one." In answer, my friend gently reflects: "I doubt it. There's never two of anything."

Home: Queenie slumps by the fire and sleeps till tomorrow, snoring loud as a human.

A trunk in the attic contains: a shoebox of ermine tails (off the opera cape of a curious lady who once rented a room in the house), coils of frazzled tinsel gone gold with age, one silver star, a brief rope of dilapidated, undoubtedly dangerous candy-like light bulbs. Excellent decorations, as far as they go, which isn't far enough: my friend wants our tree to blaze "like a Baptist window," droop with weighty snows of ornament. But we can't afford the made-in-Japan splendors at the five-and-dime. So we do what we've always done: sit for days at the kitchen table with scissors and crayons and stacks of colored paper. I make sketches and my friend cuts them out: lots of cats, fish too (because they're easy to draw), some apples, some watermelons, a few winged angels devised from saved-up sheets of Hershey-bar tin foil. We use safety pins to attach these creations to the tree; as a final touch, we sprinkle the branches with shredded cotton (picked in August for this purpose). My friend, surveying the effect, clasps her hands together. "Now honest, Buddy. Doesn't it look good enough to eat?" Queenie tries to eat an angel.

After weaving and ribboning holly wreaths for all the front windows, our next project is the fashioning of family gifts. Tie-dye scarves for the ladies, for the men a home-brewed lemon and licorice and aspirin syrup to be taken "at the first Symptoms of a Cold and after Hunting." But when it comes time for making each other's gift, my friend and I separate to work secretly. I would like to buy her a pearl-handled knife, a radio, a whole pound of chocolate-covered cherries (we tasted some once, and she always swears: "I could live on them, Buddy, Lord yes I could—and that's not taking His name in vain"). Instead, I am building her a kite. She would like to give me a bicycle (she's said so on several million occasions: "If only I could, Buddy. It's bad enough in life to do without something *you* want; but confound it, what gets my goat is not being able to give somebody something you want *them* to have. Only one of these days I will, Buddy. Locate you a bike. Don't ask how. Steal it, maybe"). Instead, I'm fairly certain that she is building me a kite—the same as last year, and the year before: the year before that we exchanged slingshots. All of which is fine by me. For we are champion kite-fliers who study the wind like sailors; my friend, more accomplished than I, can get a kite aloft when there isn't enough breeze to carry clouds.

Christmas Eve afternoon we scrape together a nickel and go to the butcher's to buy Queenie's traditional gift, a good gnawable beef bone. The bone, wrapped in funny paper, is placed high in the tree near the silver star. Queenie knows it's there. She squats at the foot of the tree staring up in a trance of greed: when bedtime arrives she refuses to budge. Her excitement is equaled by my own. I kick the covers and turn my pillow as though it were a scorching summer's night. Somewhere a rooster crows: falsely, for the sun is still on the other side of the world.

"Buddy, are you awake?" It is my friend, calling from her room, which is next to mine; and an instant later she is sitting on my bed holding a candle. "Well, I can't sleep a hoot," she declares. "My mind's jumping like a jack rabbit. Buddy, do you think Mrs. Roosevelt will serve our cake at dinner?" We huddle in the bed, and she squeezes my hand I-love-you. "Seems like your hand used to be so much smaller. I guess I hate to see you grow up. When you're grown up, will we still be friends?" I say always. "But I feel so bad, Buddy. I wanted so bad to give you a bike. I tried to sell my cameo Papa gave me. Buddy"—she hesitates, as though embarrassed—"I made you another kite." Then I confess that I made her one, too; and we laugh. The candle burns too short to hold. Out it goes, exposing the starlight, the stars spinning at the window like a visible caroling that slowly, slowly daybreak silences. Possibly we doze; but the beginnings of dawn splash us like cold water: we're up, wide-eyed and wandering while we wait for others to waken. Quite deliberately my friend drops a kettle on the kitchen floor. I tap-dance in front of closed doors. One by one the household emerges, looking as though they'd like to kill us both; but it's Christmas, so they can't. First, a gorgeous breakfast: just everything you can imagine—from flapjacks and fried squirrel to hominy grits and honey-in-the-comb. Which puts everyone in a good humor except my friend and me. Frankly, we're so impatient to get at the presents we can't eat a mouthful.

Well, I'm disappointed. Who wouldn't be? With socks, a Sunday school shirt, some handkerchiefs, a hand-me-down sweater and a year's subscription to a religious magazine for children. *The Little Shepherd.* It makes me boil. It really does.

My friend has a better haul. A sack of Satsumas, that's her best present. She is proudest, however, of a white wool shawl knitted by her married sister. But she *says* her favorite gift is the kite I built her. And it *is* very beautiful; though not as beautiful as the one she made me, which is blue and scattered with gold and green Good Conduct stars; moreover, my name is painted on it, "Buddy."

"Buddy, the wind is blowing."

The wind is blowing, and nothing will do till we've run to a pasture below the house where Queenie has scooted to bury her bone (and where, a winter hence, Queenie will be buried, too). There, plunging through the healthy waist-high grass, we unreel our kites, feel them twitching at the string like sky fish as they swim into the wind. Satisfied, sun-warmed, we sprawl in the grass and peel Satsumas and watch our kites cavort. Soon I forget the socks and hand-me-down sweater. I'm as happy as if we'd already won the fifty-thousand-dollar Grand Prize in that coffee-naming contest.

"My, how foolish I am!" my friend cries, suddenly alert, like a woman remembering too late she has biscuits in the oven. "You know what I've always thought?" she asks in a tone of discovery, and not smiling at me but a point beyond. "I've always thought a body would have to be sick and dying before they saw the Lord. And I imagined that when He came it would be like looking at the Baptist window: pretty as colored glass with the sun pouring through, such a shine you don't know it's getting dark. And it's been a comfort: to think of that shine taking away all the spooky feeling. But I'll wager it never happens. I'll wager at the very end a body realizes the Lord has already shown Himself. That things as they are"—her hand circles in a gesture that gathers clouds and kites and grass and Queenie pawing earth over her bone—"just what they've always seen, was seeing Him. As for me, I could leave the world with today in my eyes."

This is our last Christmas together.

Life separates us. Those who Know Best decide that I belong in a military school. And so follows a miserable succession of bugle-blowing prisons, grim reveille-ridden summer camps. I have a new home too. But it doesn't count. Home is where my friend is, and there I never go.

And there she remains, puttering around the kitchen. Alone with Queenie. Then alone. ("Buddy dear," she writes in her wild hard-to-read script, "yesterday Jim Macy's horse kicked Queenie bad. Be thankful she didn't feel much. I wrapped her in a Fine Linen sheet and rode her in the buggy down to Simpson's pasture where she can be with all her Bones. . . .") For a few Novembers she continues to bake her fruitcakes single-handed; not as many, but some: and, of course, she always sends me "the best of the batch." Also, in every letter she encloses a dime wadded in toilet paper: "See a picture show and write me the story." But gradually in her letters she tends to confuse me with her other friend, the Buddy who died in the 1880's; more and more thirteenths are not the only days she stays in bed: a morning arrives in November, a leafless birdless coming of winter morning, when she cannot rouse herself to exclaim: "Oh my, it's fruitcake weather!"

And when that happens, I know it. A message saying so merely confirms a piece of news some secret vein had already received, severing from me an irreplaceable part of myself, letting it loose like a kite on a broken string. That is why, walking across a school campus on this particular December morning, I keep searching the sky. As if I expected to see, rather like hearts, a lost pair of kites hurrying toward heaven.

DECEMBER NIGHT

WILLA CATHER

from DEATH COMES FOR THE ARCHBISHOP

Father Vaillant had been absent in Arizona since midsummer, and it was now December. Bishop Latour had been going through one of those periods of coldness and doubt which, from his boyhood, had occasionally settled down upon his spirit and made him feel an alien, wherever he was. He attended to his correspondence, went on his rounds among the parish priests, held services at missions that were without pastors, superintended the building of the addition to the Sisters' school: but his heart was not in these things.

One night about three weeks before Christmas he was lying in his bed, unable to sleep, with the sense of failure clutching at his heart. His prayers were empty words and brought him no refreshment. His soul had become a barren field. He had nothing within himself to give his priests or his people. His work seemed superficial, a house built upon the sands. His great diocese was still a heathen country. The Indians travelled their old road of fear and darkness, battling with evil omens and ancient shadows. The Mexicans were children who played with their religion.

As the night wore on, the bed on which the Bishop lay became a bed of thorns; he could bear it no longer. Getting up in the dark, he looked out of the window and was surprised to find that it was snowing, that the ground was already lightly covered. The full moon, hidden by veils of cloud, threw a pale phosphorescent luminousness over the heavens, and the towers of the church stood up black against this silvery fleece. Father Latour felt a longing to go into the church to pray; but instead he lay down again under his blankets. Then, realizing that it was the cold of the church he shrank from, and despising himself, he rose again, dressed quickly, and went out into the court, throwing on over his cassock that faithful old cloak that was the twin of Father Vaillant's.

They had bought the cloth for those coats in Paris, long ago, when they were young men staying at the Seminary for Foreign Missions in the rue du Bac, preparing for their first voyage to the New World. The cloth had been made up into caped riding-cloaks by a German tailor in Ohio, and lined with fox fur. Years afterward, when Father Latour was about to start on his long journey in search of his Bishopric, that same tailor had made the cloaks over and relined them with squirrel skins, as more appropriate for a mild climate. These memories and many others went through the Bishop's mind as he wrapped the trusty garment about him and crossed the court to the sacristy, with the big iron key in his hand.

The court was white with snow, and the shadows of walls and buildings stood out sharply in the faint light from the moon muffled in vapour. In the deep doorway of the sacristy he saw a crouching figure—a woman, he made out, and she was weeping bitterly. He raised her up and took her inside. As soon as he had lit a candle, he recognized her, and could have guessed her errand.

It was an old Mexican woman, called Sada, who was slave in an American family. They were Protestants, very hostile to the Roman Church, and they did not allow her to go to Mass or to receive the visits of a priest. She was carefully watched at home,—but in winter, when the heated rooms of the house were desirable to the family, she was put to sleep in a woodshed. To-night, unable to sleep for the cold, she had gathered courage for this heroic action, had slipped out through the stable door and come running up an alley-way to the House of God to pray. Finding the front doors of the church fastened, she had made her way into the Bishop's garden and come round to the sacristy, only to find that, too, shut against her.

The Bishop stood holding the candle and watching her face while she spoke her few words; a dark brown peon face, worn thin and sharp by life and sorrow. It seemed to him that he had never seen pure goodness shine out of a human countenance as it did from hers. He saw that she had no stockings under her shoes,—the cast-off rawhides of her master,—and beneath her frayed black shawl was only a thin calico dress, covered with patches. Her teeth struck together as she stood trying to control her shivering. With one movement of his free hand the Bishop took the furred cloak from his shoulders and put it about her. This frightened her. She cowered under it, murmuring, "Ah, no, no, Padre!"

"You must obey your Padre, my daughter. Draw that cloak about you, and we will go into the church to pray."

The church was utterly black except for the red spark of the sanctuary lamp before the high altar. Taking her hand, and holding the candle before him, he led her across the choir to the Lady Chapel. There he began to light the tapers before the Virgin. Old Sada fell on her knees and kissed the floor. She kissed the feet of the Holy Mother, the pedestal on which they stood, crying all the while. But from the working of her face, from the beautiful tremors which passed over it, he knew they were tears of ecstasy.

"Nineteen years, Father; nineteen years since I have seen the holy things of the altar!"

"All that is passed, Sada. You have remembered the holy things in your heart. We will pray together."

The Bishop knelt beside her, and they began, *O Holy Mary, Queen of Virgins.* . . .

More than once Father Vaillant had spoken to the Bishop of this aged captive. There had been much whispering among the devout women of the parish about her pitiful case. The Smiths, with whom she lived, were Georgia people, who had at one time lived in El Paso del Norte, and they had taken her back to their native State with them. Not long ago some disgrace had come upon this family in Georgia, they had been forced to sell all their Negro slaves and flee the State. The Mexican woman they could not sell because they had no legal title to her, her position was irregular. Now that they were back in a Mexican country, the Smiths were afraid their charwoman might escape from them and find asylum among her own people, so they kept strict watch upon her. They did not allow her to go outside their own *patio,* not even to accompany her mistress to market.

Two women of the Altar Guild had been so bold as to go into the *patio* to talk with Sada when she was washing clothes, but they had been rudely driven away by the mistress of the house. Mrs. Smith had come running out into the court, half dressed, and told them that if they had business at her *casa* they were to come in by the front door, and not sneak in through the stable to frighten a poor silly creature. When they said they had come to ask Sada to go to Mass with them, she told them she had got the poor creature out of the clutches of the priests once, and would see to it that she did not fall into them again.

Even after that rebuff a very pious neighbour woman had tried to say a word to Sada through the alley door of the stable, where she was unloading wood off the burro. But the old servant had put her finger to her lips and motioned the visitor away, glancing back over her shoulder the while with such an expression of terror that the intruder hastened off, surmising that Sada would be harshly used if she were caught speaking to anyone. The good woman went immediately to Father Vaillant with this story, and he had consulted the Bishop, declaring that something ought to be done to secure the consolations of religion for the bond-woman. But the Bishop replied that the time was not yet; for the present it was inexpedient to antagonize these people. The Smiths were the leaders of a small group of low-caste Protestants who took every occasion to make trouble for the Catholics. They hung about the door of the church on festival days with mockery and loud laughter, spoke insolently to the nuns in the street, stood jeering and blaspheming when the procession went by on Corpus Christi Sunday. There were five sons in the Smith family, fellows of low habits and evil tongues. Even the two younger boys, still children, showed a vicious disposition. Tranquilino had repeatedly driven these two boys out of the Bishop's garden, where they came with their lewd companions to rob the young pear trees or to speak filth against the priests.

When they rose from their knees, Father Latour told Sada he was glad to know that she remembered her prayers so well.

"Ah, Padre, every night I say my Rosary to my Holy Mother, no matter where I sleep!" declared the old creature passionately, looking up into his face and pressing her knotted hands against her breast.

When he asked if she had her beads with her, she was confused. She kept them tied with a cord around her waist, under her clothes, as the only place she could hide them safely.

He spoke soothingly to her. "Remember this, Sada; in the year to come, and during the Novena before Christmas, I will not forget to pray for you whenever I offer the Blessed Sacrifice of the Mass. Be at rest in your heart, for I will remember you in my silent supplications before the altar as I do my own sisters and my nieces."

Never, as he afterward told Father Vaillant, had it been permitted him to behold such deep experience of the holy joy of religion as on that pale December night. He was able to feel, kneeling beside her, the precious-ness of the things of the altar to her who was without possessions; the tapers, the image of the Virgin, the figures of the saints, the Cross that took away indignity from suffering and made pain and poverty a means of fellowship with Christ. Kneeling beside the much enduring bond-woman, he experienced those holy mysteries as he had done in his young manhood. He seemed able to feel all it meant to her to know that there was a Kind Woman in Heaven, though there were such cruel ones on earth. Old people, who had felt blows and toil and known the world's hard hand, need, even more than children do, a woman's tenderness. Only a Woman, divine, could know all that a woman can suffer.

Not often, indeed, had Jean Marie Latour come so near to the Foun-tain of all Pity as in the Lady Chapel that night; the pity that no man born of woman could ever utterly cut himself off from; that was for the murderer on the scaffold, as it was for the dying soldier or the martyr on the rack. The beautiful concept of Mary pierced the priest's heart like a sword.

"*O Sacred Heart of Mary!*" she murmured by his side, and he felt how that name was food and raiment, friend and mother to her. He received the miracle in her heart into his own, saw through her eyes, knew that his poverty was as bleak as hers. When the Kingdom of Heaven had first come into the world, into a cruel world of torture and slaves and masters, He who brought it had said, "*And whosoever is least among you, the same shall be first in the Kingdom of Heaven.*" This church was Sada's house, and he was a servant in it.

The Bishop heard the old woman's confession. He blessed her and put both hands upon her head. When he took her down the nave to let her out of the church, Sada made to lift his cloak from her shoulders. He re-strained her, telling her she must keep it for her own, and sleep in it at night. But she slipped out of it hurriedly; such a thought seemed to ter-rify her. "No, no, Father. If they were to find it on me!" More than that, she did not accuse her oppressors. But as she put it off, she stroked the old garment and patted it as if it were a living thing that had been kind to her.

Happily Father Latour bethought him of a little silver medal, with a figure of the Virgin, he had in his pocket. He gave it to her, telling her that it had been blessed by the Holy Father himself. Now she would have a treasure to hide and guard, to adore while her watchers slept. Ah, he thought, for one who cannot read—or think—the Image, the physical form of Love!

He fitted the great key into its lock, the door swung slowly back on its wooden hinges. The peace without seemed all one with the peace in his own soul. The snow had stopped, the gauzy clouds that had ribbed the arch of heaven were now all sunk into one soft white fog bank over the Sangre de Cristo mountains. The full moon shone high in the blue vault, majestic, lonely, benign. The Bishop stood in the doorway of his church, lost in thought, looking at the line of black footprints his departing visitor had left in the wet scurf of snow.

CHRISTMAS IS A SAD SEASON FOR THE POOR

JOHN CHEEVER

Christmas is a sad season. The phrase came to Charlie an instant after the alarm clock had waked him, and named for him an amorphous depression that had troubled him all the previous evening. The sky outside his window was black. He sat up in bed and pulled the light chain that hung in front of his nose. Christmas is a very sad day of the year, he thought. Of all the millions of people in New York, I am practically the only one who has to get up in the cold black of 6 A.M. on Christmas Day in the morning; I am practically the only one.

He dressed, and when he went downstairs from the top floor of the rooming house in which he lived, the only sounds he heard were the coarse sounds of sleep; the only lights burning were lights that had been forgotten. Charlie ate some breakfast in an all-night lunchwagon and took an elevated train uptown. From Third Avenue, he walked over to Sutton Place. The neighborhood was dark. House after house put into the shine of the street lights a wall of black windows. Millions and millions were sleeping, and this general loss of consciousness generated an impression of abandonment, as if this were the fall of the city, the end of time. He opened the iron-and-glass doors of the apartment building where he had been working for six months as an elevator operator, and went through the elegant lobby to a locker room at the back. He put on a striped vest with brass buttons, a false ascot, a pair of pants with a light-blue stripe on the seam, and a coat. The night elevator man was dozing on the little bench in the car. Charlie woke him. The night elevator man told him thickly that the day doorman had been taken sick and wouldn't be in that day. With the doorman sick, Charlie wouldn't have any relief for lunch, and a lot of people would expect him to whistle for cabs.

Charlie had been on duty a few minutes when 14 rang—a Mrs. Hewing, who, he happened to know, was kind of immoral. Mrs. Hewing hadn't been to bed yet, and she got into the elevator wearing a long dress under her fur coat. She was followed by her two funny-looking dogs. He took her down and watched her go out into the dark and take her dogs to the curb. She was outside for only a few minutes. Then she came in and he took her up to 14 again. When she got off the elevator, she said, "Merry Christmas, Charlie."

"Well, it isn't much of a holiday for me. Mrs. Hewing," he said. "I think Christmas is a very sad season of the year. It isn't that people around here ain't generous—I mean, I got plenty of tips—but, you see, I live alone in a furnished room and I don't have any family or anything, and Christmas isn't much of a holiday for me."

"I'm sorry, Charlie," Mrs. Hewing said. "I don't have any family myself. It is kind of sad when you're alone, isn't it?" She called her dogs and followed them into her apartment. He went down.

It was quiet then, and Charlie lighted a cigarette. The heating plant in the basement encompassed the building at that hour in a regular and profound vibration, and the sullen noises of arriving steam heat began to resound, first in the lobby and then to reverberate up through all the sixteen stories, but this was a mechanical awakening, and it didn't lighten his loneliness or his petulance. The black air outside the glass doors had begun to turn blue, but the blue light seemed to have no source; it appeared in the middle of the air. It was a tearful light, and as it picked out the empty street he wanted to cry. Then a cab drove up, and the Walsers got out, drunk and dressed in evening clothes, and he took them up to their penthouse. The Walsers got him to brooding about the difference between his life in a furnished room and the lives of the people overhead. It was terrible.

Then the early churchgoers began to ring, but there were only three of these that morning. A few more went off to church at eight o'clock, but the majority of the building remained unconscious, although the smell of bacon and coffee had begun to drift into the elevator shaft.

At a little after nine, a nursemaid came down with a child. Both the nursemaid and the child had a deep tan and had just returned, he knew, from Bermuda. He had never been to Bermuda. He, Charlie, was a prisoner, confined eight hours a day to a six-by-eight elevator cage, which was confined, in turn, to a sixteen-story shaft. In one building or another, he had made his living as an elevator operator for ten years. He estimated the average trip at about an eighth of a mile, and when he thought of the thousands of miles he had traveled, when he thought that he might have driven the car through the mists above the Caribbean and set it down on some coral beach in Bermuda, he held the narrowness of his travels against his passengers, as if it were not the nature of the elevator but the pressure of their lives that confined him, as if they had clipped his wings.

He was thinking about this when the DePauls, on 9, rang. They wished him a merry Christmas.

"Well, it's nice of you to think of me," he said as they descended, "but it isn't much of a holiday for me. Christmas is a sad season when you're poor. I live alone in a furnished room. I don't have any family."

"Who do you have dinner with, Charlie?" Mrs. DePaul asked.

"I don't have any Christmas dinner," Charlie said. "I just get a sandwich."

"Oh, Charlie!" Mrs. DePaul was a stout woman with an impulsive heart, and Charlie's plaint struck at her holiday mood as if she had been caught in a cloudburst. "I do wish we could share our Christmas dinner with you, you know," she said. "I come from Vermont, you know, and when I was a child, you know, we always used to have a great many people at our table. The mailman, you know, and the schoolteacher, and just anybody who didn't have any family of their own, you know, and I wish we could share our dinner with you the way we used to, you know, and I don't see any reason why we can't. We can't have you at the table, you know, because you couldn't leave the elevator—could you?—but just as soon as Mr. DePaul has carved the goose, I'll give you a ring, and I'll arrange a tray for you, you know, and I want you to come up and at least share our Christmas dinner."

Charlie thanked them, and their generosity surprised him, but he wondered if, with the arrival of friends and relatives, they wouldn't forget their offer.

Then old Mrs. Gadshill rang, and when she wished him a merry Christmas, he hung his head.

"It isn't much of a holiday for me, Mrs. Gadshill," he said. "Christmas is a sad season if you're poor. You see, I don't have any family. I live alone in a furnished room."

"I don't have any family either, Charlie," Mrs. Gadshill said. She spoke with a pointed lack of petulance, but her grace was forced. "That is, I don't have any children with me today. I have three children and seven grandchildren, but none of them can see their way to coming East for Christmas with me. Of course, I understand their problems. I know that it's difficult to travel with children during the holidays, although I always seemed to manage it when I was their age, but people feel differently, and we mustn't condemn them for the things we can't understand. But I know how you feel, Charlie. I haven't any family either. I'm just as lonely as you."

Mrs. Gadshill's speech didn't move him. Maybe she was lonely, but she had a ten-room apartment and three servants and bucks and bucks and diamonds and diamonds, and there were plenty of poor kids in the slums who would be happy at a chance at the food her cook threw away. Then he thought about poor kids. He sat down on a chair in the lobby and thought about them.

They got the worst of it. Beginning in the fall, there was all this excitement about Christmas and how it was a day for them. After Thanksgiving, they couldn't miss it. It was fixed so they couldn't miss it. The wreaths and decorations everywhere, and bells ringing, and trees in the park, and Santa Clauses on every corner, and pictures in the magazines and newspapers and on every wall and window in the city told them that if they were good, they would get what they wanted. Even if they couldn't read, they couldn't miss it. They couldn't miss it even if they were blind. It got into the air the poor kids inhaled. Every time they took a walk, they'd see all the expensive toys in the store windows, and they'd write letters to Santa Claus, and their mothers and fathers would promise to mail them, and after the kids had gone to sleep, they'd burn the letters in the stove. And when it came Christmas morning, how could you explain it, how could you tell them that Santa Claus only visited the rich, that he didn't know about the good? How could you face them when all you had to give them was a balloon or a lollipop?

On the way home from work a few nights earlier, Charlie had seen a woman and a little girl going down Fifty-ninth Street. The little girl was crying. He guessed she was crying, he knew she was crying, because she'd seen all the things in the toy-store windows and couldn't understand why none of them were for her. Her mother did housework, he guessed, or maybe was a waitress, and he saw them going back to a room like his, with green walls and no heat, on Christmas Eve, to eat a can of soup. And he saw the little girl hang up her ragged stocking and fall asleep, and he saw the mother looking through her purse for something to put into the stocking— This reverie was interrupted by a bell on 11. He went up, and Mr. and Mrs. Fuller were waiting. When they wished him a merry Christmas, he said, "Well, it isn't much of a holiday for me, Mrs. Fuller. Christmas is a sad season when you're poor."

"Do you have any children, Charlie?" Mrs. Fuller asked.

"Four living," he said. "Two in the grave." The majesty of his lie overwhelmed him. "Mrs. Leary's a cripple," he added.

"How sad, Charlie," Mrs. Fuller said. She started out of the elevator when it reached the lobby, and then she turned. "I want to give your children some presents, Charlie," she said. "Mr. Fuller and I are going to pay a call now, but when we come back, I want to give you some things for your children."

He thanked her. Then the bell rang on 4, and he went up to get the Westons.

"It isn't much of a Christmas for me," he told them when they wished him a merry Christmas. "Christmas is a sad season when you're poor. You see, I live alone in a furnished room."

"Poor Charlie," Mrs. Weston said. "I know just how you feel. During the war, when Mr. Weston was away, I was all alone at Christmas. I didn't have any Christmas dinner or a tree or anything. I just scrambled myself some eggs and sat there and cried." Mr. Weston, who had gone into the lobby, called impatiently to his wife. "I know just how you feel, Charlie," Mrs. Weston said.

By noon, the climate in the elevator shaft had changed from bacon and coffee to poultry and game, and the house, like an enormous and complex homestead, was absorbed in the preparations for a domestic feast. The children and their nursemaids had all returned from the Park. Grandmothers and aunts were arriving in limousines. Most of the people who came through the lobby were carrying packages wrapped in colored paper, and were wearing their best furs and new clothes. Charlie continued to complain to most of the tenants when they wished him a merry Christmas, changing his story from the lonely bachelor to the poor father, and back again, as his mood changed, but this outpouring of melancholy, and the sympathy it aroused, didn't make him feel any better.

At half past one, 9 rang, and when he went up, Mr. DePaul was standing in the door of their apartment holding a cocktail shaker and a glass. "Here's a little Christmas cheer, Charlie," he said, and he poured Charlie a drink. Then a maid appeared with a tray of covered dishes, and Mrs. DePaul came out of the living room. "Merry Christmas, Charlie," she said. "I had Mr. DePaul carve the goose early, so that you could have some, you know. I didn't want to put the dessert on the tray, because I was afraid it would melt, you know, so when we have our dessert, we'll call you."

"And what is Christmas without presents?" Mr. DePaul said, and he brought a large, flat box from the hall and laid it on top of the covered dishes.

"You people make it seem like a real Christmas to me," Charlie said. Tears started into his eyes. "Thank you, thank you."

"Merry Christmas! Merry Christmas!" they called, and they watched him carry his dinner and his present into the elevator. He took the tray and the box into the locker room when he got down. On the tray, there was a soup, some kind of creamed fish, and a serving of goose. The bell rang again, but before he answered it, he tore open the DePauls' box and saw that it held a dressing gown. Their generosity and their cocktail had begun to work on his brain, and he went jubilantly up to 12. Mrs. Gadshill's maid was standing in the door with a tray, and Mrs. Gadshill stood behind her. "Merry Christmas, Charlie!" she said. He thanked her, and tears came into his eyes again. On the way down, he drank off the glass of sherry on Mrs. Gadshill's tray. Mrs. Gadshill's contribution was a mixed grill. He ate the lamb chop with his fingers. The bell was ringing again, and he wiped his face with a paper towel and went up to 11. "Merry Christmas, Charlie," Mrs. Fuller said, and she was standing in the door with her arms full of packages wrapped in silver paper, just like a picture in an advertisement, and Mr. Fuller was beside her with an arm around her, and they both looked as if they were going to cry. "Here are some things I want you to take home to your children," Mrs. Fuller said. "And here's something for Mrs. Leary and here's something for you. And if you want to take these things out to the elevator, we'll have your dinner ready for you in a minute." He carried the things into the elevator and came back for the tray. "Merry Christmas, Charlie!" both of the Fullers called after him as he closed the door. He took their dinner and their presents into the locker room and tore open the box that was marked for him. There was an alligator wallet in it, with Mr. Fuller's initials in the corner. Their dinner was also goose, and he ate a piece of the meat with his fingers and was washing it down with a cocktail when the bell rang. He went up again. This time it was the Westons. "Merry Christmas, Charlie!" they said, and they gave him a cup of eggnog, a turkey dinner, and a present. Their gift was also a dressing gown. Then 7 rang, and when he went up, there was another dinner and some more toys. Then 14 rang, and when he went up, Mrs. Hewing was standing in the hall, in a kind of negligee, holding a pair of riding boots in one hand and some neckties in the other. She had been crying and drinking. "Merry Christmas, Charlie," she said tenderly. "I wanted to give you something, and I've been thinking about you all morning, and I've been all over the apartment, and these are the only things I could find that a man might want. These are the only things that Mr. Brewer left. I don't suppose you'd have any use for the riding boots, but wouldn't you like the neckties?" Charlie took the neckties and thanked her and hurried back to the car, for the elevator bell had rung three times.

By three o'clock, Charlie had fourteen dinners spread on the table and the floor of the locker room, and the bell kept ringing. Just as he started to eat one, he would have to go up and get another, and he was in the middle of the Parsons' roast beef when he had to go up and get the De-Pauls' dessert. He kept the door of the locker room closed, for he sensed that the quality of charity is exclusive and that his friends would have been disappointed to find that they were not the only ones to try to lessen his loneliness. There were goose, turkey, chicken, pheasant, grouse, and pigeon. There were trout and salmon, creamed scallops and oysters, lobster, crab meat, whitebait, and clams. There were plum puddings, mince pies, mousses, puddles of melted ice cream, layer cakes, *Torten,* éclairs, and two slices of Bavarian cream. He had dressing gowns, neckties, cuff links, socks, and handkerchiefs, and one of the tenants had asked for his neck size and then given him three green shirts. There were a glass teapot filled, the label said, with jasmine honey, four bottles of aftershave lotion, some alabaster bookends, and a dozen steak knives. The avalanche of charity he had precipitated filled the locker room and made him hesitant, now and then, as if he had touched some wellspring in the female heart that would bury him alive in food and dressing gowns. He had made almost no headway on the food, for all the servings were preternaturally large, as if loneliness had been counted on to generate in him a brutish appetite. Nor had he opened any of the presents that had been given to him for his imaginary children, but he had drunk everything they sent down and around him were the dregs of Martinis, Manhattans, Old-Fashioneds, champagne-and-raspberry-shrub cocktails, eggnogs, Bronxes, and Side Cars.

His face was blazing. He loved the world, and the world loved him. When he thought back over his life, it appeared to him in a rich and wonderful light, full of astonishing experiences and unusual friends. He thought that his job as an elevator operator—cruising up and down through hundreds of feet of perilous space—demanded the nerve and the intellect of a birdman. All the constraints of his life—the green walls of his room and the months of unemployment—dissolved. No one was ringing, but he got into the elevator and shot it at full speed up to the penthouse and down again, up and down, to test his wonderful mastery of space.

A bell rang on 12 while he was cruising, and he stopped in his flight long enough to pick up Mrs. Gadshill. As the car started to fall, he took his hands off the controls in a paroxysm of joy and shouted, "Strap on your safety belt, Mrs. Gadshill! We're going to make a loop-the-loop!" Mrs. Gadshill shrieked. Then, for some reason, she sat down on the floor of the elevator. Why was her face so pale, he wondered; why was she sitting on the floor? She shrieked again. He grounded the car gently, and cleverly, he thought, and opened the door. "I'm sorry if I scared you, Mrs. Gadshill," he said meekly. "I was only fooling." She shrieked again. Then she ran out into the lobby, screaming for the superintendent.

The superintendent fired Charlie and took over the elevator himself. The news that he was out of work stung Charlie for a minute. It was his first contact with human meanness that day. He sat down in the locker room and gnawed on a drumstick. His drinks were beginning to let him down, and while it had not reached him yet, he felt a miserable soberness in the offing. The excess of food and presents around him began to make him feel guilty and unworthy. He regretted bitterly the lie he had told about his children. He was a single man with simple needs. He had abused the goodness of the people upstairs. He was unworthy.

Then up through this drunken train of thought surged the sharp figure of his landlady and her three skinny children. He thought of them sitting in their basement room. The cheer of Christmas had passed them by. This image got him to his feet. The realization that he was in a position to give, that he could bring happiness easily to someone else, sobered him. He took a big burlap sack, which was used for collecting waste, and began to stuff it, first with his presents and then with the presents for his imaginary children. He worked with the haste of a man whose train is approaching the station, for he could hardly wait to see those long faces light up when he came in the door. He changed his clothes, and, fired by a wonderful and unfamiliar sense of power, he slung his bag over his shoulder like a regular Santa Claus, went out the back way, and took a taxi to the Lower East Side.

The landlady and her children had just finished off a turkey, which had been sent to them by the local Democratic Club, and they were stuffed and uncomfortable when Charlie began pounding on the door, shouting "Merry Christmas!" He dragged the bag in after him and dumped the presents for the children onto the floor. There were dolls and musical toys, blocks, sewing kits, an Indian suit, and a loom, and it appeared to him that, as he had hoped, his arrival in the basement dispelled its gloom. When half the presents had been opened, he gave the landlady a bathrobe and went upstairs to look over the things he had been given for himself.

Now, the landlady's children had already received so many presents by the time Charlie arrived that they were confused with receiving, and it was only the landlady's intuitive grasp of the nature of charity that made her allow the children to open some of the presents while Charlie was still in the room, but as soon as he had gone, she stood between the children and the presents that were still unopened. "Now, you kids have had enough already," she said. "You kids have got your share. Just look at the things you got there. Why, you ain't even played with the half of them. Mary Anne, you ain't even looked at that doll the Fire Department give you. Now, a nice thing to do would be to take all this stuff that's left over to those poor people on Hudson Street—them Deckkers. They ain't got nothing." A beatific light came into her face when she realized that she could give, that she could bring cheer, that she could put a healing finger on a case needier than hers, and—like Mrs. DePaul and Mrs. Weston, like Charlie himself and like Mrs. Deckker, when Mrs. Deckker was to think, subsequently, of the poor Shannons—first love, then charity, and then a sense of power drove her. "Now, you kids help me get all this stuff together. Hurry, hurry, hurry," she said, for it was dark then, and she knew that we are bound, one to another, in licentious benevolence for only a single day, and that day was nearly over. She was tired, but she couldn't rest, she couldn't rest.

What Was the Christmas Star?

Arthur C. Clarke

W as it a comet, or two planets in conjunction? Or could it
have been a blinding flash that started its trip toward the
earth 3,000 years before?

Go out of doors any morning this December, an hour or so before
dawn, and look up at the eastern sky. You will see there one of the most
beautiful sights in all the heavens, a blazing, blue-white beacon, ten times
brighter than Sirius, the most brilliant of the stars. Apart from the moon
itself, it is the brightest object you will ever see in the night sky. It will
still be visible even when the sun rises; indeed, you can find it at midday
if you know exactly where to look.

Ours is an age in which the glare of electric lights has hidden the stars,
so that men have forgotten many things that were familiar to their ancestors. If you take the average city dweller away from his floodlit can-
yons, lead him out to some hill in the country, and show him this
brilliant herald of the dawn, he probably will have no idea what it is. Indeed, it is safe to predict that through December there will be a flood of
flying-saucer reports from ignorant or credulous observers seeing this
dazzling point of light against the sunrise.

It is our sister world, the planet Venus, reflecting across the gulf of
space the sunlight glancing from her unbroken cloud veils. Every eighteen months she appears in the morning sky, rising shortly before the
sun.

It has been seriously suggested that Venus was the Star of Nativity,
and at least one massive book has been written in an effort to prove this

theory. However, it is a theory that makes very little sense when examined closely. To all the peoples of the Eastern world, Venus was one of the most familiar objects in the sky. Even today, she serves as a kind of alarm clock to the Arab nomads. When she rises, it is time to start moving, to make as much progress as possible before the sun begins to blast the desert with its heat. For thousands of years, shining more brilliantly than we ever see her in our northern skies, she has watched the camps struck and the caravans begin to move.

Even to uneducated Jews, there could have been nothing in the least remarkable about Venus, And the Magi were no ordinary men; they were certainly experts on astronomy, and knew the movements of the planets.

What, then, was the Star of Bethlehem—assuming that it was a natural phenomenon and not a miraculous apparition? The Bible gives us very few clues; all we can do is consider some possibilities that at this distance in time can be neither proved nor disproved. One of those possibilities—the most spectacular and awe-inspiring of all—has been suggested only in the past few years. But let us first look at some of the earlier theories.

In addition to Venus there are four other planets easily visible to the naked eye—Mercury, Mars, Jupiter and Saturn. During their movements across the sky, two planets may sometimes appear to pass very close to one another, though in fact they are millions or hundreds of millions of miles apart. Such occurrences are called "conjunctions."

On very rare occasions, the conjunctions may be so close that the planets cannot be separated by the naked eye. This happened to Mars and Venus on October 4, 1953, when for a short while the two planets appeared to be fused into a single star. Such a spectacle is rare enough to be very striking, and the great astronomer Kepler devoted much time to proving that the Star of Bethlehem was a conjunction of Jupiter and Saturn. The two planets passed very close together (remember, this was purely from Earth's point of view—in reality they were half a billion miles apart!) in May, 7 B.C., not long before the date set by some authorities for the birth of Christ. Others set it as late as 4 B.C.

Kepler's ingenious proposal, however, is as unconvincing as the Venus theory. Better calculations than he could make in his day have shown that, after all, this conjunction was not a very close one, and the planets were always far enough apart to be separated easily by the eye. Moreover, there was a still closer conjunction in 66 B.C., which, following Kepler's theory, should have brought a delegation of wise men to Bethlehem fifty-nine years too soon!

In any case, the Magi could be expected to be as familiar with such events as with all other planetary movements, and the Biblical account also indicates that the Star of Bethlehem was visible over a period of weeks (it must have taken the Magi a considerable time to reach Judea, have their interview with Herod and then go on to Bethlehem). The conjunction of two planets lasts only a few hours, since they soon separate in the sky and go on their individual ways again.

We can get around this difficulty if we assume that the Magi were astrologers and had somehow deduced the birth of the Messiah from a particular configuration of the heavens. Suppose, for example, they had decided, by some esoteric reasoning of the type on which this pseudo-science is based, that Venus or some other planet, perhaps Jupiter or Saturn, had taken a position in the Zodiac that foretold the birth of Christ. Then even when the planet concerned moved from this position, they might still refer to it as "His" star and continue to use it as a guide.

This theory is simple and plausible, for in ancient times most wise men did believe in astrology and, in consequence, many of them led somewhat precarious lives as court prophets. Because of its very simplicity, this theory can never be proved or disproved, but one would like to think that the facts are somewhat more exciting.

They may well be. It seems much more likely that the Star of the Nativity was something quite novel and unusual, and not one of the familiar planets whose behavior had been well known for thousands of years before the birth of Christ. Of course, if one accepts as literally true the statement that "the star, which they saw in the east, *went before them, till it came and stood over where the young Child was,*" no natural explanation is possible. Any heavenly body—star, planet, comet or whatever it may be—must share in the normal movement of the sky, rising in the east and setting some hours later in the west. Only the Pole Star, because it lies on the invisible axis of the turning Earth, appears unmoving in the sky and can act as a fixed and constant guide.

But the phrase "went before them," like so much else in the Bible, can be interpreted in many ways. It may be that the Star, whatever it might have been, was so close to the Sun that it could only be seen for a short period near dawn, and so would never have been visible except in the eastern sky. Like Venus when she is a morning star, it might have risen shortly before the Sun, then been lost in the glare of the new day before it could climb very far up the sky. The wise men would thus have seen it ahead of them at the beginning of each day, and then lost it in the dawn before it had veered round to the south. Many other readings are equally possible.

Very well then, can we discover some astronomical phenomenon that fits the Biblical text and is sufficiently startling to surprise men completely familiar with the movements of the stars and planets?

Let's see if a comet answers the specification. Most comets have a bright, starlike core or nucleus that is completely dwarfed by an enormous tail, a luminous appendage which may be in the shape of a narrow beam or a broad, diffuse fan. At first sight it would seem very unlikely that anyone would call such an object a star, but in old records comets are sometimes referred to, not inaptly, as "hairy stars."

It is perfectly possible that a comet appeared just before the birth of Christ. Attempts have been made, without success, to discover whether any of the known comets were visible around that date. But the number of comets whose paths and periods we do know is very small compared with the colossal number that undoubtedly exists. If a comet did shine over Bethlehem, it may not be seen again from Earth for a hundred thousand years.

We can picture it in that Oriental dawn, a band of light streaming up from the eastern horizon, perhaps stretching vertically toward the zenith. The tail of a comet always points away from the sun; the comet would appear, therefore, like a great arrow, aimed at the east. As the sun rose, the comet would fade into invisibility; but the next morning, it would be in almost the same place, still directing the travelers to their goal. It might be visible for weeks before it disappeared once more into the depths of space. The picture is a dramatic and attractive one. It may even be the correct explanation; one day, perhaps, we shall know.

But there is another theory, and this is the one most astronomers would probably accept today. It makes the other explanations look trivial and commonplace indeed, for it leads us to contemplate the most astonishing and terrifying events yet discovered in the whole realm of Nature.

We will forget now about planets and comets and the other denizens of our own tight little solar system. Let us go out across *real* space, right out to the stars—those other suns, many of them far greater than our own sun.

Most stars shine with unwavering brilliance, century after century. Sirius appears now exactly as it did to Moses, as it did to Neanderthal Man, as it did to the dinosaurs, if they ever bothered to look at the night sky. Its brilliance has changed little during the entire history of Earth, and will be the same a billion years from now.

But there are some stars, the so-called "novae" or new stars, that for no ascertainable reason suddenly turn themselves into celestial atomic bombs. Such a star may explode so violently that it leaps a hundred-thousand-fold in brilliance within a few hours. One night it may be invisible to the naked eye; on the next, it may dominate the sky.

Novae are not uncommon; many are observed every year, though few are near enough to be visible except through telescopes. They are the routine disasters of the universe.

Two or three times in every thousand years, however, there occurs something that makes a mere nova about as inconspicuous as a firefly at noon. When a star becomes a *super*nova its brilliance may increase not by a hundred thousand but by a *thousand million* times in the course of a few hours. The last time such an event was witnessed was in A.D. 1604; there was another supernova in A.D. 1572 (so brilliant that it was visible in broad daylight); and the Chinese astronomers recorded one in A.D. 1054. It is quite possible that the Star of Bethlehem was such a supernova, and if so one can draw some very surprising conclusions.

We'll assume that Supernova Bethlehem was about as bright as the nova of A.D. 1572, often called Tycho's star after the great astronomer who observed it at the time. Since this star could be seen by day, it must have been as brilliant as Venus. As we also know that a supernova is, in reality, at least a hundred million times more brilliant than our own sun, a simple calculation tells us how far away it must have been for its *apparent* brightness to equal that of Venus.

The calculation shows that Supernova Bethlehem was more than 3,000 light-years or, if you prefer, 18,000,000,000,000,000 miles away. That means its light had been traveling for at least three thousand years before it reached Earth and Bethlehem, so that the awesome cataclysm of which it was the evidence really took place five thousand years ago, when the great Pyramid was still fresh from the builders.

Let us, in imagination, cross the gulfs of space and time and go back to the moment of the catastrophe. We might find ourselves watching an ordinary star—a sun perhaps no different from our own. There may have been planets circling it; we do not know how common planets are in the Universe nor how many suns have such small companions. But there is no reason to think they are rare, and many novae must be the funeral pyres of worlds, and perhaps races, greater than ours.

There is no warning at all, only a steadily rising intensity of the sun's light. Within minutes the change is noticeable: within an hour, the nearer worlds are burning. The star is expanding like a balloon, blasting off shells of gas at a million miles an hour as it blows its outer layers into space. Within a day, it is shining with such supernal brilliance that it gives off more light than *all the other suns in the universe combined*. If it had planets, they are now no more than flecks of flame in the still expanding shells of fire. The conflagration will burn for weeks before the dying star collapses into quiescence.

But let us consider what happens to the light of the nova, which moves a hundred times more swiftly than the blast wave of the explosion. It will spread out into space, and after four or five years it will reach the next star. If there are planets circling that star, they will suddenly be illuminated by a second sun. It will give them no appreciable heat, but will be bright enough to banish night completely, for it will be more than a thousand times more luminous than our full moon. All that light will come from a single blazing point, since even from its nearest neighbor Supernova Bethlehem would appear too small to show a disc.

Century after century, the shell of light will continue to expand around its source. It will flash past countless suns and flare briefly in the skies of their planets. Indeed, by the most conservative estimate, this great new star must have shone over thousands of worlds before its light reached Earth, and to all those worlds it appeared far, far brighter than it did to the men it led to Judea.

For as the shell of light expanded, it faded also. By the time it reached Bethlehem it was spread over the surface of a sphere six thousand light-years across. A thousand years earlier, when Homer sang of Troy, the nova would have appeared twice as brilliant to any watchers farther upstream, as it were, closer to the time and place of the explosion.

That is a strange thought: there is a stranger one to come. For the light of Supernova Bethlehem is still flooding out through space. It has left Earth far behind in the twenty centuries that have elapsed since men saw it for the first and last time. Now its light is spread over a sphere ten thousand light-years across, and must be correspondingly fainter. It is simple to calculate how bright the Supernova must be to any beings who may be seeing it now as a new star in *their* skies. To them, it will still be far more brilliant than any other star in their entire heavens, for its brightness will have decreased only by 50 percent on its extra two thousand years of travel. . . .

At this very moment, therefore, the Star of Bethlehem may still be shining in the skies of countless worlds, circling far suns. Any watchers on those worlds will see its sudden appearance and its slow fading, just as the Magi may have seen it two thousand years ago when the expanding shell of light swept past Earth. And for thousands of years to come, as its radiance ebbs out toward the frontiers of the universe, Supernova Bethlehem will still have power to startle all who see it, wherever and *whatever* they may be.

Astronomy, as nothing else can do, teaches men humility. We know

now that our sun is merely one undistinguished member of a vast family of stars, and no longer think of ourselves as being at the center of Creation. Yet it is strange to think that before its light fades away below the limits of vision, we may have shared the Star of Bethlehem with the beings of perhaps a million worlds, and that to many of them, nearer to the source of the explosion, it must have been a far more wonderful sight than ever it was to human eyes. What did they make of it, and did it bring them good tidings, or ill?

CHRISTMAS IN MAINE

ROBERT P. TRISTRAM COFFIN

If you want to have a Christmas like the one we had on Paradise Farm when I was a boy, you will have to hunt up a salt-water farm on the Maine coast, with bays on both sides of it, and a road that goes around all sorts of bays, up over Misery Hill and down, and through the fir trees so close together that they brush you and your horse on both cheeks. That is the only kind of place a Christmas like that grows. You must have a clear December night, with blue Maine stars snapping like sapphires with the cold, and the big moon flooding full over Misery, and lighting up the snowy spruce boughs like crushed diamonds. You ought to be wrapped in a buffalo robe to your nose, and be sitting in a family pung, and have your breath trailing along with you as you slide over the dry, whistling snow. You will have to sing the songs we sang, "God Rest You Merry, Gentlemen" and "Joy to the World," and you will be able to see your songs around you in the air like blue smoke. That's the only way to come to a Paradise Christmas.

And you really should cross over at least one broad bay on the ice, and feel the tide rifts bounce you as the runners slide over them. And if the whole bay booms out, every now and then, and the sound echoes around the wooded islands for miles, you will be having the sort of ride we loved to take from town, the night before Christmas.

I won't insist on your having a father like ours to drive you home to your Christmas. One with a wide moustache full of icicles, and eyes like the stars of the morning. That would be impossible, anyway, for there has been only one of him in the world. But it is too bad, just the same. For you won't have the stories we had by the fireplace. You won't hear about Kitty Wells who died beautifully in song just as the sun came over the tops of the eastern mountains and just after her lover had named the wedding day, and you will not hear how Kitty's departure put an end to his mastering the banjo:

> "But death came in my cabin door
> "And took from me my joy, my pride,
> "And when they said she was no more,
> "I laid my banjo down and cried."

But you will be able to have the rooms of the farmhouse banked with emerald jewels clustered on bayberry boughs, clumps of everlasting roses with gold spots in the middle of them, tree evergreens, and the evergreen that runs all over the Maine woods and every so often puts up a bunch of palm leaves. And there will be rose-hips stuck in pine boughs. And caraway seeds in every crust and cookie in the place.

An aunt should be on hand, an aunt who believes in yarrow tea and the Bible as the two things needed to keep children well. She will read the Nativity story aloud to the family, hurrying over the really exciting parts that happened at the stable, and bearing down hard on what the angels had to say and the more edifying points that might be supposed to improve small boys who like to lie too long abed in the mornings. She will put a moral even into Christmas greens, and she will serve well as a counter-irritant to the overeating of mince pies. She will insist on all boys washing behind their ears, and that will keep her days full to the brim.

The Christmas tree will be there, and it will have a top so high that it will have to be bent over and run along the ceiling of the sitting room. It will be the best fir tree of the Paradise forests, picked from ten thousand almost perfect ones, and every bough on it will be like old-fashioned fans wide open. You will have brought it home that very morning, on the sled, from Dragonfly Spring.

Dragonfly Spring was frozen solid to the bottom, and you could look down into it and see the rainbows where you dented it with your copper-toed boots, see whole ferns caught motionless in the crystal deeps, and a frog, too, down there, with hands just like a baby's on him. Your small sister—the one with hair like new honey laid open in the middle of a honeycomb—had cried out, "Let's dig him up and take him home and warm his feet!" (She is the same sister who ate up all your more vivid pastel crayons when you were away at school, and then ate up all the things you had been pretty sure were toadstools in Bluejay Woods, when you were supposed to be keeping an eye on her, but were buried so deep

in "Mosses from an Old Manse" that you couldn't have been dug up with horses and oxen.)

Your dog, Snoozer, who is a curious and intricate combination of many merry pugs and many mournful hound-dogs, was snuffling all the time, hot on the feather-stitching the mice had made from bush to bush while you were felling the Christmas tree. A red squirrel was taking a white-pine cone apart on a hemlock bough, and telling Snoozer what he thought of him and all other dogs, the hour or so you were there.

There will be a lot of aunts in the house besides the Biblical one. Aunts of every complexion and cut. Christmas is the one time that even the most dubious of aunts take on value. One of them can make up wreaths, another can make rock candy that puts a tremble on the heart, and still another can steer your twelve-seater bob-sled—and turn it over, bottom up, with you all in just the right place for a fine spill.

There will be uncles, too, to hold one end of the molasses taffy you will pull sooner or later, yanking it out till it flashes and turns into corn-silk that almost floats in the air, tossing your end of it back and probably lassoing your uncle around his neck as you do it, and pulling out a new rope of solid honey.

The uncles will smoke, too, and that will be a help to all the younger brothers who have been smoking their acorn-pipes out in the woodshed, and who don't want their breaths to give them away. The uncles will make themselves useful in other ways. They will rig up schooners no bigger than your thumb, with shrouds like cobwebs; they will mend the bob-sled, tie up cut fingers, and sew on buttons after you shin up to the cupola in the barn; and—if you get on the good side of them—they will saw you up so much birch wood that you won't have to lay hand to a bucksaw till after New Year's.

There will be cousins by the cart load. He-ones and she-ones. The size you can sit on, and the size that can sit on you. Enough for two armies, on Little Round Top and on Big, up in the haymow. You will play Gettysburg there till your heads are full of hay chaff that will keep six aunts busy cleaning it out. And then you will come in to the house and down a whole crock of molasses cookies—the kind that go up in peaks in the middle—which somebody was foolish enough to leave the cover off.

Every holiday that came along, in my father's house, was the gathering of an Anglo-Saxon clan. My father was built for lots of people 'round him. But Christmas was a whole assembly of the West Saxons! My father wanted people in squads. There were men with wide moustaches and men with smooth places on top of their heads, women wide and narrow. Cousins of the second and third water, even, were there. Hired men, too. They were special guests and had to be handled with kid gloves, as New England hired men must. They had to have the best of everything, and you could not find fault with them, as you could with uncles, if they smacked you for upsetting their coffee into their laps. Babies were underfoot in full cry. The older children hunted in packs. The table had to be pieced out with flour barrels and bread boards and ironing boards. It was a house's length from the head of the table, where your father sat and manufactured the roast up into slivers, to your mother dishing out the pork gravy. Whole geese disappeared on the way down. The Christmas cake, which had been left sweetly to itself for a month to age into a miracle, was a narrow isthmus when it got to Mother. But Mother always said that Christmas, to her, was watching other people eat. She was the kind of mother who claimed that the neck and the back of the chicken were the tastiest parts.

The prize goose, whom you had brought up by hand and called Oliver Cromwell, Old Ironsides, or some such distinguished title, was duly carved. And Father found his wishbone snow-white and you all applauded, for that meant lots of snow and two more months of coasting on your sleds. There were mince pies by the legion. And if Uncle Tom were there, a whole raccoon baked just for him and girt around with browned sweet potatoes. Mother's wild strawberry jam was there on deck, winking at you like rubies from the holes in tarts that melted away like bubbles in the mouth. That dinner was three hours in Beulah Land!

Of course, there will be an apple pudding at such a season. Steamed in a lard bucket, and cut open with a string. A sauce of oranges and lemons to make an ocean around each steaming volcano of suet and russet apples as it falls crumbling from the loop of twine. It will have to be steamed in the boiler, if your Christmas is to be the size of ours, and cooked in a ten-pound lard pail. Better use a cod line instead of the twine of other holidays, to parcel it out to the members of the clan.

The whole nation of you in the house will go from one thing to another. The secret of the best Christmases is everybody doing the same things all at the same time. You will all fall to and string cranberries and popcorn for the tree, and the bright lines each of you has a hold on will radiate from the tree like ribbons on a maypole. Everybody will have needles and thread in the mouth, you will all get in each other's way, but that is the art of doing Christmas right. You will all bundle up together for the ride in the afternoon. You had better take the horse-sled, as the pung will not begin to hold you. And even then a dozen or so of assorted uncles and aunts and cousins will have to come trooping after through the deep snow, and wait for their turn on the straw in the sled. Smaller cousins will fall off over the sides in great knots and never be missed, and the hullabaloo will roar on and send the rabbits flying away through the woods, showing their bobbing scuts.

Everybody will hang presents on the tree at once, when the sun has dipped down into the spruces in the west and you are back home in the sitting-room. There will be no nonsense of tiptoeing up and edging a package on when nobody is looking. Everybody knows who is giving him what. There is no mystery about it. Aunt Ella has made rag dinahs for all hands and the cook—for all under fourteen years of age—and she does not care who knows it. The dinahs are all alike, except that those for the children whose lower garments are forked have forked red-flannel pants instead of red-flannel petticoats. They all have pearl button eyes and stocking toes for faces. There will be so many hands at work on the tree at once that the whole thing will probably go over two or three times, and it will be well to make it fast with a hawser or so.

And then you will turn right around and take the presents off again, the minute you have got them all on and have lighted the candles up. There will be no waiting, with small children sitting around with aching hearts. The real candles will be a problem, in all that mass of spills.

Boughs will take fire here and there. But there will be plenty of uncles around to crush out the small bonfires in their big brown hands. All the same, it would be well to have an Uncle Thomas who can take up a live coal in his thumb and finger, and light his pipe from it, cool as a cucumber. Better turn the extinguishing of the tree over to him.

There will be boughten presents, to be sure—a turtle of cardboard in a glassed, dainty box; hung on springs and swimming for dear life with all four feet, and popguns with their barrels ringed and streaked with red and yellow lines. Why popguns should be painted like broomsticks is one of the mysteries, along with the blue paint you always find on Maine cartwheels. Somebody will probably get one of those Swiss music-boxes that will eke out a ghostly "Last Rose of Summer," if tenderly cranked. There should be those little bottles of transparent candies, with real syrup in them, which I used to live for through the years. And there must be a German doll for every last girl, with mountains of yellow hair and cheeks looking as if life were a continuous blowing of bubbles. Boughten things are all right.

But if it is going to be our kind of Christmas, most of the presents will be home-made. Socks knit by the aunt who swears only by useful gifts. You have seen those socks growing up from their white toes for the last two weeks. Wristers, always red. A box of Aunt Louise's candied orange peel that she will never let on to anybody how she makes. Your father will have made a sled for every mother's son and daughter of you, with a bluebird, or robin redbreast, more real than life, painted on each one and your name underneath. You will never have another present to match that, though you grow up and become Midases. Popcorn balls, big as muskmelons, will be common ware. They will be dripping with molasses, and will stick your wristers and socks and other treasures together.

But the pith of the party is not reached until the whole nation of you sits down in rocking chairs, or lies down on their bellies in front of the six-foot gulf of the fireplace. The presents are all stowed, heaped and tucked away, stuck fast with cornballs. The last lamps are out. The firelight dances on the ceiling. It lights up the steel engraving of Major McCulloch leaping from Kentucky to Ohio, with ten thousand mounted redskins yelling and reining in their steeds behind him. It lights up Daniel Boone's daughters as they lean away towards their boat's end and scream their silent screams and drop their water lilies, while Indian head after Indian head grins up at them from the river of the Dark and Bloody Ground.

All the babies will be hushed and put away. All the younger fry will be more than half asleep. The toasted cheese and red herring will go 'round. The herring, by the way,—if you are worthy to wear my shoes after me—which you yourself have smoked with green oak, and have gotten your own two eyes so that they looked like two burnt holes in a blanket while doing it, and have hugely enjoyed every hour of it all.

Then you had best find a fair substitute for my father. Give him the best chair in the house—and the way to find *that* is to push the cat out of it—and let him tear! He will begin by telling you about such people as the brilliant young ladies of Philadelphia who had a piano too big to fit their house, so they put it on the porch and played on it through the open window. Then he will sit back and work his way to the Caliph of Bagdad, who had a daughter so homely that she had to wear a sack on her head when her suitors came awooing, and how she fell down a well and made herself a great fortune, and won the handsomest husband that ever wore a turban. That story, by the way, you will not find in the "Arabian Nights" even though you look for it, as I have done, till you have gray hairs in your head.

The firelight will get into your father's eyes and on his hair. He will move on from Bagdad to Big Bethel, and tell you all how the Yankee campfires looked like the high Milky Way itself, all night long before the battle; how the dew silvered every sleeping soldier's face and the stacked rifles, as the dawn came up with the new day and death. And you will hug your knees and hear the wind outside going its rounds among the snowy pines, and you will listen on till the story you are hearing becomes a part of the old winds of the world and the motion of the bright stars. And probably it will take two uncles at least to carry you to bed.

THE CHRISTMAS TREE

SAMUEL T. COLERIDGE

Ratzeburg, Germany, 1799

There is a Christmas custom here which pleased and interested me. The children make little presents to their parents, and to each other; and the parents to the children. For three or four months before Christmas the girls are all busy, and the boys save up their pocket-money, to make or purchase these presents. What the present is to be is cautiously kept secret, and the girls have a world of contrivances to conceal it—such as working when they are out on visits, and the others are not with them; getting up in the morning before day-light, and the like. Then, on the evening before Christmas Day, one of the parlours is lighted up by the children, into which the parents must not go. A great yew bough is fastened on the table at a little distance from the wall, a multitude of little tapers are fastened in the bough, but so as not to catch it till they are nearly burnt out, and coloured paper hangs and flutters from the twigs. Under this bough the children lay out in great order the presents they mean for their parents, still concealing in their pockets what they intend for each other. Then the parents are introduced, and each presents his little gift, and then bring out the rest one by one from their pockets, and present them with kisses and embraces. Where I witnessed this scene there were eight or nine children, and the eldest daughter and the mother wept aloud for joy and tenderness; and the tears ran down the face of the father, and he clasped all his children so tight to his breast, it seemed as if he did it to stifle the sob that was rising within him. I was very much affected. The shadow of the bough and its appendages on the wall, and arching over on the ceiling, made a pretty picture; and then the raptures of the very little ones, when at last the twigs and their needles began to take fire and snap!—Oh, it was a delight for them! On the next day, in the great parlour, the parents lay out on the table the presents for the children: a scene of more sober joy succeeds, as on this day, after an old custom, the mother says privately to each of her daughters, and the father to his sons, that which he has observed most praiseworthy, and that which was most faulty in their conduct. Formerly, and still in all the smaller towns and villages throughout North Germany, these presents were sent by all the parents to some one fellow, who in high buskins, a white robe, a mask, and an enormous flax wig, personates *Knecht Rupert,* the servant Rupert. On Christmas night he goes round to every house, and says that Jesus Christ his master sent him thither; the parents and elder children receive him with great pomp of reverence, while the little ones are most terribly frightened. He then inquires for the children, and, according to the character which he hears from the parent, he gives them the intended presents, as if they came out of heaven from Jesus Christ. Or, if they should have been bad children, he gives the parents a rod, and in the name of his master recommends them to use it frequently. About seven or eight years old the children are let into the secret, and it is curious to observe how faithfully they keep it.

CHRISTMAS EVE

ALISTAIR COOKE

from LETTERS FROM AMERICA

A modern American poet has written: "From the new earth the dead return no more," meaning that in America there are no ghost stories. Is that so? Well, I beg to amend the record and tell you what can happen, what did happen two hundred years ago, and again only one year ago, in a country place up the Hudson which was settled by Dutchmen who brought over and transformed the oldest legend about Santa Claus.

In the seventeenth century the Dutch crews who used to drop anchor in the Hudson heard about some buried treasure. For several generations headstrong men would go out digging for it in the near-by hills. The man I have in mind was one Rambout Van Dam, who got obsessed with gold and nearly lost his daughters. That may sound like a contradiction in terms. I had better explain it gently by beginning at the beginning.

If anybody had asked Rambout if he was a good father he would have laughed aloud. He had three adored daughters, one beautiful, one very homely, and one like you and me. They were all, however, intelligent, which is much more of a threat to parenthood than the other vices. Ram Van Dam was a gay dog in a quiet way, and a little less quiet after his wife died. He had a fine streak of curiosity, which two of his daughters inherited. The beautiful one didn't need to. All the curiosity came her way.

Well, Ram sat and moped for a while as a widower. And then he took to rowing up the Hudson every Saturday night across a fine stretch of water called the Tappan Zee. He would tie up and tramp off to a tavern and a few hours later would untie and have quite a time of it rowing back home. One night at the tavern he heard about the buried treasure. And in the next year, having a small income from farming land his wife had left him, he had a lot of time on his hands to mooch around for gold. Maybe he was told, or maybe he just connected the buried treasure with the place he'd heard about, but he grew convinced as the months went by that the Rockland Hills were the place to explore. One summer and fall he spent almost every day there and the week before Christmas he had done nothing about chopping down a Christmas tree or preparing to make merry. So far as his daughters could see, he didn't mean to.

The more he went away from home, the more he made it up to his guilty conscience by being stricter and stricter with his daughters. He had the sense to see that they were growing and ripening before his eyes. He noticed that the beautiful one was always seeming to run into young men she knew, either in the village store or sometimes nearer home. So he gave out an order: no men, no visitors, whenever he went away. He barred the storm windows and he locked the doors and took the key away with him.

This Christmas week, two hundred years ago, he went off as usual with his rowboat and a pail and a spade. Christmas Eve came in with dull grey skies, but he rowed off just the same. He didn't get very far. The skies lowered and the snow came down, and he put into a little cove and waited to sit the storm out. But the snow came down heavier and in the middle of the afternoon he pushed his rowboat out into the Hudson again and bent before the whirling storm and pulled for home. He forgot all about the buried treasure. He began to get maudlin as he thought of the locked-up treasure of his daughters. As he rowed he sweated and as he sweated he wept. He had never loved his daughters so much in his life, now that he seemed near to never seeing them again. He could see no landing lights anywhere across the dizzy falling snow. And there came to him a quick, horrible fear.

His daughters had been very quiet and complacent that morning. They had done everything he asked. His crullers were baked when he came downstairs. His tea was hot. His cheese was pungent. A little pot of rum was already poured for him. His daughters had never behaved so like good daughters in the storybooks. He was an experienced parent after all, and he knew this was a bad sign.

Soon the night came on with that terrible gentleness of any night that brings disaster. He knew his own landing-place without stopping to think but he saw no glimmer of light between the pines. He tied up the boat with shaking fingers and climbed up the bank and plodded knee-deep through the snow. He hadn't even noticed that the snow had stopped. But it was deep and very still now. And what was worse, the great looming ghost of his house was still and dark.

Was it possible that his beloved daughters had gone looking for him and suffered he daren't think what sort of fate? He pulled out the great key to the front door. But he didn't need it and he knew as he chattered there that he might never need it again. The door was ajar. It creaked as he pushed it, and he heard it in his head as a squeaking demon laugh, a sort of sick chuckle from another world. He lit the lamp in the hallway and shouted out their names. There was no answer, no light, no sound but the door creaking back with a sigh. "Gone, old man, gone for good," the door said.

He ran into the living-room and lit another lamp. As the flame leaped up, he saw under it a piece of paper. He did not have to read what had been written down on it so painstakingly. He saw only the words: "and so, dear Father, and on account of this unhappy neglect"; and he jumped two lines to read: "have taken the stagecoach to New York City, there, as we intend, to abandon ourselves to a life of merry shame."

He fell in silly sobs over the torn page. After a while he heard a church bell strike and he moved fast. He tossed off a noggin of rum. He threw on a greatcoat and plodded back to the stable and saddled his horse. He took a lantern. He knew the roads as well as any farmer in the Hudson Valley and it was his guess that the stage had plunged into a snowdrift. It left, he remembered, at four o'clock. And it was now eight. He rode off through the snow into the dark.

He was luckily right. He found the stage five miles down the road, with the passengers all gone to an inn two miles away. He turned and rode on. Not to sicken you further, he found his daughters. They were surrounded by sturdy, cheerful-looking men and they were drinking hot rum toddies, with cinnamon sticks stuck shamelessly in big pewter mugs. It took a little time and a private interview in a back room to get the daughters weeping. But they wept copiously, not because they had recanted about the prospect of a life of merry shame, but because they had never seen their father look so old, so red in the nose, so pathetic. I mean, they had never seen him cry.

He borrowed another horse and galloped back home with them. By the time they were home they promised him everlasting obedience and all sorts of virtues he hadn't so far noticed in them. But he looked them in the eye and they looked him straight back. And he knew that New York was still a pleasing prospect and a date in their diaries. They went sorrowfully to bed.

They were all asleep when the church bell struck a deep, challenging, throbbing twelve. If they had not all been so exhausted, they would have died of fright in their beds. For there was a strange ringing of little bells across the fields, followed soon by a scraping sound at the chimney, and a dislodged brick fell down the roofing and thudded into the snow. The living-room, and the tree they had dragged in and put up, were crackling with light. Then the light went out and the chimneystack made the same scraping sound, and the bells vanished across the fields.

Next morning when they came down, at the foot of the tree were three packages. They each contained a dowry. This was enough to abolish the thrilling prospect of a life of merry shame. The very plain one married the stagecoach-man. And the in-between one married her dowry. And the beautiful one took her time and married the Mayor of New York City and settled down to a life of merry respectability. But Ram Van Dam never again went rowing up the Hudson for gold. The word got around that a stranger had come on Christmas Eve and restored the old man to his daughters, and vice versa. Everyone in the Hudson Valley the next year put up a tree and left little baskets and other suitable containers for dowries for their own daughters. For a time they called the invisible stranger simply The Stranger, but since he came on Saint Nicholas' Eve they got to calling him at first Nick; then, when he left no dowries, Old Nick; then Saint 'Claus, and finally Santa Claus, a horrid Americanism that the rest of the world first execrated and then, as is its custom, adopted. Such dreadful anxieties were set up in the valley children that a few kindly parents started sneaking in bits of money and little presents to put under the tree at midnight. This too got to be taken for granted. So that today many a grumpy father, going off to empty his earnings on a pile of presents, refers to Santa Claus simply as That Dam Ghost.

This might have been all there is to tell of this Hudson Valley legend if life ended as the fairy stories do. But I regret to say that Ram Van Dam again got to taking his daughters for granted. And one fine Saturday night he rowed up the river and across the waters of the Tappan Zee. He carried his pail and spade with him. We do not know for certain what happened to him, but he never came back. And if you go down to the Hudson shore on Christmas Eve, and however crisp and bright the night, you will see nothing; but you will hear all night long, if you care to stay, the faint splashing, the weary dipping of oars, up and down the waters of the Tappan Zee.

This was the fate of the father who took his children for granted and tried the fatal, though familiar, experiment of "molding their characters."

There was a further warning given to all of us last year when a certain Raymond Van Dam, who lives in those parts, threatened to repeat the error of his ancestor's way. He is an upright, cultivated man, but of the sort who has been educated about two degrees (A.B. and Ph.D.) above his intelligence. I hate to bring nationalism into this but it will explain a very eccentric trait of his: he was half-English and hated American radio. He too had three daughters. From their earliest childhood he banned all radio sets from his house. Like many another tyrant masquerading as a "sensitive man," he thought this would give his children no taste for the stuff. But he was wrong, and he learned it just in time.

A few weeks before Christmas, while his daughters were in school, he saw a postcard addressed to the beautiful one on the letter tray in the hall. Same house, by the way. As he shuffled through his own mail, the postcard fell face-down. He was, as I say, a moral man. But he believed there was a special dispensation that made it all right to read other people's postcards. He read it. It was from a theatrical agency. It said that a television network had agreed to the proposition of the three girls to take an audition for a sister act, a close-harmony trio! Mr. Raymond Van Dam replaced the letter. And he did not go out to saddle his horse. But he moved as fast as his ancestor. He got out his car and drove into Tarrytown and headed for a big, bright department store.

On Christmas Eve the bells were heard again, and the scraping sound, and a brick fell off the roof. Next morning, when the girls came down, they found to their astonishment three huge packages. One was a television set, one was a radio, and the third was a phonograph with a three-speed player.

They now watch television every night and play the radio and phonograph every morning. Mr. Van Dam has never had it so peaceful.

Mr. Van Dam received the embraces of his daughters all day long. But he had a testy gleam in his eye. And the next day he wrote a tart letter to a certain doctor friend—a friend no more—a psychiatrist attached to the World Health Organization. This doctor, I understand, is trying to get the United Nations to agree to undertake a propaganda campaign to belittle, deplore, and in time abolish Santa Claus from the national customs and the folklore of all the signatory nations. Santa Claus, this psychiatrist says, is a dangerous sentimental father-figure, who is expected to satisfy "unreasonable wants," and who by that very expectation delays "the necessary adjustment of the preadolescent child to the world of reality."

Did I say Mr. Van Dam wrote a letter? I'm sorry. His temper was much too short for that. He sent a telegram. It read:

MERRY CHRISTMAS STOP YOU ARE A DAMN FOOL STOP VAN DAM.

THE CHRISTMAS GIFT
A Memory of Stalingrad

JOAN COONS

Her grandmother was dead. Nadia did not cry when the old women told her, nor was she afraid. She was sorry, of course, for she'd miss the stories her grandmother used to tell, but she was not afraid. Death was nothing to fear. Her father had told her that. Her mother was dead, as were many of the people she had known. No, death was nothing. There were worse things. The Germans were worse . . . trying to force their way into Stalingrad. Nadia listened. She could hear the distant roar of the guns, the thunder of bombs. The Germans were less than ten miles away.

"It is better to be dead," a woman muttered hopelessly. "When there is only fighting and bloodshed for the young, what can we old ones ask for?" She looked at the listening child, shook her head sorrowfully. "You're to sleep in my shack now," she said, turning away.

Nadia didn't answer. She was thinking of her grandmother. They'd put her in the farthest shack with the other bodies. There was no time for burials, no implements to dig a grave. Besides, the earth was frozen. The old women had kept Nadia away from the shed, but she went there now, to say good-bye to her grandmother.

It was cold in the shed, but her grandmother would not mind. They were all cold . . . hungry too. Nadia's father had said they should be glad of the cold, for it helped save Russia from the Germans. The Germans hated General Winter, as they called this deadly foe.

There was no odor of decay in the shed, for the cold had preserved the bodies. Later, the shack would be burned, with the bodies in it. But not now. They couldn't have any fires or lights that might attract the Germans. These scattered little shacks must be kept secret. Even the German planes had not discovered them, hidden there in the hills.

The Germans wouldn't bother with these shacks anyway, would dismiss them as the shelters of old people and children. And they'd be right; only they wouldn't know that here the great Russian flyer Petrovich met his comrades to discuss plans to save Russia. And Petrovich was Nadia's father.

"He's coming tonight," the child whispered to the dead about her. "My father's coming tonight." She drew close to her grandmother, touched the old woman's stiff face.

"It's Christmas Eve, you know," Nadia said wistfully, recalling the stories her grandmother had told her about the Christmas celebrations she'd known as a girl. That was in the old Russia, the Russia that had died, even as the grandmother herself had died. Nadia bent over the silent figure on the floor.

"He'll find you," she said softly, "I know He will." Her grandmother had believed the Christ Child came for the souls of the dead, and had been afraid He wouldn't find hers among so many dead and dying, afraid she would be overlooked and carried to the underworld by evil spirits.

Nadia sighed as she turned toward the door. She would not come again. It did no good to cling to the dead. Those were her father's words. She thought again of her father, pretended she was to buy him a present, and tried to decide what she would choose. Intent on these imaginings, she followed the trail into the hills, forgetting her father's rule that she must never go out of sight of the shacks.

Nadia came upon the light suddenly. A man had it, a stranger whose crouched figure was almost completely concealed by the ledge above him.

"Oh a fire!" she cried with pleasure, instinctively stretching out her hands toward it, and adding quickly, "Put it out!"

Startled, the man almost fell over. He hadn't heard her approach. His hand went automatically to the knife in his belt, stopped as the child spoke again.

"It's not allowed, you know," she said, fixing her eyes longingly on the candle where a moment before the man had been warming his cold hands.

The man did not reply. Fool that he'd been to stop! But who'd expect anyone here, especially a child? Now what was to be done with her?

"It's warm, isn't it?" Nadia said wistfully.

"Yes," the man replied, peering at her sharply. "Here, come closer and warm your hands a second. Then we'll put it out."

Nadia crept under the ledge beside him, held her hands cupped about the small flame, smiled at the man, the shy, appealing smile of a six-year-old.

"It's alive," she told him softly.

"Yes," he answered gruffly.

"It would make a lovely gift." She sighed. "Such a lovely Christmas gift."

The man reached over and pinched out the small flame. "A gift," he asked, "for whom?"

"My father."

"Oh." Still the man watched the child thoughtfully.

"He's coming tonight." Nadia paused. She'd been warned not to speak to strangers, most of all not to mention her father. But this man spoke Russian, not the hated German, and he was kind. He'd shared the candle with her. A German wouldn't have done that.

"Coming tonight?" the man asked, a sudden interest evident in his voice. "Coming," he repeated, "from where?"

The child leaned closer, her great dark eyes studied him for a moment. "From Stalingrad," she confided.

"No one can come from Stalingrad," her companion remarked shortly, without thinking. "The Germans will not let one escape."

"He will come," the little girl replied firmly. "The Germans cannot stop him. My father's Petrovich," she added proudly.

The moment the words were out, Nadia knew she had betrayed her father's secret. Quick tears filled the dark eyes. "You will tell no one?" she implored anxiously. "It's a secret. I shouldn't have told."

"It's all right," the man assured her. "Petrovich's meeting place is safe with me."

At the words meeting place Nadia looked up. Maybe the man knew all about the discussions held in the shacks. Maybe she hadn't given anything away after all.

"You know my father?" she asked hopefully.

"Yes," the other replied with fervor. "Yes, I know Petrovich."

Relief spread rapidly over the child's pinched little face. "Oh, it's all right then," she suggested eagerly.

"Yes, it's all right," he repeated, smiling at her. He picked up the candle, held it out to her. "A present," he said, "for your father, for Petrovich."

Nadia hesitated, intense longing in the dark eyes. The man was giving her the candle! It wasn't possible. No one gave away anything. People hadn't enough for themselves.

"Take it!" The man put the candle in her hand. "It's a magic candle," he told her.

"Magic?"

"In a way. You see," he explained, "it's been blessed."

"In a church?" Nadia interrupted. She held the candle carefully.

"Yes, in a church," he replied. "It will bring a blessing to the house where it burns . . . and to those who sleep beneath the roof of that house. You must put it in the window tonight, after your father is asleep."

"Have you forgotten," the child reminded him, "we cannot have lights?"

"This is different," the man said sharply, added more gently, "A blessed candle on Christmas Eve lights the Christ Child to the door. No harm can come then . . . not even from the Germans." This last was uttered in a whisper, low, intense.

Nadia laid the candle against her cheek, remembering the warmth it had shed but a few minutes before. "You are kind," she murmured, "so kind . . . to give it to me."

"It is for Petrovich, the greatest flyer in all Russia."

That explained everything. Nadia smiled happily. The man had given her the candle because he loved her father. Everyone loved her father. All Russia loved Petrovich.

"But you must not tell your father about the candle or me," the man went on slowly. "The candle would lose its power if you did. You must tell no one. You must not speak of it at all."

"I know," she agreed. "The evil spirits might overhear and steal the blessing."

"Yes." The man lifted her back onto the path, watched her hide the candle beneath her shawl. "You must not say you have seen me . . . until tomorrow," he added hastily, seeing the surprise on her face.

"Tomorrow?"

"Yes . . . tomorrow I shall be with Petrovich," he told her slowly. "I'd like to tell him myself . . . about our meeting, I mean. I want to explain . . ." He broke off, smiled at her. Nadia smiled back. "Run along now," he told her, "before they miss you."

The child started down the path, stopped and looked back. "Goodbye," she said, waving to him.

"Goodbye," he answered. "Goodbye . . . little one."

"I'm Nadia," the child replied, turning away.

"Goodbye, Nadia," the man murmured, watching the little girl until she disappeared from view. He shrugged, muttered an oath, and started off into the hills.

The man stopped before the entrance of a cave, hidden by trees and almost buried under drifted snow.

"I'm back, Karl," he called, stooping to crawl through the narrow opening. He spoke in German, and the man in the cave, the man called Karl, answered in the same tongue.

"I thought something must have happened to you . . . you were gone so long. Did you get a good look at the shacks, Hans?" he asked eagerly as the other came to sit beside him.

"Yes. They're the ones all right," Hans replied flatly.

"Good!" Karl was excited. "I was right. If only we knew when the next meeting . . ."

"Tonight," Hans put in abruptly.

"Tonight! How do you know?"

Hans smiled, but it wasn't a happy smile. He told Karl about the candle, the Christmas gift for Petrovich.

"It was a stroke of luck, our stumbling on this place," Karl said when Hans had finished. "It'll make it all worth-while . . . all this." He glanced about the cave. "This hole . . . the days and nights we've lain here . . . waiting . . . waiting . . . and the cold . . ." He shivered. "Yes, even this damnable cold."

"We'll carry the gun to the hill above the sheds," Hans said tonelessly. "I found a good site this afternoon."

Karl touched the gun beside him. "We've only the one shell," he said, "but it won't be wasted now. They'd have found us sooner or later, and if they didn't we'd starve anyway." He shrugged. "The shacks are scattered. We could easily have picked the wrong one. There'd be no chance of a second shot . . . even if we had the shell," he added thoughtfully. "The first sound will bring every Russian in these hills after us." He paused, went on. "But we'll die knowing we brought down Russia's greatest flyer."

"Do you mind dying, Karl?" the other asked, thinking how young the boy was, not more than twenty at the most.

"Mind?" Karl's voice was vibrant. "Death is nothing," he said. "I would prefer to live to serve our leader and Germany, but I die to protect the Fatherland. It is my duty!"

"My duty," Hans muttered softly, under his breath. "It was my duty, little Nadia. Can a child like you understand that?"

"What are you mumbling about?" Karl asked impatiently.

"Nothing."

"I don't understand you sometimes," the boy began, but Hans interrupted him.

"We'll go as soon as it is dark," he remarked.

"Are you sure she'll light the candle?" Karl asked, doubtful for a moment.

"Yes," the older man assured him quietly. "I'm sure Nadia will light the candle."

Nadia held the candle in her hand, anticipating the warmth the small flame would give. Her father and his companions had sent her out while they talked, but now they were all asleep in the straw in the loft of the large shed. The men, posted to watch, would pay no attention to her. Nadia smiled to herself.

She hesitated a moment. The man's words came back to her. "It's a blessed candle. No harm can come."

Nadia slipped into the shed, struck the flint she carried. A few seconds later she was on her way to the old woman's cabin where she was to sleep. Pausing, she looked back at the lighted candle, pleased by the bit of flame.

"There it is!"

From the top of the hill, Karl peered through the sights of the gun, finding the range carefully, precisely. It had been a struggle, getting the gun there, making no sound that might carry to the people below. Time and again they had stopped, scarcely daring to breathe, fearing they'd been discovered.

"Ready," Karl said at last, then, as Hans did not answer, made no move, "What is the matter with you?"

"You're sure it's set?" Hans asked instead of replying.

"It's set," the boy said coldly. "It's not much of a light, but I found it."

Hans slid the shell in silently, peered through the sights briefly, then moved his hand mechanically. The sound of the exploding shell burst into the night. The aim had been perfect. A real blaze replaced the tiny flame of the candle.

Nadia stood beside the blackened ruins of the shed the next morning. The Germans were dead, both of them, and her father was already on his way to safety. He'd left as soon as the explosion awakened him, not waiting to help put out the fire. There were other men to do that. Petrovich was needed for greater things.

Nadia sighed. Her father had been angry at first, when she'd told him about the candle, but afterwards he'd understood. She turned at the sound of a footstep behind her.

"Whatever made you do it, child?" the old woman asked, going to Nadia, pulling the child to her comfortingly.

"He said it was a blessed candle," the little girl replied, "that it would light the Christ Child to the door." Tears rolled down her cheeks, sparkled on the front of her shawl.

"But why did you change your mind and put it in this shack?" the other asked, then added, "Though it's a blessing you did."

"Grandmother was so worried that the Christ wouldn't find her soul when there were so many," Nadia explained. "I thought my father wouldn't mind if I put the candle in her shack instead of his." She sobbed as the old woman led her away from the charred timbers.

A Christmas Dinner Won in Battle

STEPHEN CRANE

T om had set up a plumbing shop in the prairie town of Levelville as soon as the people learned to care more about sanitary conditions than they did about the brand of tobacco smoked by the inhabitants of Mars. Nevertheless he was a wise young man for he was only one week ahead of the surveyors. A railroad, like a magic wand, was going to touch Levelville and change it to a great city. In an incredibly short time, the town had a hotel, a mayor, a board of aldermen and more than a hundred real estate agents, besides a blue print of the plans for a street railway three miles long. When the cowboys rode in with their customary noise to celebrate the fact that they had been paid, their efforts were discouraged by new policemen in uniform. Levelville had become a dignified city.

As the town expanded in marvelous circles out over the prairies, Tom bestrode the froth of the wave of progress. He was soon one of the first citizens. These waves carry men to fortune with sudden sweeping movements, and Tom had the courage, the temerity and the assurance to hold his seat like a knight errant.

In the democratic and genial atmosphere of this primary boom, he became an intimate acquaintance of Colonel Fortman, the president of the railroad, and with more courage, temerity and assurance, had already fallen violently in love with his daughter, the incomparable Mildred. He carried his intimacy with the colonel so far as to once save his life from the flying might of the 5.30 express. It seems that the colonel had ordered the engineer of the 5.30 to make his time under all circumstances; to make his time if he had to run through fire, flood and earthquake.

The engineer decided that the usual rule relating to the speed of trains when passing through freight yards could not concern an express that was ordered to slow down for nothing but the wrath of heaven and in consequence, at the time of this incident, the 5.30 was shrieking through the Levelville freight yard at fifty miles an hour, roaring over the switches and screaming along the lines of box cars. The colonel and Tom were coming from the shops. They had just rounded the corner of a car and stepped out upon the main track when this whirring, boiling, howling demon of an express came down upon them. Tom had an instant in which to drag his companion off the rails; the train whistled past them like an enormous projectile. "Damn that fellow—he's making his time," panted the old colonel gazing after the long speeding shadow with its two green lights. Later he said very soberly: "I'm much obliged to you for that, Tom old boy."

When Tom went to him a year later, however, to ask for the hand of Mildred, the colonel replied: "My dear man, I think you are insane. Mildred will have over a million dollars at my death, and while I don't mean to push the money part of it too far forward, yet Mildred with her beauty, her family name and her wealth, can marry the finest in the land. There isn't anyone too great for her. So you see, my dear man, it is impossible that she could consider you for a moment."

Whereupon Tom lost his temper. He had the indignation of a good, sound-minded, fearless-eyed young fellow who is assured of his love and assured almost of the love of the girl. Moreover, it filled him with unspeakable rage to be called "My dear man."

They then accused each other of motives of which neither was guilty, and Tom went away. It was a serious quarrel. The colonel told Tom never to dare to cross his threshold. They passed each other on the street without a wink of an eye to disclose the fact that one knew that the other existed. As time went on the colonel became more massively aristocratic and more impenetrably stern. Levelville had developed about five grades of society, and the Fortmans mingled warily with the dozen families that formed the highest and iciest grades. Once when the colonel and Mildred were driving through town, the girl bowed to a young man who passed them.

"Who the deuce was that?" said the colonel airily. "Seems to me I ought to know that fellow."

"That's the man that saved your life from the 5.30," replied Mildred.

"See here, young lady," cried the colonel angrily, "don't you take his part against me."

About a year later came the great railway strike. The papers of the city foreshadowed it vaguely from time to time, but no one apparently took the matter in a serious way. There had been threats and rumors of threats but the general public had seemed to view them as idle bombast. At last, however, the true situation displayed itself suddenly and vividly. Almost the entire force of the great P.C.C. and W.U. system went on strike. The people of the city awoke one morning to find the grey sky of dawn splashed with a bright crimson color. The strikers had set ablaze one of the company's shops in the suburbs and the light from it flashed out a red ominous signal of warning foretelling the woe and despair of the struggle that was to ensue. Rumors came that the men usually so sober, industrious and imperturbable were running in a wild mob, raving and destroying. Whereupon, the people who had laughed to scorn any idea of being prepared for this upheaval began to assiduously abuse the authorities for not being ready to meet it.

That morning Tom, in his shirt sleeves, went into the back part of his shop to direct some of his workmen about a certain job, and when he came out he was well covered by as honest a coating of grime and soot as was ever worn by journeyman. He went to the sink to dispose of this adornment and while there he heard his men talking of the strike. One was saying: "Yes, sir; sure as th' dickens! They say they're goin' t' burn th' president's house an' everybody in it." Tom's body stiffened at these words. He felt himself turn cold. A moment later he left the shop forgetting his coat, forgetting his covering of soot and grime.

In the main streets of the city there was no evident change. The horses of the jangling street cars still slipped and strained in the deep mud into which the snow had been churned. The store windows were gay with the color of Christmas. Innumerable turkeys hung before each butcher's shop. Upon the walks the business men had formed into little eager groups discussing the domestic calamity. Against the leaden-hued sky, over the tops of the buildings, arose a great leaning pillar of smoke marking the spot upon which stood the burning shop.

Tom hurried on through that part of town which was composed of little narrow streets with tiny grey houses on either side. There he saw a concourse of Slavs, Polacs, Italians and Hungarians, laborers of the company, floundering about in the mud and raving, conducting a riot in their own inimitable way. They seemed as blood-thirsty, pitiless, mad, as starved wolves. And Tom presented a figure no less grim as he ran through the crowd, coatless and now indeed hatless, with pale skin showing through the grime. He went until he came to a stretch of commons across which he could see the Fortmans' house standing serenely with no evidences of riot about it. He moderated his pace then.

When he had gone about half way across this little snow-covered common, he looked back, for he heard cries. Across the white fields, winding along the muddy road, there came a strange procession. It resembled a parade of Parisians at the time of the first revolution. Fists were wildly waving and at times hoarse voices rang out. It was as if this crowd was delirious from drink. As it came nearer Tom could see women—gaunt and ragged creatures with inflamed visages and rolling eyes. There were men with dark sinister faces whom Tom had never before seen. They had emerged from the earth, so to speak, to engage in this carousal of violence. And from this procession there came continual threatening ejaculations, shrill cries for revenge, and querulous voices of hate, that made a sort of barbaric hymn, a pagan chant of savage battle and death.

Tom waited for them. Those in the lead evidently considered him to be one of their number since his face was grimed and his garments dishevelled. One gigantic man with bare and brawny arms and throat, gave him invitation with a fierce smile. "Come ahn, Swipsey, while we go roast 'em."

A raving grey-haired woman, struggling in the mud, sang a song which consisted of one endless line:

> "We'll burn th' foxes out,
> We'll burn th' foxes out,
> We'll burn th' foxes out."

As for the others, they babbled and screamed in a vast variety of foreign tongues. Tom walked along with them listening to the cries that came from the terrible little army, marching with clenched fists and with gleaming eyes fastened upon the mansion that upreared so calmly before them.

When they arrived, they hesitated a moment, as if awed by the impassive silence of the structure with closed shutters and barred doors, which stolidly and indifferently confronted them.

Then from the centre of the crowd came the voice of the grey-headed old woman: "Break in th' door! Break in th' door!" And then it was that Tom displayed the desperation born of his devotion to the girl within the house. Although he was perhaps braver than most men, he had none of that magnificent fortitude, that gorgeous tranquility amid upheavals and perils which is the attribute of people in plays; but he stepped up on the porch and faced the throng. His face was wondrously pallid and his hands trembled but he said: "You fellows can't come in here."

There came a great sarcastic howl from the crowd. "Can't we?" They broke into laughter at this wildly ridiculous thing. The brawny, bare-armed giant seized Tom by the arm. "Get outa th' way, you yap," he said between his teeth. In an instant Tom was punched and pulled and knocked this way and that way, and amid the pain of these moments he was conscious that members of the mob were delivering thunderous blows upon the huge doors. Directly indeed they crashed down and he felt the crowd sweep past him and into the house. He clung to a railing; he had no more sense of balance than a feather. A blow in the head had made him feel that the ground swirled and heaved around him. He had no further interest in rioting, and such scenes of excitement. Gazing out over the common he saw two patrol wagons, loaded with policemen, and the lashed horses galloping in the mud. He wondered dimly why they were in such a hurry.

But at that moment a scream rang from the house out through the open doors. He knew the voice, and like an electric shock it aroused him from his semi-stupor. Once more alive, he turned and charged into the house as valiant and as full of rage as a Roman. Pandemonium reigned within. There came yells and roars, splinterings, cracklings, crashes. The scream of Mildred again rang out; this time he knew it came from the dining-room before whose closed door four men were as busy as miners with improvised pick and drill.

Tom grasped a heavy oaken chair that stood ornamentally in the hall and, elevating it above his head, ran madly at the four men. When he was almost upon them, he let the chair fly. It seemed to strike all of them. A heavy oak chair of the old English type is one of the most destructive of weapons. Still, there seemed to be enough of the men left for they flew at him from all sides like dragons. In the dark of the hallway, Tom put down his head and half-closed his eyes and plied his fists. He knew he had but a moment in which to stand up, but there was a sort of grim joy in knowing that the most terrific din of this affray was going straight through the dining-room door, and into the heart of Mildred and when she knew that her deliverer was—— He saw a stretch of blood-red sky flame under his lids and then sank to the floor, blind, deaf, and nerveless.

When the old colonel arrived in one of the patrol wagons, he did not wait to see the police attack in front but ran around to the rear. As he passed the dining-room windows he saw his wife's face. He shouted, and when they opened a window he clambered with great agility into the room. For a minute they deluged each other with shouts of joy and tears. Then finally the old colonel said: "But they did not get in here. How was that?"

"Oh, papa," said Mildred, "they were trying to break in when somebody came and fought dreadfully with them and made them stop."

"Heavens, who could it have been?" said the colonel. He went to the door and opened it. A group of police became visible hurrying about the wide hall but near the colonel's feet lay a body with a white still face.

"Why, it's—it's——" ejaculated the colonel in great agitation.

"It's Tom," cried Mildred.

When Tom came to his senses he found that his fingers were clasped tightly by a soft white hand which by some occult power of lovers he knew at once.

"Tom," said Mildred.

And the old colonel from further away said: "Tom, my boy!"

But Tom was something of an obstinate young man. So as soon as he felt himself recovered sufficiently, he arose and went unsteadily toward the door.

"Tom, where are you going?" cried Mildred.

"Where are you going, Tom?" called the colonel.

"I'm going home," said Tom doggedly. "I didn't intend to cross this threshold—I——" He swayed unsteadily and seemed about to fall. Mildred screamed and ran toward him. She made a prisoner of him. "You shall not go home," she told him.

"Well," began Tom weakly yet persistently, "I——"

"No, no, Tom," said the colonel, "you are to eat a Christmas dinner with us to-morrow and then I wish to talk with you about—about——"

"About what?" said Tom.

"About—about—damnitall, about marrying my daughter," cried the colonel.

little tree

E. E. CUMMINGS

little tree
little silent Christmas tree
you are so little
you are more like a flower

who found you in the green forest
and were you very sorry to come away?
see   i will comfort you
because you smell so sweetly

i will kiss your cool bark
and hug you safe and tight
just as your mother would,
only don't be afraid

look   the spangles
that sleep all the year in a dark box
dreaming of being taken out and allowed to shine,
the balls the chains red and gold the fluffy threads,

put up your little arms
and i'll give them all to you to hold
every finger shall have its ring
and there won't be a single place dark or unhappy

then when you're quite dressed
you'll stand in the window for everyone to see
and how they'll stare!
oh but you'll be very proud

and my little sister and i will take hands
and looking up at our beautiful tree
we'll dance and sing
"Noel Noel"

SANTA CLAUS

WALTER DE LA MARE

On wool-soft feet he peeps and creeps,
  While in the moon-blanched snow,
Tossing their sled-belled antlered heads,
  His reindeer wait below.
Bright eyes, peaked beard, and bulging sack,
  He stays to listen, and look, because
A child lies sleeping out of sight,
  And this is Santa Claus.

"Hast thou, in Fancy, trodden where lie
Leagues of ice beneath the sky?
Where bergs, like palaces of light,
Emerald, sapphire, crystal white,
Glimmer in the polar night?
Hast thou heard in dead of dark
The mighty Sea-lion's shuddering bark?
Seen, shuffling through the crusted snow,
The blue-eyed Bears a-hunting go?
And in leagues of space o'erhead——
Radiant Aurora's glory spread?
Hast thou?" "Why?" "My child, because
  There dwells thy loved Santa Claus."

A CHRISTMAS CHAPTER

CHARLES DICKENS

from THE PICKWICK PAPERS

A good-humoured Christmas Chapter, containing an Account of a Wedding, and some other Sports beside: which although in their way, even as good Customs as Marriage itself, are not quite so religiously kept up, in these degenerate Times

As brisk as bees, if not altogether as light as fairies, did the four Pickwickians assemble on the morning of the twenty-second day of December, in the year of grace in which these, their faithfully-recorded adventures, were undertaken and accomplished. Christmas was close at hand, in all his bluff and hearty honesty; it was the season of hospitality, merriment, and open-heartedness; the old year was preparing, like an ancient philosopher, to call his friends around him, and amidst the sound of feasting and revelry to pass gently and calmly away. Gay and merry was the time, and gay and merry were at least four of the numerous hearts that were gladdened by its coming.

And numerous indeed are the hearts to which Christmas brings a brief season of happiness and enjoyment. How many families, whose members have been dispersed and scattered far and wide, in the restless struggles of life, are then reunited, and meet once again in that happy state of companionship and mutual good-will, which is a source of such pure and unalloyed delight, and one so incompatible with the cares and sorrows of the world, that the religious belief of the most civilised nations, and the rude traditions of the roughest savages, alike number it among the first joys of a future condition of existence, provided for the blest and happy!

How many old recollections, and how many dormant sympathies, does Christmas time awaken!

We write these words now, many miles distant from the spot at which, year after year, we met on that day, a merry and joyous circle. Many of the hearts that throbbed so gaily then, have ceased to beat; many of the looks that shone so brightly then, have ceased to glow; the hands we grasped, have grown cold; the eyes we sought, have hid their lustre in the grave; and yet the old house, the room, the merry voices and smiling faces, the jest, the laugh, the most minute and trivial circumstances connected with those happy meetings, crowd upon our mind at each recurrence of the season, as if the last assemblage had been but yesterday! Happy, happy Christmas, that can win us back to the delusions of our childish days; that can recall to the old man the pleasures of his youth; that can transport the sailor and the traveller, thousands of miles away, back to his own fire-side and his quiet home!

But we are so taken up and occupied with the good qualities of this saint Christmas, that we are keeping Mr Pickwick and his friends waiting in the cold on the outside of the Muggleton coach, which they have just attained, well wrapped up in great-coats, shawls, and comforters. The portmanteaus and carpet-bags have been stowed away, and Mr Weller and the guard are endeavouring to insinuate into the fore-boot a huge cod-fish several sizes too large for it—which is snugly packed up, in a long brown basket, with a layer of straw over the top, and which has been left to the last, in order that he may repose in safety on the half-dozen barrels of real native oysters, all the property of Mr Pickwick, which have been arranged in regular order at the bottom of the receptacle. The interest displayed in Mr Pickwick's countenance is most intense, as Mr Weller and the guard try to squeeze the cod-fish into the boot, first head first, and then tail first, and then top upward, and then bottom upward, and then side-ways, and then long-ways, all of which artifices the implacable cod-fish sturdily resists, until the guard accidentally hits him in the very middle of the basket, whereupon he suddenly disappears into the boot, and with him, the head and shoulders of the guard himself, who, not calculating upon so sudden a cessation of the passive resistance of the cod-fish, experiences a very unexpected shock, to the unsmotherable delight of all the porters and bystanders. Upon this, Mr Pickwick smiles with great good-humour, and drawing a shilling from his waistcoat pocket, begs the guard, as he picks himself out of the boot, to drink his health in a glass of hot brandy and water; at which the guard smiles too, and Messrs Snodgrass, Winkle, and Tupman, all smile in company. The guard and Mr Weller disappear for five minutes: most probably to get the hot brandy and water, for they smell very strongly of it; when they return, the coachman mounts to the box, Mr Weller jumps up behind, the Pickwickians pull their coats round their legs and their shawls over their noses, the helpers pull the horse-cloths off, the coachman shouts out a cheery 'All right,' and away they go.

They have rumbled through the streets, and jolted over the stones, and at length reach the wide and open country. The wheels skim over the hard and frosty ground: and the horses, bursting into a canter at a smart crack of the whip, step along the road as if the load behind them: coach, passengers, cod-fish, oyster barrels, and all: were but a feather at their heels. They have descended a gentle slope, and enter upon a level, as compact and dry as a solid block of marble, two miles long. Another crack of the whip, and on they speed, at a smart gallop: the horses tossing their heads and rattling the harness, as if in exhilaration at the rapidity of the motion: while the coachman, holding whip and reins in one hand, takes off his hat with the other, and resting it on his knees, pulls out his handkerchief, and wipes his forehead: partly because he has a habit of doing it, and partly because it's as well to show the passengers how cool he is, and what an easy thing it is to drive four-in-hand, when you have had as much practice as he has. Having done this very leisurely (otherwise the effect would be materially impaired), he replaces his handkerchief, pulls on his hat, adjusts his gloves, squares his elbows, cracks the whip again, and on they speed, more merrily than before.

A few small houses, scattered on either side of the road, betoken the entrance to some town or village. The lively notes of the guard's key-bugle vibrate in the clear cold air, and wake up the old gentleman inside, who, carefully letting down the window-sash half-way, and standing sentry over the air, takes a short peep out, and then carefully pulling it up again, informs the other inside that they're going to change directly; on which the other inside wakes himself up, and determines to postpone his next nap until after the stoppage. Again the bugle sounds lustily forth, and rouses the cottager's wife and children, who peep out at the house-door, and watch the coach till it turns the corner, when they once more crouch round the blazing fire, and throw on another log of wood against father comes home; while father himself, a full mile off, has just exchanged a friendly nod with the coachman, and turned round to take a good long stare at the vehicle as it whirls away.

And now the bugle plays a lively air as the coach rattles through the ill-paved streets of a country-town; and the coachman, undoing the buckle which keeps his ribands together, prepares to throw them off the moment he stops. Mr Pickwick emerges from his coat collar, and looks about him with great curiosity; perceiving which, the coachman informs Mr Pickwick of the name of the town, and tells him it was market-day yesterday, both of which pieces of information Mr Pickwick re-tails to his fellow-passengers; whereupon they emerge from their coat collars too, and look about them also. Mr Winkle, who sits at the ex-treme edge, with one leg dangling in the air, is nearly precipitated into the street, as the coach twists round the sharp corner by the cheese-monger's shop, and turns into the market-place; and before Mr Snod-grass, who sits next to him, has recovered from his alarm, they pull up at the inn yard, where the fresh horses, with cloths on, are already waiting. The coachman throws down the reins and gets down himself, and the other outside passengers drop down also: except those who have no great confidence in their ability to get up again: and they remain where they are, and stamp their feet against the coach to warm them—looking, with longing eyes and red noses, at the bright fire in the inn bar, and the sprigs of holly with red berries which ornament the window.

But the guard has delivered at the corn-dealer's shop the brown paper packet he took out of the little pouch which hangs over his shoulder by a leathern strap; and has seen the horses carefully put to; and has thrown on the pavement the saddle which was brought from London on the coach-roof; and has assisted in the conference between the coachman and the hostler about the grey mare that hurt her off-fore-leg last Tuesday; and he and Mr Weller are all right behind, and the coachman is all right in front, and the old gentleman inside, who has kept the window down full two inches all this time, has pulled it up again, and the cloths are off, and they are all ready for starting, except the 'two stout gentlemen,' whom the coachman inquires after with some impatience. Hereupon the coach-man, and the guard, and Sam Weller, and Mr Winkle, and Mr Snodgrass, and all the hostlers, and every one of the idlers, who are more in number than all the others put together, shout for the missing gentlemen as loud as they can bawl. A distant response is heard from the yard, and Mr Pick-wick and Mr Tupman come running down it, quite out of breath, for they have been having a glass of ale a-piece, and Mr Pickwick's fingers are so cold that he has been full five minutes before he could find the six-pence to pay for it. The coachman shouts an admonitory 'Now then, gen'lm'n!' the guard re-echoes it; the old gentleman inside thinks it a very extraordinary thing that people *will* get down when they know there isn't time for it; Mr Pickwick struggles up on one side, Mr Tupman on the other; Mr Winkle cries 'All right'; and off they start. Shawls are pulled up, coat collars are re-adjusted, the pavement ceases, the houses disappear, and they are once again dashing along the open road, with the fresh clear air blowing in their faces, and gladdening their very hearts within them.

Such was the progress of Mr Pickwick and his friends by the Muggleton Telegraph, on their way to Dingley Dell; and at three o'clock that afternoon they all stood, high and dry, safe and sound, hale and hearty, upon the steps of the Blue Lion, having taken on the road quite enough of ale and brandy to enable them to bid defiance to the frost that was binding up the earth in its iron fetters, and weaving its beautiful network upon the trees and hedges. Mr Pickwick was busily engaged in counting the barrels of oysters and superintending the disinterment of the cod-fish, when he felt himself gently pulled by the skirts of the coat. Looking round, he discovered that the individual who resorted to this mode of catching his attention was no other than Mr Wardle's favourite page, better known to the readers of this unvarnished history, by the distinguishing appellation of the fat boy.

'Aha!' said Mr Pickwick.

'Aha!' said the fat boy.

As he said it, he glanced from the cod-fish to the oyster-barrels, and chuckled joyously. He was fatter than ever.

'Well, you look rosy enough, my young friend,' said Mr Pickwick.

'I've been asleep, right in front of the tap-room fire,' replied the fat boy, who had heated himself to the colour of a new chimney-pot, in the course of an hour's nap. 'Master sent me over with the shay-cart, to carry your luggage up to the house. He'd ha' sent some saddle-horses, but he thought you'd rather walk, being a cold day.'

'Yes, yes,' said Mr Pickwick, hastily, for he remembered how they had travelled over nearly the same ground on a previous occasion. 'Yes, we would rather walk. Here, Sam!'

'Sir,' said Mr Weller.

'Help Mr Wardle's servant to put the packages into the cart, and then ride on with him. We will walk forward at once.'

Having given this direction, and settled with the coachman, Mr Pickwick and his three friends struck into the footpath across the fields, and walked briskly away, leaving Mr Weller and the fat boy confronted together for the first time. Sam looked at the fat boy with great astonishment, but without saying a word; and began to stow the luggage rapidly away in the cart, while the fat boy stood quietly by, and seemed to think it a very interesting sort of thing to see Mr Weller working by himself.

'There,' said Sam, throwing in the last carpet-bag. 'There they are!'

'Yes,' said the fat boy, in a very satisfied tone, 'there they are.'

'Vell, young twenty stun,' said Sam, 'you're a nice specimen of a prize boy, you are!'

'Thank'ee,' said the fat boy.

'You ain't got nothin' on your mind as makes you fret yourself, have you?' inquired Sam.

'Not as I knows on,' replied the fat boy.

'I should rayther ha' thought, to look at you, that you was a labourin' under an unrequited attachment to some young 'ooman,' said Sam.

The fat boy shook his head.

'Vell,' said Sam, 'I'm glad to hear it. Do you ever drink anythin'?'

'I likes eating, better,' replied the boy.

'Ah,' said Sam, 'I should ha' s'posed that; but what I mean is, should you like a drop of anythin' as 'd warm you? but I s'pose you never was cold, with all them elastic fixtures, was you?'

'Sometimes,' replied the boy; 'and I likes a drop of something, when it's good.'

'Oh, you do, do you?' said Sam, 'come this way, then!'

The Blue Lion tap was soon gained and the fat boy swallowed a glass of liquor without so much as winking; a feat which considerably advanced him in Mr Weller's good opinion. Mr Weller having transacted a similar piece of business on his own account, they got into the cart.

'Can you drive?' said the fat boy.

'I should rayther think so,' replied Sam.

'There, then,' said the fat boy, putting the reins in his hand, and pointing up a lane, 'it's as straight as you can go; you can't miss it.'

With these words, the fat boy laid himself affectionately down by the side of the cod-fish: and placing an oyster-barrel under his head for a pillow, fell asleep instantaneously.

'Well,' said Sam, 'of all the cool boys ever I set my eyes on, this here young gen'l'm'n is the coolest. Come, wake up young dropsy!'

But as young dropsy evinced no symptoms of returning animation, Sam Weller sat himself down in front of the cart, and starting the old horse with a jerk of the rein, jogged steadily on, towards Manor Farm.

Meanwhile, Mr Pickwick and his friends having walked their blood into active circulation, proceeded cheerfully on. The paths were hard; the grass was crisp and frosty; the air had a fine, dry, bracing coldness; and the rapid approach of the grey twilight (slate-coloured is a better term in frosty weather) made them look forward with pleasant anticipation to the comforts which awaited them at their hospitable entertainer's. It was the sort of afternoon that might induce a couple of elderly gentlemen, in a lonely field, to take off their great-coats and play at leap-frog in pure lightness of heart and gaiety; and we firmly believe that had Mr Tupman at that moment proffered 'a back,' Mr Pickwick would have accepted his offer with the utmost avidity.

However, Mr Tupman did not volunteer any such accommodation, and the friends walked on, conversing merrily. As they turned into a lane they had to cross, the sound of many voices burst upon their ears; and before they had even had time to form a guess to whom they belonged, they walked into the very centre of the party who were expecting their arrival—a fact which was first notified to the Pickwickians, by the loud 'Hurrah,' which burst from old Wardle's lips, when they appeared in sight.

First, there was Wardle himself, looking, if possible, more jolly than ever; then there were Bella and her faithful Trundle; and, lastly, there were Emily and some eight or ten young ladies, who had all come down to the wedding, which was to take place next day, and who were in as happy and important a state as young ladies usually are, on such momentous occasions; and they were, one and all, startling the fields and lanes, far and wide, with their frolic and laughter.

The ceremony of introduction, under such circumstances, was very soon performed, or we should rather say that the introduction was soon over, without any ceremony at all. In two minutes thereafter, Mr Pickwick was joking with the young ladies who wouldn't come over the stile while he looked—or who, having pretty feet and unexceptionable ankles, preferred standing on the top-rail for five minutes or so, declaring that they were too frightened to move—with as much ease and absence of reserve or constraint, as if he had known them for life. It is worthy of remark, too, that Mr Snodgrass offered Emily far more assistance than the absolute terrors of the stile (although it was full three feet high, and had only a couple of stepping-stones) would seem to require; while one black-eyed young lady in a very nice little pair of boots with fur round the top, was observed to scream very loudly, when Mr Winkle offered to help her over.

All this was very snug and pleasant. And when the difficulties of the stile were at last surmounted, and they once more entered on the open field, old Wardle informed Mr Pickwick how they had all been down in a body to inspect the furniture and fittings-up of the house, which the young couple were to tenant, after the Christmas holidays; at which communication Bella and Trundle both coloured up, as red as the fat boy after the tap-room fire; and the young lady with the black eyes and the fur round the boots, whispered something in Emily's ear, and then glanced archly at Mr Snodgrass: to which Emily responded that she was a foolish girl, but turned very red, notwithstanding; and Mr Snodgrass, who was as modest as all great geniuses usually are, felt the crimson rising to the crown of his head, and devoutly wished in the inmost recesses of his own heart that the young lady aforesaid, with her black eyes, and her archness, and her boots with the fur round the top, were all comfortably deposited in the adjacent county.

But if they were social and happy outside the house, what was the warmth and cordiality of their reception when they reached the farm! The very servants grinned with pleasure at sight of Mr Pickwick; and Emma bestowed a half-demure, half-impudent, and all pretty, look of recognition, on Mr Tupman, which was enough to make the statue of Bonaparte in the passage, unfold his arms, and clasp her within them.

The old lady was seated in customary state in the front parlour, but she was rather cross, and, by consequence, most particularly deaf. She never went out herself, and like a great many other old ladies of the same stamp, she was apt to consider it an act of domestic treason, if anybody else took the liberty of doing what she couldn't. So, bless her old soul, she sat as upright as she could, in her great chair, and looked as fierce as might be—and that was benevolent after all.

'Mother,' said Wardle, 'Mr Pickwick. You recollect him?'

'Never mind,' replied the old lady with great dignity. 'Don't trouble Mr Pickwick about an old creetur like me. Nobody cares about me now, and it's very nat'ral they shouldn't.' Here the old lady tossed her head, and smoothed down her lavender-coloured silk dress, with trembling hands.

'Come, come, ma'am,' said Mr Pickwick, 'I can't let you cut an old friend in this way. I have come down expressly to have a long talk, and another rubber with you; and we'll show these boys and girls how to dance a minuet, before they're eight-and-forty hours older.'

The old lady was rapidly giving way, but she did not like to do it all at once; so she only said, 'Ah! I can't hear him!'

'Nonsense, mother,' said Wardle. 'Come, come, don't be cross, there's a good soul. Recollect Bella; come, you must keep her spirits up, poor girl.'

The good old lady heard this, for her lip quivered as her son said it. But age has its little infirmities of temper, and she was not quite brought round yet. So, she smoothed down the lavender-coloured dress again, and turning to Mr Pickwick said, 'Ah, Mr Pickwick, young people was very different, when I was a girl.'

'No doubt of that, ma'am,' said Mr Pickwick, 'and that's the reason why I would make much of the few that have any traces of the old stock,'—and saying this, Mr Pickwick gently pulled Bella towards him, and bestowing a kiss upon her forehead, bade her sit down on the little stool at her grandmother's feet. Whether the expression of her countenance, as it was raised towards the old lady's face, called up a thought of old times, or whether the old lady was touched by Mr Pickwick's affectionate good nature, or whatever was the cause, she was fairly melted; so she threw herself on her granddaughter's neck, and all the little ill-humour evaporated in a gush of silent tears.

A happy party they were, that night. Sedate and solemn were the score of rubbers in which Mr Pickwick and the old lady played together; uproarious was the mirth of the round table. Long after the ladies had retired, did the hot elder wine, well qualified with brandy and spice, go round, and round, and round again; and sound was the sleep and pleasant were the dreams that followed. It is a remarkable fact that those of Mr Snodgrass bore constant reference to Emily Wardle; and that the principal figure in Mr Winkle's visions was a young lady with black eyes, an arch smile, and a pair of remarkably nice boots with fur round the tops.

Mr Pickwick was awakened, early in the morning, by a hum of voices and a pattering of feet, sufficient to rouse even the fat boy from his heavy slumbers. He sat up in bed and listened. The female servants and female visitors were running constantly to and fro; and there were such multitudinous demands for hot water, such repeated outcries for needles and thread, and so many half-suppressed entreaties of 'Oh, do come and tie me, there's a dear!' that Mr Pickwick in his innocence began to imagine that something dreadful must have occurred: when he grew more awake, and remembered the wedding. The occasion being an important one he dressed himself with peculiar care, and descended to the breakfast room.

There were all the female servants in a brand new uniform of pink muslin gowns with white bows in their caps, running about the house in a state of excitement and agitation which it would be impossible to describe. The old lady was dressed out in a brocaded gown which had not seen the light for twenty years, saving and excepting such truant rays as had stolen through the chinks in the box in which it had been lain by, during the whole time. Mr Trundle was in high feather and spirits, but a little nervous withal. The hearty old landlord was trying to look very cheerful and unconcerned, but failing signally in the attempt. All the girls were in tears and white muslin, except a select two or three who were being honoured with a private view of the bride and bridesmaids, up stairs. All the Pickwickians were in most blooming array; and there was a terrific roaring on the grass in front of the house, occasioned by all the men, boys, and hobbledehoys attached to the farm, each of whom had got a white bow in his button-hole, and all of whom were cheering with might and main: being incited thereunto, and stimulated therein, by the precept and example of Mr Samuel Weller, who had managed to become mighty popular already, and was as much at home as if he had been born on the land.

A wedding is a licensed subject to joke upon, but there really is no great joke in the matter after all;—we speak merely of the ceremony, and beg it to be distinctly understood that we indulge in no hidden sarcasm upon a married life. Mixed up with the pleasure and joy of the occasion, are the many regrets at quitting home, the tears of parting between parent and child, the consciousness of leaving the dearest and kindest friends of the happiest portion of human life, to encounter its cares and troubles with others still untried and little known: natural feelings which we would not render this chapter mournful by describing, and which we should be still more unwilling to be supposed to ridicule.

Let us briefly say, then, that the ceremony was performed by the old clergyman, in the parish church of Dingley Dell, and that Mr Pickwick's name is attached to the register, still preserved in the vestry thereof; that the young lady with the black eyes signed her name in a very unsteady and tremulous manner; that Emily's signature, as the other bridesmaid, is nearly illegible; that it all went off in very admirable style; that the young ladies generally thought it far less shocking than they had expected; and that although the owner of the black eyes and the arch smile informed Mr Winkle that she was sure she could never submit to anything so dreadful, we have the very best reasons for thinking she was mistaken. To all this, we may add, that Mr Pickwick was the first who saluted the bride, and that in so doing, he threw over her neck a rich gold watch and chain, which no mortal eyes but the jeweller's had ever beheld before. Then, the old church bell rang as gaily as it could, and they all returned to breakfast.

'Vere does the mince pies go, young opium eater?' said Mr Weller to the fat boy, as he assisted in laying out such articles of consumption as had not been duly arranged on the previous night.

The fat boy pointed to the destination of the pies.

'Wery good,' said Sam, 'stick a bit o' Christmas in 'em. T'other dish opposite. There; now we look compact and comfortable, as the father said ven he cut his little boy's head off, to cure him o' squintin'.'

As Mr Weller made the comparison, he fell back a step or two, to give full effect to it, and surveyed the preparations with the utmost satisfaction.

'Wardle,' said Mr Pickwick, almost as soon as they were all seated, 'a glass of wine, in honour of this happy occasion!'

'I shall be delighted, my boy,' said Wardle. 'Joe—damn that boy, he's gone to sleep.'

'No, I ain't, sir,' replied the fat boy, starting up from a remote corner, where, like the patron saint of fat boys—the immortal Horner—he had been devouring a Christmas pie: though not with the coolness and deliberation which characterised that young gentleman's proceedings.

'Fill Mr Pickwick's glass.'

'Yes, sir.'

The fat boy filled Mr Pickwick's glass, and then retired behind his master's chair, from whence he watched the play of the knives and forks, and the progress of the choice morsels from the dishes to the mouths of the company, with a kind of dark and gloomy joy that was most impressive.

'God bless you, old fellow!' said Mr Pickwick.

'Same to you, my boy,' replied Wardle; and they pledged each other, heartily.

'Mrs Wardle,' said Mr Pickwick, 'we old folks must have a glass of wine together, in honour of this joyful event.'

The old lady was in a state of great grandeur just then, for she was sitting at the top of the table in the brocaded gown, with her newly-married granddaughter on one side and Mr Pickwick on the other, to do the carving. Mr Pickwick had not spoken in a very loud tone, but she understood him at once, and drank off a full glass of wine to his long life and happiness; after which the worthy old soul launched forth into a minute and particular account of her own wedding, with a dissertation on the fashion of wearing high-heeled shoes, and some particulars concerning the life and adventures of the beautiful Lady Tollimglower, deceased: at all of which the old lady herself laughed very heartily indeed, and so did the young ladies too, for they were wondering among themselves what on earth grandma was talking about. When they laughed, the old lady laughed ten times more heartily, and said that these always had been considered capital stories: which caused them all to laugh again, and put the old lady into the very best of humours. Then, the cake was cut, and passed through the ring; the young ladies saved pieces to put under their pillows to dream of their future husbands on; and a great deal of blushing and merriment was thereby occasioned.

'Mr Miller,' said Mr Pickwick to his old acquaintance the hard-headed gentleman, 'a glass of wine?'

'With great satisfaction, Mr Pickwick,' replied the hard-headed gentleman, solemnly.

'You'll take me in?' said the benevolent old clergyman.

'And me,' interposed his wife.

'And me, and me,' said a couple of poor relations at the bottom of the table, who had eaten and drank very heartily, and laughed at everything.

Mr Pickwick expressed his heartfelt delight at every additional suggestion; and his eyes beamed with hilarity and cheerfulness.

'Ladies and gentlemen,' said Mr Pickwick, suddenly rising.

'Hear, hear! Hear, hear! Hear, hear!' cried Mr Weller, in the excitement of his feelings.

'Call in all the servants,' cried old Wardle, interposing to prevent the public rebuke which Mr Weller would otherwise most indubitably have received from his master. 'Give them a glass of wine each, to drink the toast in. Now, Pickwick.'

Amidst the silence of the company, the whispering of the women servants, and the awkward embarrassment of the men, Mr Pickwick proceeded.

'Ladies and gentlemen—no, I won't say ladies and gentlemen, I'll call you my friends, my dear friends, if the ladies will allow me to take so great a liberty'——

Here Mr Pickwick was interrupted by immense applause from the ladies, echoed by the gentlemen, during which the owner of the eyes was distinctly heard to state that she could kiss that dear Mr Pickwick. Whereupon Mr Winkle gallantly inquired if it couldn't be done by deputy: to which the young lady with the black eyes replied, 'Go away'—and accompanied the request with a look which said as plainly as a look could do—'if you can.'

'My dear friends,' resumed Mr Pickwick, 'I am going to propose the health of the bride and bridegroom—God bless 'em (cheers and tears). My young friend, Trundle, I believe to be a very excellent and manly fellow; and his wife I know to be a very amiable and lovely girl, well qualified to transfer to another sphere of action the happiness which for twenty years she has diffused around her, in her father's house. (Here, the fat boy burst forth into stentorian blubberings, and was led forth by the coat collar, by Mr Weller.) I wish,' added Mr Pickwick, 'I wish I was young enough to be her sister's husband (cheers), but, failing that, I am happy to be old enough to be her father; for, being so, I shall not be suspected of any latent designs when I say, that I admire, esteem, and love them both (cheers and sobs). The bride's father, our good friend there, is a noble person, and I am proud to know him (great uproar). He is a kind, excellent, independent-spirited, fine-hearted, hospitable, liberal man (enthusiastic shouts from the poor relations, at all the adjectives; and especially at the two last). That his daughter may enjoy all the happiness, even he can desire; and that he may derive from the contemplation of her felicity all the gratification of heart and peace of mind which he so well deserves, is, I am persuaded, our united wish. So, let us drink their healths, and wish them prolonged life, and every blessing!'

Mr Pickwick concluded amidst a whirlwind of applause; and once more were the lungs of the supernumeraries, under Mr Weller's command, brought into active and efficient operation. Mr Wardle proposed Mr Pickwick; Mr Pickwick proposed the old lady. Mr Snodgrass proposed Mr Wardle; Mr Wardle proposed Mr Snodgrass. One of the poor relations proposed Mr Tupman, and the other poor relation proposed Mr Winkle; all was happiness and festivity, until the mysterious disappearance of both the poor relations beneath the table, warned the party that it was time to adjourn.

At dinner they met again, after a five-and-twenty-mile walk, undertaken by the males at Wardle's recommendation, to get rid of the effects of the wine at breakfast. The poor relations had kept in bed all day, with the view of attaining the same happy consummation, but, as they had been unsuccessful, they stopped there. Mr Weller kept the domestics in a state of perpetual hilarity; and the fat boy divided his time into small alternate allotments of eating and sleeping.

The dinner was as hearty an affair as the breakfast, and was quite as noisy, without the tears. Then came the dessert and some more toasts. Then came the tea and coffee; and then, the ball.

The best sitting room at Manor Farm was a good, long, dark-panelled room with a high chimney-piece, and a capacious chimney, up which you could have driven one of the new patent cabs, wheels and all. At the upper end of the room, seated in a shady bower of holly and evergreens, were the two best fiddlers, and the only harp, in all Muggleton. In all sorts of recesses, and on all kinds of brackets, stood massive old silver candlesticks with four branches each. The carpet was up, the candles burnt bright, the fire blazed and crackled on the hearth, and merry voices and light-hearted laughter rang through the room. If any of the old English yeomen had turned into fairies when they died, it was just the place in which they would have held their revels.

If anything could have added to the interest of this agreeable scene, it would have been the remarkable fact of Mr Pickwick's appearing without his gaiters, for the first time within the memory of his oldest friends.

'You mean to dance?' said Wardle.

'Of course I do,' replied Mr Pickwick. 'Don't you see I am dressed for the purpose?' Mr Pickwick called attention to his speckled silk stockings, and smartly tied pumps.

'*You* in silk stockings!' exclaimed Mr Tupman jocosely.

'And why not, sir—why not?' said Mr Pickwick, turning warmly upon him.

'Oh, of course there is no reason why you shouldn't wear them,' responded Mr Tupman.

'I imagine not sir, I imagine not,' said Mr Pickwick in a very peremptory tone.

Mr Tupman had contemplated a laugh, but he found it was a serious matter; so he looked grave, and said they were a pretty pattern.

'I hope they are,' said Mr Pickwick fixing his eyes upon his friend. 'You see nothing extraordinary in the stockings, *as* stockings, I trust sir?'

'Certainly not. Oh certainly not,' replied Mr Tupman. He walked away; and Mr Pickwick's countenance resumed its customary benign expression.

'We are all ready, I believe,' said Mr Pickwick, who was stationed with the old lady at the top of the dance, and had already made four false starts, in his excessive anxiety to commence.

'Then begin at once,' said Wardle. 'Now!'

Up struck the two fiddles and the one harp, and off went Mr Pickwick into hands across, when there was a general clapping of hands, and a cry of 'Stop, stop!'

'What's the matter!' said Mr Pickwick, who was only brought to, by the fiddles and harp desisting, and could have been stopped by no other earthly power, if the house had been on fire.

'Where's Arabella Allen?' cried a dozen voices.

'And Winkle?' added Mr Tupman.

'Here we are!' exclaimed that gentleman, emerging with his pretty companion from the corner; as he did so, it would have been hard to tell which was the redder in the face, he or the young lady with the black eyes.

'What an extraordinary thing it is, Winkle,' said Mr Pickwick, rather pettishly, 'that you couldn't have taken your place before.'

'Not at all extraordinary,' said Mr Winkle.

'Well,' said Mr Pickwick, with a very expressive smile, as his eyes rested on Arabella, 'well, I don't know that it *was* extraordinary, either, after all.'

However, there was no time to think more about the matter, for the fiddles and harp began in real earnest. Away went Mr Pickwick—hands across—down the middle to the very end of the room, and half-way up the chimney, back again to the door—poussette everywhere—loud stamp on the ground—ready for the next couple—off again—all the figure over once more—another stamp to beat out the time—next couple, and the next, and the next again—never was such going! At last, after they had reached the bottom of the dance, and full fourteen couple after the old lady had retired in an exhausted state, and the clergyman's wife had been substituted in her stead, did that gentleman, when there was no demand whatever on his exertions, keep perpetually dancing in his place, to keep time to the music: smiling on his partner all the while with a blandness of demeanour which baffles all description.

Long before Mr Pickwick was weary of dancing, the newly-married couple had retired from the scene. There was a glorious supper down-stairs, notwithstanding, and a good long sitting after it; and when Mr Pickwick awoke, late the next morning, he had a confused recollection of having, severally and confidentially, invited somewhere about five-and-forty people to dine with him at the George and Vulture, the very first time they came to London; which Mr Pickwick rightly considered a pretty certain indication of his having taken something besides exercise, on the previous night.

'And so your family has games in the kitchen to-night, my dear, has they?' inquired Sam of Emma.

'Yes, Mr Weller,' replied Emma; 'we always have on Christmas eve. Master wouldn't neglect to keep it up on any account.'

'Your master's a wery pretty notion of keepin' anythin' up, my dear,' said Mr Weller; 'I never see such a sensible sort of man as he is, or such a reg'lar gen'l'm'n.'

'Oh, that he is!' said the fat boy, joining in the conversation; 'don't he breed nice pork!' The fat youth gave a semi-cannibalic leer at Mr Weller, as he thought of the roast legs and gravy.

'Oh, you've woke up, at last, have you?' said Sam.

The fat boy nodded.

'I'll tell you what it is, young boa constructer,' said Mr Weller, impressively; 'if you don't sleep a little less, and exercise a little more, wen you comes to be a man you'll lay yourself open to the same sort of personal inconwenience as was inflicted on the old gen'l'm'n as wore the pigtail.'

'What did they do to him?' inquired the fat boy, in a faltering voice.

'I'm a-goin' to tell you,' replied Mr Weller; 'he was one o' the largest patterns as was ever turned out—reg'lar fat man, as hadn't caught a glimpse of his own shoes for five-and-forty-year.'

'Lor!' exclaimed Emma.

'No, that he hadn't, my dear,' said Mr Weller; 'and if you'd put an exact model of his own legs on the dinin' table afore him, he wouldn't ha' known 'em. Well, he always walks to his office with a wery handsome gold watch-chain hanging out, about a foot and a quarter, and a gold watch in his fob pocket as was worth—I'm afraid to say how much, but as much as a watch can be—a large, heavy, round manafacter, as stout as a watch, as he was for a man, and with a big face in proportion. "You'd better not carry that 'ere watch," says the old gen'l'm'n's friends, "you'll be robbed on it," says they. "Shall I?" says he. "Yes, you will," says they. "Vell," says he, "I should like to see the thief as could get this here watch out, for I'm blest if I ever can, it's such a tight fit," says he; "and venever I wants to know what's o'clock, I'm obliged to stare into the bakers' shops," he says. Well, then he laughs as hearty as if he was a goin' to pieces, and out he walks agin' with his powdered head and pigtail, and rolls down the Strand vith the chain hangin' out furder than ever, and the great round watch almost bustin' through his grey kersey smalls. There warn't a pickpocket in all London as didn't take a pull at that chain, but the chain 'ud never break, and the watch 'ud never come out, so they soon got tired o' dragging such a heavy old gen'l'm'n along the pavement, and he'd go home and laugh till the pigtail wibrated like the penderlum of a Dutch clock. At last, one day the old gen'l'm'n was a rollin' along, and he sees a pickpocket as he know'd by sight, a-comin' up, arm in arm vith a little boy with a wery large head. "Here's a game," says the old gen'l'm'n to himself, "they're a-goin' to have another try, but it won't do!" So he begins a-chucklin' wery hearty, wen, all of a sudden, the little boy leaves hold of the pickpocket's arm, and rushes headforemost straight into the old gen'l'm'n's stomach, and for a moment doubles him right up vith the pain. "Murder!" says the old gen'l'm'n. "All right, sir," says the pickpocket, a wisperin' in his ear. And wen he come straight agin, the watch and chain was gone, and what's worse than that, the old gen'l'm'n's digestion was all wrong ever artervards, to the wery last day of his life; so just you look about you, young feller, and take care you don't get too fat.'

As Mr Weller concluded this moral tale, with which the fat boy appeared much affected, they all three repaired to the large kitchen, in which the family were by this time assembled, according to annual custom on Christmas eve, observed by old Wardle's forefathers from time immemorial.

From the centre of the ceiling of this kitchen, old Wardle had just suspended, with his own hands, a huge branch of mistletoe, and this same branch of mistletoe instantaneously gave rise to a scene of general and most delightful struggling and confusion; in the midst of which, Mr Pickwick, with a gallantry that would have done honour to a descendant of Lady Tollimglower herself, took the old lady by the hand, led her beneath the mystic branch, and saluted her in all courtesy and decorum. The old lady submitted to this piece of practical politeness with all the dignity which befitted so important and serious a solemnity, but the younger ladies, not being so thoroughly imbued with a superstitious veneration for the custom: or imagining that the value of a salute is very much enhanced if it cost a little trouble to obtain it: screamed and struggled, and ran into corners, and threatened and remonstrated, and did everything but leave the room, until some of the less adventurous gentlemen were on the point of desisting, when they all at once found it useless to resist any longer, and submitted to be kissed with a good grace. Mr Winkle kissed the young lady with the black eyes, and Mr Snodgrass kissed Emily, and Mr Weller, not being particular about the form of being under the mistletoe, kissed Emma and the other female servants, just as he caught them. As to the poor relations, they kissed everybody, not even excepting the plainer portions of the young-lady visitors, who, in their excessive confusion, ran right under the mistletoe, as soon as it was hung up, without knowing it! Wardle stood with his back to the fire, surveying the whole scene, with the utmost satisfaction; and the fat boy took the opportunity of appropriating to his own use, and summarily devouring, a particularly fine mince-pie, that had been carefully put by, for somebody else.

Now, the screaming had subsided, and faces were in a glow, and curls in a tangle, and Mr Pickwick, after kissing the old lady as before mentioned, was standing under the mistletoe, looking with a very pleased countenance on all that was passing around him, when the young lady with the black eyes, after a little whispering with the other young ladies, made a sudden dart forward, and, putting her arm round Mr Pickwick's neck, saluted him affectionately on the left cheek; and before Mr Pickwick distinctly knew what was the matter, he was surrounded by the whole body, and kissed by every one of them.

It was a pleasant thing to see Mr Pickwick in the centre of the group, now pulled this way, and then that, and first kissed on the chin, and then on the nose, and then on the spectacles: and to hear the peals of laughter which were raised on every side; but it was a still more pleasant thing to see Mr Pickwick, blinded shortly afterwards with a silk handkerchief, falling up against the wall, and scrambling into corners, and going through all the mysteries of blind-man's buff, with the utmost relish for the game, until at last he caught one of the poor relations, and then had to evade the blind-man himself, which he did with a nimbleness and agility that elicited the admiration and applause of all beholders. The poor relations caught the people who they thought would like it, and, when the game flagged, got caught themselves. When they were all tired of blind-man's buff, there was a great game at snapdragon, and when fingers enough were burned with that, and all the raisins were gone, they sat down by the huge fire of blazing logs to a substantial supper, and a mighty bowl of wassail, something smaller than an ordinary wash-house copper, in which the hot apples were hissing and bubbling with a rich look, and a jolly sound, that were perfectly irresistible.

'This,' said Mr Pickwick, looking round him, 'this is, indeed, comfort.'

'Our invariable custom,' replied Mr Wardle. 'Everybody sits down with us on Christmas eve, as you see them now—servants and all; and here we wait, until the clock strikes twelve, to usher Christmas in, and beguile the time with forfeits and old stories. Trundle, my boy, rake up the fire.'

Up flew the bright sparks in myriads as the logs were stirred. The deep red blaze sent forth a rich glow, that penetrated into the furthest corner of the room, and cast its cheerful tint on every face.

'Come,' said Wardle, 'a song—a Christmas song! I'll give you one, in default of a better.'

'Bravo!' said Mr Pickwick.

'Fill up,' cried Wardle. 'It will be two hours, good, before you see the bottom of the bowl through the deep rich colour of the wassail; fill up all round, and now for the song.'

Thus saying, the merry old gentleman, in a good, round, sturdy voice, commenced without more ado:

A CHRISTMAS CAROL

I care not for Spring; on his fickle wing
Let the blossoms and buds be borne:
He woos them amain with his treacherous rain,
And he scatters them ere the morn.
An inconstant elf, he knows not himself,
Nor his own changing mind an hour,
He'll smile in your face, and, with wry grimace,
He'll wither your youngest flower.

Let the Summer sun to his bright home run,
He shall never be sought by me;
When he's dimmed by a cloud I can laugh aloud,
And care not how sulky he be!
For his darling child is the madness wild
That sports in fierce fever's train;
And when love is too strong, it don't last long,
As many have found to their pain.

A mild harvest night, by the tranquil light
Of the modest and gentle moon,
Has a far sweeter sheen, for me, I ween,
Than the broad and unblushing noon.
But every leaf awakens my grief,
As it lieth beneath the tree;
So let Autumn air be never so fair,
It by no means agrees with me.

But my song I troll out, for CHRISTMAS stout,
The hearty, the true, and the bold;
A bumper I drain, and with might and main
Give three cheers for this Christmas old!
We'll usher him in with a merry din
That shall gladden his joyous heart,
And we'll keep him up, while there's bite or sup,
And in fellowship good, we'll part.

In his fine honest pride, he scorns to hide,
One jot of his hard-weather scars;
They're no disgrace, for there's much the same trace
On the cheeks of our bravest tars.

Then again I sing 'till the roof doth ring,
And it echoes from wall to wall——
To the stout old wight, fair welcome to-night,
As the King of the Seasons all!

This song was tumultuously applauded—for friends and dependents make a capital audience—and the poor relations, especially, were in perfect ecstasies of rapture. Again was the fire replenished, and again went the wassail round.

'How it snows!' said one of the men, in a low tone.

'Snows, does it?' said Wardle.

'Rough, cold night, sir,' replied the man; 'and there's a wind got up, that drifts it across the fields, in a thick white cloud.'

'What does Jem say?' inquired the old lady. 'There ain't anything the matter, is there?'

'No, no, mother,' replied Wardle; 'he says there's a snow-drift, and a wind that's piercing cold. I should know that, by the way it rumbles in the chimney.'

'Ah!' said the old lady, 'there was just such a wind, and just such a fall of snow, a good many years back, I recollect—just five years before your poor father died. It was a Christmas eve, too; and I remember that on that very night he told us the story about the goblins that carried away old Gabriel Grub.'

'The story about what?' said Mr Pickwick.

'Oh, nothing, nothing,' replied Wardle. 'About an old sexton, that the good people down here suppose to have been carried away by goblins.'

'Suppose!' ejaculated the old lady. 'Is there any body hardy enough to disbelieve it? Suppose! Haven't you heard ever since you were a child, that he *was* carried away by the goblins, and don't you know he was?'

'Very well, mother, he was, if you like,' said Wardle, laughing. 'He *was* carried away by goblins, Pickwick; and there's an end of the matter.'

'No, no,' said Mr Pickwick, 'not an end of it, I assure you; for I must hear how, and why, and all about it.'

Wardle smiled, as every head was bent forward to hear; and filling out the wassail with no stinted hand, nodded a health to Mr Pickwick, and began as follows:

But bless our editorial heart, what a long chapter we have been betrayed into! We had quite forgotten all such petty restrictions as chapters, we solemnly declare. So here goes, to give the goblin a fair start in a new one! A clear stage and no favour for the goblins, ladies and gentlemen, if you please.

THE HOLLY-TREE

First Branch/Myself

CHARLES DICKENS

from THE CHRISTMAS STORIES

I have kept one secret in the course of my life. I am a bashful man. Nobody would suppose it, nobody ever does suppose it, nobody ever did suppose it, but I am naturally a bashful man. This is the secret which I have never breathed until now.

I might greatly move the reader by some account of the innumerable places I have not been to, the innumerable people I have not called upon or received, the innumerable social evasions I have been guilty of, solely because I am by original constitution and character a bashful man. But I will leave the reader unmoved, and proceed with the object before me.

That object is to give a plain account of my travels and discoveries in the Holly-Tree Inn; in which place of good entertainment for man and beast I was once snowed up.

It happened in the memorable year when I parted for ever from Angela Leath, whom I was shortly to have married, on making the discovery that she preferred my bosom friend. From our school-days I had freely admitted Edwin, in my own mind, to be far superior to myself; and, though I was grievously wounded at heart, I felt the preference to be natural, and tried to forgive them both. It was under these circumstances that I resolved to go to America—on my way to the Devil.

Communicating my discovery neither to Angela nor to Edwin, but resolving to write each of them an affecting letter conveying my blessing and forgiveness, which the steam-tender for shore should carry to the post when I myself should be bound for the New World, far beyond recall—I say, locking up my grief in my own breast, and consoling myself as I could with the prospect of being generous, I quietly left all I held dear, and started on the desolate journey I have mentioned.

The dead winter-time was in full dreariness when I left my chambers for ever, at five o'clock in the morning. I had shaved by candlelight, of course, and was miserably cold, and experienced that general all-pervading sensation of getting up to be hanged which I have usually found inseparable from untimely rising under such circumstances.

How well I remember the forlorn aspect of Fleet-street when I came out of the Temple! The street-lamps flickering in the gusty north-east wind, as if the very gas were contorted with cold; the white-topped houses; the bleak, star-lighted sky; the market people and other early stragglers, trotting to circulate their almost frozen blood; the hospitable light and warmth of the few coffee-shops and public-houses that were open for such customers; the hard, dry, frosty rime with which the air was charged (the wind had already beaten it into every crevice), and which lashed my face like a steel whip.

It wanted nine days to the end of the month, and end of the year. The Post-office packet for the United States was to depart from Liverpool, weather permitting, on the first of the ensuing month, and I had the intervening time on my hands. I had taken this into consideration, and had resolved to make a visit to a certain spot (which I need not name) on the farther borders of Yorkshire. It was endeared to me by my having first seen Angela at a farmhouse in that place, and my melancholy was gratified by the idea of taking a wintry leave of it before my expatriation. I ought to explain, that, to avoid being sought out before my resolution should have been rendered irrevocable by being carried into full effect, I had written to Angela overnight, in my usual manner, lamenting that urgent business, of which she should know all particulars by-and-by— took me unexpectedly away from her for a week or ten days.

There was no Northern Railway at that time, and in its place there were stage-coaches; which I occasionally find myself, in common with some other people, affecting to lament now, but which everybody dreaded as a very serious penance then. I had secured the box-seat on the fastest of these, and my business in Fleet-street was to get into a cab with my portmanteau, so to make the best of my way to the Peacock at Islington, where I was to join this coach. But when one of our Temple watchmen, who carried my portmanteau into Fleet-street for me, told me about the huge blocks of ice that had for some days past been floating in the river, having closed up in the night, and made a walk from the Temple Gardens over to the Surrey shore, I began to ask myself the question, whether the box-seat would not be likely to put a sudden and a frosty end to my unhappiness. I was heart-broken, it is true, and yet I was not quite so far gone as to wish to be frozen to death.

When I got up to the Peacock,—where I found everybody drinking hot purl, in self-preservation,—I asked if there were an inside seat to spare. I then discovered that, inside or out, I was the only passenger. This gave me a still livelier idea of the great inclemency of the weather, since that coach always loaded particularly well. However, I took a little purl (which I found uncommonly good), and got into the coach. When I was seated, they built me up with straw to the waist, and, conscious of making a rather ridiculous appearance, I began my journey.

It was still dark when we left the Peacock. For a little while, pale, uncertain ghosts of houses and trees appeared and vanished, and then it was hard, black, frozen day. People were lighting their fires; smoke was mounting straight up high into the rarefied air; and we were rattling for Highgate Archway over the hardest ground I have ever heard the ring of iron shoes on. As we got into the country, everything seemed to have grown old and gray. The roads, the trees, thatched roofs of cottages and homesteads, the ricks in farmers' yards. Out-door work was abandoned, horse-troughs at roadside inns were frozen hard, no stragglers lounged about, doors were close shut, little turnpike houses had blazing fires inside, and children (even turnpike people have children, and seem to like them) rubbed the frost from the little panes of glass with their chubby arms, that their bright eyes might catch a glimpse of the solitary coach going by. I don't know when the snow began to set in; but I know that we were changing horses somewhere when I heard the guard remark, "That the old lady up in the sky was picking her geese pretty hard today." Then, indeed, I found the white down falling fast and thick.

The lonely day wore on, and I dozed it out, as a lonely traveller does. I was warm and valiant after eating and drinking,—particularly after dinner; cold and depressed at all other times. I was always bewildered as to time and place, and always more or less out of my senses. The coach and horses seemed to execute in chorus Auld Lang Syne, without a moment's intermission. They kept the time and tune with the greatest regularity, and rose into the swell at the beginning of the Refrain, with a precision that worried me to death. While we changed horses, the guard and coachman went stumping up and down the road, printing off their shoes in the snow, and poured so much liquid consolation into themselves without being any the worse for it, that I began to confound them, as it darkened again, with two great white casks standing on end. Our horses tumbled down in solitary places, and we got them up,—which was the pleasantest variety I had, for it warmed me. And it snowed and snowed, and still it snowed, and never left off snowing. All night long we went on in this manner. Thus we came round the clock, upon the Great North Road, to the performance of Auld Lang Syne all day again. And it snowed and snowed, and still it snowed, and never left off snowing.

I forget now where we were at noon on the second day, and where we ought to have been; but I know that we were scores of miles behind-hand, and that our case was growing worse every hour. The drift was becoming prodigiously deep; landmarks were getting snowed out; the road and the fields were all one; instead of having fences and hedge-rows to guide us, we went crunching on over an unbroken surface of ghastly white that might sink beneath us at any moment and drop us down a whole hillside. Still the coachman and guard—who kept together on the box, always in council, and looking well about them—made out the track with astonishing sagacity.

When we came in sight of a town, it looked, to my fancy, like a large drawing on a slate, with abundance of slate-pencil expended on the churches and houses where the snow lay thickest. When we came within a town, and found the church clocks all stopped, the dial-faces choked with snow, and the inn-signs blotted out, it seemed as if the whole place were overgrown with white moss. As to the coach, it was a mere snow-ball; similarly, the men and boys who ran along beside us to the town's end, turning our clogged wheels and encouraging our horses, were men and boys of snow; and the bleak wild solitude to which they at last dismissed us was a snowy Sahara. One would have thought this enough: notwithstanding which, I pledge my word that it snowed and snowed, and still it snowed, and never left off snowing.

We performed Auld Lang Syne the whole day; seeing nothing, out of towns and villages, but the track of stoats, hares, and foxes, and sometimes of birds. At nine o'clock at night, on a Yorkshire moor, a cheerful burst from our horn, and a welcome sound of talking, with a glimmering and moving about of lanterns, roused me from my drowsy state. I found that we were going to change.

They helped me out, and I said to a waiter, whose bare head became as white as King Lear's in a single minute, "What Inn is this?"

"The Holly-Tree, Sir," said he.

"Upon my word, I believe," said I, apologetically, to the guard and coachman, "that I must stop here."

Now the landlord, and the landlady, and the ostler, and the post-boy, and all the stable authorities, had already asked the coachman, to the wide-eyed interest of all the rest of the establishment, if he meant to go on. The coachman had already replied, "Yes, he'd take her through it,"—meaning by Her the coach,—"if so be as George would stand by him." George was the guard, and he had already sworn that he *would* stand by him. So the helpers were already getting the horses out.

My declaring myself beaten, after this parley, was not an announcement without preparation. Indeed, but for the way to the announcement being smoothed by the parley, I more than doubt whether, as an innately bashful man, I should have had the confidence to make it. As it was, it received the approval even of the guard and coachman. Therefore, with many confirmations of my inclining, and many remarks from one bystander to another, that the gentleman could go for'ard by the mail tomorrow, whereas to-night he would only be froze, and where was the good of a gentleman being froze,—ah, let alone buried alive (which latter clause was added by a humorous helper as a joke at my expense, and was extremely well received), I saw my portmanteau got out stiff, like a frozen body; did the handsome thing by the guard and coachman; wished them good-night and a prosperous journey; and, a little ashamed of myself, after all, for leaving them to fight it out alone, followed the landlord, landlady, and waiter of the Holly-Tree upstairs.

I thought I had never seen such a large room as that into which they showed me. It had five windows, with dark red curtains that would have absorbed the light of a general illumination; and there were complications of drapery at the top of the curtains, that went wandering about the wall in a most extraordinary manner. I asked for a smaller room, and they told me there was no smaller room. They could screen me in, however, the landlord said. They brought a great old japanned screen, with natives (Japanese, I suppose) engaged in a variety of idiotic pursuits all over it; and left me roasting whole before an immense fire.

My bedroom was some quarter of a mile off, up a great staircase at the end of a long gallery; and nobody knows what a misery this is to a bashful man who would rather not meet people on the stairs. It was the grimmest room I have ever had the nightmare in; and all the furniture, from the four posts of the bed to the two old silver candlesticks, was tall, high-shouldered, and spindle-waisted. Below, in my sitting-room, if I looked round my screen, the wind rushed at me like a mad bull; if I stuck to my armchair, the fire scorched me to the colour of a new brick. The chimneypiece was very high, and there was a bad glass—what I may call a wavy glass—above it, which, when I stood up, just showed me my anterior phrenological developments,—and these never look well, in any subject, cut short off at the eyebrow. If I stood with my back to the fire, a gloomy vault of darkness above and beyond the screen insisted on being looked at; and, in its dim remoteness, the drapery of the ten curtains of the five windows went twisting and creeping about, like a nest of gigantic worms.

I suppose that what I observe in myself must be observed by some other men of similar character in *themselves;* therefore I am emboldened to mention, that, when I travel, I never arrive at a place but I immediately want to go away from it. Before I had finished my supper of broiled fowl and mulled port, I had impressed upon the waiter in detail my arrangements for departure in the morning. Breakfast and bill at eight. Fly at nine. Two horses, or, if needful, even four.

Tired though I was, the night appeared about a week long. In oases of nightmare, I thought of Angela, and felt more depressed than ever by the reflection that I was on the shortest road to Gretna Green. What had *I* to do with Gretna Green? I was not going *that* way to the Devil, but by the American route, I remarked in my bitterness.

In the morning I found that it was snowing still, that it had snowed all night, and that I was snowed up. Nothing could get out of that spot on the moor, or could come at it, until the road had been cut out by labourers from the market-town. When they might cut their way to the Holly-Tree nobody could tell me.

It was now Christmas-eve. I should have had a dismal Christmas-time of it anywhere, and consequently that did not so much matter; still, being snowed up was like dying of frost, a thing I had not bargained for. I felt very lonely. Yet I could no more have proposed to the landlord and landlady to admit me to their society (though I should have liked it very much) than I could have asked them to present me with a piece of plate. Here my great secret, the real bashfulness of my character, is to be observed. Like most bashful men, I judge of other people as if they were bashful too. Besides being far too shamefaced to make the proposal myself, I really had a delicate misgiving that it would be in the last degree disconcerting to them.

Trying to settle down, therefore, in my solitude, I first of all asked what books there were in the house. The waiter brought me a *Book of Roads,* two or three old Newspapers, a little Song-Book, terminating in a collection of Toasts and Sentiments, a little Jest-Book, an odd volume of *Peregrine Pickle,* and the *Sentimental Journey.* I knew every word of the two last already, but I read them through again, then tried to hum all the songs (Auld Lang Syne was among them); went entirely through the jokes,—in which I found a fund of melancholy adapted to my state of mind; proposed all the toasts, enunciated all the sentiments, and mastered the papers. The latter had nothing in them but stock advertisements, a meeting about a county rate, and a highway robbery. As I am a greedy reader, I could not make this supply hold out until night; it was exhausted by tea-time. Being then entirely cast upon my own resources, I got through an hour in considering what to do next. Ultimately, it came into my head (from which I was anxious by any means to exclude Angela and Edwin), that I would endeavour to recall my experience of Inns, and would try how long it lasted me. I stirred the fire, moved my chair a little to one side of the screen,—not daring to go far, for I knew the wind was waiting to make a rush at me, I could hear it growling,—and began.

My first impressions of an Inn dated from the Nursery; consequently I went back to the Nursery for a starting-point, and found myself at the knee of a sallow woman with a fishy eye, an aquiline nose, and a green gown, whose specialty was a dismal narrative of a landlord by the roadside, whose visitors unaccountably disappeared for many years, until it was discovered that the pursuit of his life had been to convert them into pies. For the better devotion of himself to this branch of industry, he had constructed a secret door behind the head of the bed; and when the visitor (oppressed with pie) had fallen asleep, this wicked landlord would look softly in with a lamp in one hand and a knife in the other, would cut his throat, and would make him into pies; for which purpose he had coppers, underneath a trap-door, always boiling; and rolled out his pastry in the dead of the night. Yet even he was not insensible to the stings of conscience, for he never went to sleep without being heard to mutter, "Too much pepper!" which was eventually the cause of his being brought to justice. I had no sooner disposed of this criminal than there started up another of the same period, whose profession was originally housebreaking; in the pursuit of which art he had had his right ear chopped off one night, as he was burglariously getting in at a window, by a brave and lovely servant-maid (whom the aquiline-nosed woman, though not at all answering the description, always mysteriously implied to be herself). After several years, this brave and lovely servant-maid was married to the landlord of a country Inn; which landlord had this remarkable characteristic, that he always wore a silk nightcap, and never would on any consideration take it off. At last, one night, when he was fast asleep, the brave and lovely woman lifted up his silk nightcap on the right side, and found that he had no ear there; upon which she sagaciously perceived that he was the clipped housebreaker, who had married her with the intention of putting her to death. She immediately heated the poker and terminated his career, for which she was taken to King George upon his throne, and received the compliments of royalty on her great discretion and valour. This same narrator, who had a Ghoulish pleasure, I have long been persuaded, in terrifying me to the utmost confines of my reason, had another authentic anecdote within her own experience, founded, I now believe, upon *Raymond and Agnes, or the Bleeding Nun.* She said it happened to her brother-in-law, who was immensely rich,—which my father was not; and immensely tall,—which my father was not. It was always a point with this Ghoul to present my dearest relations and friends to my youthful mind under circumstances of disparaging contrast. The brother-in-law was riding once through a forest on a magnificent horse (we had no magnificent horse at our house), attended by a favourite and valuable Newfoundland dog (we had no dog), when he found himself benighted, and came to an Inn. A dark woman opened the door, and he asked her if he could have a bed there. She answered yes, and put his horse in the stable, and took him into a room where there were two dark men. While he was at supper, a parrot in the room began to talk, saying, "Blood, blood! Wipe up the blood!" Upon which one of the dark men wrung the parrot's neck, and said he was fond of roasted parrots, and he meant to have this one for breakfast in the morning. After eating and drinking heartily, the immensely rich, tall brother-in-law went up to bed; but he was rather vexed, because they had shut his dog in the stable, saying that they never allowed dogs in the house. He sat very quiet for more than an hour, thinking and thinking, when, just as his candle was burning out, he heard a scratch at the door. He opened the door, and there was the Newfoundland dog! The dog came softly in, smelt about him, went straight to some straw in the corner which the dark men had said covered apples, tore the straw away, and disclosed two sheets steeped in blood. Just at that moment the candle went out, and the brother-in-law, looking through a chink in the door, saw the two dark men stealing upstairs; one armed with a dagger that long (about five feet); the other carrying a chopper, a sack, and a spade. Having no remembrance of the close of this adventure, I suppose my faculties to have been always so frozen with terror at this stage of it, that the power of listening stagnated within me for some quarter of an hour.

These barbarous stories carried me, sitting there on the Holly-Tree hearth, to the Roadside Inn, renowned in my time in a sixpenny book with a folding plate, representing in a central compartment of oval form the portrait of Jonathan Bradford, and in four corner compartments four incidents of the tragedy with which the name is associated,—coloured with a hand at once so free and economical, that the bloom of Jonathan's complexion passed without any pause into the breeches of the ostler, and, smearing itself off into the next division, became rum in a bottle. Then I remembered how the landlord was found at the murdered traveller's bedside, with his own knife at his feet, and blood upon his hand; how he was hanged for the murder, notwithstanding his protestation that he had indeed come there to kill the traveller for his saddle-bags, but had been stricken motionless on finding him already slain; and how the ostler, years afterwards, owned the deed. By this time I had made myself quite uncomfortable. I stirred the fire, and stood with my back to it as long as I could bear the heat, looking up at the darkness beyond the screen, and at the wormy curtains creeping in and creeping out, like the worms in the ballad of Alonzo the Brave and the Fair Imogene.

There was an Inn in the cathedral town where I went to school, which had pleasanter recollections about it than any of these. I took it next. It was the Inn where friends used to put up, and where we used to go to see parents and to have salmon and fowls, and be tipped. It had an ecclesiastical sign,—the Mitre,—and a bar that seemed to be the next best thing to a bishopric, it was so snug. I loved the landlord's youngest daugher to distraction,—but let that pass. It was in this Inn that I was cried over by my rosy little sister, because I had acquired a black eye in a fight. And though she had been, that Holly-Tree night, for many a long year where all tears are dried, the Mitre softened me yet.

"To be continued tomorrow," said I, when I took my candle to go to bed. But my bed took it upon itself to continue the train of thought that night. It carried me away, like the enchanted carpet, to a distant place (though still in England), and there, alighting from a stage-coach at another Inn in the snow, as I had actually done some years before, I repeated in my sleep a curious experience I had really had here. More than a year before I made the journey in the course of which I put up at that Inn, I had lost a very near and dear friend by death. Every night since, at home or away from home, I had dreamed of that friend; sometimes as still living; sometimes as returning from the world of shadows to comfort me; always as being beautiful, placid, and happy, never in association with any approach to fear or distress. It was at a lonely Inn in a wide moorland place, that I halted to pass the night. When I had looked from my bedroom window over the waste of snow on which the moon was shining, I sat down by my fire to write a letter. I had always, until that hour, kept it within my own breast that I dreamed every night of the dear lost one. But in the letter that I wrote I recorded the circumstance, and added that I felt much interested in proving whether the subject of my dream would still be faithful to me, travel-tired, and in that remote place. No. I lost the beloved figure of my vision in parting with the secret. My sleep has never looked upon it since, in sixteen years, but once. I was in Italy, and awoke (or seemed to awake), the well-remembered voice distinctly in my ears, conversing with it. I entreated it, as it rose above my bed and soared up to the vaulted roof of the old room, to answer me a question I had asked touching the Future Life. My hands were still outstretched towards it as it vanished, when I heard a bell ringing by the garden wall, and a voice in the deep stillness of the night calling on all good Christians to pray for the souls of the dead; it being All Souls' Eve.

To return to the Holly-Tree. When I awoke next day, it was freezing hard, and the lowering sky threatened more snow. My breakfast cleared away, I drew my chair into its former place, and, with the fire getting so much the better of the landscape that I sat in twilight, resumed my Inn remembrances.

That was a good Inn down in Wiltshire where I put up once, in the days of the hard Wiltshire ale, and before all beer was bitterness. It was on the skirts of Salisbury Plain, and the midnight wind that rattled my lattice window came moaning at me from Stonehenge. There was a hanger-on at that establishment (a supernaturally preserved Druid I believe him to have been, and to be still), with long white hair, and a flinty blue eye always looking afar off; who claimed to have been a shepherd, and who seemed to be ever watching for the reappearance, on the verge of the horizon, of some ghostly flock of sheep that had been mutton for many ages. He was a man with a weird belief in him that no one could count the stones of Stonehenge twice, and make the same number of them; likewise, that any one who counted them three times nine times, and then stood in the centre and said, "I dare!" would behold a tremendous apparition, and be stricken dead. He pretended to have seen a bustard (I suspect him to have been familiar with the dodo), in manner following: He was out upon the plain at the close of a late autumn day, when he dimly discerned, going on before him at a curious fitfully bounding pace, what he at first supposed to be a gig-umbrella that had been blown from some conveyance, but what he presently believed to be a lean dwarf man upon a little pony. Having followed this object for some distance without gaining on it, and having called to it many times without receiving any answer, he pursued it for miles and miles, when, at length coming up with it, he discovered it to be the last bustard in Great Britain, degenerated into a wingless state, and running along the ground. Resolved to capture him or perish in the attempt, he closed with the bustard; but the bustard, who had formed a counter-resolution that he should do neither, threw him, stunned him, and was last seen making off due west. This weird man, at that stage of metempsychosis, may have been a sleep-walker or an enthusiast or a robber; but I awoke one night to find him in the dark at my bedside, repeating the Athanasian Creed in a terrific voice. I paid my bill next day, and retired from the county with all possible precipitation.

That was not a commonplace story which worked itself out at a little Inn in Switzerland, while I was staying there. It was a very homely place, in a village of one narrow zigzag street, among mountains, and you went in at the main door through the cow-house, and among the mules and the dogs and the fowls, before ascending a great bare staircase to the rooms; which were all of unpainted wood, without plastering or papering,—like rough packing-cases. Outside there was nothing but the straggling street, a little toy church with a copper-coloured steeple, a pine forest, a torrent, mists, and mountain-sides. A young man belonging to this Inn had disappeared eight weeks before (it was winter-time), and was supposed to have had some undiscovered love affair, and to have gone for a soldier. He had got up in the night, and dropped into the village street from the loft in which he slept with another man; and he had done it so quietly, that his companion and fellow-labourer had heard no movement when he was awakened in the morning, and they said, "Louis, where is Henri?" They looked for him high and low, in vain, and gave him up. Now, outside this Inn, there stood, as there stood outside every dwelling in the village, a stack of firewood; but the stack belonging to the Inn was higher than any of the rest, because the Inn was the richest house, and burnt the most fuel. It began to be noticed, while they were looking high and low, that a Bantam cock, part of the live stock of the

Inn, put himself wonderfully out of his way to get to the top of this wood-stack; and that he would stay there for hours and hours, crowing, until he appeared in danger of splitting himself. Five weeks went on,—six weeks,—still this terrible Bantam, neglecting his domestic affairs, was always on the top of the wood-stack, crowing the very eyes out of his head. By this time it was perceived that Louis had become inspired with a violent animosity towards the terrible Bantam, and one morning he was seen by a woman, who sat nursing her goître at a little window in a gleam of sun, to catch up a rough billet of wood, with a great oath, hurl it at the terrible Bantam crowing on the wood-stack, and bring him down dead. Hereupon the woman, with a sudden light in her mind, stole round to the back of the wood-stack, and, being a good climber, as all those women are, climbed up, and soon was seen upon the summit, screaming, looking down the hollow within, and crying, "Seize Louis, the murderer! Ring the church bell! Here is the body!" I saw the murderer that day, and I saw him as I sat by my fire at the Holly-Tree Inn, and I see him now, lying shackled with cords on the stable litter, among the mild eyes and the smoking breath of the cows, waiting to be taken away by the police, and stared at by the fearful village. A heavy animal,—the dullest animal in the stables,—with a stupid head, and a lumpish face devoid of any trace of sensibility, who had been, within the knowledge of the murdered youth, an embezzler of certain small moneys belonging to his master, and who had taken this hopeful mode of putting a possible accuser out of his way. All of which he confessed next day, like a sulky wretch who couldn't be troubled any more, now that they had got hold of him, and meant to make an end of him. I saw him once again, on the day of my departure from the Inn. In that Canton the headsman still does his office with a sword; and I came upon this murderer sitting bound to a chair, with his eyes bandaged, on a scaffold in a little market-place. In that instant, a great sword (loaded with quicksilver in the thick part of the blade) swept round him like a gust of wind or fire, and there was no such creature in the world. My wonder was, not that he was so suddenly dispatched, but that any head was left unreaped, within a radius of fifty yards of that tremendous sickle.

That was a good Inn, too, with the kind, cheerful landlady and the honest landlord, where I lived in the shadow of Mont Blanc, and where one of the apartments has a zoological papering on the walls, not so accurately joined but that the elephant occasionally rejoices in a tiger's hind legs and tail, while the lion puts on a trunk and tusks, and the bear, moulting as it were, appears as to portions of himself like a leopard. I made several American friends at that Inn, who all called Mont Blanc Mount Blank,—except one good-humoured gentleman, of a very sociable nature, who became on such intimate terms with it that he spoke of it familiarly as "Blank"; observing, at breakfast, "Blank looks pretty tall this morning"; or considerably doubting in the courtyard in the evening, whether there warn't some go-ahead naters in our country, Sir, that would make out the top of Blank in a couple of hours from first start—now!

Once I passed a fortnight at an Inn in the North of England, where I was haunted by the ghost of a tremendous pie. It was a Yorkshire pie, like a fort,—an abandoned fort with nothing in it; but the waiter had a fixed idea that it was a point of ceremony at every meal to put the pie on the table. After some days I tried to hint, in several delicate ways, that I considered the pie done with; as for example, by emptying fag-ends of glasses of wine into it; putting cheese-plates and spoons into it, as into a basket; putting wine-bottles into it, as into a cooler; but always in vain, the pie being invariably cleaned out again and brought up as before. At last, beginning to be doubtful whether I was not the victim of a spectral illusion, and whether my health and spirits might not sink under the horrors of an imaginary pit, I cut a triangle out of it, fully as large as the musical instrument of that name in a powerful orchestra. Human prevision could not have foreseen the result—but the waiter mended the pie. With some effectual species of cement, he adroitly fitted the triangle in again, and I paid my reckoning and fled.

The Holly-Tree was getting rather dismal. I made an overland expedition beyond the screen, and penetrated as far as the fourth window. Here I was driven back by stress of weather. Arrived at my winter-quarters once more, I made up the fire, and took another Inn.

It was in the remotest part of Cornwall. A great annual Miner's Feast was being holden at the Inn, when I and my travelling companions presented ourselves at night among the wild crowd that were dancing before it by torchlight. We had had a break-down in the dark, on a stony morass some miles away; and I had the honour of leading one of the unharnessed post-horses. If any lady or gentleman, on perusal of the present lines, will take any very tall post-horse with his traces hanging about his legs, and will conduct him by the bearing-rein into the heart of a country dance of a hundred and fifty couples, that lady or gentleman will then, and only then, form an adequate idea of the extent to which that post-horse will tread on his conductor's toes. Over and above which, the post-horse, finding three hundred people whirling about him, will probably rear, and also lash out with his hind legs, in a manner incompatible with dignity or self-respect on his conductor's part. With such little drawbacks on my usually impressive aspect, I appeared at this Cornish

Inn, to the unutterable wonder of the Cornish Miners. It was full, and twenty times full, and nobody could be received but the post-horse,—though to get rid of that noble animal was something. While my fellow-travellers and I were discussing how to pass the night and so much of the next day as must intervene before the jovial blacksmith and the jovial wheelwright would be in a condition to go out on the morass and mend the coach, an honest man stepped forth from the crowd and proposed his unlet floor of two rooms, with supper of eggs and bacon, ale and punch. We joyfully accompanied him home to the strangest of clean houses, where we were well entertained to the satisfaction of all parties. But the novel feature of the entertainment was, that our host was a chairmaker, and that the chairs assigned to us were mere frames, altogether without bottoms of any sort; so that we passed the evening on perches. Nor was this the absurdest consequence; for when we unbent at supper, and any one of us gave way to laughter, he forgot the peculiarity of his position, and instantly disappeared. I myself, doubled up into an attitude from which self-extrication was impossible, was taken out of my frame, like a clown in a comic pantomime who has tumbled into a tub, five times by the taper's light during the eggs and bacon.

The Holly-Tree was fast reviving within me a sense of loneliness. I began to feel conscious that my subject would never carry on until I was dug out. I might be a week here,—weeks!

There was a story with a singular idea in it, connected with an Inn I once passed a night at in a picturesque old town on the Welsh border. In a large double-bedded room of this Inn there had been a suicide committed by poison, in one bed, while a tired traveller slept unconscious in the other. After that time, the suicide bed was never used, but the other constantly was; the disused bedstead remaining in the room empty, though as to all other respects in its old state. The story ran, that whoever slept in this room, though never so entire a stranger, from never so far off, was invariably observed to come down in the morning with an impression that he smelt Laudanum, and that his mind always turned upon the subject of suicide; to which, whatever kind of man he might be, he was certain to make some reference if he conversed with any one. This went on for years, until it at length induced the landlord to take the disused bedstead down, and bodily burn it,—bed, hangings, and all. The strange influence (this was the story) now changed to a fainter one, but never changed afterwards. The occupant of that room, with occasional but very rare exceptions, would come down in the morning, trying to recall a forgotten dream he had had in the night. The landlord, on his mentioning his perplexity, would suggest various commonplace subjects, not one of which, as he very well knew, was the true subject. But the moment the landlord suggested "Poison," the traveller started, and cried, "Yes!" He never failed to accept that suggestion, and he never recalled any more of the dream.

This reminiscence brought the Welsh Inns in general before me; with the women in their round hats, and the harpers with their white beards (venerable, but humbugs, I am afraid), playing outside the door while I took my dinner. The transition was natural to the Highland Inns, with the oatmeal bannocks, the honey, the venison steaks, the trout from the loch, the whisky, and perhaps (having the materials so temptingly at hand) the Athol brose. Once was I coming south from the Scottish Highlands in hot haste, hoping to change quickly at the station at the bottom of a certian wild historical glen, when these eyes did with mortification see the landlord come out with a telescope and sweep the whole prospect for the horses; which horses were away picking up their own living, and did not heave in sight under four hours. Having thought of the loch-trout, I was taken by quick association to the Anglers' Inns of England (I have assisted at innumerable feats of angling by lying in the bottom of the boat, whole summer days, doing nothing with the greatest perseverance; which I have generally found to be as effectual towards the taking of fish as the finest tackle and the utmost science), and to the pleasant white, clean, flower-pot-decorated bedrooms of those inns, overlooking the river, and the ferry, and the green ait, and the church-spire, and the country bridge; and to the peerless Emma with the bright eyes and the pretty smile, who waited, bless her! with a natural grace that would have converted Blue-Beard. Casting my eyes upon my Holly-Tree fire, I next discerned among the glowing coals the pictures of a score or more of those wonderful English posting-inns which we are all so sorry to have lost, which were so large and so comfortable, and which were such monuments of British submission to rapacity and extortion. He who would see these houses pining away, let him walk from Basingstoke, or even Windsor, to London, by way of Hounslow, and moralise on their perishing remains; the stables crumbling to dust; unsettled labourers and wanderers bivouacking in the outhouses; grass growing in the yards; the rooms, where erst so many hundred beds of down were made up, let off to Irish lodgers at eighteenpence a week; a little ill-looking beer-shop shrinking in the tap of former days, burning coach-house gates for firewood, having one of its two windows bunged up, as if it had received punishment in a fight with the Railroad; a low, bandy-legged, brick-making bulldog standing in the doorway. What could I next see in my fire so naturally as the new railway-house of these times near the dismal country station; with nothing particular on draught but cold air and damp, nothing worth mentioning in the larder but new mortar, and no business doing beyond a conceited affectation of luggage in the hall? Then I came to the Inns of Paris, with the pretty apartment of four pieces up one hundred and seventy-five waxed stairs, the privilege of ringing the bell all day long without influencing anybody's mind or body but your own, and the not-too-much-for-dinner, considering the price. Next to the provincial Inns of France, with the great church-tower rising above the courtyard, the horse-bells jingling merrily up and down the street beyond, and the clocks of all descriptions in all the rooms, which are never right, unless taken at the precise minute when, by getting exactly twelve hours too fast or too slow, they unintentionally become so. Away I went, next, to the lesser roadside Inns of Italy; where all the dirty clothes in the house (not in wear) are always lying in your anteroom; where the mosquitoes make a raisin pudding of your face in summer, and the cold bites it blue in winter; where you get what you can, and forget what you can't; where I should again like to be boiling my tea in a pocket-handkerchief dumpling, for want of a teapot. So to the old palace Inns and old monastery Inns, in towns and cities of the same bright country; with their massive quadrangular staircases, whence you may look from among clustering pillars high into the blue vault of heaven; with their stately banqueting-rooms, and vast refectories; with their labyrinths of ghostly bedchambers, and their glimpses into gorgeous streets that have no appearance of reality or possibility. So to the close little Inns of the Malaria districts, with their pale attendants, and their peculiar smell of never letting in the air. So to the immense fantastic Inns of Venice, with the cry of the gondolier below, as he skims the corner; the grip of the watery odours on one particular little bit of the bridge of your nose (which is never released while you stay there); and the great bell of St. Mark's Cathedral tolling midnight. Next I put up for a minute at the restless Inns upon the Rhine, where your going to bed, no matter at what hour, appears to be the tocsin for everybody else's getting up; and where, in the table-d'hôte room at the end of the long table (with several Towers of Babel on it at the other end, all made of white plates), one knot of stoutish men, entirely dressed in jewels and dirt, and having nothing else upon them, *will* remain all night, clinking glasses, and singing about the river that flows, and the grape that grows, and Rhine wine that beguiles, and Rhine woman that smiles and hi drink drink my friend and ho drink drink my brother, and all the rest of it. I departed thence, as a matter of course, to other German Inns, where all the eatables are soddened down to the same flavour, and where the mind is disturbed by the apparition of hot puddings, and boiled cherries, sweet and slab, at awfully unexpected periods of the repast. After a draught of sparkling beer from a foaming glass jug, and a glance of recognition through the windows of the student beer-houses at Heidelberg and elsewhere, I put out to sea for the Inns of America, with their four hundred beds apiece, and their eight or nine hundred ladies and gentlemen at dinner every day. . . .

THE FESTIVAL OF ST. NICHOLAS

MARY MAPES DODGE

from HANS BRINKER, OR THE SILVER SKATES

Christmas Day is devoted by the Hollanders to church rites and pleasant family visiting. It is on Saint Nicholas' Eve that their young people become half wild with joy and expectation. To some of them it is a sorry time, for the saint is very candid, and if any of them have been bad during the past year, he is quite sure to tell them so. Sometimes he carries a birch rod under his arm and advises the parents to give them scoldings in place of confections, and floggings instead of toys.

It was well that the boys hastened to their abodes on that bright winter evening, for in less than an hour afterward, the saint made his appearance in half the homes of Holland. He visited the king's palace and in the selfsame moment appeared in Annie Bouman's comfortable home. Probably one of our silver half dollars would have purchased all that his saintship left at the peasant Bouman's; but a half dollar's worth will sometimes do for the poor what hundreds of dollars may fail to do for the rich; it makes them happy and grateful, fills them with new peace and love.

Hilda van Gleck's little brothers and sisters were in a high state of excitement that night. They had been admitted into the grand parlor; they were dressed in their best, and had been given two cakes apiece at supper. Hilda was as joyous as any. Why not? Saint Nicholas would never cross a girl of fourteen from his list, just because she was tall and looked almost like a woman. On the contrary, he would probably exert himself to do honor to such an august-looking damsel. Who could tell? So she sported

and laughed and danced as gaily as the youngest, and was the soul of all their merry games. Father, mother and grandmother looked on approvingly; so did grandfather, before he spread his large red handkerchief over his face, leaving only the top of his skullcap visible. This kerchief was his ensign of sleep.

Earlier in the evening all had joined in the fun. In the general hilarity, there had seemed to be a difference only in bulk between grandfather and the baby. Indeed a shade of solemn expectation, now and then flitting across the faces of the younger members, had made them seem rather more thoughtful than their elders.

Now the spirit of fun reigned supreme. The very flames danced and capered in the polished grate. A pair of prim candles that had been staring at the astral lamp began to wink at other candles far away in the mirrors. There was a long bellrope suspended from the ceiling in the corner, made of glass beads netted over a cord nearly as thick as your wrist. It generally hung in the shadow and made no sign; but tonight it twinkled from end to end. Its handle of crimson glass sent reckless dashes of red at the papered wall, turning its dainty blue stripes into purple. Passers-by halted to catch the merry laughter floating, through curtain and sash, into the street, then skipped on their way with a startled consciousness that the village was wide awake. At last matters grew so uproarious that the grandsire's red kerchief came down from his face with a jerk. What decent old gentleman could sleep in such a racket! Mynheer van Gleck regarded his children with astonishment. The baby even showed symptoms of hysterics. It was high time to attend to business. Madame suggested that if they wished to see the good Saint Nicholas they should sing the same loving invitation that had brought him the year before.

The baby stared and thrust his fist into his mouth as Mynheer put him down upon the floor. Soon he sat erect, and looked with a sweet scowl at the company. With his lace and embroideries, and his crown of blue ribbon and whalebone (for he was not quite past the tumbling age), he looked like the king of the babies.

The other children, each holding a pretty willow basket, formed at once in a ring, and moved slowly around the little fellow, lifting their eyes, meanwhile, for the saint to whom they were about to address themselves was yet in mysterious quarters.

Madame commenced playing softly upon the piano; soon the voices rose—gentle, youthful voices—rendered all the sweeter for their tremor:

"Welcome, friend! Saint Nicholas, welcome!
　　Bring no rod for us, tonight!
While our voices bid thee, welcome,
　　Every heart with joy is light!

　　　　Tell us every fault and failing,
　　　　We will bear thy keenest railing,
　　　　So we sing—so we sing—
　　　　Thou shalt tell us everything!

Welcome, friend! Saint Nicholas, welcome!
　　Welcome to this merry band!
Happy children greet thee, welcome!
　　Thou art glad'ning all the land!

　　　　Fill each empty hand and basket,
　　　　'Tis thy little ones who ask it,
　　　　So we sing—so we sing—
　　　　Thou wilt bring us everything!"

During the chorus, sundry glances, half in eagerness, half in dread, had been cast toward the polished folding doors. Now a loud knocking was heard. The circle was broken in an instant. Some of the little ones, with a strange mixture of fear and delight, pressed against their mother's knee. Grandfather bent forward, with his chin resting upon his hand; grandmother lifted her spectacles; Mynheer van Gleck, seated by the fireplace, slowly drew his meerschaum from his mouth, while Hilda and the other children settled themselves beside him in an expectant group.

The knocking was heard again.

"Come in," said madame softly.

The door slowly opened, and Saint Nicholas, in full array, stood before them.

You could have heard a pin drop!

Soon he spoke. What a mysterious majesty in his voice! what kindliness in his tones!

"Karel van Gleck, I am pleased to greet thee, and thy honored vrouw Kathrine, and thy son and his good vrouw Annie!

"Children, I greet ye all! Hendrick, Hilda, Broom, Katy, Huygens, and Lucretia! And thy cousins, Wolfert, Diedrich, Mayken, Voost, and Katrina! Good children ye have been, in the main, since I last accosted ye. Diedrich was rude at the Haarlem fair last fall, but he has tried to atone for it since. Mayken has failed of late in her lessons, and too many sweets and trifles have gone to her lips, and too few stivers to her charity box. Diedrich, I trust, will be a polite, manly boy for the future, and Mayken will endeavor to shine as a student. Let her remember, too, that economy and thrift are needed in the foundation of a worthy and generous life. Little Katy has been cruel to the cat more than once. Saint Nicholas can hear the cat cry when its tail is pulled. I will forgive her if she will remember from this hour that the smallest dumb creatures have feeling and must not be abused."

As Katy burst into a frightened cry, the saint graciously remained silent until she was soothed.

"Master Broom," he resumed, "I warn thee that boys who are in the habit of putting snuff upon the foot stove of the schoolmistress may one day be discovered and receive a flogging—— But thou art such an excellent scholar, I shall make thee no further reproof.

"Thou, Hendrick, didst distinguish thyself in the archery match last spring, and hit the Doel, though the bird was swung before it to unsteady thine eye. I give thee credit for excelling in manly sport and exercise—though I must not unduly countenance thy boat racing since it leaves thee too little time for thy proper studies.

"Lucretia and Hilda shall have a blessed sleep tonight. The consciousness of kindness to the poor, devotion in their souls, and cheerful, hearty obedience to household rule will render them happy.

"With one and all I avow myself well content. Goodness, industry, benevolence and thrift have prevailed in your midst. Therefore, my blessing upon you—and may the New Year find all treading the paths of obedience, wisdom and love. Tomorrow you shall find more substantial proofs that I have been in your midst. Farewell!"

With these words came a great shower of sugarplums, upon a linen sheet spread out in front of the doors. A general scramble followed. The children fairly tumbled over each other in their eagerness to fill their baskets. Madame cautiously held the baby down in their midst, till the chubby little fists were filled. Then the bravest of the youngsters sprang up and burst open the closed doors—in vain they peered into the mysterious apartment—Saint Nicholas was nowhere to be seen.

A LITTLE BOY AT CHRIST'S CHRISTMAS TREE

FEODOR DOSTOEVSKY

from THE DIARY OF A WRITER, 1876

But I am a novelist, and it seems that one "story" I did invent myself. Why did I say "it seems," since I know for certain that I did actually invent it; yet I keep fancying that this happened somewhere, once upon a time, precisely on Christmas Eve, in *some* huge city during a bitter frost.

I dreamed of a little boy—very little—about six, or even younger. This little boy woke up one morning in a damp, cold basement. He was clad in a shabby dressing gown of some kind, and he was shivering. Sitting in the corner on a chest, wearily he kept blowing out his breath, letting it escape from his mouth, and it amused him to watch the vapor flow through the air. But he was very hungry.

Several times that morning he came to the bedstead, where his sick mother lay on bedding thin as a pancake, with a bundle of some sort under her head for a pillow.

How did she happen to be here?—She may have come with her little boy from some faraway town, and then suddenly she had fallen ill.

Two days ago the landlady of this wretched hovel had been seized by the police; most of the tenants had scattered in all directions—it was the holiday season—and now there remained only two. The peddler was still there, but he had been lying in a drunken stupor for more than twenty-four hours, not even having waited for the holiday to come. In another corner of the lodging an eighty-year-old woman was moaning with rheumatism. In days past she had been a children's nurse somewhere. Now she was dying in solitude, moaning and sighing continuously and grumbling at the boy so that he grew too frightened to come near her. Somehow he had managed to find water in the entrance hall, with which to appease his thirst; but nowhere was he able to discover as much as a crust of bread. Time after time he came up to his mother, trying in vain to awaken her. As it grew dark, dread fell upon him. Though it was late evening, the candle was not yet lit. Fumbling over his mother's face he began to wonder why she lay so quiet, and why she felt as cold as the wall. "It's rather chilly in here," he said to himself . . . For a moment he stood still, unconsciously resting his hand on the shoulder of the dead woman. Then he began to breathe on his tiny fingers in an attempt to warm them, and, suddenly, coming upon his little cap that lay on the bedstead, he groped along cautiously and quietly made his way out of the basement. This he would have done earlier had he not been so afraid of the big dog upstairs on the staircase, which kept howling all day long in front of a neighbor's door. Now the dog was gone, and in a moment he was out in the street.

"My God, what a city!"—Never before had he seen anything like this. There, in the place from which he had come, at night, everything was plunged into dark gloom—just a single lamp-post in the whole street! Humble wooden houses were closed in by shutters; no sooner did dusk descend than there was no one in sight; people locked themselves up in their homes, and only big packs of dogs—hundreds and thousands of them—howled and barked all night. Ah, but out there it was so warm, and there he had been given something to eat, while here . . . "Dear God, I do wish I had something to eat!"—And here—what a thundering noise! What dazzling light! What crowds of people and horses and carriages! And what biting frost! What frost! Vapor, which at once turned cold, burst forth in thick clouds from the horses' hot-breathing muzzles. Horseshoes tinkle as they strike the stones through the fluffy snow. And men pushing each other about . . . "But, good heavens, how hungry I am! I wish I had just a tiny bit of something to eat!" And suddenly he felt a sharp pain in his little fingers.

A policeman passed by and turned his head away, so as not to take notice of the boy.

"And here is another street.—Oh, how wide it is! Here I'll surely be run over! And how people shout and run and drive along! And what floods of light! Light everywhere! Look, what's this?—Oh, what a huge window and, beyond it, a hall with a tree reaching up to the ceiling. It's a Christmas tree covered with gleaming lights, with sparkling bits of gold paper and apples, and all around are little dolls, toy-horses. Lots of beautifully dressed, neat children running about the hall; they laugh and play,

and they eat and drink something. And see, over there, that little girl—now she starts to dance with a boy! What a pretty little girl she is! And just listen to the music! You can hear it from inside, coming through the window!"

The little boy gazes and gazes and wonders; he even starts laughing, but . . . his toes begin to hurt, while the little fingers on his hand have grown quite red—they won't bend any longer, and it hurts to move them. And when at last he became fully aware of the sharp pain in his fingers, he burst into tears and set off running.

Presently, through another window, he catches sight of a room, with trees standing in it, and tables loaded with cakes, all sorts of cakes—almond cakes, red cakes, yellow cakes! . . . Four beautifully dressed ladies

are sitting in the room; whoever enters it is given a cake . . . Every minute the door opens, and many gentlemen come in from the outside to
visit these ladies.

The boy stole up, quickly pushed the door open, and sidled in. Oh,
how they started shouting at him and motioning him out! One of the
ladies hurried toward him, thrust a small copper coin into his hand, but
she opened the door into the street. How frightened he was! The coin
rolled from his hand, bouncing down the steps, he was just unable to
bend his little red fingers to hold on to it.

Very fast, the little boy ran away, and quickly he started going, but he
himself did not know whither to go. Once more he was ready to cry, but
he was so frightened that he just kept on running and running, and
blowing on his cold little hands. How dreadfully lonesome he felt, and
suddenly despair clutched at his heart.

But lo!—What's going on here?—In front of a window people are
standing crowded together, lost in admiration . . . Inside they see three
tiny dolls, all dressed up in little red and green frocks, so real that they
seem alive! A kindly-looking old man is sitting there, as if playing on a
big violin; and next to him—two other men are playing small violins,
swinging their heads to the rhythm of the music; they look at each other,
their lips move, and they talk—they really do, but one simply can't hear
them through the window pane.

At first the little boy thought that these moving figures were alive, but
when at last he realized that they were only small puppets, he burst into
laughter. He had never seen such figurines, and he didn't even know that
such existed! He felt like crying, and yet the dolls looked so funny to
him—oh, how funny!

Suddenly he felt as if somebody grabbed him by his dressing gown: a
big bully of a boy, standing close by, without warning, struck him on the
head, tore off his cap and kicked him violently. The little fellow fell
down, and the people around began shouting. Scared to death, he
jumped quickly to his feet and scampered off. All of a sudden he found
himself in a strange courtyard under the vault of a gateway, and leaped
behind a pile of kindling wood. "Here they won't find me! Besides, it's
dark here!"

He sank down and huddled himself up in a small heap, but he could
hardly catch his breath for fright. But presently a sensation of happiness
crept over his whole being: his little hands and feet suddenly stopped
aching, and once more he felt as comfortable and warm as on a hearth.
But hardly a moment later a shudder convulsed him: "Ah, I almost fell
asleep. Well, I'll stay here awhile, and then I'll get back to look at the
puppets"—the little boy said to himself, and the memory of the pretty

dolls made him smile: "They seem just as though they're alive!" And all of a sudden he seemed to hear the voice of his mother, leaning over him and singing a song. "Mother dear, I'm just dozing. Oh, how wonderful it is to sleep here!"

Then a gentle voice whispered above him: "Come, little boy, come along with me! Come to see a Christmas tree!"

His first thought was that it might be his mama still speaking to him, but no—this wasn't she. Who, then, could it be? He saw no one, and yet, in the darkness, someone was hovering over him and tenderly clasping him in his arms . . . The little boy stretched out his arms and . . . an instant later—"Oh, what dazzling light! Oh, what a Christmas tree! Why, it can't be a Christmas tree,"—for he had never seen such trees.

Where is he now?—Everything sparkles and glitters and shines, and scattered all over are tiny dolls—no, they are little boys and girls, only they are so luminous, and they all fly around him; they embrace him and lift him up; they carry him along, and now he flies, too. And he sees: yonder is his mother; she looks at him, smiling at him so happily. "Oh, Mother! Mother! How beautiful it is here!"—exclaimed the little boy, and again he begins to kiss the children; he can hardly wait to tell them about those wee puppets behind the glass of the window.

"Who are you, little boys? Who are you, little girls?"—he asks them, smilingly, and he feels that he loves them all.

"This is Christ's Christmas Tree,"—they tell him. "On this day of the year Christ always has a Christmas Tree for those little children who have no Christmas tree of their own."

And then he learned that these little boys and girls were all once children like himself, but some of them have frozen to death in those baskets in which they had been left at the doors of Petersburg officials; others had perished in miserable hospital wards; still others had died at the dried-up breasts of their famine-stricken mothers (during the Samara famine); these, again, had choked to death from stench in third-class railroad cars. Now they are all here, all like little angels, and they are all with Christ, and He is in their midst, holding out His hands to them and to their sinful mothers . . . And the mothers of these babes, they all stand there, a short distance off, and weep: each one recognizes her darling— her little boy, or her little girl—and they fly over to their mothers and kiss them and brush away their tears with their little hands, begging them not to cry, for they feel so happy here . . .

Next morning, down in the courtyard, porters found the tiny body of a little boy who had hidden behind the piles of kindling wood, and there had frozen to death. They also found his mother. She died even before he had passed away.

Now they are again united in God's Heaven.

And why did I invent such a story, one that conforms so little to an ordinary, reasonable diary—especially a writer's diary? And that, after having promised to write stories pre-eminently about actual events! But the point is that I keep fancying that all this could actually have happened—I mean, the things which happened in the basement and behind the piles of kindling wood. Well, and as regards Christ's Christmas Tree—I really don't know what to tell you, and I don't know whether or not this could have happened. Being a novelist, I have to invent things.

AN IOWA CHRISTMAS

PAUL ENGLE

Every Christmas should begin with the sound of bells, and when I
was a child mine always did. But they were sleigh bells, not
church bells, for we lived in a part of Cedar Rapids, Iowa, where
there were no churches. My bells were on my father's team of horses as he
drove up to our horse-headed hitching post with the bobsled that would
take us to celebrate Christmas on the family farm ten miles out in the
country. My father would bring the team down Fifth Avenue at a smart
trot, flicking his whip over the horses' rumps and making the bells double their light, thin jangling over the snow, whose radiance threw back a
brilliance like the sound of bells.

There are no such departures any more: the whole family piling into
the bobsled with a foot of golden oat straw to lie in and heavy buffalo
robes to lie under, the horses stamping the soft snow, and at every motion of their hoofs the bells jingling, jingling. My father sat there with
the reins firmly held, wearing a long coat made from the hide of a favorite family horse, the deep chestnut color still glowing, his mittens also
from the same hide. It always troubled me as a boy of eight that the
horses had so indifferent a view of their late friend appearing as a warm
overcoat on the back of the man who put the iron bit in their mouths.

There are no streets like those any more: the snow sensibly left on the
road for the sake of sleighs and easy travel. We could hop off and ride the
heavy runners as they made their hissing, tearing sound over the packed
snow. And along the streets we met other horses, so that we moved from
one set of bells to another, from the tiny tinkle of the individual bells on
the shafts to the silvery, leaping sound of the long strands hung over the

harness. There would be an occasional brass-mounted automobile laboring on its narrow tires and as often as not pulled up the slippery hills by a horse, and we would pass it with a triumphant shout for an awkward nuisance which was obviously not here to stay.

The country road ran through a landscape of little hills and shallow valleys and heavy groves of timber, including one of great towering black walnut trees which were all cut down a year later to be made into gunstocks for the First World War. The great moment was when we left the road and turned up the long lane on the farm. It ran through fields where watermelons were always planted in the summer because of the fine sandy soil, and I could go out and break one open to see its Christmas colors of green skin and red inside. My grandfather had been given some of that farm as bounty land for service as a cavalryman in the Civil War.

Near the low house on the hill, with oaks on one side and apple trees on the other, my father would stand up, flourish his whip, and bring the bobsled right up to the door of the house with a burst of speed.

There are no such arrivals any more: the harness bells ringing and clashing, the horses whinnying at the horses in the barn and receiving a great, trumpeting whinny in reply, the dogs leaping into the bobsled and burrowing under the buffalo robes, a squawking from the hen house, a yelling of "Whoa, whoa," at the excited horses, boy and girl cousins howling around the bobsled, and the descent into the snow with the Christmas basket carried by my mother.

While my mother and sisters went into the house, the team was un-hitched and taken to the barn, to be covered with blankets and given a little grain. That winter odor of a barn is a wonderfully complex one, rich and warm and utterly unlike the smell of the same barn in summer: the body heat of many animals weighing a thousand pounds and more; pigs in one corner making their dark, brown-sounding grunts; milk cattle still nuzzling the manger for wisps of hay; horses eying the new-comers and rolling their deep, oval eyes white; oats, hay, and straw tangy still with the live August sunlight; the manure steaming; the sharp odor of leather harness rubbed with neat's-foot oil to keep it supple; the molasses-sweet odor of ensilage in the silo where the fodder was almost ferment-ing. It is a smell from strong and living things, and my father always said it was the secret of health, that it scoured out a man's lungs; and he would stand there, breathing deeply, one hand on a horse's rump, watch-ing the steam come out from under the blankets as the team cooled down from their rapid trot up the lane. It gave him a better appetite, he argued, than plain fresh air, which was thin and had no body to it.

A barn with cattle and horses is the place to begin Christmas; after all, that's where the original event happened, and that same smell was the first air that the Christ Child breathed.

By the time we reached the house my mother and sisters were wearing aprons and busying in the kitchen, as red-faced as the women who had been there all morning. The kitchen was the biggest room in the house and all family life save sleeping went on there. My uncle even had a couch along one wall where he napped and where the children lay when they were ill. The kitchen range was a tremendous black and gleaming one called a Smoke Eater, with pans bubbling over the holes above the firebox and a reservoir of hot water at the side, lined with dull copper, from which my uncle would dip a basin of water and shave above the sink, turning his lathered face now and then to drop a remark into the women's talk, waving his straight-edged razor as if it were a threat to make them believe him. My job was to go to the woodpile out back and keep the fire burning, splitting the chunks of oak and hickory, watching how cleanly the ax went through the tough wood.

It was a handmade Christmas. The tree came from down in the grove, and on it were many paper ornaments made by my cousins, as well as beautiful ones brought from the Black Forest, where the family had orig-inally lived. There were popcorn balls, from corn planted on the sunny slope next the watermelons, paper horns with homemade candy, and apples from the orchard. The gifts tended to be hand-knit socks, or wool ties, or fancy crocheted "yokes" for nightgowns, tatted collars for blouses, doilies with fancy flower patterns for tables, tidies for chairs, and once I received a brilliantly polished cow horn with a cavalryman crudely but bravely carved on it. And there would usually be a cornhusk doll, perhaps with a prune or walnut for a face, and a gay dress of an old corset-cover scrap with its ribbons still bright. And there were real candles burning with real flames, every guest sniffing the air for the smell of scorching pine needles. No electrically lit tree has the warm and primitive presence of a tree with a crown of living fires over it, suggesting whatever true flame Joseph may have kindled on that original cold night.

There are no dinners like that any more: every item from the farm itself, with no deep-freezer, no car for driving into town for packaged food. The pies had been baked the day before, pumpkin, apple, and mince; as we ate them, we could look out the window and see the cornfield where the pumpkins grew, the trees from which the apples were picked. There was cottage cheese, with the dripping bags of curds still hanging from the cold cellar ceiling. The bread had been baked that morning, heating up the oven for the meat, and as my aunt hurried by I could smell in her apron the freshest of all odors with which the human nose is honored— bread straight from the oven. There would be a huge brown crock of beans with smoked pork from the hog butchered every November. We would see, beyond the crock, the broad black iron kettle in a corner of the barnyard, turned upside down, the innocent hogs stopping to scratch on it.

There would be every form of preserve: wild grape from the vines in the grove, crabapple jelly, wild blackberry and tame raspberry, strawberry from the bed in the garden, sweet and sour pickles with dill from the edge of the lane where it grew wild, pickles from the rind of the same watermelon we had cooled in the tank at the milkhouse and eaten on a hot September afternoon.

Cut into the slope of the hill behind the house, with a little door of its own, was the vegetable cellar, from which came carrots, turnips, cabbages, potatoes, squash. Sometimes my scared cousins were sent there for punishment, to sit in darkness and meditate on their sins; but never on Christmas Day. For days after such an ordeal they could not endure biting into a carrot.

And of course there was the traditional sauerkraut, with flecks of caraway seed. I remember one Christmas Day, when a ten-gallon crock of it in the basement, with a stone weighting down the lid, had blown up, driving the stone against the floor of the parlor, and my uncle had exclaimed, "Good God, the piano's fallen through the floor."

All the meat was from the home place too. Most useful of all, the goose—the very one which had chased me the summer before, hissing and darting out its bill at the end of its curving neck like a feathered snake. Here was the universal bird of an older Christmas: its down was plucked, washed, and hung in bags in the barn to be put into pillows; its awkward body was roasted until the skin was crisp as a fine paper; and the grease from its carcass was melted down, a little camphor added, and rubbed on the chests of coughing children. We ate, slept on, and wore that goose.

I was blessed as a child with a remote uncle from the nearest railroad town, Uncle Ben, who was admiringly referred to as a "railroad man," working the run into Omaha. Ben had been to Chicago; just often enough, as his wife Minnie said with a sniff in her voice, "to ruin the fool, not often enough to teach him anything useful." Ben refused to eat fowl in any form, and as a Christmas token a little pork roast would be put in the oven just for him, always referred to by the hurrying ladies in the kitchen as "Ben's chunk." Ben would make frequent trips to the milkhouse, returning each time a little redder in the face, usually with one of the men toward whom he had jerked his head. It was not many years before I came to associate Ben's remarkably fruity breath not only with the mince pie, but with the jug I found sunk in the bottom of the cooling tank with a stone tied to its neck. He was a romantic person in my life for his constant travels and for that dignifying term "railroad man," so much more impressive than farmer or lawyer. Yet now I see that he was a short man with a fine natural shyness, giving us knives and guns because he had no children of his own.

And of course the trimmings were from the farm too: the hickory nut cake made with nuts gathered in the grove after the first frost and hulled out by my cousins with yellowed hands; the black walnut cookies, sweeter than any taste; the fudge with butternuts crowding it. In the mornings we would be given a hammer, a flatiron, and a bowl of nuts to crack and pick out for the homemade ice cream.

And there was the orchard beyond the kitchen window, the Wealthy, the Russet, the Wolf with its giant-sized fruit, and an apple romantically called the Northern Spy as if it were a suspicious character out of the Civil War.

All families had their special Christmas food. Ours was called Dutch Bread, made from a dough halfway between bread and cake, stuffed with citron and every sort of nut from the farm—hazel, black walnut, hickory, butternut. A little round one was always baked for me in a Clabber Girl baking soda can, and my last act on Christmas Eve was to put it by the tree so that Santa Claus would find it and have a snack—after all, he'd come a long, cold way to our house. And every Christmas morning he would have eaten it. My aunt made the same Dutch Bread and we smeared over it the same butter she had been churning from their own Jersey (highest butterfat content) milk that same morning.

To eat in the same room where food is cooked—that is the way to thank the Lord for His abundance. The long table, with its different levels where additions had been made for the small fry, ran the length of the kitchen. The air was heavy with odors not only of food on plates but of the act of cooking itself, along with the metallic smell of heated iron from the hard-working Smoke Eater, and the whole stove offered us its yet uneaten prospects of more goose and untouched pies. To see the giblet gravy made and poured into a gravy boat, which had painted on its sides winter scenes of boys sliding and deer bounding over snow, is the surest way to overeat its swimming richness.

The warning for Christmas dinner was always an order to go to the milkhouse for cream, where we skimmed from the cooling pans of fresh milk the cream which had the same golden color as the flanks of the Jersey cows which had given it. The last deed before eating was grinding the coffee beans in the little mill, adding that exotic odor to the more native ones of goose and spiced pumpkin pie. Then all would sit at the table and my uncle would ask the grace, sometimes in German, but later, for the benefit of us ignorant children, in English:

> Come, Lord Jesus, be our guest,
> Share this food that you have blessed.

There are no blessings like that any more: every scrap of food for which my uncle had asked the blessing was the result of his own hard work. What he took to the Lord for Him to make holy was the plain substance that an Iowa farm could produce in an average year with decent rainfall and proper plowing and manure.

The first act of dedication on such a Christmas was to the occasion which had begun it, thanks to the Child of a pastoral couple who no doubt knew a good deal about rainfall and grass and the fattening of animals. The second act of dedication was to the ceremony of eating. My aunt kept a turmoil of food circulating, and to refuse any of it was somehow to violate the elevated nature of the day. We were there not only to celebrate a fortunate event for mankind but also to recognize that suffering is the natural lot of men—and to consume the length and breadth of that meal was to suffer! But we all faced the ordeal with courage. Uncle Ben would let out his belt—a fancy western belt with steer heads and silver buckle—with a snap and a sigh. The women managed better by always getting up from the table and trotting to the kitchen sink or the Smoke Eater or outdoors for some item left in the cold. The men sat there grimly enduring the glory of their appetites.

After dinner, late in the afternoon, the women would make despairing gestures toward the dirty dishes and scoop up hot water from the reservoir at the side of the range. The men would go to the barn and look after the livestock. My older cousin would take his new .22 rifle and stalk out across the pasture with the remark, "I saw that fox just now looking for his Christmas goose." Or sleds would be dragged out and we would slide in a long snake, feet hooked into the sled behind, down the hill and across the westward sloping fields into the sunset. Bones would be thrown to dogs, suet tied in the oak trees for the juncos and winter-defying chickadees, a saucer of skimmed milk set out for the cats, daintily and disgustedly picking their padded feet through the snow, and crumbs scattered on a bird feeder where already crimson cardinals would be dropping out of the sky like blood. Then back to the house for a final warming up before leaving.

There was usually a song around the tree before we were all bundled up, many thanks all around for gifts, the basket as loaded as when it came, more so, for leftover food had been piled in it. My father and uncle would have brought up the team from the barn and hooked them into the double shafts of the bobsled, and we would all go out into the freezing air of early evening.

On the way to the door I would walk under a photograph of my grandfather, his cavalry saber hung over it (I had once sneaked it down from the wall and in a burst of gallantry had killed a mouse with it behind the corncrib). With his long white beard he looked like one of the prophets in Hurlbut's illustrated *Story of the Bible,* and it was years before I discovered that as a young man he had not been off fighting the Philistines but the painted Sioux. It was hard to think of that gentle man, whose family had left Germany in protest over military service, swinging that deadly blade and yelling in a cavalry charge. But he had done just that, in some hard realization that sometimes the way to have peace and a quiet life on a modest farm was to go off and fight for them.

And now those bells again as the horses, impatient from their long standing in the barn, stamped and shook their harness, my father holding them back with a soft clucking in his throat and a hard pull on the reins. The smell of wood smoke flavoring the air in our noses, the cousins shivering with cold, "Good-bye, good-bye," called out from everyone, and the bobsled would move off, creaking over the frost-brittle snow. All of us, my mother included, would dig down in the straw and pull the buffalo robes up to our chins. As the horses settled into a steady trot, the bells gently chiming in their rhythmical beat, we would fall half asleep, the hiss of the runners comforting. As we looked up at the night sky through half-closed eyelids, the constant bounce and swerve of the runners would seem to shake the little stars as if they would fall into our laps. But that one great star in the East never wavered. Nothing could shake it from the sky as we drifted home on Christmas.

A CHRISTMAS GIFT OF MUSIC, LONG AGO

HANS FANTEL

I cannot say how much of my life I spent listening to phonographs, but the most unforgettable of these many hours came on Christmas Eve just 40 years ago. I was then in my late teens and, being racially obnoxious to Hitler's government, I had become a fugitive and outlaw and had to be hidden. In a remote village in the Tatra Mountains I found shelter, for a fee, in the house of an elderly grain dealer. He loosely supported the local resistance movement, but firmly hated Hitler. So he could be trusted.

In happier days he had sold his produce at the commodities exchange in Brno, gone to the opera there, and fallen under the spell of music. In consequence, he owned one of the few radios to be found at the time in the uplands of Slovakia, where even plumbing was rare and water had to be fetched from a pump. Since the village had no electricity, the radio ran on batteries and reception was erratic. But when the weather was right, my host told me, he used to be able to hear concerts from Prague, relayed by the transmitter at Kosice.

The radio was silent now. Batteries, along with almost anything else, were unavailable in wartime. Besides, the government frowned on private ownership of radios, preferring to entertain the populace with loudspeaker trucks parked in the village square, which blared out martial music interspersed with triumphant news of German victories from Norway to Greece. In fact as in its songs, the Third Reich proclaimed dominions over the earth.

But beyond earshot of the sound trucks, our village rested in stillness broken only by the occasional lowing of a cow. Yet, we knew the world as turbulent and terrible, that the stillness would end and we, too, would be engulfed in the nightmare.

It didn't matter about the batteries because my host was no longer in the mood for music. His business had collapsed when the Germans confiscated the crops and there was no grain to sell. His wife was dead and his son, with a snug job in the Nazi-sponsored bureaucracy at Bratislava, had nothing to say to him. Much of the day he sat in an elaborately carved high-backed chair—a relic of bygone opulence—and stared at the wall. I kept out of his way and busied myself in the garden, pruning trees or—for some perverse pleasure—beheading snails, or worked my way systematically through an old German encyclopedia I found on his shelves. Europe raced in the maelstrom. History tumbled in its cataclysm. For us, the hours didn't move. Time had stopped.

The two of us lived in the house that way for several months. A peasant woman came to cook and clean. Her son was with the partisans, so she wouldn't betray me either. She spoke no German, so I couldn't talk with her. And, of course, I could not go out. I had no legal existence and hence no right to live. To be seen was dangerous.

In the silence and solitude of my days I developed the habit of trying to hear music inside my head. I tried to reconstruct from memory the music I had so often heard at home when my father systematically acquainted me with his record collection. Those were the years when the mainstays of the repertoire were being recorded for the first time, the electric phonograph just having made it possible to capture music sound with tolerable verisimilitude. Each new release was an event in our lives. We waited eagerly for another Mozart symphony from Sir Thomas Beecham, for the next album in Weingartner's Beethoven cycle, and for Bruno Walter's Brahms. We discovered the existence of faraway places like Boston and Philadelphia through the recordings of Serge Koussevitsky and Leopold Stokowski and marveled at the magnificent performances of Toscanini in New York. Those evenings with the phonograph, back home, had been my happiest times, sharing in concentrated attention the experience of music with my father, who soon afterward vanished forever in the Gestapo dragnet during the invasion of Austria.

Now, in the little Slovak village, I was trying to put together pieces of remembered music like a jigsaw puzzle. Often they didn't fit. Bits of Schubert's Trout would get right into the middle of a Rasumovsky quartet. And sometimes the music would simply break off. I couldn't remember the rest.

This frightened me and made me desperate. For, without realizing it at the time, I must have harbored the notion that if I could put all the music I had heard at home back together in my head, in one seamless continuity, my father would come back. I suppose that is why I felt that the whole world was going to come right, after all, when I discovered that I could—in my mind—get through the Meistersinger prelude all the way from beginning to end.

It was easier in the summer when I could be in the garden. But the cold weather comes early in the mountains, and indoors it was harder to think of the tunes. It was as if the low ceilings and thick walls, the meager windows and prevalent gloom of the house had quenched the music of my imagination, and I knew it could be re-kindled only by hearing real music once again. Without the music, I too began to despair—to lose the links between one day and the next. I no longer sensed the connection between where I was and the days with my father.

By November everything had grown dark. The mists rarely lifted. The towering bulk of the High Tatras kept the low sun out of our valley. You couldn't see inside the house by mid-afternoon. We had no petroleum for the lamps and insufficient candles.

The approaching winter also darkened our lives in other ways. The Germans had taken the cows when they were driven back down from their mountain pastures after the first frost; so, there was even less to eat. More soldiers loitered about after Slovakia opened its roads to the German army, allowing access to the oilfields in nearby Rumania. Occasionally, we saw a black Mercedes carrying black-clad men with silver skulls on their caps—the SS. In a neighboring town, we were told, the Germans had taken away all members of the resistance and their families. Their names, the peasant woman said, had been betrayed by someone under torture. The loudspeakers in the square told of Hitler's new friendship with Japan and boasted of the burning of London. The horror now spanned the globe, and our valley was a trap.

Later in the year, my host asked me what I would like for Christmas. I am not sure he liked me much, but he was a kind man. I said I would like to hear some music.

I said it almost without thinking, but my eyes shifted to the radio. Perhaps, without being aware of it, I hoped that my host's well-connected son might use his influence to get a set of batteries in Bratislava. But I certainly never would have suggested this. The old grain dealer just nodded.

We had no Christmas tree. On December 24, the peasant woman brought several boughs of fir and we lit some extra candles. I thought of midnight mass in the village church. The organ would be playing. I trembled at the imagined sound of the big bass pipes, the fullness of the great chords, and the miracle of melody rising from it all. But I could not go to church. It was too risky to be seen, especially now that there were so many more Germans in the district.

Still, I had my Christmas wish. On the table in the dining room, on the thick ochre rug that usually covered it between meals, stood an ancient and rather ramshackle phonograph. But its brass horn was freshly polished and the tattered green felt covering the turntable was more or less sewn together. The old man had remembered the phonograph, fetched it from the rumpus room, and the peasant woman had helped him fix it up. It hadn't been used since they began broadcasting music from Kosice. The radio sounded better, he said. But he still had some records and even a box of needles.

So, on Christmas Eve, 1940, I listened to Fritz Kreisler play the Beethoven violin concerto with the orchestra of the Berlin State Opera conducted by Leo Blech. I have no recollection how it sounded. But I remember having to wind up the phonograph after each side—10 times in all. Curiously, this was no real interruption of the music. On the contrary, it was as if the music swelled to boundless force in those intervals. As I turned the crank, it set in motion engines of war all over the world that threw back and cut down the armies of the enemy.

THE FIRST CHRISTMAS TREE

EUGENE FIELD

Once upon a time the forest was in a great commotion. Early in the evening the wise old cedars had shaken their heads ominously and predicted strange things. They had lived in the forest many, many years; but never had they seen such marvellous sights as were to be seen now in the sky, and upon the hills, and in the distant village.

"Pray tell us what you see," pleaded a little vine; "we who are not as tall as you can behold none of these wonderful things. Describe them to us, that we may enjoy them with you."

"I am filled with such amazement," said one of the cedars, "that I can hardly speak. The whole sky seems to be aflame, and the stars appear to be dancing among the clouds; angels walk down from heaven to the earth, and enter the village or talk with the shepherds upon the hills."

The vine listened in mute astonishment. Such things never before had happened. The vine trembled with excitement. Its nearest neighbor was a tiny tree, so small it scarcely ever was noticed; yet it was a very beautiful little tree, and the vines and ferns and mosses and other humble residents of the forest loved it dearly.

"How I should like to see the angels!" sighed the little tree, "and how I should like to see the stars dancing among the clouds! It must be very beautiful."

As the vine and the little tree talked of these things, the cedars watched with increasing interest the wonderful scenes over and beyond the confines of the forest. Presently they thought they heard music, and they were not mistaken, for soon the whole air was full of the sweetest harmonies ever heard upon earth.

"What beautiful music!" cried the little tree. "I wonder whence it comes."

"The angels are singing," said a cedar; "for none but angels could make such sweet music."

"But the stars are singing, too," said another cedar; "yes, and the shepherds on the hill join in the song, and what a strangely glorious song it is!"

The trees listened to the singing, but they did not understand its meaning: it seemed to be an anthem, and it was of a Child that had been born; but further than this they did not understand. The strange and glorious song continued all the night; and all that night the angels walked to and fro, and the shepherd-folk talked with the angels, and the stars danced and carolled in high heaven. And it was nearly morning when the cedars cried out, "They are coming to the forest! the angels are coming to the forest!" And, surely enough, this was true. The vine and the little tree were very terrified, and they begged their older and stronger neighbors to protect them from harm. But the cedars were too busy with their own fears to pay any heed to the faint pleadings of the humble vine and the little tree. The angels came into the forest, singing the same glorious anthem about the Child, and the stars sang in chorus with them, until every part of the woods rang with echoes of that wondrous song. There was nothing in the appearance of this angel host to inspire fear; they were clad all in white, and there were crowns upon their fair heads, and golden harps in their hands; love, hope, charity, compassion, and joy beamed from their beautiful faces, and their presence seemed to fill the forest with a divine peace. The angels came through the forest to where the little tree stood, and gathering around it, they touched it with their hands, and kissed its little branches, and sang even more sweetly than before. And their song was about the Child, the Child, the Child that had been born. Then the stars came down from the skies and danced and hung upon the branches of the tree, and they, too, sang that song—the song of the Child. And all the other trees and the vines and the ferns and the mosses beheld in wonder; nor could they understand why all these things were being done, and why this exceeding honor should be shown the little tree.

When the morning came the angels left the forest—all but one angel, who remained behind and lingered near the little tree. Then a cedar asked: "Why do you tarry with us, holy angel?" And the angel answered: "I stay to guard this little tree, for it is sacred, and no harm shall come to it."

The little tree felt quite relieved by this assurance, and it held up its head more confidently than ever before. And how it thrived and grew, and waxed in strength and beauty! The cedars said they never had seen the like. The sun seemed to lavish its choicest rays upon the little tree, heaven dropped its sweetest dew upon it, and the winds never came to the forest that they did not forget their rude manners and linger to kiss the little tree and sing it their prettiest songs. No danger ever menaced it, no harm threatened; for the angel never slept—through the day and through the night the angel watched the little tree and protected it from all evil. Oftentimes the trees talked with the angel; but of course they understood little of what he said, for he spoke always of the Child who was to become the Master; and always when thus he talked, he caressed the little tree, and stroked its branches and leaves, and moistened them with his tears. It all was so very strange that none in the forest could understand.

So the years passed, the angel watching his blooming charge. Sometimes the beasts strayed toward the little tree and threatened to devour its tender foliage; sometimes the woodman came with his axe, intent upon hewing down the straight and comely thing; sometimes the hot, consuming breath of drought swept from the south, and sought to blight the forest and all its verdure: the angel kept them from the little tree. Serene and beautiful it grew, until now it was no longer a little tree, but the pride and glory of the forest.

One day the tree heard someone coming through the forest. Hitherto the angel had hastened to its side when men approached; but now the angel strode away and stood under the cedars yonder.

"Dear angel," cried the tree, "can you not hear the footsteps of someone approaching? Why do you leave me?"

"Have no fear," said the angel; "for He who comes is the Master."

The Master came to the tree and beheld it. He placed His hands upon its smooth trunk and branches, and the tree was thrilled with a strange and glorious delight. Then He stooped and kissed the tree, and then He turned and went away.

Many times after that the Master came to the forest, and when He came it always was to where the tree stood. Many times He rested beneath the tree and enjoyed the shade of its foliage, and listened to the music of the wind as it swept through the rustling leaves. Many times He slept there, and the tree watched over Him, and the forest was still, and all its voices were hushed. And the angel hovered near like a faithful sentinel.

Ever and anon men came with the Master to the forest, and sat with Him in the shade of the tree, and talked with Him of matters which the tree never could understand; only it heard that the talk was of love and charity and gentleness, and it saw that the Master was beloved and venerated by the others. It heard them tell of the Master's goodness and humility—how He had healed the sick and raised the dead and bestowed inestimable blessings wherever He walked. And the tree loved the Master for His beauty and His goodness; and when He came to the forest it was full of joy, but when He came not it was sad. And the other trees of the forest joined in its happiness and its sorrow, for they, too, loved the Master. And the angel always hovered near.

The Master came one night alone into the forest, and His face was pale with anguish and wet with tears, and He fell upon His knees and prayed. The tree heard Him, and all the forest was still, as if it were standing in the presence of death. And when the morning came, lo! the angel had gone.

Then there was a great confusion in the forest. There was a sound of rude voices, and a clashing of swords and staves. Strange men appeared, uttering loud oaths and cruel threats, and the tree was filled with terror. It called aloud for the angel, but the angel came not.

"Alas," cried the vine, "they have come to destroy the tree, the pride and glory of the forest!"

The forest was sorely agitated, but it was in vain. The strange men plied their axes with cruel vigor, and the tree was hewn to the ground. Its beautiful branches were cut away and cast aside, and its soft, thick foliage was strewn to the tenderer mercies of the winds.

"They are killing me!" cried the tree; "why is not the angel here to protect me?"

But no one heard the piteous cry—none but the other trees of the forest; and they wept, and the little vine wept too.

Then the cruel men dragged the despoiled and hewn tree from the forest, and the forest saw that beauteous thing no more.

But the night wind that swept down from the City of the Great King that night to ruffle the bosom of distant Galilee, tarried in the forest awhile to say that it had seen that day a cross upraised on Calvary—the tree on which was stretched the body of the dying Master.

CHRISTMAS TREES
A Christmas Circular Letter

ROBERT FROST

The city had withdrawn into itself
And left at last the country to the country;
When between whirls of snow not come to lie
And whirls of foliage not yet laid, there drove
A stranger to our yard, who looked the city,
Yet did in country fashion in that there
He sat and waited till he drew us out
A-buttoning coats to ask him who he was.
He proved to be the city come again
To look for something it had left behind
And could not do without and keep its Christmas.
He asked if I would sell my Christmas trees;
My woods—the young fir balsams like a place
Where houses all are churches and have spires.
I hadn't thought of them as Christmas trees.
I doubt if I was tempted for a moment
To sell them off their feet to go in cars
And leave the slope behind the house all bare,
Where the sun shines now no warmer than the moon.
I'd hate to have them know it if I was.
Yet more I'd hate to hold my trees except
As others hold theirs or refuse for them,
Beyond the time of profitable growth,
The trial by market everything must come to.

I dallied so much with the thought of selling.
Then whether from mistaken courtesy
And fear of seeming short of speech, or whether
From hope of hearing good of what was mine,
I said, 'There aren't enough to be worth while.'

'I could soon tell how many they would cut,
You let me look them over.'

                         'You could look.
But don't expect I'm going to let you have them.'
Pasture they spring in, some in clumps too close
That lop each other of boughs, but not a few
Quite solitary and having equal boughs
All round and round. The latter he nodded 'Yes' to,
Or paused to say beneath some lovelier one,
With a buyer's moderation, 'That would do.'
I thought so too, but wasn't there to say so.
We climbed the pasture on the south, crossed over,
And came down on the north.

                         He said, 'A thousand.'

'A thousand Christmas trees!—at what apiece?'

He felt some need of softening that to me:
'A thousand trees would come to thirty dollars.'

Then I was certain I had never meant
To let him have them. Never show surprise!
But thirty dollars seemed so small beside
The extent of pasture I should strip, three cents
(For that was all they figured out apiece),
Three cents so small beside the dollar friends
I should be writing to within the hour
Would pay in cities for good trees like those,
Regular vestry-trees whole Sunday Schools
Could hang enough on to pick off enough.

A thousand Christmas trees I didn't know I had!
Worth three cents more to give away than sell

As may be shown by a simple calculation.
Too bad I couldn't lay one in a letter.
I can't help wishing I could send you one,
In wishing you herewith a Merry Christmas.

DULCE DOMUM

KENNETH GRAHAME

from THE WIND IN THE WILLOWS

The sheep ran huddling together against the hurdles, blowing out thin nostrils and stamping with delicate forefeet, their heads thrown back and a light steam rising from the crowded sheep-pen into the frosty air, as the two animals hastened by in high spirits, with much chatter and laughter. They were returning across country after a long day's outing with Otter, hunting and exploring on the wide uplands where certain streams tributary to their own river had their first small beginnings; and the shades of the short winter day were closing in on them, and they had still some distance to go. Plodding at random across the plough, they had heard the sheep and had made for them; and now, leading from the sheep-pen, they found a beaten track that made walking a lighter business, and responded, moreover, to that small inquiring something which all animals carry inside them, saying unmistakably, 'Yes, quite right; *this* leads home!'

'It looks as if we were coming to a village,' said the Mole somewhat dubiously, slackening his pace, as the track, that had in time become a path and then had developed into a lane, now handed them over to the charge of a well-metalled road. The animals did not hold with villages, and their own highways, thickly frequented as they were, took an independent course, regardless of church, post office, or public-house.

'Oh, never mind,' said the Rat. 'At this season of the year they're all safe indoors by this time, sitting round the fire; men, women, and children, dogs and cats and all. We shall slip through all right, without any bother or unpleasantness, and we can have a look at them through their windows if you like, and see what they're doing.'

The rapid nightfall of mid-December had quite beset the little village as they approached it on soft feet over a thin fall of powdery snow. Little was visible but squares of a dusky orange-red on either side of the street, where the firelight or lamplight of each cottage overflowed through the casements into the dark world without. Most of the low latticed windows were innocent of blinds, and to the lookers-in from outside, the inmates, gathered round the tea-table, absorbed in handiwork, or talking with laughter and gesture, had each that happy grace which is the last thing the skilled actor shall capture—the natural grace which goes with perfect unconsciousness of observation. Moving at will from one theatre to another, the two spectators, so far from home themselves, had something of wistfulness in their eyes as they watched a cat being stroked, a sleepy child picked up and huddled off to bed, or a tired man stretch and knock out his pipe on the end of a smouldering log.

But it was from one little window, with its blind drawn down, a mere blank transparency on the night, that the sense of home and the little curtained world within walls—the larger stressful world of outside Nature shut out and forgotten—most pulsated. Close against the white blind hung a bird-cage, clearly silhouetted, every wire, perch, and appurtenance distinct and recognisable, even to yesterday's full-edged lump of sugar. On the middle perch the fluffy occupant, head tucked well into feathers, seemed so near to them as to be easily stroked, had they tried; even the delicate tips of his plumped-out plumage pencilled plainly on the illuminated screen. As they looked, the sleepy little fellow stirred uneasily, woke, shook himself, and raised his head. They could see the gape of his tiny beak as he yawned in a bored sort of way, looked round, and then settled his head into his back again, while the ruffled feathers gradually subsided into perfect stillness. Then a gust of bitter wind took them in the back of the neck, a small sting of frozen sleet on the skin woke them as from a dream, and they knew their toes to be cold and their legs tired, and their own home distant a weary way.

Once beyond the village, where the cottages ceased abruptly, on either side of the road they could smell through the darkness the friendly fields again; and they braced themselves for the last long stretch, the home stretch, the stretch that we know is bound to end, some time, in the rattle of the door-latch, the sudden firelight, and the sight of familiar things greeting us as long-absent travellers from far oversea. They plodded along steadily and silently, each of them thinking his own thoughts. The

Mole's ran a good deal on supper, as it was pitch-dark, and it was all a strange country to him as far as he knew, and he was following obediently in the wake of the Rat, leaving the guidance entirely to him. As for the Rat, he was walking a little way ahead, as his habit was, his shoulders humped, his eyes fixed on the straight grey road in front of him; so he did not notice poor Mole when suddenly the summons reached him, and took him like an electric shock.

We others, who have long lost the more subtle of the physical senses, have not even proper terms to express an animal's intercommunications with his surroundings, living or otherwise, and have only the word 'smell,' for instance, to include the whole range of delicate thrills which murmur in the nose of the animal night and day, summoning, warning, inciting, repelling. It was one of these mysterious fairy calls from out the void that suddenly reached Mole in the darkness, making him tingle through and through with its very familiar appeal, even while as yet he could not clearly remember what it was. He stopped dead in his tracks, his nose searching hither and thither in its efforts to recapture the fine filament, the telegraphic current, that had so strongly moved him. A moment, and he had caught it again; and with it this time came recollection in fullest flood.

Home! That was what they meant, those caressing appeals, those soft touches wafted through the air, those invisible little hands pulling and tugging, all one way! Why, it must be quite close by him at that moment, his old home that he had hurriedly forsaken and never sought again, that day when he first found the river! And now it was sending out its scouts and its messengers to capture him and bring him in. Since his escape on that bright morning he had hardly given it a thought, so absorbed had he been in his new life, in all its pleasures, its surprises, its fresh and captivating experiences. Now, with a rush of old memories, how clearly it stood up before him, in the darkness! Shabby indeed, and small and poorly furnished, and yet his, the home he had made for himself, the home he had been so happy to get back to after his day's work. And the home had been happy with him, too, evidently, and was missing him, and wanted him back, and was telling him so, through his nose, sorrowfully, reproachfully, but with no bitterness or anger; only with plaintive reminder that it was there, and wanted him.

The call was clear, the summons was plain. He must obey it instantly, and go. 'Ratty!' he called, full of joyful excitement, 'hold on! Come back! I want you, quick!'

'O, *come* along, Mole, do!' replied the Rat cheerfully, still plodding along.

'*Please* stop, Ratty!' pleaded the poor Mole, in anguish of heart. 'You don't understand! It's my home, my old home! I've just come across the smell of it, and it's close by here, really quite close. And I *must* go to it, I must, I must! O, come back, Ratty! Please, please come back!'

The Rat was by this time very far ahead, too far to hear clearly what the Mole was calling, too far to catch the sharp note of painful appeal in his voice. And he was much taken up with the weather, for he too could smell something—something suspiciously like approaching snow.

'Mole, we mustn't stop now, really!' he called back. 'We'll come for it to-morrow, whatever it is you've found. But I daren't stop now—it's late, and the snow's coming on again, and I'm not sure of the way! And I want your nose, Mole, so come on quick, there's a good fellow!' And the Rat pressed forward on his way without waiting for an answer.

Poor Mole stood alone in the road, his heart torn asunder, and a big sob gathering, gathering, somewhere low down inside him, to leap up to the surface presently, he knew, in passionate escape. But even under such a test as this his loyalty to his friend stood firm. Never for a moment did he dream of abandoning him. Meanwhile, the wafts from his old home pleaded, whispered, conjured, and finally claimed him imperiously. He dared not tarry longer within their magic circle. With a wrench that tore his very heartstrings he set his face down the road and followed submissively in the track of the Rat, while faint, thin little smells, still dogging his retreating nose, reproached him for his new friendship and his callous forgetfulness.

With an effort he caught up the unsuspecting Rat, who began chattering cheerfully about what they would do when they got back, and how jolly a fire of logs in the parlour would be, and what a supper he meant to eat; never noticing his companion's silence and distressful state of mind. At last, however, when they had gone some considerable way further, and were passing some tree-stumps at the edge of a copse that bordered the road, he stopped and said kindly, 'Look here, Mole, old chap, you seem dead tired. No talk left in you, and your feet dragging like lead. We'll sit down here for a minute and rest. The snow has held off so far, and the best part of our journey is over.'

The Mole subsided forlornly on a tree-stump and tried to control himself, for he felt it surely coming. The sob he had fought with so long refused to be beaten. Up and up, it forced its way to the air, and then another, and another, and others thick and fast; till poor Mole at last gave up the struggle, and cried freely and helplessly and openly, now that he knew it was all over and he had lost what he could hardly be said to have found.

The Rat, astonished and dismayed at the violence of Mole's paroxysm of grief, did not dare to speak for a while. At last he said, very quietly and sympathetically, 'What is it, old fellow? Whatever can be the matter? Tell us your trouble, and let me see what I can do.'

Poor Mole found it difficult to get any words out between the upheavals of his chest that followed one upon another so quickly and held back speech and choked it as it came. 'I know it's a—shabby, dingy little place,' he sobbed forth at last, brokenly: 'not like—your cosy quarters—or Toad's beautiful hall—or Badger's great house—but it was my own little home—and I was fond of it—and I went away and forgot all about it—and then I smelt it suddenly—on the road, when I called and you wouldn't listen, Rat—and everything came back to me with a rush—and I *wanted* it!—O dear, O dear!—and when you *wouldn't* turn back, Ratty—and I had to leave it, though I was smelling it all the time—I thought my heart would break—We might have just gone and had one look at it, Ratty—only one look—it was close by—but you wouldn't turn back, Ratty, you wouldn't turn back! O dear, O dear!'

Recollection brought fresh waves of sorrow, and sobs again took full charge of him, preventing further speech.

The Rat stared straight in front of him, saying nothing, only patting Mole gently on the shoulder. After a time he muttered gloomily, 'I see it all now! What a *pig* I have been! A pig—that's me! Just a pig—a plain pig!'

He waited till Mole's sobs became gradually less stormy and more rhythmical; he waited till at last sniffs were frequent and sobs only intermittent. Then he rose from his seat, and, remarking carelessly, 'Well, now we'd really better be getting on, old chap!' set off up the road again, over the toilsome way they had come.

'Wherever are you (hic) going to (hic), Ratty?' cried the tearful Mole, looking up in alarm.

'We're going to find that home of yours, old fellow,' replied the Rat pleasantly; 'so you had better come along, for it will take some finding, and we shall want your nose.'

'O, come back, Ratty, do!' cried the Mole, getting up and hurrying after him. 'It's no good, I tell you! It's too late, and too dark, and the place is too far off, and the snow's coming! And—and I never meant to let you know I was feeling that way about it—it was all an accident and a mistake! And think of River Bank, and your supper!'

'Hang River Bank, and supper too!' said the Rat heartily. 'I tell you, I'm going to find this place now, if I stay out all night. So cheer up, old chap, and take my arm, and we'll very soon be back there again.'

Still snuffling, pleading, and reluctant, Mole suffered himself to be dragged back along the road by his imperious companion, who by a flow of cheerful talk and anecdote endeavoured to beguile his spirits back and make the weary way seem shorter. When at last it seemed to the Rat that they must be nearing that part of the road where the Mole had been 'held up,' he said, 'Now, no more talking. Business! Use your nose, and give your mind to it.'

They moved on in silence for some little way, when suddenly the Rat was conscious, through his arm that was linked in Mole's, of a faint sort of electric thrill that was passing down that animal's body. Instantly he disengaged himself, fell back a pace, and waited, all attention.

The signals were coming through!

Mole stood a moment rigid, while his uplifted nose, quivering slightly, felt the air.

Then a short, quick run forward—a fault—a check—a try back; and then a slow, steady, confident advance.

The Rat, much excited, kept close to his heels as the Mole, with something of the air of a sleepwalker, crossed a dry ditch, scrambled through a hedge, and nosed his way over a field open and trackless and bare in the faint starlight.

Suddenly, without giving warning, he dived; but the Rat was on the alert, and promptly followed him down the tunnel to which his unerring nose had faithfully led him.

It was close and airless, and the earthy smell was strong, and it seemed a long time to Rat ere the passage ended and he could stand erect and stretch and shake himself. The Mole struck a match, and by its light the Rat saw that they were standing in an open space, neatly swept and sanded underfoot, and directly facing them was Mole's little front door, with 'Mole End' painted, in Gothic lettering, over the bell-pull at the side.

Mole reached down a lantern from a nail on the wall and lit it, and the Rat, looking round him, saw that they were in a sort of fore-court. A garden-seat stood on one side of the door, and on the other, a roller; for the Mole, who was a tidy animal when at home, could not stand having his ground kicked up by other animals into little runs that ended in earth-heaps. On the walls hung wire baskets with ferns in them, alternating with brackets carrying plaster statuary—Garibaldi, and the infant Samuel, and Queen Victoria, and other heroes of modern Italy. Down one side of the fore-court ran a skittle-alley, with benches along it and little wooden tables marked with rings that hinted at beer-mugs. In the middle was a small round pond containing goldfish and surrounded by a cockle-shell border. Out of the centre of the pond rose a fanciful erection clothed in more cockle-shells and topped by a large silvered glass ball that reflected everything all wrong and had a very pleasing effect.

Mole's face beamed at the sight of all these objects so dear to him, and he hurried Rat through the door, lit a lamp in the hall, and took one glance round his old home. He saw the dust lying thick on everything, saw the cheerless, deserted look of the long-neglected house, and its narrow, meagre dimensions, its worn and shabby contents—and collapsed again on a hall-chair, his nose in his paws. 'O, Ratty!' he cried dismally, 'why ever did I do it? Why did I bring you to this poor, cold little place, on a night like this, when you might have been at River Bank by this time, toasting your toes before a blazing fire, with all your own nice things about you!'

The Rat paid no heed to his doleful self-reproaches. He was running here and there, opening doors, inspecting rooms and cupboards, and lighting lamps and candles and sticking them up everywhere. 'What a capital little house this is!' he called out cheerily. 'So compact! So well planned! Everything here and everything in its place! We'll make a jolly night of it. The first thing we want is a good fire; I'll see to that—I always know where to find things. So this is the parlour? Splendid! Your own idea, those little sleeping-bunks in the wall? Capital! Now, I'll fetch the wood and the coals, and you get a duster, Mole—you'll find one in the drawer of the kitchen table—and try and smarten things up a bit. Bustle about, old chap!'

Encouraged by his inspiriting companion, the Mole roused himself and dusted and polished with energy and heartiness, while the Rat, running to and fro with armfuls of fuel, soon had a cheerful blaze roaring up the chimney. He hailed the Mole to come and warm himself; but Mole promptly had another fit of the blues, dropping down on a couch in dark despair and burying his face in his duster.

'Rat,' he moaned, 'how about your supper, you poor, cold, hungry, weary animal? I've nothing to give you—nothing—not a crumb!'

'What a fellow you are for giving in!' said the Rat reproachfully. 'Why, only just now I saw a sardine-opener on the kitchen dresser, quite distinctly; and everybody knows that means there are sardines about somewhere in the neighbourhood. Rouse yourself! pull yourself together, and come with me and forage.'

They went and foraged accordingly, hunting through every cupboard and turning out every drawer. The result was not so very depressing after all, though of course it might have been better; a tin of sardines—a box of captain's biscuits, nearly full—and a German sausage encased in silver paper.

'There's a banquet for you!' observed the Rat, as he arranged the table.
'I know some animals who would give their ears to be sitting down to
supper with us tonight!'

'No bread!' groaned the Mole dolorously; 'no butter, no—'

'No *pâté de foie gras,* no champagne!' continued the Rat, grinning.
'And that reminds me—what's that little door at the end of the passage?
Your cellar, of course! Every luxury in this house! Just you wait a min-
ute.'

He made for the cellar door, and presently reappeared, somewhat
dusty, with a bottle of beer in each paw and another under each arm.
'Self-indulgent beggar you seem to be, Mole,' he observed. 'Deny yourself
nothing. This is really the jolliest little place I ever was in. Now, wherever did you pick up those prints? Make the place look so home-like, they
do. No wonder you're so fond of it, Mole. Tell us all about it, and how
you came to make it what it is.'

Then, while the Rat busied himself fetching plates, and knives and
forks, and mustard which he mixed in an egg-cup, the Mole, his bosom
still heaving with the stress of his recent emotion, related—somewhat
shyly at first, but with more freedom as he warmed to his subject—how
this was planned, and how that was thought out, and how this was got
through a windfall from an aunt, and that was a wonderful find and
a bargain, and this other thing was bought out of laborious savings
and a certain amount of 'going without.' His spirits finally quite restored,
he must needs go and caress his possessions, and take a lamp and show
off their points to his visitor and expatiate on them, quite forgetful of
the supper they both so much needed; Rat, who was desperately hungry
but strove to conceal it, nodding seriously, examining with a puckered
brow, and saying, 'Wonderful,' and 'Most remarkable,' at intervals, when
the chance for an observation was given him.

At last the Rat succeeded in decoying him to the table, and had just
got seriously to work with the sardine-opener when sounds were heard
from the fore-court without—sounds like the scuffling of small feet in
the gravel and a confused murmur of tiny voices, while broken sentences
reached them—'Now, all in a line—hold the lantern up a bit,
Tommy—clear your throats first—no coughing after I say one, two,
three.—Where's young Bill?—Here, come on, do, we're all a-wait-
ing—'

'What's up?' inquired the Rat, pausing in his labours.

'I think it must be the field-mice,' replied the Mole, with a touch of
pride in his manner. 'They go round carol-singing regularly at this time
of the year. They're quite an institution in these parts. And they never
pass me over—they come to Mole End last of all; and I used to give them

hot drinks, and supper too sometimes, when I could afford it. It will be like old times to hear them again.'

'Let's have a look at them!' cried the Rat, jumping up and running to the door.

It was a pretty sight, and a seasonable one, that met their eyes when they flung the door open. In the fore-court, lit by the dim rays of a horn lantern, some eight or ten little field-mice stood in a semicircle, red worsted comforters round their throats, their fore-paws thrust deep into their pockets, their feet jigging for warmth. With bright beady eyes they glanced shyly at each other, sniggering a little, sniffing and applying coat-sleeves a good deal. As the door opened, one of the elder ones that carried the lantern was just saying, 'Now then, one, two, three!' and forthwith their shrill little voices uprose on the air, singing one of the old-time carols that their forefathers composed in fields that were fallow and held by frost, or when snow-bound in chimney corners, and handed down to be sung in the miry streets to lamp-lit windows at Yule-time.

© 1959 Ernest H. Shepard

CAROL

Villagers all, this frosty tide,
Let your doors swing open wide,
Though wind may follow, and snow beside,
Yet draw us in by your fire to bide;
    Joy shall be yours in the morning!

Here we stand in the cold and the sleet,
Blowing fingers and stamping feet,
Come from far away you to greet—
You by the fire and we in the street—
    Bidding you joy in the morning!

For ere one half of the night was gone,
Sudden a star has led us on,
Raining bliss and benison—
Bliss to-morrow and more anon,
    Joy for every morning!

Goodman Joseph toiled through the snow—
Saw the star o'er a stable low;
Mary she might not further go—
Welcome thatch, and litter below!
    Joy was hers in the morning!

And then they heard the angels tell
'Who were the first to cry Nowell?
Animals all, as it befell,
In the stable where they did dwell!
    Joy shall be theirs in the morning!'

The voices ceased, the singers, bashful but smiling, exchanged sidelong glances, and silence succeeded—but for a moment only. Then, from up above and far away, down the tunnel they had so lately travelled was borne to their ears in a faint musical hum the sound of distant bells ringing a joyful and clangorous peal.

'Very well sung, boys!' cried the Rat heartily. 'And now come along in, all of you, and warm yourselves by the fire, and have something hot!'

'Yes, come along, field-mice,' cried the Mole eagerly. 'This is quite like old times! Shut the door after you. Pull up that settle to the fire. Now, you just wait a minute, while we——O, Ratty!' he cried in despair, plumping down on a seat, with tears impending. 'Whatever are we doing? We've nothing to give them!'

'You leave all that to me,' said the masterful Rat. 'Here, you with the lantern! Come over this way. I want to talk to you. Now, tell me, are there any shops open at this hour of the night?'

'Why certainly, sir,' replied the field-mouse respectfully. 'At this time of the year our shops keep open to all sorts of hours.'

'Then look here!' said the Rat. 'You go off at once, you and your lantern, and you get me—'

Here much muttered conversation ensued, and the Mole only heard bits of it, such as—'Fresh, mind!—no, a pound of that will do—see you get Buggins's, for I won't have any other—no, only the best—if you can't get it there, try somewhere else—yes, of course, home-made, no tinned stuff—well then, do the best you can!' Finally, there was a chink of coin passing from paw to paw, the field-mouse was provided with an ample basket for his purchases, and off he hurried, he and his lantern.

The rest of the field-mice, perched in a row on the settle, their small legs swinging, gave themselves up to enjoyment of the fire, and toasted their chilblains till they tingled; while the Mole, failing to draw them into easy conversation, plunged into family history and made each of them recite the names of his numerous brothers, who were too young, it appeared, to be allowed to go out a-carolling this year, but looked forward very shortly to winning the parental consent.

The Rat, meanwhile, was busy examining the label on one of the beer-bottles. 'I perceive this to be Old Burton,' he remarked approvingly. '*Sensible* Mole! The very thing! Now we shall be able to mull some ale! Get the things ready, Mole, while I draw the corks.'

It did not take long to prepare the brew and thrust the tin heater well into the red heart of the fire; and soon every field-mouse was sipping and coughing and choking (for a little mulled ale goes a long way) and wiping his eyes and laughing and forgetting he had ever been cold in all his life.

'They act plays too, these fellows,' the Mole explained to the Rat. 'Make them up all by themselves, and act them afterwards. And very well they do it, too! They gave us a capital one last year, about a field-mouse who was captured at sea by a Barbary corsair, and made to row in a galley; and when he escaped and got home again, his lady-love had gone into a convent. Here, *you!* You were in it, I remember. Get up and recite a bit.'

The field-mouse addressed got up on his legs, giggled shyly, looked round the room, and remained absolutely tongue-tied. His comrades cheered him on, Mole coaxed and encouraged him, and the Rat went so far as to take him by the shoulders and shake him; but nothing could overcome his stage-fright. They were all busily engaged on him like water men applying the Royal Humane Society's regulations to a case of long submersion, when the latch clicked, the door opened, and the field-mouse with the lantern reappeared, staggering under the weight of his basket.

There was no more talk of play-acting once the very real and solid contents of the basket had been tumbled out on the table. Under the generalship of Rat, everybody was set to do something or to fetch something. In a very few minutes supper was ready, and Mole, as he took the head of the table in a sort of dream, saw a lately barren board set thick with savoury comforts; saw his little friends' faces brighten and beam as they fell to without delay; and then let himself loose—for he was famished indeed—on the provender so magically provided, thinking what a happy homecoming this had turned out, after all. As they ate, they talked of old times, and the field-mice gave him the local gossip up to date, and answered as well as they could the hundred questions he had to ask them. The Rat said little or nothing, only taking care that each guest had what he wanted, and plenty of it, and that Mole had no trouble or anxiety about anything.

They clattered off at last, very grateful and showering wishes of the season, with their jacket pockets stuffed with remembrances for the small brothers and sisters at home. When the door had closed on the last of them and the chink of the lanterns had died away, Mole and Rat kicked the fire up, drew their chairs in, brewed themselves a last nightcap of mulled ale, and discussed the events of the long day. At last the Rat, with a tremendous yawn, said, 'Mole, old chap, I'm ready to drop. Sleepy is simply not the word. That your own bunk over on that side? Very well, then, I'll take this. What a ripping little house this is! Everything so handy!'

He clambered into his bunk and rolled himself well up in the blankets, and slumber gathered him forthwith, as a swath of barley is folded into the arms of the reaping-machine.

The weary Mole also was glad to turn in without delay, and soon had his head on his pillow, in great joy and contentment. But ere he closed his eyes he let them wander round his old room, mellow in the glow of the firelight that played or rested on familiar and friendly things which had long been unconsciously a part of him, and now smilingly received him back, without rancour. He was now in just the frame of mind that the tactful Rat had quietly worked to bring about in him. He saw clearly how plain and simple—how narrow, even—it all was; but clearly, too, how much it all meant to him, and the special value of some such anchorage in one's existence. He did not at all want to abandon the new life and its splendid spaces, to turn his back on sun and air and all they offered him and creep home and stay there; the upper world was all too strong, it called to him still, even down there, and he knew he must return to the larger stage. But it was good to think he had this to come back to, this place which was all his own, these things which were so glad to see him again and could always be counted upon for the same simple welcome.

THE OXEN

THOMAS HARDY

Christmas Eve, and twelve of the clock.
    "Now they are all on their knees,"
An elder said as we sat in a flock
    By the embers in hearthside ease.

We pictured the meek mild creatures where
    They dwelt in their strawy pen,
Nor did it occur to one of us there
    To doubt they were kneeling then.

So fair a fancy few would weave
    In these years! Yet, I feel,
If someone said on Christmas Eve,
    "Come; see the oxen kneel,

"In the lonely barton by yonder coomb
    Our childhood used to know,"
I should go with him in the gloom,
    Hoping it might be so.

1915

MELLSTOCK-LANE

THOMAS HARDY

from UNDER THE GREENWOOD TREE

To dwellers in a wood almost every species of tree has its voice as well as its feature. At the passing of the breeze the fir-trees sob and moan no less distinctly than they rock; the holly whistles as it battles with itself; the ash hisses amid its quiverings; the beech rustles while its flat boughs rise and fall. And winter, which modifies the note of such trees as shed their leaves, does not destroy its individuality.

On a cold and starry Christmas-eve within living memory a man was passing up a lane towards Mellstock Cross in the darkness of a plantation that whispered thus distinctively to his intelligence. All the evidences of his nature were those afforded by the spirit of his footsteps, which succeeded each other lightly and quickly, and by the liveliness of his voice as he sang in a rural cadence:

> With the rose and the lily
> And the daffodowndilly,
> The lads and the lasses a-sheep-shearing go.

The lonely lane he was following connected one of the hamlets of Mellstock parish with Upper Mellstock and Lewgate, and to his eyes, casually glancing upward, the silver and black-stemmed birches with their characteristic tufts, the pale grey boughs of beech, the dark-creviced elm, all appeared now as black and flat outlines upon the sky, wherein the white stars twinkled so vehemently that their flickering seemed like the flapping of wings. Within the woody pass, at a level anything lower than the horizon, all was dark as the grave. The copse-wood forming the sides of the bower interlaced its branches so densely, even at this season of the year, that the draught from the north-east flew along the channel with scarcely an interruption from lateral breezes.

After passing the plantation and reaching Mellstock Cross the white surface of the lane revealed itself between the dark hedgerows like a ribbon jagged at the edges; the irregularity being caused by temporary accumulations of leaves extending from the ditch on either side.

The song (many times interrupted by flitting thoughts which took the place of several bars, and resumed at a point it would have reached had its continuity been unbroken) now received a more palpable check, in the shape of 'Ho-i-i-i-i-i!' from the crossing lane to Lower Mellstock, on the right of the singer who had just emerged from the trees.

'Ho-i-i-i-i-i!' he answered, stopping and looking round, though with no idea of seeing anything more than imagination pictured.

'Is that thee, young Dick Dewy?' came from the darkness.

'Ay, sure, Michael Mail.'

'Then why not stop for fellow-craters—going to thy own father's house too, as we be, and knowen us so well?'

Dick Dewy faced about and continued his tune in an under-whistle, implying that the business of his mouth could not be checked at a moment's notice by the placid emotion of friendship.

Having come more into the open he could now be seen rising against the sky, his profile appearing on the light background like the portrait of a gentleman in black cardboard. It assumed the form of a low-crowned hat, an ordinary-shaped nose, an ordinary chin, an ordinary neck, and ordinary shoulders. What he consisted of further down was invisible from lack of sky low enough to picture him on.

Shuffling, halting, irregular footsteps of various kinds were now heard coming up the hill, and presently there emerged from the shade severally five men of different ages and gaits, all of them working villagers of the parish of Mellstock. They, too, had lost their rotundity with the daylight, and advanced against the sky in flat outlines, which suggested some processional design on Greek or Etruscan pottery. They represented the chief portion of Mellstock parish choir.

The first was a bowed and bent man, who carried a fiddle under his arm, and walked as if engaged in studying some subject connected with the surface of the road. He was Michael Mail, the man who had hallooed to Dick.

The next was Mr. Robert Penny, boot- and shoe-maker; a little man who, though rather round-shouldered, walked as if that fact had not come to his own knowledge, moving on with his back very hollow and his face fixed on the north-east quarter of the heavens before him, so that his lower waistcoat-buttons came first, and then the remainder of his figure. His features were invisible; yet when he occasionally looked round, two faint moons of light gleamed for an instant from the precincts of his eyes, denoting that he wore spectacles of a circular form.

The third was Elias Spinks, who walked perpendicularly and dramatically. The fourth outline was Joseph Bowman's, who had now no distinctive appearance beyond that of a human being. Finally came a weak lath-like form, trotting and stumbling along with one shoulder forward and his head inclined to the left, his arms dangling nervelessly in the wind as if they were empty sleeves. This was Thomas Leaf.

'Where be the boys?' said Dick to this somewhat indifferently-matched assembly.

The eldest of the group, Michael Mail, cleared his throat from a great depth.

'We told them to keep back at home for a time, thinken they wouldn't be wanted yet awhile; and we could choose the tuens, and so on.'

'Father and grandfather William have expected ye a little sooner. I have just been for a run round by Ewelease Stile and Hollow Hill to warm my feet.'

'To be sure father did! To be sure 'a did expect us—to taste the little barrel beyond compare that he's going to tap.'

' 'Od rabbit it all! Never heard a word of it!' said Mr Penny, gleams of delight appearing upon his spectacle-glasses, Dick meanwhile singing parenthetically—

The lads and the lasses a-sheep-shearing go.

'Neighbours, there's time enough to drink a sight of drink now afore bedtime?' said Mail.

'True, true—time enough to get as drunk as lords!' replied Bowman cheerfully.

This opinion being taken as convincing they all advanced between the varying hedges and the trees dotting them here and there, kicking their toes occasionally among the crumpled leaves. Soon appeared glimmering indications of the few cottages forming the small hamlet of Upper Mellstock for which they were bound, whilst the faint sound of church-bells ringing a Christmas peal could be heard floating over upon the breeze from the direction of Longpuddle and Weatherbury parishes on the other side of the hills. A little wicket admitted them to the garden, and they proceeded up the path to Dick's house.

GOING THE ROUNDS

THOMAS HARDY

from UNDER THE GREENWOOD TREE

Shortly after ten o'clock the singing-boys arrived at the tranter's house,* which was invariably the place of meeting, and preparations were made for the start. The older men and musicians wore thick coats, with stiff perpendicular collars, and coloured handkerchiefs wound round and round the neck till the end came to hand, over all which they just showed their ears and noses, like people looking over a wall. The remainder, stalwart ruddy men and boys, were dressed mainly in snow-white smock-frocks, embroidered upon the shoulders and breasts in ornamental forms of hearts, diamonds, and zigzags. The cider-mug was emptied for the ninth time, the music-books were arranged, and the pieces finally decided upon. The boys in the meantime put the old horn-lanterns in order, cut candles into short lengths to fit the lanterns; and, a thin fleece of snow having fallen since the early part of the evening, those who had no leggings went to the stable and wound wisps of hay round their ankles to keep the insidious flakes from the interior of their boots.

Mellstock was a parish of considerable acreage, the hamlets composing it lying at a much greater distance from each other than is ordinarily the case. Hence several hours were consumed in playing and singing within hearing of every family, even if but a single air were bestowed on each. There was Lower Mellstock, the main village; half a mile from this were the church and vicarage, and a few other houses, the spot being rather

*Tranter: an irregular carrier.

lonely now, though in past centuries it had been the most thickly-populated quarter of the parish. A mile north-east lay the hamlet of Upper Mellstock, where the tranter lived; and at other points knots of cottages, besides solitary farmsteads and dairies.

Old William Dewy, with the violoncello, played the bass; his grandson Dick the treble violin; and Reuben and Michael Mail the tenor and second violins respectively. The singers consisted of four men and seven boys, upon whom devolved the task of carrying and attending to the lanterns, and holding the books open for the players. Directly music was the theme, old William ever and instinctively came to the front.

'Now mind, neighbors,' he said, as they all went out one by one at the door, he himself holding it ajar and regarding them with a critical face as they passed, like a shepherd counting out his sheep. 'You two counter-boys, keep your ears open to Michael's fingering, and don't ye go straying into the treble part along o' Dick and his set, as ye did last year; and mind this especially when we be in "Arise, and hail." Billy Chimlen, don't you sing quite so raving mad as you fain would; and, all o' ye, whatever ye do, keep from making a great scuffle on the ground when we go in at people's gates; but go quietly, so as to strike up all of a sudden, like spirits.'

'Farmer Ledlow's first?'

'Farmer Ledlow first; the rest as usual.'

'And, Voss,' said the tranter terminatively, 'you keep house here till about half-past two; then heat the metheglin and cider in the warmer you'll find turned up upon the copper; and bring it wi' the victuals to church-hatch, as th'st know.'

Just before the clock struck twelve they lighted the lanterns and started. The moon, in her third quarter, had risen since the snowstorm; but the dense accumulation of snow-cloud weakened her power to a faint twi-light which was rather pervasive of the landscape than traceable to the sky. The breeze had gone down, and the rustle of their feet and tones of their speech echoed with an alert rebound from every post, boundary-stone, and ancient wall they passed, even where the distance of the echo's origin was less than a few yards. Beyond their own slight noises nothing was to be heard save the occasional bark of foxes in the direction of Yal-bury Wood, or the brush of a rabbit among the grass now and then as it scampered out of their way.

Most of the outlying homesteads and hamlets had been visited by about two o'clock; they then passed across the outskirts of a wooded park toward the main village, nobody being at home at the Manor. Pursuing no recognized track, great care was necessary in walking lest their faces should come in contact with the low-hanging boughs of the old lime-trees, which in many spots formed dense overgrowths of interlaced branches.

'Times have changed from the times they used to be,' said Mail, regarding nobody can tell what interesting old panoramas with an inward eye, and letting his outward glance rest on the ground because it was as convenient a position as any. 'People don't care much about us now! I've been thinking we must be almost the last left in the county of the old string players? Barrel-organs, and the things next door to 'em that you blow wi' your foot, have come in terribly of late years.'

'Ay!' said Bowman shaking his head; and old William on seeing him did the same thing.

'More's the pity,' replied another. 'Time was—long and merry ago now!—when not one of the varmits was to be heard of; but it served some of the quires right. They should have stuck to strings as we did, and kept out clarinets, and done away with serpents. If you'd thrive in musical religion, stick to strings, says I.'

'Strings be safe soul-lifters, as far as that do go,' said Mr Spinks.

'Yet there's worse things than serpents,' said Mr Penny. 'Old things pass away, 'tis true; but a serpent was a good old note: a deep rich note was the serpent.'

'Clar'nets, however, be bad at all times,' said Michael Mail. 'One Christmas—years agone now, years—I went the rounds wi' the Weatherbury quire. 'Twas a hard frosty night, and the keys of all the clar'nets froze—ah, they did freeze!—so that 'twas like drawing a cork every time a key was opened; and the players o' 'em had to go into a hedger-and-ditcher's chimley-corner, and thaw their clar'nets every now and then. An icicle o' spet hung down from the end of every man's clar'net a span long; and as to fingers—well, there, if ye'll believe me, we had no fingers at all, to our knowing.'

'I can well bring back to my mind,' said Mr Penny, 'what I said to poor Joseph Ryme (who took the treble part in Chalk-Newton Church for two-and-forty year) when they thought of having clar'nets there. "Joseph," I said says I, "depend upon't, if so be you have them tooting clar'nets you'll spoil the whole set-out. Clar'nets were not made for the service of the Lard; you can see it by looking at 'em," I said. And what came o't? Why, souls, the parson set up a barrel-organ on his own account within two years o' the time I spoke, and the old quire went to nothing.'

'As far as look is concerned,' said the tranter, 'I don't for my part see that a fiddle is much nearer heaven than a clar'net. 'Tis further off. There's always a rakish, scampish twist about a fiddle's looks that seems to say the Wicked One had a hand in making o'en; while angels be supposed to play clar'nets in heaven, or som'at like 'em if ye may believe picters.'

'Robert Penny, you was in the right,' broke in the eldest Dewy. 'They should ha' stuck to strings. Your brass-man is a rafting dog—well and good; your reed-man is a dab at stirring ye—well and good; your drumman is a rare bowel-shaker—good again. But I don't care who hears me say it, nothing will spak to your heart wi' the sweetness o' the man of strings!'

'Strings for ever!' said little Jimmy.

'Strings alone would have held their ground against all the new comers in creation.' ('True, true!' said Bowman.) 'But clarinets was death.' ('Death they was!' said Mr Penny.) 'And harmonions,' William continued in a louder voice, and getting excited by these signs of approval, 'harmonions and barrel-organs' ('Ah!' and groans from Spinks) 'be miserable—what shall I call 'em?—miserable—'

'Sinners,' suggested Jimmy, who made large strides like the men and did not lag behind with the other little boys.

'Miserable dumbledores!'

'Right, William, and so they be—miserable dumbledores!' said the choir with unanimity.

By this time they were crossing to a gate in the direction of the school which, standing on a slight eminence at the junction of three ways, now rose in unvarying and dark flatness against the sky. The instruments were retuned, and all the band entered the school enclosure, enjoined by old William to keep upon the grass.

'Number seventy-eight,' he softly gave out as they formed round in a semicircle, the boys opening the lanterns to get a clearer light, and directing their rays on the books.

Then passed forth into the quiet night an ancient and time-worn hymn, embodying a quaint Christianity in words orally transmitted from father to son through several generations down to the present characters, who sang them out right earnestly:

> Remember Adam's fall,
>   O thou Man:
> Remember Adam's fall
>   From Heaven to Hell.
> Remember Adam's fall;
>   How he hath condemn'd all
> In Hell perpetual
>   There for to dwell.

Remember God's goodnesse,
  O thou Man:
Remember God's goodnesse,
  His promise made.
Remember God's goodnesse;
He sent His Son sinlesse
Our ails for to redress;
  Be not afraid!

In Bethlehem He was born,
  O thou Man:
In Bethlehem He was born,
  For mankind's sake.
In Bethlehem He was born,
Christmas-day i' the morn:
Our Saviour thought no scorn
  Our faults to take.

Give thanks to God alway,
  O thou Man:
Give thanks to God alway
  With heart-most joy.
Give thanks to God alway
On this our joyful day:
Let all men sing and say,
  Holy, Holy!

Having concluded the last note they listened for a minute or two, but found that no sound issued from the schoolhouse.

'Four breaths, and then, "O, what unbounded goodness!" number fifty-nine,' said William.

This was duly gone through, and no notice whatever seemed to be taken of the performance.

'Good guide us, surely 'tisn't a' empty house, as befell us in the year thirty-nine and forty-three!' said old Dewy.

'Perhaps she's jist come from some musical city, and sneers at our doings?' the tranter whispered.

' 'Od rabbit her!' said Mr Penny, with an annihilating look at a corner of the school chimney. 'I don't quite stomach her, if this is it. Your plain music well done is as worthy as your other sort done bad, a' b'lieve, souls; so say I.'

'Four breaths, and then the last,' said the leader authoritatively. ' "Re-joice, ye Tenants of the Earth," number sixty-four.'

At the close, waiting yet another minute, he said in a clear loud voice, as he had said in the village at that hour and season for the previous forty years—

'A merry Christmas to ye!'

THE LISTENERS

THOMAS HARDY

from UNDER THE GREENWOOD TREE

When the expectant stillness consequent upon the exclamation had nearly died out of them all, an increasing light made itself visible in one of the windows of the upper floor. It came so close to the blind that the exact position of the flame could be perceived from the outside. Remaining steady for an instant, the blind went upward from before it, revealing to thirty concentrated eyes a young girl framed as a picture by the window architrave, and unconsciously illuminating her countenance to a vivid brightness by a candle she held in her left hand, close to her face, her right hand being extended to the side of the window. She was wrapped in a white robe of some kind, whilst down her shoulders fell a twining profusion of marvellously rich hair, in a wild disorder which proclaimed it to be only during the invisible hours of the night that such a condition was discoverable. Her bright eyes were looking into the grey world outside with an uncertain expression, oscillating between courage and shyness, which, as she recognized the semicircular group of dark forms gathered before her, transformed itself into pleasant resolution.

Opening the window, she said lightly and warmly—

'Thank you, singers, thank you!'

Together went the window quickly and quietly, and the blind started downward on its return to its place. Her fair forehead and eyes vanished; her little mouth; her neck and shoulders; all of her. Then the spot of candlelight shone nebulously as before; then it moved away.

'How pretty!' exclaimed Dick Dewy.

'If she'd been rale wexwork she couldn't ha' been comelier,' said Michael Mail.

'As near a thing to a spiritual vision as ever *I* wish to see!' said tranter* Dewy.

'O, sich I never, never see!' said Leaf fervently.

All the rest, after clearing their throats and adjusting their hats, agreed that such a sight was worth singing for.

'Now to Farmer Shiner's, and then replenish our insides, father?' said the tranter.

'Wi' all my heart,' said old William, shouldering his bass-viol.

Farmer Shiner's was a queer lump of a house, standing at the corner of a lane that ran into the principal thoroughfare. The upper windows were much wider than they were high, and this feature, together with a broad bay-window where the door might have been expected, gave it by day the aspect of a human countenance turned askance, and wearing a sly and wicked leer. Tonight nothing was visible but the outline of the roof upon the sky.

The front of this building was reached, and the preliminaries arranged as usual.

'Four breaths, and number thirty-two, "Behold the Morning Star," ' said old William.

They had reached the end of the second verse, and the fiddlers were doing the up bow-stroke previously to pouring forth the opening chord of the third verse, when, without a light appearing or any signal being given a roaring voice exclaimed—

'Shut up, woll 'ee! Don't make your blaring row here! A feller wi' a headache enough to split his skull likes a quiet night!'

Slam went the window.

'Hullo, that's a' ugly blow for we!' said the tranter, in a keenly appreciative voice, and turning to his companions.

'Finish the carrel, all who be friends of harmony!' commanded old William; and they continued to the end.

'Four breaths, and number nineteen!' said William firmly. 'Give it him well; the quire can't be insulted in this manner!'

A light now flashed into existence, the window opened, and the farmer stood revealed as one in a terrific passion.

'Drown en!—drown en!' the tranter cried, fiddling frantically. 'Play fortissimy, and drown his spaking!'

Tranter: an irregular carrier.

'Fortissimy!' said Michael Mail, and the music and singing waxed so loud that it was impossible to know what Mr Shiner had said, was saying, or was about to say; but wildly flinging his arms and body about in the forms of capital Xs and Ys, he appeared to utter enough invectives to consign the whole parish to perdition.

'Very onseemly—very!' said old William, as they retired. 'Never such a dreadful scene in the whole round o' my carrel practice—never! And he a churchwarden!'

'Only a drap o' drink got into his head,' said the tranter. 'Man's well enough when he's in his religious frame. He's in his worldly frame now. Must ask en to our bit of a party tomorrow night, I suppose, and so put en in humour again. We bear no mortal man ill-will.'

They now crossed Mellstock Bridge, and went along an embowered path beside the Froom towards the church and vicarage, meeting Voss with the hot mead and bread-and-cheese as they were approaching the churchyard. This determined them to eat and drink before proceeding further, and they entered the church and ascended to the gallery. The lanterns were opened, and the whole body sat round against the wall on benches and whatever else was available, and made a hearty meal. In the pauses of conversation there could be heard through the floor overhead a little world of undertones and creaks from the halting clockwork, which never spread further than the tower they were born in, and raised in the more meditative minds a fancy they were born in, and raised in the more meditative minds a fancy that here lay the direct pathway of Time.

Having done eating and drinking they again tuned the instruments, and once more the party emerged into the night air.

'Where's Dick?' said old Dewy.

Every man looked round upon every other man, as if Dick might have been transmuted into one or the other; and then they said they didn't know.

'Well now, that's what I call very nasty of Master Dicky, that I do,' said Michael Mail.

'He've clinked off home-along, depend upon't,' another suggested, though not quite believing that he had.

'Dick!' exclaimed the tranter, and his voice rolled sonorously forth among the yews.

He suspended his muscles rigid as stone whilst listening for an answer, and finding he listened in vain, turned to the assemblage.

'The treble man too! Now if he'd been a tenor or counter chap, we might ha' contrived the rest o't without en, you see. But for a quire to lose the treble, why, my sonnies, you may so well lose your ...' The

tranter paused, unable to mention an image vast enough for the occasion.

'Your head at once,' suggested Mr Penny.

The tranter moved a pace as if it were puerile of people to complete sentences when there were more pressing things to be done.

'Was ever heard such a thing as a young man leaving his work half done and turning tail like this!'

'Never,' replied Bowman, in a tone signifying that he was the last man in the world to wish to withhold the formal finish required of him.

'I hope no fatal tragedy has overtook the lad!' said his grandfather.

'O no,' replied tranter Dewy placidly. 'Wonder where he's put that there fiddle of his. Why that fiddle cost thirty shillings, and good words besides. Somewhere in the damp, without doubt; that instrument will be unglued and spoilt in ten minutes—ten! ay, two.'

'What in the name o' righteousness can have happened?' said old William, more uneasily. 'Perhaps he's drownded!'

Leaving their lanterns and instruments in the belfry they retraced their steps along the waterside track. 'A strapping lad like Dick d'know better than let anything happen onawares,' Reuben remarked. 'There's sure to be some poor little scram reason for't staring us in the face all the while.' He lowered his voice to a mysterious tone: 'Neighbours, have ye noticed any sign of a scornful woman in his head, or suchlike?'

'Not a glimmer of such a body. He's as clear as water yet.'

'And Dicky said he should never marry,' cried Jimmy, 'but live at home always along wi' mother and we!'

'Ay, ay, my sonny; every lad has said that in his time.'

They had now again reached the precincts of Mr Shiner's, but hearing nobody in that direction, one or two went across to the schoolhouse. A light was still burning in the bedroom, and though the blind was down the window had been slightly opened, as if to admit the distant notes of the carollers to the ears of the occupant of the room.

Opposite the window, leaning motionless against a beech tree, was the lost man, his arms folded, his head thrown back, his eyes fixed upon the illuminated lattice.

'Why, Dick, is that thee? What b'st doing here?'

Dick's body instantly flew into a more rational attitude, and his head was seen to turn east and west in the gloom as if endeavouring to discern some proper answer to that question; and at last he said in rather feeble accents—

'Nothing, father.'

'Th'st take long enough time about it then, upon my body,' said the tranter as they all turned anew towards the vicarage.

'I thought you hadn't done having snap in the gallery,' said Dick.

'Why, we've been traypsing and rambling about, looking everywhere, and thinking you'd done fifty deathly things, and here have you been at nothing at all!'

'The stupidness lies in that point of it being nothing at all,' murmured Mr Spinks.

The vicarage front was their next field of operation, and Mr Maybold, the lately-arrived incumbent, duly received his share of the night's harmonies. It was hoped that by reason of his profession he would have been led to open the window, and an extra carol in quick time was added to draw him forth. But Mr Maybold made no stir.

'A bad sign!' said old William, shaking his head.

However, at that same instant a musical voice was heard exclaiming from inner depths of bedclothes—

'Thanks, villagers!'

'What did he say?' asked Bowman, who was rather dull of hearing. Bowman's voice, being therefore loud, had been heard by the vicar within.

'I said, "Thanks, villagers!" ' cried the vicar again.

'Oh, we didn't hear 'ee the first time!' cried Bowman.

'Now don't for heaven's sake spoil the young man's temper by answering like that!' said the tranter.

'You won't do that, my friends!' the vicar shouted.

'Well to be sure, what ears!' said Mr Penny in a whisper. 'Beats any horse or dog in the parish, and depend upon't that's a sign he's a proper clever chap.'

'We shall see that in time,' said the tranter.

Old William, in his gratitude for such thanks from a comparatively new inhabitant, was anxious to play all the tunes over again; but renounced his desire on being reminded by Reuben that it would be best to leave well alone.

'Now putting two and two together,' the tranter continued, as they went their way over the hill, and across to the last remaining houses; 'that is, in the form of that young female vision we zeed just now, and this young tenor-voiced parson, my belief is she'll wind en round her finger, and twist the pore young feller about like the figure of 8—that she will, my sonnies.'

HOW SANTA CLAUS CAME TO SIMPSON'S BAR

BRET HARTE

I t had been raining in the valley of the Sacramento. The North Fork had overflowed its banks, and Rattlesnake Creek was impassable. The few boulders that had marked the summer ford at Simpson's Crossing were obliterated by a vast sheet of water stretching to the foothills. The upstage was stopped at Granger's; the last mail had been abandoned in the tules, the rider swimming for his life. "An area," remarked the *Sierra Avalanche,* with pensive local pride, "as large as the State of Massachusetts is now under water."

Nor was the weather any better in the foothills. The mud lay deep on the mountain road; wagons that neither physical force nor moral objurgation could move from the evil ways into which they had fallen encumbered the track, and the way to Simpson's Bar was indicated by broken-down teams and hard swearing. And further on, cut off and inaccessible, rained upon and bedraggled, smitten by high winds and threatened by high water, Simpson's Bar, on the eve of Christmas Day, 1862, clung like a swallow's nest to the rocky entablature and splintered capitals of Table Mountain, and shook in the blast.

As night shut down on the settlement, a few lights gleamed through the mist from the windows of cabins on either side of the highway, now crossed and gullied by lawless streams and swept by marauding winds. Happily most of the population were gathered at Thompson's store, clustered around a red-hot stove, at which they silently spat in some accepted sense of social communion that perhaps rendered conversation unnecessary. Indeed, most methods of diversion had long since been exhausted on Simpson's Bar; high water had suspended the regular occupations on gulch and on river, and a consequent lack of money and whiskey had taken the zest from most illegitimate recreation. Even Mr. Hamlin was fain to leave the Bar with fifty dollars in his pocket—the only amount actually realized of the large sums won by him in the successful exercise of his arduous profession. "Ef I was asked," he remarked somewhat later—"ef I was asked to pint out a purty little village where a retired sport as didn't care for money could exercise hisself, frequent and lively, I'd say Simpson's Bar; but for a young man with a large family depending on his exertions, it don't pay." As Mr. Hamlin's family consisted mainly of female adults, this remark is quoted rather to show the breadth of his humor than the exact extent of his responsibilities.

Howbeit, the unconscious objects of this satire sat that evening in the listless apathy begotten of idleness and lack of excitement. Even the sudden splashing of hoofs before the door did not arouse them. Dick Bullen alone paused in the act of scraping out his pipe, and lifted his head, but no other one of the group indicated any interest in, or recognition of, the man who entered.

It was a figure familiar enough to the company, and known in Simpson's Bar as "The Old Man." A man of perhaps fifty years; grizzled and scant of hair, but still fresh and youthful of complexion. A face full of ready but not very powerful sympathy, with a chameleonlike aptitude for taking on the shade and color of contiguous moods and feelings. He had evidently just left some hilarious companions, and did not at first notice the gravity of the group, but clapped the shoulder of the nearest man jocularly, and threw himself into a vacant chair.

"Jest heard the best thing out, boys! Ye know Smiley, over yar—Jim Smiley—funniest man in the Bar? Well, Jim was jest telling the richest yarn about"—

"Smiley's a——fool," interrupted a gloomy voice.

"A particular——skunk," added another in sepulchral accents.

A silence followed these positive statements. The Old Man glanced quickly around the group. Then his face slowly changed. "That's so," he said reflectively, after a pause, "certainly a sort of a skunk and suthin' of a fool. In course." He was silent for a moment, as in painful contemplation of the unsavoriness and folly of the unpopular Smiley. "Dismal weather, ain't it?" he added, now fully embarked on the current of prevailing sentiment. "Mighty rough papers on the boys, and no show for money this season. And tomorrow's Christmas."

There was a movement among the men at this announcement, but whether of satisfaction or disgust was not plain. "Yes," continued the Old Man in the lugubrious tone he had within the last few moments unconsciously adopted—"yes, Christmas, and tonight's Christmas Eve.

Ye see, boys, I kinder thought—that is, I sorter had an idee, jest passin' like, you know—that maybe ye'd all like to come over to my house to-night and have a sort of tear round. But I suppose, now, you wouldn't? Don't feel like it, maybe?" he added with anxious sympathy, peering into the faces of his companions.

"Well, I don't know," responded Tom Flynn with some cheerfulness. "P'r'aps we may. But how about your wife, Old Man? What does *she* say to it?"

The Old Man hesitated. His conjugal experience had not been a happy one, and the fact was known to Simpson's Bar. His first wife, a delicate, pretty little woman, had suffered keenly and secretly from the jealous suspicions of her husband, until one day he invited the whole Bar to his house to expose her infidelity. On arriving, the party found the shy, petite creature quietly engaged in her household duties, and retired abashed and discomfited. But the sensitive woman did not easily recover from the shock of this extraordinary outrage. It was with difficulty she regained her equanimity sufficiently to release her lover from the closet in which he was concealed, and escape with him. She left a boy of three years to comfort her bereaved husband. The Old Man's present wife had been his cook. She was large, loyal, and aggressive.

Before he could reply, Joe Dimmick suggested with great directness that it was the "Old Man's house," and that, invoking the Divine Power, if the case were his own, he would invite whom he pleased, even if in so doing he imperiled his salvation. The Powers of Evil, he further remarked, should contend against him vainly. All this delivered with a terseness and vigor lost in this necessary translation.

"In course. Certainly. Thet's it," said the Old Man with a sympathetic frown. "Thar's no trouble about thet. It's my own house, built every stick on it myself. Don't you be afeard o' her, boys. She *may* cut up a trifle rough—ez wimmin do—but she'll come round." Secretly the Old Man trusted to the exaltation of liquor and the power of courageous example to sustain him in such an emergency.

As yet, Dick Bullen, the oracle and leader of Simpson's Bar, had not spoken. He now took his pipe from his lips. "Old Man, how's that yer Johnny gettin' on? Seems to me he didn't look so peart last time I seed him on the bluff heavin' rocks at Chinamen. Didn't seem to take much interest in it. Thar was a gang of 'em by yar yesterday—drownded out up the river—and I kinder thought o' Johnny, and how he'd miss 'em! Maybe now, we'd be in the way ef he wus sick?"

The father, evidently touched not only by this pathetic picture of Johnny's deprivation, but by the considerate delicacy of the speaker, hastened to assure him that Johnny was better, and that a "little fun might 'liven him up." Whereupon Dick arose, shook himself, and saying, "I'm ready. Lead the way, Old Man: here goes," himself led the way with a leap, a characteristic howl, and darted out into the night. As he passed through the outer room he caught up a blazing brand from the hearth. The action was repeated by the rest of the party, closely following and elbowing each other, and before the astonished proprietor of Thompson's grocery was aware of the intention of his guests, the room was deserted.

The night was pitchy dark. In the first gust of wind their temporary torches were extinguished, and only the red brands dancing and flitting in the gloom like drunken will-o'-the-wisps indicated their whereabouts. Their way led up Pine Tree Canyon, at the head of which a broad, low, bark-thatched cabin burrowed in the mountainside. It was the home of the Old Man, and the entrance to the tunnel in which he worked when he worked at all. Here the crowd paused for a moment, out of delicate deference to their host, who came up panting in the rear.

"P'r'aps ye'd better hold on a second out yer, whilst I go in and see that things is all right," said the Old Man, with an indifference he was far from feeling. The suggestion was graciously accepted, the door opened and closed on the host, and the crowd, leaning their backs against the wall and cowering under the eaves, waited and listened.

For a few moments there was no sound but the dripping of water from the eaves and the stir and rustle of wrestling boughs above them. Then the men became uneasy, and whispered suggestion and suspicion passed from the one to the other. "Reckon she's caved in his head the first lick!" "Decoyed him inter the tunnel and barred him up, likely." "Got him down and sittin' on him." "Prob'ly biling suthin' to heave on us: stand clear the door, boys!" For just then the latch clicked, the door slowly opened, and a voice said, "Come in out o' the wet."

The voice was neither that of the Old Man nor of his wife. It was the voice of a small boy, its weak treble broken by that preternatural hoarseness which only vagabondage and the habit of premature self-assertion can give. It was the face of a small boy that looked up at theirs—a face that might have been pretty, and even refined, but that it was darkened by evil knowledge from within, and dirt and hard experience from without. He had a blanket around his shoulders, and had evidently just risen from his bed. "Come in," he repeated, "and don't make no noise. The Old Man's in there talking to mar," he continued, pointing to an adjacent room which seemed to be a kitchen, from which the Old Man's voice came in deprecating accents. "Let me be," he added querulously to Dick Bullen, who had caught him up, blanket and all, and was affecting to toss him into the fire, "let go o' me, you d—d old fool, d'ye hear?"

Thus adjured, Dick Bullen lowered Johnny to the ground with a smothered laugh, while the men, entering quietly, ranged themselves around a long table of rough boards which occupied the center of the room. Johnny then gravely proceeded to a cupboard and brought out several articles, which he deposited on the table. "Thar's whiskey. And crackers. And red herons. And cheese." He took a bite of the latter on his way to the table. "And sugar." He scooped up a mouthful en route with a small and very dirty hand. "And terbacker. Thar's dried appils too on the shelf, but I don't admire 'em. Appils is swellin'. Thar," he concluded, "now wade in, and don't be afeard. *I* don't mind the old woman. She don't b'long to *me*. S'long."

He had stepped to the threshold of a small room, scarcely larger than a closet, partitioned off from the main apartment, and holding in its dim recess a small bed. He stood there a moment looking at the company, his bare feet peeping from the blanket, and nodded.

"Hello, Johnny! You ain't goin' to turn in again, are ye?" said Dick.

"Yes, I are," responded Johnny decidedly.

"Why, wot's up, old fellow?"

"I'm sick."

"How sick?"

"I've got a fevier. And childblains. And roomatiz," returned Johnny, and vanished within. After a moment's pause, he added in the dark, apparently from under the bedclothes—"And biles!"

There was an embarrassing silence. The men looked at each other and at the fire. Even with the appetizing banquet before them, it seemed as if they might again fall into the despondency of Thompson's grocery, when the voice of the Old Man, incautiously lifted, came deprecatingly from the kitchen.

"Certainly! Thet's so. In course they is. A gang o' lazy, drunken loafers, and that ar Dick Bullen's the ornariest of all. Didn't hev no more *sabe* than to come round yar with sickness in the house and no provision. Thet's what I said: 'Bullen,' sez I, 'it's crazy drunk you are, or a fool,' sez I, 'to think o' such a thing.' 'Staples,' I sez, 'be you a man, Staples, and 'spect to raise h—ll under my roof and invalids lyin' round?' But they would come—they would. Thet's wot you must 'spect o' such trash as lays round the Bar."

A burst of laughter from the men followed this unfortunate exposure. Whether it was overheard in the kitchen, or whether the Old Man's irate companion had just then exhausted all other modes of expressing her contemptuous indignation, I cannot say, but a back door was suddenly slammed with great violence. A moment later and the Old Man reap-

peared, haply unconscious of the cause of the late hilarious outburst, and smiled blandly.

"The old woman thought she'd jest run over to Mrs. MacFadden's for a sociable call," he explained with jaunty indifference, as he took a seat at the board.

Oddly enough it needed this untoward incident to relieve the embarrassment that was beginning to be felt by the party, and their natural audacity returned with their host. I do not propose to record the convivialities of that evening. The inquisitive reader will accept the statement that the conversation was characterized by the same intellectual exaltation, the same cautious reverence, the same fastidious delicacy, the same rhetorical precision, and the same logical and coherent discourse somewhat later in the evening, which distinguish similar gatherings of the masculine sex in more civilized localities and under more favorable auspices. No glasses were broken in the absence of any; no liquor was uselessly spilt on the floor or table in the scarcity of that article.

It was nearly midnight when the festivities were interrupted. "Hush," said Dick Bullen, holding up his hand. It was the querulous voice of Johnny from his adjacent closet: "O dad!"

The Old Man arose hurriedly and disappeared in the closet. Presently he reappeared. "His rheumatiz is coming on agin bad," he explained, "and he wants rubbin'." He lifted the demijohn of whiskey from the table and shook it. It was empty. Dick Bullen put down his tin cup with an embarrassed laugh. So did the others. The Old Man examined their contents and said hopefully, "I reckon that's enough; he don't need much. You hold on all o' you for a spell, and I'll be back"; and vanished in the closet with an old flannel shirt and the whiskey. The door closed but imperfectly, and the following dialogue was distinctly audible:

"Now, sonny, whar does she ache worst?"

"Sometimes over yar and sometimes under yer; but it's most powerful from yer to yer. Rub yer, dad."

A silence seemed to indicate a brisk rubbing. Then Johnny:

"Hevin' a good time out yer, dad?"

"Yes, sonny."

"Tomorrer's Chrismiss—ain't it?"

"Yes, sonny. How does she feel now?"

"Better. Rub a little furder down. Wot's Chrismiss, anyway? Wot's it all about?"

"Oh, it's a day."

This exhaustive definition was apparently satisfactory, for there was a silent interval of rubbing. Presently Johnny again:

"Mar sez that everywhere else but yer everybody gives things to everybody Chrismiss, and then she jist waded inter you. She sez thar's a man they call Sandy Claws, not a white man, you know, but a kind o' Chinemin, comes down the chimbley night afore Chrismiss and gives things to chillern—boys like me. Puts 'em in their butes! Thet's what she tried to play upon me. Easy now, pop, whar are you rubbin' to—thet's a mile from the place. She jest made that up, didn't she, jest to aggrewate me and you? Don't rub thar.... Why, dad!"

In the great quiet that seemed to have fallen upon the house the sigh of the near pines and the drip of leaves without was very distinct. Johnny's voice, too, was lowered as he went on, "Don't you take on now, for I'm gettin' all right fast. Wot's the boys doin' out thar?"

The Old Man partly opened the door and peered through. His guests were sitting there sociably enough, and there were a few silver coins and a lean buckskin purse on the table. "Bettin' on suthin'—some little game or 'nother. They're all right," he replied to Johnny, and recommenced his rubbing.

"I'd like to take a hand and win some money," said Johnny reflectively after a pause.

The Old Man glibly repeated what was evidently a familiar formula, that if Johnny would wait until he struck it rich in the tunnel he'd have lots of money, etc., etc.

"Yes," said Johnny, "but you don't. And whether you strike it or I win it, it's about the same. It's all luck. But it's mighty cur'o's about Chrismiss—ain't it? Why do they call it Chrismiss?"

Perhaps from some instinctive deference to the overhearing of his guests, or from some vague sense of incongruity, the Old Man's reply was so low as to be inaudible beyond the room.

"Yes," said Johnny, with some slight abatement of interest, "I've heard o' *him* before. Thar, that'll do, dad. I don't ache near so bad as I did. Now wrap me tight in this yer blanket. So. Now," he added in a muffled whisper, "sit down yer by me till I go asleep." To assure himself of obedience, he disengaged one hand from the blanket, and grasping his father's sleeve, again composed himself to rest.

For some moments the Old Man waited patiently. Then the unwonted stillness of the house excited his curiosity, and without moving from the bed he cautiously opened the door with his disengaged hand, and looked into the main room. To his infinite surprise it was dark and deserted. But even then a smoldering log on the hearth broke, and by the upspringing blaze he saw the figure of Dick Bullen sitting by the dying embers.

"Hello!"

Dick started, rose, and came somewhat unsteadily toward him.

"Whar's the boys?" said the Old Man.

"Gone up the canyon on a little *pasear*. They're coming back for me in a minit. I'm waitin' round for 'em. What are you starin' at, Old Man?" he added, with a forced laugh; "do you think I'm drunk?"

The Old Man might have been pardoned the supposition, for Dick's eyes were humid and his face flushed. He loitered and lounged back to the chimney, yawned, shook himself, buttoned up his coat, and laughed. "Liquor ain't so plenty as that, Old Man. Now don't you get up," he continued, as the Old Man made a movment to release his sleeve from Johnny's hand. "Don't you mind manners. Sit jest whar you be; I'm goin' in a jiffy. Thar, that's them now."

There was a low tap at the door. Dick Bullen opened it quickly, nodded "good night" to his host, and disappeared. The Old Man would have followed him but for the hand that still unconsciously grasped his sleeve. He could have easily disengaged it: it was small, weak, and emaciated. But perhaps because it *was* small, weak, and emaciated he changed his mind, and drawing his chair closer to the bed, rested his head upon it. In this defenseless attitude the potency of his earlier potations surprised him. The room flickered and faded before his eyes, reappeared, faded again, went out, and left him—asleep.

Meantime Dick Bullen, closing the door, confronted his companions. "Are you ready?" said Staples. "Ready," said Dick; "what's the time?" "Past twelve," was the reply; "can you make it?—it's nigh on fifty miles, the round trip hither and yon." "I reckon," returned Dick shortly. "Whar's the mare?" "Bill and Jack's holdin' her at the crossin'." "Let 'em hold on a minit longer," said Dick.

He turned and re-entered the house softly. By the light of the guttering candle and dying fire he saw that the door of the little room was open. He stepped toward it on tiptoe and looked in. The Old Man had fallen back in his chair, snoring, his helpless feet thrust out in a line with his collapsed shoulders, and his hat pulled over his eyes. Beside him, on a narrow wooden bedstead, lay Johnny, muffled tightly in a blanket that hid all save a strip of forehead and a few curls damp with perspiration. Dick Bullen made a step forward, hesitated, and glanced over his shoulder into the deserted room. Everything was quiet. With a sudden resolution he parted his huge mustaches with both hands and stooped over the sleeping boy. But even as he did so a mischievous blast, lying in wait, swooped down the chimney, rekindled the hearth, and lit up the room with a shameless glow from which Dick fled in bashful terror.

His companions were already waiting for him at the crossing. Two of them were struggling in the darkness with some strange misshapen bulk, which as Dick came nearer took the semblance of a great yellow horse.

It was the mare. She was not a pretty picture. From her Roman nose to her rising haunches, from her arched spine hidden by the stiff *machillas* of a Mexican saddle, to her thick, straight bony legs, there was not a line of equine grace. In her half-blind but wholly vicious white eyes, in her protruding underlip, in her monstrous color, there was nothing but ugliness and vice.

"Now then," said Staples, "stand cl'ar of her heels, boys, and up with you. Don't miss your first holt of her mane, and mind ye get your off stirrup *quick*. Ready!"

There was a leap, a scrambling struggle, a bound, a wild retreat of the crowd, a circle of flying hoofs, two springless leaps that jarred the earth, a rapid play and jingle of spurs, a plunge, and then the voice of Dick somewhere in the darkness. "All right!"

"Don't take the lower road back unless you're hard pushed for time! Don't hold her in downhill! We'll be at the ford at five. G'lang! Hoopa! Mula! GO!"

A splash, a spark struck from the ledge in the road, a clatter in the rocky cut beyond, and Dick was gone.

Sing, O Muse, the ride of Richard Bullen! Sing, O Muse, of chivalrous men! the sacred quest, the doughty deeds, the battery of low churls, the fearsome ride and gruesome perils of the Flower of Simpson's Bar! Alack! she is dainty, this Muse! She will have none of this bucking brute and swaggering, ragged rider, and I must fain follow him in prose, afoot!

It was one o'clock, and yet he had only gained Rattlesnake Hill. For in that time Jovita had rehearsed to him all her imperfections and practiced all her vices. Thrice had she stumbled. Twice had she thrown up her Roman nose in a straight line with the reins, and resisting bit and spur, struck out madly across country. Twice had she reared, and rearing, fallen backward; and twice had the agile Dick, unharmed, regained his seat before she found her vicious legs again. And a mile beyond them, at the foot of a long hill, was Rattlesnake Creek. Dick knew that here was the crucial test of his ability to perform his enterprise, set his teeth grimly, put his knees well into her flanks, and changed his defensive tactics to brisk aggression. Bullied and maddened, Jovita began the descent of the hill. Here the artful Richard pretended to hold her in with ostentatious objurgation and well-feigned cries of alarm. It is unnecessary to add that Jovita instantly ran away. Nor need I state the time made in the descent; it is written in the chronicles of Simpson's Bar. Enough that in another moment, as it seemed to Dick, she was splashing on the overflowed banks of Rattlesnake Creek. As Dick expected, the momentum she had acquired carried her beyond the point of balking, and holding her well together for a mighty leap, they dashed into the middle of the swiftly flowing current. A few moments of kicking, wading, and swimming, and Dick drew a long breath on the opposite bank.

The road from Rattlesnake Creek to Red Mountain was tolerably level. Either the plunge in Rattlesnake Creek had dampened her baleful fire, or the art which led to it had shown her the superior wickedness of her rider, for Jovita no longer wasted her surplus energy in wanton conceits. Once she bucked, but it was from force of habit; once she shied, but it was from a new, freshly painted meetinghouse at the crossing of the county road. Hollows, ditches, gravelly deposits, patches of freshly springing grasses, flew from beneath her rattling hoofs. She began to smell unpleasantly, once or twice she coughed slightly, but there was no abatement of her strength or speed. By two o'clock he had passed Red Mountain and begun the descent to the plain. Ten minutes later the driver of the fast Pioneer coach was overtaken and passed by a "man on a pinto hoss"—an event sufficiently notable for remark. At half-past two Dick rose in his stirrups with a great shout. Stars were glittering through the rifted clouds, and beyond him, out of the plain, rose two spires, a flagstaff, and a straggling line of black objects. Dick jingled his spurs and swung his *riata,* Jovita bounded forward, and in another moment they swept into Tuttleville, and drew up before the wooden piazza of "The Hotel of All Nations."

What transpired that night at Tuttleville is not strictly a part of this record. Briefly I may state, however, that after Jovita had been handed over to a sleepy ostler, whom she at once kicked into unpleasant consciousness, Dick sallied out with the barkeeper for a tour of the sleeping town. Lights still gleamed from a few saloons and gambling houses; but avoiding these, they stopped before several closed shops, and by persistent tapping and judicious outcry roused the proprietors from their beds, and made them unbar the doors of their magazines and expose their wares. Sometimes they were met by curses, but oftener by interest and some concern in their needs, and the interview was invariably concluded by a drink. It was three o'clock before this pleasantry was given over, and with a small waterproof bag of India rubber strapped on his shoulders, Dick returned to the hotel. But here he was waylaid by Beauty—Beauty opulent in charms, affluent in dress, persuasive in speech, and Spanish in accent! In vain she repeated the invitation in "Excelsior," happily scorned by all Alpine-climbing youth, and rejected by this child of the Sierras—a rejection softened in this instance by a laugh and his last gold coin. And then he sprang to the saddle and dashed down the lonely street and out into the lonelier plain, where presently the lights, the black line of houses, the spires, and the flagstaff sank into the earth behind him again and were lost in the distance.

The storm had cleared away, the air was brisk and cold, the outlines of adjacent landmarks were distinct, but it was half-past four before Dick reached the meetinghouse and the crossing of the county road. To avoid the rising grade he had taken a longer and more circuitous road, in whose viscid mud Jovita sank fetlock deep at every bound. It was a poor preparation for a steady ascent of five miles more; but Jovita, gathering her legs under her, took it with her usual blind, unreasoning fury, and a half-hour later reached the long level that led to Rattlesnake Creek. Another half-hour would bring him to the creek. He threw the reins lightly upon the neck of the mare, chirruped to her, and began to sing.

Suddenly Jovita shied with a bound that would have unseated a less practiced rider. Hanging to her rein was a figure that had leaped from the bank, and at the same time from the road before her arose a shadowy horse and rider.

"Throw up your hands," commanded the second apparition, with an oath.

Dick felt the mare tremble, quiver, and apparently sink under him. He knew what it meant and was prepared.

"Stand aside, Jack Simpson. I know you, you d—d thief! Let me pass, or—"

He did not finish the sentence. Jovita rose straight in the air with a terrific bound, throwing the figure from her bit with a single shake of her vicious head, and charged with deadly malevolence down on the impediment before her. An oath, a pistol shot, horse and highwayman rolled over in the road, and the next moment Jovita was a hundred yards away. But the good right arm of her rider, shattered by a bullet, dropped helplessly at his side.

Without slacking his speed he shifted the reins to his left hand. But a few moments later he was obliged to halt and tighten the saddle girths that had slipped in the onset. This in his crippled condition took some time. He had no fear of pursuit, but looking up he saw that the eastern stars were already paling, and that the distant peaks had lost their ghostly whiteness and now stood out blackly against a lighter sky. Day was upon him. Then completely absorbed in a single idea, he forgot the pain of his wound, and mounting again dashed on toward Rattlesnake Creek. But now Jovita's breath came broken by gasps, Dick reeled in his saddle, and brighter and brighter grew the sky.

Ride, Richard; run, Jovita; linger, O day!

For the last few rods there was a roaring in his ears. Was it exhaustion from loss of blood, or what? He was dazed and giddy as he swept down the hill, and did not recognize his surroundings. Had he taken the wrong road, or was this Rattlesnake Creek?

It was. But the brawling creek he had swum a few hours before had risen, more than doubled its volume, and now rolled a swift and resistless river between him and Rattlesnake Hill. For the first time that night Richard's heart sank within him. The river, the mountain, the quickening east, swam before his eyes. He shut them to recover his self-control. In that brief interval, by some fantastic mental process, the little room at Simpson's Bar and the figures of the sleeping father and son rose upon him. He opened his eyes wildly, cast off his coat, pistol, boots, and saddle, bound his precious pack tightly to his shoulders, grasped the bare flanks of Jovita with his bared knees, and with a shout dashed into the yellow water. A cry rose from the opposite bank as the head of a man and horse struggled for a few moments against the battling current, and then were swept away amidst uprooted trees and whirling driftwood.

The Old Man started and woke. The fire on the hearth was dead, the candle in the outer room flickering in its socket, and somebody was rapping at the door. He opened it, but fell back with a cry before the dripping, half-naked figure that reeled against the doorpost.

"Dick?"

"Hush! Is he awake yet?"

"No; but, Dick—"

"Dry up, you old fool! Get me some whiskey, *quick!*" The Old Man flew and returned with—an empty bottle! Dick would have sworn, but his strength was not equal to the occasion. He staggered, caught at the handle of the door, and motioned to the Old Man.

"Thar's suthin' in my pack yer for Johnny. Take it off. I can't."

The Old Man unstrapped the pack, and laid it before the exhausted man.

"Open it, quick."

He did so with trembling fingers. It contained only a few poor toys—cheap and barbaric enough, goodness knows, but bright with paint and tinsel. One of them was broken; another, I fear, was irretrievably ruined by water, and on the third—ah me! there was a cruel spot.

"It don't look like much, that's a fact," said Dick ruefully. . . ."But it's the best we could do. . . . Take 'em, Old Man, and put 'em in his stocking, and tell him—tell him, you know—hold me, Old Man—" The Old Man caught at his sinking figure. "Tell him," said Dick, with a weak little laugh—"tell him Sandy Claus has come."

And even so, bedraggled, ragged, unshaven and unshorn, with one arm hanging helplessly at his side, Santa Claus came to Simpson's Bar and fell fainting on the first threshold. The Christmas dawn came slowly after, touching the remoter peaks with the rosy warmth of ineffable love. And it looked so tenderly on Simpson's Bar that the whole mountain, as if caught in a generous action, blushed to the skies.

GIFTS OF THE MAGI

O. HENRY

Title and story as they appeared originally in the New York World

One dollar and eighty-seven cents. That was all. And 60 cents of it was in pennies. Pennies saved one and two at a time by bull-dozing the grocer and the vegetable man and the butcher until one's cheeks burned with the silent imputation of parsimony that such close dealing implied. Three times Della counted it. One dollar and eighty-seven cents. And the next day would be Christmas.

There was clearly nothing to do but flop down on the shabby little couch and howl. So Della did it. Which instigates the moral reflection that life is made up of sobs, sniffles and smiles, with sniffles predominating.

While the mistress of the home is gradually subsiding from the first stage to the second take a look at the home. A furnished flat at $8 per week. It did not exactly beggar description, but it certainly had that word on the lookout for the mendicancy squad.

In the vestibule below belonged to this flat a letter-box into which no letter would go, and an electric button from which no mortal finger could coax a ring. Also appertaining thereunto was a card bearing the name "Mr. James Dillingham Young."

The "Dillingham" had been flung to the breeze during a former period of prosperity when its possessor was being paid $30 per week. Now, when the income was shrunk to $20, the letters of "Dillingham" looked blurred, as though they were thinking seriously of contracting to a modest and unassuming D. But whenever Mr. James Dillingham Young came home and reached his flat above he was called "Jim" and greatly hugged by Mrs. James Dillingham Young, already introduced to you as Della. Which is all very good.

Della finished her cry and attended to her cheeks with the powder rag. She stood by the window and looked out dully at a gray cat walking a gray fence in a gray backyard. Tomorrow would be Christmas Day, and she had ony $1.87 with which to buy Jim a present. She had been saving every penny she could for months, with this result. Twenty dollars a week doesn't go far. Expenses had been greater than she had calculated. They always are. Only $1.87 to buy a present for Jim. Her Jim. Many a happy hour she had spent planning for something nice for him. Something fine and rare and sterling—something just a little bit near to being worthy of the honor of being owned by Jim.

There was a pier-glass between the windows of the room. Perhaps you have seen a pier-glass in an $8 flat. A very thin and very agile person may, by observing his reflection in a rapid sequence of longitudinal strips, obtain a fairly accurate conception of his looks. Della, being slender, had mastered the art.

Suddenly she whirled from the window and stood before the glass. Her eyes were shining brilliantly, but her face had lost its color within twenty seconds. Rapidly she pulled down her hair and let it fall to its full length.

Now, there were two possessions of the James Dillingham Youngs in which they both took a mighty pride. One was Jim's gold watch that had been his father's and his grandfather's. The other was Della's hair. Had the Queen of Sheba lived in the flat across the airshaft Della would have let her hair hang out the window some day to dry and mocked at Her Majesty's jewels and gifts. Had King Solomon been the janitor, with all his treasures piled up in the basement, Jim would have pulled out his watch every time he passed, just to see him pluck at his beard from envy.

So now Della's beautiful hair fell about her, rippling and shining like a cascade of brown waters. It reached below her knee and made itself almost a garment for her. And then she did it up again nervously and quickly. Once she faltered for a minute and stood still while a tear or two splashed on the worn red carpet.

On went her old brown jacket; on went her old brown hat. With a whirl of skirts and with the brilliant sparkle still in her eyes, she fluttered out the door and down the stairs to the street.

Where she stopped the sign read: "Mme. Sofronie. Hair Goods of All Kinds." One flight up Della ran, and collected herself, panting, before Madame, large, too white, chilly and hardly looking the "Sofronie."

"Will you buy my hair?" asked Della.

"I buy hair," said Madame. "Take yer hat off and let's have a sight at the looks of it."

Down rippled the brown cascade.

"Twenty dollars," said Madame, lifting the mass with a practised hand.

"Give it to me quick," said Della.

Oh, and the next two hours tripped by on rosy wings. Forget the hashed metaphor. She was ransacking the stores for Jim's present.

She found it at last. It surely had been made for Jim and no one else. There was none other like it in any of the stores, and she had turned all of them inside out. It was a platinum fob chain simple and chaste in design, properly proclaiming its value by substance alone and not by meretricious ornamentation—as all good things should do. It was even worthy of The Watch. As soon as she saw it she knew that it must be Jim's. It was like him. Quietness and value—the description applied to both. Twenty-one dollars they took from her for it, and she hurried home with the 87 cents. With that chain on his watch Jim might be properly anxious about the time in any company. Grand as the watch was, he sometimes looked at it on the sly on account of the old leather strap that he used in place of a chain.

When Della reached home her intoxication gave way a little to prudence and reason. She got out her curling irons and lighted the gas and went to work repairing the ravages made by generosity added to love. Which is always a tremendous task, dear friends—a mammoth task.

Within forty minutes her head was covered with tiny, close-lying curls that made her look wonderfully like a truant schoolboy. She looked at her reflection in the mirror long, carefully and critically.

"If Jim doesn't kill me," she said to herself, "before he takes a second look at me, he'll say I look like a Coney Island chorus girl. But what could I do—oh, what could I do with a dollar and eighty-seven cents!"

At 7 o'clock the coffee was made and the frying pan was on the back of the stove hot and ready to cook the chops.

Jim was never late. Della doubled the fob chain in her hand and sat on the corner of the table near the door that he always entered. Then she heard his step on the stair away down on the first flight, and she turned white for just a moment. She had a habit of saying little silent prayers about the simplest everyday things, and now she whispered: "Please, God, make him think I am still pretty."

The door opened and Jim stepped in and closed it. He looked thin and very serious. Poor fellow, he was only twenty-two—and to be burdened with a family! He needed a new overcoat and he was without gloves.

Jim stopped inside the door, as immovable as a setter at the scent of quail. His eyes were fixed upon Della, and there was an expression in them that she could not read, and it terrified her. It was not anger, nor surprise, nor disapproval, nor horror, nor any of the sentiments that she had been prepared for. He simply stared at her fixedly with that peculiar expression on his face.

Della wriggled off the table and went for him.

"Jim, darling," she cried, "don't look at me that way. I had my hair cut off and sold it because I couldn't have lived through Christmas without giving you a present. It'll grow again—you won't mind, will you? I just had to do it. My hair grows awfully fast. Say 'Merry Christmas!' Jim, and let's be happy. You don't know what a nice—what a beautiful, nice gift I've got for you."

"You've cut off your hair?" asked Jim, laboriously, as if he had not arrived at that patent fact yet even after the hardest mental labor.

"Cut if off and sold it," said Della. "Don't you like me just as well, anyhow? I'm me without my hair, ain't I?"

Jim looked about the room curiously.

"You say your hair is gone?" he said, with an air almost of idiocy.

"You needn't look for it," said Della. "It's sold, I tell you—sold and gone too. It's Christmas Eve, boy. Be good to me, for it went for you. Maybe the hairs of my head were numbered," she went on with a sudden serious sweetness, "but nobody could ever count my love for you. Shall I put the chops on, Jim?"

Out of his trance Jim seemed to quickly wake. He enfolded his Della. For ten seconds let us regard with discreet scrutiny some inconsequential object in the other direction. Eight dollars a week or a million a year—what is the difference? A mathematician or a wit would give you the wrong answer. The magi brought valuable gifts, but that was not among them. This dark assertion will be illuminated later on.

Jim drew a package from his overcoat pocket and threw it upon the table.

"Don't make any mistake, Dell," he said, "about me. I don't think there's anything in the way of a haircut or a shave or a shampoo that could make me like my girl any less. But if you'll unwrap that package you may see why you had me going awhile at first."

White fingers and nimble tore at the string and paper. And then an ecstatic scream of joy; and then alas! a quick feminine change to hysterical tears and wails, necessitating the immediate employment of all the comforting powers of the lord of the flat.

For there lay The Combs—the set of combs, side and back, that Della had worshipped for long in a Broadway window. Beautiful combs, pure tortoise shell, with jewelled rims—just the shade to wear in the beautiful vanished hair. They were expensive combs, she knew, and her heart had simply craved and yearned over them without the least hope of possession. And now, they were hers, but the tresses that should have adorned the coveted adornments were gone.

But she hugged them to her bosom, and at length she was able to look up with dim eyes and a smile and say: "My hair grows so fast, Jim!"

And then Della leaped up like a little singed cat and cried, "Oh, oh!"

Jim had not yet seen his beautiful present. She held it out to him eagerly upon her open palm. The dull, precious metal seemed to flash with a reflection of her bright and ardent spirit.

"Isn't it a dandy, Jim? I hunted all over town to find it. You'll have to look at the time a hundred times a day now. Give me your watch. I want to see how it looks on it."

Instead of obeying, Jim tumbled down on the couch and put his hands under the back of his head and smiled.

"Dell," said he, "let's put our Christmas presents away and keep 'em a while. They're too nice to use just at present. I sold the watch to get the money to buy your combs. And now suppose you put the chops on."

The magi, as you know, were wise men—wonderfully wise men—who brought gifts to the Babe in the manger. They invented the art of giving Christmas gifts. Being wise, their gifts were no doubt wise ones, possibly bearing the privilege of exchange in case of duplication. And here I have lamely related to you the uneventful chronicle of two foolish children in a flat who most unwisely sacrificed for each other the greatest treasures of their house. But in a last word to the wise of these days let it be said that of all who give gifts these two were of the wisest. Of all who give and receive gifts, such as they are wisest. Everywhere they are wisest. They are the magi.

CEREMONIES FOR CANDELMAS

ROBERT HERRICK

from *HESPERIDES,* 1648

Down with the rosemary and bays,
   Down with the mistletoe;
Instead of holly, now up-raise
   The green box, for show.

The holly hitherto did sway;
   Let box now domineer;
Until the dancing Easter-day,
   On Easter's eve appear.

Then youthful box, which now hath grace,
   Your houses to renew;
Grown old, surrender must his place,
   Unto the crispèd yew.

When yew is out, then birch comes in,
   And many flowers beside;
Both of a fresh and fragrant kin
   To honor Whitsuntide.

Green rushes then, and sweetest bents,
   With cooler oaken boughs,
Come in for comely ornaments
   To re-adorn the house.

Thus times do shift; each thing his turn does hold;
New things succeed, as former things grow old.

* * *

Down with the rosemary, and so
Down with the bays and mistletoe;
Down with the holly, ivy, all,
Wherewith ye dressed the Christmas Hall:
That so the superstitious find
No one least branch there left behind:
For look how many leaves there be
Neglected, there (maids, trust to me)
So many goblins you shall see.

On Lending a Punch-Bowl

OLIVER WENDELL HOLMES

This ancient silver bowl of mine, it tells of good old times,
Of joyous days and jolly nights, and merry Christmas times;
They were a free and jovial race, but honest, brave, and true,
Who dipped their ladle in the punch when this old bowl was new.

A Spanish galleon brought the bar,—so runs the ancient tale;
'Twas hammered by an Antwerp smith, whose arm was like a flail;
And now and then between the strokes, for fear his strength should fail,
He wiped his brow and quaffed a cup of good old Flemish ale.

'Twas purchased by an English squire to please his loving dame,
Who saw the cherubs, and conceived a longing for the same;
And oft as on the ancient stock another twig was found,
'Twas filled with candle spiced and hot, and handed smoking round.

But, changing hands, it reached at length a Puritan divine,
Who used to follow Timothy, and take a little wine,
But hated punch and prelacy; and so it was, perhaps,
He went to Leyden, where he found conventicles and schnapps.

And then, of course, you know what's next: it left the Dutchman's
    shore
With those that in the Mayflower came,—a hundred souls and more,—
Along with all the furniture, to fill their new abodes,—
To judge by what is still on hand, at least a hundred loads.

'Twas on a dreary winter's eve, the night was closing dim,
When brave Miles Standish took the bowl, and filled it to the brim;
The little Captain stood and stirred the posset with his sword,
And all his sturdy men-at-arms were ranged about the board.

He poured the fiery Hollands in,—the man that never feared,—
He took a long and solemn draught, and wiped his yellow beard;
And one by one the musketeers—the men that fought and prayed—
All drank as 'twere their mother's milk, and not a man afraid.

That night, affrighted from his nest, the screaming eagle flew.
He heard the Pequot's ringing whoop, the soldier's wild halloo;
And there the sachem learned the rule he taught to kith and kin,
"Run from the white man when you find he smells of Hollands gin!"

A hundred years, and fifty more, had spread their leaves and snows,
A thousand rubs had flattened down each little cherub's nose,
When once again the bowl was filled, but not in mirth or joy,—
'Twas mingled by a mother's hand to cheer her parting boy.

Drink, John, she said, 'twill do you good,—poor child, you'll never
    bear
This working in the dismal trench, out in the midnight air;
And if—God bless me!—you were hurt, 'twould keep away the chill.
So John *did* drink,—and well he wrought that night at Bunker's Hill!

I tell you, there was generous warmth in good old English cheer;
I tell you, 'twas a pleasant thought to bring its symbol here.
'Tis but the fool that loves excess; hast thou a drunken soul?

THE INEXHAUSTIBILITY OF THE SUBJECT OF CHRISTMAS

LEIGH HUNT

So many things have been said of late years about Christmas, that it is supposed by some there is no saying more. Oh, they of little faith! What? Do they suppose that everything has been said that *can* be said, about any one Christmas thing?

About beef, for instance
About plum-pudding
About mince-pie
About holly
About ivy
About rosemary
About mistletoe (Good God! what an immense
number of things need to be said about mistletoe!)
About Christmas Eve
About hunt-the-slipper
About hot cockles
About blind-man's-buff
About shoeing-the-wild-mare
About thread-the-needle
About he-can-do-little-that-can't-do-this
About puss-in-the-corner
About snapdragon
About forfeits
About Miss Smith
About the bell-man
About the waits

About chilblains
About carols
About the fire
About the block on it
About schoolboys
About their mothers
About Christmas boxes
About turkeys
About Hogmanay
About goose-pie
About mumming
About saluting the apple-trees
About brawn
About plum-porridge
About hobby-horse
About hoppings
About wakes
About "feed-the-dove"
About hackins
About Yule doughs
About going-a-gooding
About loaf-stealing
About julklaps (Who has exhausted that subject,
   we should like to know?)
About wad-shooting
About elder wine
About pantomimes
About cards
About New-Year's day
About gifts
About wassail
About twelfth-cake
About king and queen
About characters
About eating too much
About aldermen
About the doctor
About all being in the wrong
About charity
About all being in the right
About Faith, Hope and Endeavour
About the Greatest Plum-pudding for the Greatest Number?

New-Fashioned Christmas

Aldous Huxley

The name is still the same; but the thing is almost unrecognizably different from what Charles Dickens meant by 'Christmas.' For example, there was no tree at Dingley Dell, and, except for five shillings to Sam Weller, not a single present was given. Christmas, for Mr. Pickwick and his friends, was an affair of copious eating and still more copious drinking, interrupted by bouts of home-made fun and purely domestic horseplay.

For us, three generations later, the word connotes the Prince Consort's imported Teutonic evergreen; connotes all those endless presents, which it is such a burden to buy and such an embarrassment to receive; connotes restaurants, dance halls, theatres, cabarets—all the highly organized, professional entertainments provided by the astute business men who run the amusement industry. Only the name connects the new-fashioned Christmas with the Pickwickian festival.

The tree, of course, was a mere accident. If Queen Victoria had married a Frenchman we should probably be giving one another *étrennes* and ushering in the year with a series of calls on the most remote and the most personally antipathetic of our innumerable relations. (Relations, in France, *are* innumerable.) As it was, she took to herself a prince from the land of tannenbaums. It is therefore to a tannenbaum's green branches, and upon Christmas Day, that we attach our gifts.

The tree, I repeat, was an accident, a thing outside the realm of determinism, a product of personal idiosyncrasy. But all the other changes in our Christmas habits, which have taken place since Dickens wrote of Dingley Dell, are the results of great impersonal processes. During

Dickens's lifetime, and still more rapidly after his death, industrial production enormously and continuously increased. But production cannot increase unless there is a corresponding increase in consumption. It became necessary to stimulate consumption, to provide the home public with reasons, or, better still, with compelling unreasons, for consuming. Hence the rise of advertisement, and hence the gradual and, as time went on, the more and more deliberate canalization into industrially profitable channels of all such common human impulses and emotions as lent themselves to the process.

The producer who succeeds in thus canalizing some universal human urge opens up for himself and his successors an inexhaustible gold mine. Thus, art and industry have flourished from time immemorial in the rich soil of bereavement and the fear of death. Weddings have been almost as profitable to commerce as funerals, and within the last few years an American man of genius has discovered how even filial affection may be made a justification for increased consumption; the florists and candy manufacturers of the United States have reason to bless the inventor of Mother's Day.

The love of excitement is as deeply planted in human nature as the love of a mother; the desire for change, for novelty, for a relief from the monotony of every day, as strong as sexual desire or the terror of death. Men have instituted festivals and holidays to satisfy these cravings. Mr. Pickwick's Christmas was a typical feast day of the old style—a time of jollification and excitement, a gaudily glittering 'captain jewel in the carcanet' of grey, uneventful days. Psychologically, it performed its function. Not economically, however—that is, so far as *we* are concerned. The Pickwickian Christmas did very little to stimulate consumption; it was mainly a gratuitous festivity. A few vintners and distillers and poulterers were the only people whom it greatly profited financially. This was a state of things which an ever-increasingly efficient industrialism could not possibly afford to tolerate. Christmas, accordingly, was canalized. The deep festal impulse of man was harnessed and made to turn a very respectable little wheel in the mills of industry. To-day Christmas is an important economic event. The distributors of goods spend large sums in advertising potential gifts, and (since the man who pays the piper calls the tune) the newspapers reinforce their advertisements by fostering a notion that the mutual goodwill of modern Christians can be expressed only by the exchange of manufactured articles.

The last thirty years have witnessed the promotion of innkeeping and showmanship to the rank of major commercial enterprises. Major commercial enterprises spend money on advertising. Therefore, newspapers are always suggesting that a good time can be enjoyed only by those who take what is offered them by entertainment manufacturers. The Dickensian Christmas-at-Home receives only perfunctory lip-service from a press which draws a steady income from the catering and amusement trades. Home-made fun is gratuitous, and gratuitousness is something which an industrialized world cannot afford to tolerate.

CHRISTMAS EVE

WASHINGTON IRVING

from THE SKETCH BOOK

I t was a brilliant moonlight night, but extremely cold; our chaise whirled rapidly over the frozen ground; the post-boy smacked his whip incessantly, and a part of the time his horses were on a gallop. "He knows where he is going," said my companion, laughing, "and is eager to arrive in time for some of the merriment and good cheer of the servants' hall. My father, you must know, is a bigoted devotee of the old school, and prides himself upon keeping up something of old English hospitality. He is a tolerable specimen of what you will rarely meet with nowadays in its purity, the old English country gentleman; for our men of fortune spend so much of their time in town, and fashion is carried so much into the country, that the strong rich peculiarities of ancient rural life are almost polished away. My father, however, from early years, took honest Peacham for his text book, instead of Chesterfield: he determined, in his own mind, that there was no condition more truly honourable and enviable than that of a country gentleman on his paternal lands, and, therefore, passes the whole of his time on his estate. He is a strenuous advocate for the revival of the old rural games and holiday observances, and is deeply read in the writers, ancient and modern, who have treated on the subject. Indeed, his favourite range of reading is among the authors who flourished at least two centuries since; who, he insists, wrote and thought more like true Englishmen than any of their successors. He even regrets sometimes that he had not been born a few centuries earlier, when England was itself, and had its peculiar manners and customs. As he lives at some distance from the main road, in rather a lonely part of the country, without any rival gentry near him, he has that most enviable of all blessings to an Englishman, an opportunity of indulging the bent of his own humour without molestation. Being representative of the oldest family in the neighbourhood, and a great part of the peasantry being his tenants, he is much looked up to and, in general, is known simply by the appellation of 'The Squire'; a title which has been accorded to the head of the family since time immemorial. I think it best to give you these hints about my worthy old father, to prepare you for any little eccentricities that might otherwise appear absurd."

We had passed for some time along the wall of a park, and at length the chaise stopped at the gate. It was in a heavy magnificent old style, of iron bars, fancifully wrought at top into flourishes and flowers. The huge square columns that supported the gate were surmounted by the family crest. Close adjoining was the porter's lodge, sheltered under dark fir-trees, and almost buried in shrubbery.

The post-boy rang a large porter's bell, which resounded through the still frosty air, and was answered by the distant barking of dogs, with which the mansion-house seemed garrisoned. An old woman immediately appeared at the gate. As the moonlight fell strongly upon her, I had a full view of a little primitive dame, dressed very much in the antique taste, with a neat kerchief and stomacher, and her silver hair peeping from under a cap of snowy whiteness. She came curtseying forth, with many expressions of simple joy at seeing her young master. Her husband, it seems, was up at the house keeping Christmas eve in the servants' hall; they could not do without him, as he was the best hand at a song and story in the household.

My friend proposed that we should alight and walk through the park to the hall, which was at no great distance, while the chaise should follow on. Our road wound through a noble avenue of trees, among the naked branches of which the moon glittered as she rolled through the deep vault of a cloudless sky. The lawn beyond was sheeted with a slight covering of snow, which here and there sparkled as the moonbeams caught a frosty crystal; and at a distance might be seen a thin transparent vapour, stealing up from the low grounds, and threatening gradually to shroud the landscape.

My companion looked round him with transport:—"How often," said he, "have I scampered up this avenue, on returning home on school vacations! How often have I played under these trees when a boy! I feel a degree of filial reverence for them, as we look up to those who have cherished us in childhood. My father was always scrupulous in exacting our holidays, and having us around him on family festivals. He used to direct and superintend our games with the strictness that some parents do the studies of their children. He was very particular that we should play the old English games according to their original form; and consulted old books for precedent and authority for every 'merrie disport'; yet I assure you there never was pedantry so delightful. It was the policy of the good old gentleman to make his children feel that home was the happiest place in the world; and I value this delicious home-feeling as one of the choicest gifts a parent can bestow."

We were interrupted by a clangour of a troop of dogs of all sorts and sizes, "mongrel, puppy, whelp and hound, and curs of low degree," that, disturbed by the ringing of the porter's bell, and the rattling of the chaise, came bounding, open-mouthed, across the lawn.

—"The little dogs and all,
Tray, Blanch, and Sweetheart—see they bark at me!"

cried Bracebridge, laughing. At the sound of his voice the bark was changed into a yelp of delight, and in a moment he was surrounded and almost overpowered by the caresses of the faithful animals.

We had now come in full view of the old family mansion, partly thrown in deep shadow, and partly lit up by the cold moonshine. It was an irregular building of some magnitude, and seemed to be of the architecture of different periods. One wing was evidently very ancient, with heavy stone-shafted bow windows jutting out and overrun with ivy, from among the foliage of which the small diamond-shaped panes of glass glittered with the moonbeams. The rest of the house was in the French taste of Charles the Second's time, having been repaired and altered, as my friend told me, by one of his ancestors, who returned with that monarch at the Restoration. The grounds about the house were laid out in the old formal manner of artificial flower-beds, clipped shrubberies, raised terraces, and heavy stone balustrades, ornamented with urns, a leaden statue or two, and a jet of water. The old gentleman, I was told, was extremely careful to preserve this obsolete finery in all its original state. He admired this fashion in gardening; it had an air of magnificence, was courtly and noble, and befitting good old family style. The boasted imitation of nature in modern gardening had sprung up with modern republican notions, but did not suit a monarchical government; it smacked of the levelling system.—I could not help smiling at this introduction of politics into gardening, though I expressed some apprehension that I should find the old gentleman rather intolerant in his creed.—Frank assured me, however, that it was almost the only instance in which he had ever heard his father meddle with politics; and he believed that he had got this notion from a member of parliament who once passed a few weeks with him. The Squire was glad of any argument to defend his clipped yew-trees and formal terraces, which had been occasionally attacked by modern landscape-gardeners.

As we approached the house, we heard the sound of music, and now and then a burst of laughter from one end of the building. This, Bracebridge said, must proceed from the servants' hall, where a great deal of revelry was permitted, and even encouraged, by the Squire throughout

the twelve days of Christmas, provided everything was done conformably to ancient usage. Here were kept up the old games of hoodman blind, shoe the wild mare, hot cockles, steal the white loaf, bob apple, and snap-dragon: the Yule log and Christmas candle were regularly burnt, and the mistletoe, with its white berries, hung up to the imminent peril of all the pretty housemaids.

So intent were the servants upon their sports, that we had to ring repeatedly before we could make ourselves heard. On our arrival being announced, the Squire came out to receive us, accompanied by his two other sons; one a young officer in the army, home on leave of absence; the other an Oxonian, just from the university. The Squire was a fine, healthy-looking old gentleman, with silver hair curling lightly round an open florid countenance; in which a physiognomist, with the advantage, like myself, of a previous hint or two, might discover a singular mixture of whim and benevolence.

The family meeting was warm and affectionate; as the evening was far advanced, the Squire would not permit us to change our travelling dresses, but ushered us at once to the company, which was assembled in a large old-fashioned hall. It was composed of different branches of a numerous family connection, where there were the usual proportion of old uncles and aunts, comfortably married dames, superannuated spinsters, blooming country cousins, half-fledged striplings, and bright-eyed boarding-school hoydens. They were variously occupied; some at a round game of cards; others conversing around the fireplace; at one end of the hall was a group of the young folks, some nearly grown up, others of a more tender and budding age, fully engrossed by a merry game; and a profusion of wooden horses, penny trumpets, and tattered dolls, about the floor, showed traces of a troop of little fairy beings, who having frolicked through a happy day, had been carried off to slumber through a peaceful night.

While the mutual greetings were going on between Bracebridge and his relatives, I had time to scan the apartment. I have called it a hall, for so it had certainly been in old times, and the Squire had evidently endeavoured to restore it to something of its primitive state. Over the heavy projecting fireplace was suspended a picture of a warrior in armour, standing by a white horse, and on the opposite wall hung helmet, buckler, and lance. At one end an enormous pair of antlers were inserted in the wall, the branches serving as hooks on which to suspend hats, whips, and spurs; and in the corners of the apartment were fowling-pieces, fishing-rods, and other sporting implements. The furniture was of the cumbrous workmanship of former days, though some articles of modern convenience had been added, and the oaken floor had been carpeted; so that the whole presented an odd mixture of parlour and hall.

The grate had been removed from the wide overwhelming fireplace, to make way for a fire of wood, in the midst of which was an enormous log glowing and blazing, and sending forth a vast volume of light and heat; this I understood was the Yule-log, which the Squire was particular in having brought in and illumined on a Christmas eve, according to ancient custom.

It was really delightful to see the old Squire seated in his hereditary elbow-chair by the hospitable fireside of his ancestors, and looking around him like the sun of a system, beaming warmth and gladness to every heart. Even the very dog that lay stretched at his feet, as he lazily shifted his position and yawned, would look fondly up in his master's face, wag his tail against the floor, and stretch himself again to sleep, confident of kindness and protection. There is an emanation from the heart in genuine hospitality which cannot be described, but is immediately felt, and puts the stranger at once at his ease. I had not been seated many minutes by the comfortable hearth of the worthy cavalier before I found myself as much at home as if I had been one of the family.

Supper was announced shortly after our arrival. It was served up in a spacious oaken chamber, the panels of which shone with wax, and around which were several family portraits decorated with holly and ivy. Beside the accustomed lights, two great wax tapers, called Christmas candles, wreathed with greens, were placed on a highly-polished buffet among the family plate. The table was abundantly spread with substantial fare; but the Squire made his supper of frumenty, a dish made of wheat cakes boiled in milk with rich spices, being a standing dish in old times for Christmas eve. I was happy to find my old friend, minced-pie, in the retinue of the feast; and finding him to be perfectly orthodox, and that I need not be ashamed of my predilection, I greeted him with all the warmth wherewith we usually greet an old and very genteel acquaintance.

The mirth of the company was greatly promoted by the humours of an eccentric personage whom Mr. Bracebridge always addressed with the quaint appellation of Master Simon. He was a tight, brisk little man, with the air of an arrant old bachelor. His nose was shaped like the bill of a parrot; his face slightly pitted with the small-pox, with a dry perpetual bloom on it, like a frost-bitten leaf in autumn. He had an eye of great quickness and vivacity, with a drollery and lurking waggery of expression that was irresistible. He was evidently the wit of the family, dealing very much in sly jokes and innuendoes with the ladies, and making infinite merriment by harpings upon old themes; which, unfortunately, my ignorance of the family chronicles did not permit me to enjoy. It seemed to be his great delight during supper to keep a young girl next him in a continual agony of stifled laughter, in spite of her awe of the reproving looks of her mother, who sat opposite. Indeed, he was the idol of the younger part of the company, who laughed at everything he said or did, and at every turn of his countenance. I could not wonder at it; for he must have been a miracle of accomplishments in their eyes. He could imitate Punch and Judy; make an old woman of his hand, with the assistance of a burnt cork and pocket-handkerchief: and cut an orange into such a ludicrous caricature, that the young folks were ready to die with laughing.

I was let briefly into his history by Frank Bracebridge. He was an old bachelor of a small independent income, which by careful management was sufficient for all his wants. He revolved through the family system like a vagrant comet in its orbit; sometimes visiting one branch, and sometimes another quite remote; as is often the case with gentlemen of extensive connections and small fortunes in England. He had a chirping, buoyant disposition, always enjoying the present moment; and his frequent change of scene and company prevented his acquiring those rusty unaccommodating habits with which old bachelors are so uncharitably charged. He was a complete family chronicle, being versed in the genealogy, history, and intermarriages of the whole house of Bracebridge, which made him a great favourite with the old folks; he was a beau of all the elder ladies and superannuated spinsters, among whom he was habitually considered rather a young fellow, and he was a master of the revels among the children; so that there was not a more popular being in the sphere in which he moved than Mr. Simon Bracebridge. Of late years he had resided almost entirely with the Squire, to whom he had become a factotum, and whom he particularly delighted by jumping with his humour in respect to old times, and by having a scrap of an old song to suit every occasion. We had presently a specimen of his last-mentioned talent; for no sooner was supper removed, and spiced wines and other beverages peculiar to the season introduced, than Master Simon was called on for a good old Christmas song. He bethought himself for a moment, and then, with a sparkle of the eye, and a voice that was by no means bad, excepting that it ran occasionally into a falsetto, like the notes of a split reed, he quavered forth a quaint old ditty,—

"Now Christmas is come,
    Let us beat up the drum,
And call all our neighbours together;
    And when they appear,
    Let us make them such cheer
As will keep out the wind and the weather," etc.

The supper had disposed every one to gaiety, and an old harper was summoned from the servants' hall, where he had been strumming all the evening, and to all appearance comforting himself with some of the Squire's home-brewed. He was a kind of hanger-on, I was told, of the establishment, and though ostensibly a resident of the village, was oftener to be found in the Squire's kitchen than his own home, the old gentleman being fond of the sound of "harp in hall."

The dance, like most dances after supper, was a merry one; some of the older folks joined in it, and the Squire himself figured down several couples with a partner with whom he affirmed he had danced at every Christmas for nearly half-a-century. Master Simon, who seemed to be a kind of connecting link between the old times and the new, and to be withal a little antiquated in the taste of his accomplishments, evidently piqued himself on his dancing, and was endeavouring to gain credit by the heel and toe, rigadoon, and other graces of the ancient school; but he had unluckily assorted himself with a little romping girl from boarding-school, who, by her wild vivacity, kept him continually on the stretch, and defeated all his sober attempts at elegance;—such are the ill-assorted matches to which antique gentlemen are unfortunately prone!

The young Oxonian, on the contrary, had led out one of his maiden aunts, on whom the rogue played a thousand little knaveries with impunity; he was full of practical jokes, and his delight was to tease his aunts and cousins; yet, like all madcap youngsters, he was a universal favourite among the women. The most interesting couple in the dance was the young officer and a ward of the Squire's, a beautiful blushing girl of seventeen. From several shy glances which I had noticed in the course of the evening, I suspected there was a little kindness growing up between them; and, indeed, the young soldier was just the hero to captivate a romantic girl. He was tall, slender, and handsome, and like most young British offi-

cers of late years, had picked up various small accomplishments on the Continent—he could talk French and Italian—draw landscapes, sing very tolerably—dance divinely; but, above all, he had been wounded at Waterloo:—what girl of seventeen, well read in poetry and romance, could resist such a mirror of chivalry and perfection!

The moment the dance was over, he caught up a guitar, and lolling against the old marble fireplace, in an attitude which I am half inclined to suspect was studied, began the little French air of the Troubadour. The Squire, however, exclaimed against having anything on Christmas eve but good old English; upon which the young minstrel, casting up his eye for a moment, as if in an effort of memory, struck into another strain, and, with a charming air of gallantry, gave Herrick's "Night-Piece to Julia":—

> "Her eyes the glow-worm lend thee,
>   The shooting stars attend thee,
>   And the elves also,
>   Whose little eyes glow
> Like the sparks of fire, befriend thee.

No Will-o'-the-Wisp mislight thee;
Nor snake or glow-worm bite thee;
   But on, on thy way,
   Not making a stay,
Since ghost there is none to affright thee.

Then let not the dark thee cumber;
What though the moon does slumber,
   The stars of the night
   Will lend thee their light,
Like tapers clear without number.

Then, Julia, let me woo thee,
Thus, thus to come unto me;
   And when I shall meet
   Thy silvery feet,
My soul I'll pour into thee."

The song might have been intended in compliment to the fair Julia, for so I found his partner was called, or it might not; she, however, was certainly unconscious of any such application, for she never looked at the singer, but kept her eyes cast upon the floor. Her face was suffused, it is true, with a beautiful blush, and there was a gentle heaving of the bosom, but all that was doubtless caused by the exercise of the dance; indeed, so great was her indifference, that she was amusing herself with plucking to pieces a choice bouquet of hothouse flowers, and by the time the song was concluded, the nosegay lay in ruins on the floor.

The party now broke up for the night with the kind-hearted old custom of shaking hands. As I passed through the hall, on the way to my chamber, the dying embers of the *Yule-log* still sent forth a dusky glow; and had it not been the season when "no spirit dares stir abroad," I should have been half tempted to steal from my room at midnight, and peep whether the fairies might not be at their revels about the hearth.

My chamber was in the old part of the mansion, the ponderous furniture of which might have been fabricated in the days of the giants. The room was panelled with cornices of heavy carved work, in which flowers and grotesque faces were strangely intermingled; and a row of black-looking portraits stared mournfully at me from the walls. The bed was of rich though faded damask, with a lofty tester, and stood in a niche opposite a bow-window. I had scarcely got into bed when a strain of music seemed to break forth in the air just below the window. I listened, and found it proceeded from a band, which I concluded to be the waits from some neighbouring village. They went round the house, playing under the windows. I drew aside the curtains, to hear them more distinctly. The moonbeams fell through the upper part of the casement, partially lighting up the antiquated apartment. The sounds, as they receded, became more soft and aerial, and seemed to accord with quiet and moonlight. I listened and listened—they became more and more tender and remote, and, as they gradually died away, my head sank upon the pillow and I fell asleep.

PARIS, CHRISTMAS, 1876

HENRY JAMES

The excerpt is from an article James wrote for the New York Tribune

I have never seen Paris so charming as on this last Christmas Day. The weather put in a claim to a share in the fun, the sky was radiant and the air as soft and pure as a southern spring. It was a day to spend in the streets and all the world did so. I passed it strolling half over the city and wherever I turned I found the entertainment that a pedestrian relishes. What people love Paris for became almost absurdly obvious: charm, beguilement, diversion were stamped upon everything. I confess that, privately, I kept thinking of Prince Bismarck and wishing he might take a turn upon the boulevards. Not that they would have flustered him much, I suppose, for, after all, the boulevards are not human; but the whole spectacle seemed a supreme reminder of the fact so constantly present at this time to the reflective mind—the amazing elasticity of France. Beaten and humiliated on a scale without precedent, despoiled, dishonored, bled to death financially—all this but yesterday—Paris is today in outward aspect as radiant, as prosperous, as instinct with her own peculiar genius as if her sky had never known a cloud. The friendly stranger cannot refuse an admiring glance to this mystery of wealth and thrift and energy and good spirits. I don't know how Berlin looked on Christmas Day, though Christmas-keeping is a German specialty, but I greatly doubt whether its aspect would have appealed so irresistibly to the sympathies of the impartial observer. With the approach of Christmas here the whole line of the boulevards is bordered on each side with a row of little booths for the sale—for the sale of everything conceivable. The width of the classic asphalt is so ample that they form no serious obstruction, and the scene, in the evening especially, presents a picturesque combination of the rustic fair and the highest Parisian civilization. You may buy anything in the line of trifles in the world, from a cotton nightcap to an orange neatly pricked in blue letters with the name of the young lady—Adèle or Ernestine—to whom you may gallantly desire to present it. On the other side of the crowded channel the regular shops present their glittering portals, decorated for the occasion with the latest refinements of the trade. The confectioners in particular are amazing; the rows of marvelous *bonbonnières* look like precious sixteenth-century caskets and reliquaries, chiseled by Florentine artists, in the glass cases of great museums. The *bonbonnière,* in its elaborate and impertinent uselessness, is certainly the consummate flower of material luxury; it seems to bloom, with its petals of satin and its pistils of gold, upon the very apex of the tree of civilization.

CHRISTMAS EVE

JAMES JOYCE

There is no complete manuscript of this story, begun by Joyce in the fall of 1904 and apparently intended as part of Dubliners

Mr. Callanan felt homely. There was a good fire burning in the grate and he knew that it was cold outside. He had been about town all day shopping with Mrs. Callanan and he had met many friends. These friends had been very friendly, exchanging the compliments of the season, joking with Mrs. Callanan about her number of parcels, and pinching Katsey's cheek. Some said that Katsey was like her mother but others said she was like her father—only better-looking: she was a rather pretty child. The Callanans—that is, the father and mother and Katsey and an awkward brother named Charlie—had then gone into a cake-shop and taken four cups of coffee. After that the turkey had been bought and safely tucked under Mr. Callanan's arm. As they were making for their crowded tram Mr. Callanan's 'boss' passed and saluted. The salute was generously returned.

—That's the 'boss'. He saluted—did you see?—

—That man?—

—Ah, he's not a bad sort after all if you know how to take him. But you mustn't rub him the wrong way.—

There was wood in the fire. Every Christmas Mr. Callanan got a present of a small load of wooden blocks from a friend of his in a timber-yard near Ringsend. Christmas would not have been Christmas without a wood-fire. Two of these blocks were laid crosswise on the top of the fire and were beginning to glow. The brave light of the fire lit up a small, well-kept room with bees-waxed borders arranged cleanly round a bright square carpet. The table in the middle of the room had a shaded lamp upon it. The shade set obliquely sprayed the light of the lamp upon one of the walls, revealing a gilt-framed picture of a curly-headed child in a nightdress playing with a collie. The picture was called "Can't you talk?"

Mr. Callanan felt homely but he had himself a more descriptive phrase for his condition: he felt mellow. He was a blunt figure as he sat in his arm-chair; short thick legs resting together like block pipes, short thick arms hardly crossing over his chest, and a heavy red face nestling upon all. His scanty hair was deciding for grey and he looked a man who had come near his comfortable winter as he blinked his blue eyes thoughtfully at the burning blocks. His mind was vacant. He had calculated all his expenses and discovered that all had been done well within the margin. This discovery had resulted in a mood of general charity and in particular desire for some fellow-spirit to share his happiness, some of his old cronies, one of the right sort.

Someone might drop in: Hooper perhaps. Hooper and he were friends from long ago and both had been many years in the same profession. Hooper was a clerk in a solicitor's office in Eustace St. and Mr. Callanan was a clerk in a solicitor's office close by on Wellington Quay. They used often to meet at Swan's public-house where each went every day at lunch-time to get a fourpenny snack and a pint and when they met they compared notes astutely for they were legal rivals. But still they were friends and could forget the profession for one night. Mr. Callanan felt he would like to hear Hooper's gruff voice call in at the door "Hello Tom! How's the body?"

The kettle was put squatting on the fire to boil for punch and soon began to puff. Mr. Callanan stood up to fill his pipe and while filling it he gave a few glances at Katsey who was diligently stoning some raisins on a plate. Many people thought she would turn out a nun but there could be no harm in having her taught the typewriter; time enough after the holidays. Mr. Callanan began to toss the water from tumbler to tumbler in a manner that suggested technical difficulties and just at that moment Mrs. Callanan came in from the hall.

—Tom! here's Mr. Hooper!—

—Bring him in! Bring him in! I wouldn't doubt you, Paddy, when there's punch going—

—I'm sure I'm in the way . . . busy night with you, Mrs. Callanan . . . —

—Not at all, Mr. Hooper. You're as welcome as the flowers in May. How is Mrs. Hooper? —

—Ah! we can't complain. Just a touch of the old trouble, you know
. . . indigestion—
—Nasty thing it is! She is quite strong otherwise?—
—O, yes, tip-top—
—Well, sit down, my hearty and make yourself at home—
—I'll try to, Tom—

A Letter at Christmastime

JOHN KEATS

The excerpt is from a letter Keats wrote to his brother George and sister-in-law Georgiana in America following the death of brother Tom on December 1, 1818. Keats spent Christmas with Fanny Brawne, a day she later described as the happiest in her life

Shall I give you Miss Brawne? She is about my height—with a fine style of countenance of the lengthen'd sort—she wants sentiment in every feature—she manages to make her hair look well—her nostrils are fine—though a little painful—her mouth is bad and good—her Profil is better than her full-face which indeed is not full but pale and thin without showing any bone—Her shape is very graceful and so are her movements—her Arms are good her hands baddish—her feet tolerable—she is not seventeen—but she is ignorant—monstrous in her behaviour flying out in all directions, calling people such names—that I was forced lately to make use of the term *Minx*—this is I think not from any innate vice but from a penchant she has for acting stylishly. I am however tired of such style and shall decline any more of it. . . .

A SCHOOLBOY'S HOLIDAY

CHARLES LAMB

Let us have leave to remember the festivities at Christmas, when the richest of us would club our stock to have a gaudy day, sitting round the fire, replenished to the height with logs, and the pennyless, and he that could contribute nothing, partook in all the mirth, and in some of the substantialities of the feasting; the carol sung by night at that time of the year, which, when a young boy, I have so often lain awake to hear from seven (the hour of going to bed) till ten when it was sung by the older boys and monitors, and have listened to it, in their rude chaunting, till I have been transported in fancy to the fields of Bethlehem, and the song which was sung at that season, by angels' voices to the shepherds.

1813

OLD FOLKS' CHRISTMAS

RING LARDNER

Tom and Grace Carter sat in their living-room on Christmas Eve, sometimes talking, sometimes pretending to read and all the time thinking things they didn't want to think. Their two children, Junior, aged nineteen, and Grace, two years younger, had come home that day from their schools for the Christmas vacation. Junior was in his first year at the university and Grace attending a boarding-school that would fit her for college.

I won't call them Grace and Junior any more, though that is the way they had been christened. Junior had changed his name to Ted and Grace was now Caroline, and thus they insisted on being addressed, even by their parents. This was one of the things Tom and Grace the elder were thinking of as they sat in their living-room Christmas Eve.

Other university freshmen who had lived here had returned on the twenty-first, the day when the vacation was supposed to begin. Ted had telegraphed that he would be three days late owing to a special examination which, if he passed it, would lighten the terrific burden of the next term. He had arrived at home looking so pale, heavy-eyed and shaky that his mother doubted the wisdom of the concentrated mental effort, while his father secretly hoped the stuff had been non-poisonous and would not have lasting effects. Caroline, too, had been behind schedule, explaining that her laundry had gone astray and she had not dared trust others to trace it for her.

Grace and Tom had attempted, with fair success, to conceal their disappointment over this delayed home-coming and had continued with their preparations for a Christmas that would thrill their children and consequently themselves. They had bought an imposing lot of presents, costing twice or three times as much as had been Tom's father's annual income when Tom was Ted's age, or Tom's own income a year ago, before General Motors' acceptance of his new weather-proof paint had enabled him to buy this suburban home and luxuries such as his own parents and Grace's had never dreamed of, and to give Ted and Caroline advantages that he and Grace had perforce gone without.

Behind the closed door of the music-room was the elaborately decked tree. The piano and piano bench and the floor around the tree were covered with beribboned packages of all sizes, shapes and weights, one of them addressed to Tom, another to Grace, a few to the servants and the rest to Ted and Caroline. A huge box contained a sealskin coat for Caroline, a coat that had cost as much as the Carters had formerly paid a year for rent. Even more expensive was a "set" of jewelry consisting of an opal brooch, a bracelet of opals and gold filigree, and an opal ring surrounded by diamonds.

Grace always had preferred opals to any other stone, but now that she could afford them, some inhibition prevented her from buying them for herself; she could enjoy them much more adorning her pretty daughter. There were boxes of silk stockings, lingerie, gloves and handkerchiefs. And for Ted, a three-hundred-dollar watch, a de-luxe edition of Balzac, an expensive bag of shiny, new steel-shafted golf-clubs and the last word in portable phonographs.

But the big surprise for the boy was locked in the garage, a black Gorham sedan, a model more up to date and better-looking than Tom's own year-old car that stood beside it. Ted could use it during the vacation if the mild weather continued and could look forward to driving it around home next spring and summer, there being a rule at the university forbidding undergraduates the possession or use of private automobiles.

Every year for sixteen years, since Ted was three and Caroline one, it had been the Christmas Eve custom of the Carters to hang up their children's stockings and fill them with inexpensive toys. Tom and Grace had thought it would be fun to continue the custom this year; the contents of the stockings—a mechanical negro dancing doll, music-boxes, a kitten that meowed when you pressed a spot on her back, et cetera—would make the "kids" laugh. And one of Grace's first pronouncements to her returned offspring was that they must go to bed early so Santa Claus would not be frightened away.

But it seemed they couldn't promise to make it so terribly early. They both had long-standing dates in town. Caroline was going to dinner and a play with Beatrice Murdock and Beatrice's nineteen-year-old brother Paul. The latter would call for her in his car at half past six. Ted had accepted an invitation to see the hockey match with two classmates, Herb Castle and Bernard King. He wanted to take his father's Gorham, but Tom told him untruthfully that the foot-brake was not working; Ted must be kept out of the garage till tomorrow morning.

Ted and Caroline had taken naps in the afternoon and gone off together in Paul Murdock's stylish roadster, giving their word that they would be back by midnight or a little later and that tomorrow night they would stay home.

And now their mother and father were sitting up for them, because the stockings could not be filled and hung till they were safely in bed, and also because trying to go to sleep is a painful and hopeless business when you are kind of jumpy.

"What time is it?" asked Grace, looking up from the third page of a book that she had begun to "read" soon after dinner.

"Half past two," said her husband. (He had answered the same question every fifteen or twenty minutes since midnight.)

"You don't suppose anything could have happened?" said Grace.

"We'd have heard if there had," said Tom.

"It isn't likely, of course," said Grace, "but they might have had an accident some place where nobody was there to report it or telephone or anything. We don't know what kind of a driver the Murdock boy is."

"He's Ted's age. Boys that age may be inclined to drive too fast, but they drive pretty well."

"How do you know?"

"Well, I've watched some of them drive."

"Yes, but not all of them."

"I doubt whether anybody in the world has seen every nineteen-year-old boy drive."

"Boys these days seem so kind of irresponsible."

"Oh, don't worry! They probably met some of their young friends and stopped for a bite to eat or something." Tom got up and walked to the window with studied carelessness. "It's a pretty night," he said. "You can see every star in the sky."

But he wasn't looking at the stars. He was looking down the road for headlights. There were none in sight and after a few moments he returned to his chair.

"What time is it?" asked Grace.

"Twenty-two of," he said.

"Of what?"

"Of three."

"Your watch must have stopped. Nearly an hour ago you told me it was half past two."

"My watch is all right. You probably dozed off."

"I haven't closed my eyes."

"Well, it's time you did. Why don't you go to bed?"

"Why don't *you?*"

"I'm not sleepy."

"Neither am I. But honestly, Tom, it's silly for you to stay up. I'm just doing it so I can fix the stockings, and because I feel so wakeful. But there's no use of your losing your sleep."

"I couldn't sleep a wink till they're home."

"That's foolishness! There's nothing to worry about. They're just having a good time. You were young once yourself."

"That's just it! When I was young, I was young." He picked up his paper and tried to get interested in the shipping news.

"What time is it?" asked Grace.

"Five minutes of three."

"Maybe they're staying at the Murdocks' all night."

"They'd have let us know."

"They were afraid to wake us up, telephoning."

At three-twenty a car stopped at the front gate.

"There they are!"

"I told you there was nothing to worry about."

Tom went to the window. He could just discern the outlines of the Murdock boy's roadster, whose lighting system seemed to have broken down.

"He hasn't any lights," said Tom. "Maybe I'd better go out and see if I can fix them."

"No, don't!" said Grace sharply. "He can fix them himself. He's just saving them while he stands still."

"Why don't they come in?"

"They're probaby making plans."

"They can make them in here. I'll go out and tell them we're still up."

"No, don't!" said Grace as before, and Tom obediently remained at the window.

It was nearly four when the car lights flashed on and the car drove away. Caroline walked into the house and stared dazedly at her parents.

"Heavens! What are you doing up?"

Tom was about to say something, but Grace forestalled him.

"We were talking over old Christmases," she said. "Is it very late?"

"I haven't any idea," said Caroline.

"Where is Ted?"

"Isn't he home? I haven't seen him since we dropped him at the hockey place."

"Well, you go right to bed," said her mother. "You must be worn out."

"I am, kind of. We danced after the play. What time is breakfast?"

"Eight o'clock."

"Oh, Mother, can't you make it nine?"

"I guess so. You used to want to get up early on Christmas."

"I know, but—"

"Who brought you home?" asked Tom.

"Why, Paul Murdock—and Beatrice."

"You look rumpled."

"They made me sit in the 'rumple' seat."

She laughed at her joke, said good night and went upstairs. She had not come even within hand-shaking distance of her father and mother.

"The Murdocks," said Tom, "must have great manners, making their guest ride in that uncomfortable seat."

Grace was silent.

"You go to bed, too," said Tom. "I'll wait for Ted."

"You couldn't fix the stockings."

"I won't try. We'll have time for that in the morning; I mean, later in the morning."

"I'm not going to bed till you do," said Grace.

"All right, we'll both go. Ted ought not to be long now. I suppose his friends will bring him home. We'll hear him when he comes in."

There was no chance not to hear him when, at ten minutes before six, he came in. He had done his Christmas shopping late and brought home a package.

Grace was downstairs again at half past seven, telling the servants breakfast would be postponed till nine. She nailed the stockings beside the fireplace, went into the music-room to see that nothing had been disturbed and removed Ted's hat and overcoat from where he had carefully hung them on the hall floor.

Tom appeared a little before nine and suggested that the children ought to be awakened.

"I'll wake them," said Grace, and went upstairs. She opened Ted's door, looked, and softly closed it again. She entered her daughter's room and found Caroline semiconscious.

"Do I have to get up now? Honestly I can't eat anything. If you could just have Molla bring me some coffee. Ted and I are both invited to the Murdocks' for breakfast at half past twelve, and I could sleep for another hour or two."

"But dearie, don't you know we have Christmas dinner at one?"

"It's a shame, Mother, but I thought of course our dinner would be at night."

"Don't you want to see your presents?"

"Certainly I do, but can't they wait?"

Grace was about to go to the kitchen to tell the cook that dinner would be at seven instead of one, but she remembered having promised Signe the afternoon and evening off, as a cold, light supper would be all anyone wanted after the heavy midday meal.

Tom and Grace breakfasted alone and once more sat in the living-room, talking, thinking and pretending to read.

"You ought to speak to Caroline," said Tom.

"I will, but not today. It's Christmas."

"And I intend to say a few words to Ted."

"Yes, dear, you must. But not today."

"I suppose they'll be out again tonight."

"No, they promised to stay home. We'll have a nice cozy evening."

"Don't bet too much on that," said Tom.

At noon the "children" made their entrance and responded to their parents' salutations with almost the proper warmth. Ted declined a cup of coffee and he and Caroline apologized for making a "breakfast" date at the Murdocks'.

"Sis and I both thought you'd be having dinner at seven, as usual."

"We've always had it at one o'clock on Christmas," said Tom.

"I'd forgotten it was Christmas," said Ted.

"Well, those stockings ought to remind you."

Ted and Caroline looked at the bulging stockings.

"Isn't there a tree?" asked Caroline.

"Of course," said her mother. "But the stockings come first."

"We've only a little time," said Caroline. "We'll be terribly late as it is. So can't we see the tree now?"

"I guess so," said Grace, and led the way into the music-room.

The servants were summoned and the tree stared at and admired.

"You must open your presents," said Grace to her daughter.

"I can't open them all now," said Caroline. "Tell me which is special."

The cover was removed from the huge box and Grace held up the coat.

"Oh, Mother!" said Caroline. "A sealskin coat!"

"Put it on," said her father.

"Not now. We haven't time."

"Then look at this!" said Grace, and opened the case of jewels.

"Oh, Mother! Opals!" said Caroline.

"They're my favorite stone," said Grace quietly.

"If nobody minds," said Ted, "I'll postpone my personal investigation till we get back. I know I'll like everything you've given me. But if we have no car in working order, I've got to call a taxi and catch a train."

"You can drive in," said his father.

"Did you fix the brake?"

"I think it's all right. Come up to the garage and we'll see."

Ted got his hat and coat and kissed his mother good-by.

"Mother," he said, "I know you'll forgive me for not having any presents for you and Dad. I was so rushed the last three days at school. And I thought I'd have time to shop a little when we got in yesterday, but I was in too much of a hurry to be home. Last night, everything was closed."

"Don't worry," said Grace. "Christmas is for young people. Dad and I have everything we want."

The servants had found their gifts and disappeared, expressing effusive Scandinavian thanks.

Caroline and her mother were left alone.

"Mother, where did the coat come from?"

"Lloyd and Henry's."

"They keep all kinds of furs, don't they?"

"Yes."

"Would you mind horribly if I exchanged this?"

"Certainly not, dear. You pick out anything you like, and if it's a little more expensive, it won't make any difference. We can go in town to-morrow or next day. But don't you want to wear your opals to the Murdocks'?"

"I don't believe so. They might get lost or something. And I'm not— well, I'm not so crazy about——"

"I think they can be exchanged, too," said Grace. "You run along now and get ready to start."

Caroline obeyed with alacrity, and Grace spent a welcome moment by herself.

Tom opened the garage door.

"Why, you've got two cars!" said Ted.

"The new one isn't mine," said Tom.

"Whose is it?"

"Yours. It's the new model."

"Dad, that's wonderful! But it looks just like the old one."

"Well, the old one's pretty good. Just the same, yours is better. You'll find that out when you drive it. Hop in and get started. I had her filled with gas."

"I think I'd rather drive the old one."

"Why?"

"Well, what I really wanted, Dad, was a Barnes sport roadster, something like Paul Murdock's, only a different color scheme. And if I don't drive this Gorham at all, maybe you could get them to take it back or make some kind of a deal with the Barnes people."

Tom didn't speak till he was sure of his voice. Then: "All right, son. Take my car and I'll see what can be done about yours."

Caroline, waiting for Ted, remembered something and called to her mother. "Here's what I got for you and Dad," she said. "It's two tickets to 'Jolly Jane,' the play I saw last night. You'll love it!"

"When are they for?" asked Grace.

"Tonight," said Caroline.

"But dearie," said her mother, "we don't want to go out tonight, when you promised to stay home."

"We'll keep our promise," said Caroline, "but the Murdocks may drop in and bring some friends and we'll dance and there'll be music. And Ted and I both thought you'd rather be away somewhere so our noise wouldn't disturb you."

"It was sweet of you to do this," said her mother, "but your father and I don't mind noise as long as you're enjoying yourselves."

"It's time anyway that you and Dad had a treat."

"The real treat," said Grace, "would be to spend a quiet evening here with just you two."

"The Murdocks practically invited themselves and I couldn't say no after they'd been so nice to me. And honestly, Mother, you'll love this play!"

"Will you be home for supper?"

"I'm pretty sure we will, but if we're a little late, don't you and Dad wait for us. Take the seven-twenty so you won't miss anything. The first act is really the best. We probably won't be hungry, but have Signe leave something out for us in case we are."

Tom and Grace sat down to the elaborate Christmas dinner and didn't make much impression on it. Even if they had had any appetite, the sixteen-pound turkey would have looked almost like new when they had eaten their fill. Conversation was intermittent and related chiefly to Signe's excellence as a cook and the mildness of the weather. Children and Christmas were barely touched on.

Tom merely suggested that on account of its being a holiday and their having theatre tickets, they ought to take the six-ten and eat supper at the Metropole. His wife said no; Ted and Caroline might come home and be disappointed at not finding them. Tom seemed about to make some remark, but changed his mind.

The afternoon was the longest Grace had ever known. The children were still absent at seven and she and Tom taxied to the train. Neither talked much on the way to town. As for the play, which Grace was sure to love, it turned out to be a rehash of "Cradle Snatchers" and "Sex," retaining the worst features of each.

When it was over, Tom said: "Now I'm inviting you to the Cove Club. You didn't eat any breakfast or dinner or supper and I can't have you starving to death on a feast-day. Besides, I'm thirsty as well as hungry."

They ordered the special *table d'hôte* and struggled hard to get away with it. Tom drank six high-balls, but they failed to produce the usual effect of making him jovial. Grace had one high-ball and some kind of cordial that gave her a warm, contented feeling for a moment. But the warmth and contentment left her before the train was half way home.

The living-room looked as if Von Kluck's army had just passed through. Ted and Caroline had kept their promise up to a certain point. They had spent part of the evening at home, and the Murdocks must have brought all their own friends and everybody else's, judging from the results. The tables and floors were strewn with empty glasses, ashes and cigaret stubs. The stockings had been torn off their nails and the wrecked contents were all over the place. Two sizable holes had been burnt in Grace's favorite rug.

Tom took his wife by the arm and led her into the music-room.

"You never took the trouble to open your own present," he said.

"And I think there's one for you, too," said Grace. "They didn't come in here," she added, "so I guess there wasn't much dancing or music."

Tom found his gift from Grace, a set of diamond studs and cuff buttons for festive wear. Grace's present from him was an opal ring.

"Oh, Tom!" she said.

"We'll have to go out somewhere tomorrow night, so I can break these in," said Tom.

"Well, if we do that, we'd better get a good night's rest."

"I'll beat you upstairs," said Tom.

JOY IN FREETOWN

EDNA LEWIS

from THE TASTE OF COUNTRY COOKING

Around Christmastime the kitchens of Freetown, Virginia, would grow fragrant with the baking of cakes, fruit puddings, cookies, and candy. Exchanging gifts was not a custom at that time, but we did look forward to hanging our stockings from the mantel and finding them filled on Christmas morning with tasty "imported" nuts from Lahore's, our favorite hard candies with the cinnamon-flavored red eye, and oranges whose special Christmas aroma reached us at the top of the stairs. And for us four girls, there would also be little celluloid dolls with movable arms and legs that we so loved, and new paper dolls with their fascinating clip-on wardrobes. But mainly getting ready for Christmas meant preparing all kinds of delicious foods that we would enjoy with our families and friends during the days between Christmas Eve and New Year's Day.

There was a special excitement in the kitchens, as many of the things we prepared were foods we tasted only at Christmas. This was the only time in the year when we had oranges, almonds, Brazil nuts, and raisins that came in clusters. And although we were miles from the sea, at Christmas one of the treats we always looked forward to was oysters. The oysters were delivered to Lahore's in barrels on Christmas Eve day, and late on Christmas Eve we would climb the steps over the pasture fence and walk along the path through the woods to the store, carrying our covered tin pails. Mr. Jackson, the storekeeper, would fill some of our pails with oysters. And before we left he always filled our hands with nuts and candy.

We were excited by all the preparations for Christmas, but my own favorite chores were chopping the nuts and raisins for Mother and stirring the wonderful-smelling dark mixtures of fruits and brandy that would go into the fruitcake and plum pudding, and decorating the house with evergreens.

Just before Christmas a green lacy vine called running cedar appeared in the woods around Freetown and we would gather yards and yards of it. We draped everything in the house with it: windows, doors, even the large gilded frames that held the pictures of each of my aunts and uncles. We picked the prickly branches of a giant holly tree—the largest holly I've ever seen—which grew on the top of a nearby hill, and we cut armloads of pine boughs and juniper. My mother always gave the fireplace and hearth a fresh whitewashing the day before Christmas, and washed, starched, and ironed the white lace curtains. On Christmas Eve my father would set up the tree in one corner of the room and we would decorate it with pink, white, and blue strings of popcorn that we had popped, dipped in colored sugar water, and carefully threaded. Small white candles nestled on tufts of cotton were the last decorations to be placed on the tree.

I loved the way the greens looked set off by the white hearth and walls and the stiff white curtains which they draped. In the evenings the soft orange glow from the fire and from the candlelight and the fragrance of the cedar and juniper mingling with the smell of chestnuts roasting always made me wish that Christmas week would last until spring, though I suspected that my mother did not share my wish.

The celebration of Christmas Day began before daybreak with the shooting off of Roman candles. With a great roaring noise they exploded into balls of red fire arcing into the still-dark sky. After they had all been set off, my father would light sparklers for us. We could never imagine Christmas without Roman candles and sparklers; for us it was the most important part of the whole day.

Finally we would go back into the warmth of the house for breakfast. There would be eggs and sausages and plates of hot biscuits with my mother's best preserves, and pan-fried oysters which would taste so sweet, crispy, and delicious. The familiar smell of hot coffee and cocoa mixed with the special aroma of bourbon, which was part of every holiday breakfast. We were allowed to smell, but never to taste this special drink of the menfolk.

We all dressed in our Sunday dresses for Christmas dinner. Dinner was at noon so that we would be finished in time for the men to feed the animals before dark. My mother would have been in the kitchen since five o'clock and half of the night as well, and when the dinner was ready we would gather round the table and sit for hours enjoying all the things she had prepared.

Christmas week was spent visiting back and forth, as at this time of year the men were able to take off some time. The women enjoyed tasting each other's baking and the men took pleasure in comparing the wines they had made at harvest time—wild plum, elderberry, dandelion, and grape. And they usually managed to enjoy a taste of that bourbon as well.

Every household had a sideboard or a food safe, and these would be laden throughout the week with all the foods that had been made for the holiday. Ours would hold baked ham, smothered rabbit, a pan of mixed small birds that had been trapped in the snow, braised guinea hen, liver pudding, and sometimes a roasted wild turkey that had grown up with our own flock (but usually a fat roast hen), and all the sweet and pungent pickles my mother had made from cucumbers and watermelon rind, crab apples and peaches. The open shelf of the sideboard would be lined with all the traditional holiday cakes: caramel and coconut layer cakes, pound cake, and my mother's rich, dark, flavorful fruitcake. There were plates of fudge and peanut brittle and crocks filled with crisp sugar cookies. The food safe was filled with mince pies, and fruit pies made with the canned fruit of summer.

Although there were no exceptions to our usual custom of sitting down together three times a day for meals, during Christmas week we were free to return to the food safe as many times a day as we liked and my mother would never say a word. But at the end of holiday week we were all given a home-brewed physic which was really vile! It was so vile I've never quite forgotten the taste of it.

On New Year's Day when all the Christmas decorations were taken down, we felt sad and let down; to us our house looked drab and naked, and although the visiting back and forth would continue until winter came to an end, Christmas was over.

VALLEY FORGE: 24 DECEMBER 1777

F. VAN WYCK MASON

Corporal Timothy Maddox of Smallwood's Maryland Cavalry, presently detailed to the Commander-in-Chief's bodyguard, stood disgustedly considering the armful of fir boughs he had dropped at the rear of the General's weather-beaten marquee. In evident disappointment Sergeant Hiram Toulmin considered the fruits of his corporal's labors.

"And is that all ye have to show for a half hour's rummagin'?"

"Yer cussed right," the Corporal grunted, retying the length of cotton cord serving him in place of a belt. "I had to get mighty 'cute to find as much. Only two days here and there ain't an evergreen within a mile o' here but's been stripped clean."

The Sergeant blew on grimy, reddish-blue fingers. "I believe ye, Maddox, but I'd been hopin' fer more. That much won't bank above five feet of the marquee. Wish to God we could come across some hay. The wind beats in cruel sharp under them canvas bottoms, and to-night bein' Christmas Eve His Excellency will be expectin' guests, no doubt."

"Even so," Maddox observed, "the General'd never let us use them boughs for banking, Christmas Eve or no Christmas Eve—not with a third o' the Army setting up all night around fires for lack o' beddin'."

Mechanically, Sergeant Toulmin's smoke-reddened eyes sought the campfires of the Blue Hen's Chickens—General Billy Maxwell's Delaware troops. In the fading yellow-gray sunset he could see that the smoke of their campfires veered ever more sharply away to the southwest. A veteran of White Plains and Brandywine, he noticed subconsciously that the fires they had built were too big and hot by far. Even now the huddled soldiers began to move away—roasted on one side and half frozen on the other.

Beyond the trampled fields to his right, Conway's and Huntington's ragged battalions were faring better. Quite a few rough huts had been near enough completed for occupancy, and a dogwood grove afforded them a measure of shelter.

Despite the plans of Colonel Duportail, that competent if irascible Frenchman, for a permanent arrangement, there was no order about the way in which the campfires had been kindled; dozens upon dozens of them glowed within easy eyeshot, and farther across the weed-tufted expanse of meadows more fires winked and blinked. These marked the camp's outer line of defenses.

The snowy ground between the General's marquee and the outer defenses had, during the day, become heavily crisscrossed by caisson and forage wagon wheels, splashed with dark groups of horse droppings, and trampled by the feet of nearly nine thousand men.

A gust of wind stirred sere brown leaves clinging doggedly to the branches of some oaks growing between the temporary headquarters and an old schoolhouse standing at the intersection of Gulph and Baptist roads.

The Corporal sniffed a clear drop back into his nose. "Lay you two to one, Sergeant, if that blasted wind holds out o' the northeast we'll get a three-day blizzard. As if we ain't been nipped raw already."

"Don't want an easy bet, do ye?" Though his effort was hardly more than a gesture, Sergeant Toulmin knelt, commenced carefully to arrange the fir boughs along the base of the marquee's windward side. So few branches would not go very far towards dispelling the frost-laden wind now beginning to dislodge remnants of old snow from the tops of tall oaks.

Plague take it! Why did the General persist in being so careless of his own comfort? Why, Generals Varnum, Wayne, Patterson, and even tough old Teufel Piet Muhlenberg had long since ensconced themselves, more or less comfortably, in various sturdy stone or wood farmhouses of the neighborhood. Lord, how the General's aide, Major Alexander Hamilton, had cursed—out of his superior's earshot—when the General had refused courteously but firmly to occupy Mrs. Deborah Hewes's well-constructed mansion. Under no conditions, the General had declared, would he occupy a comfortable billet while his rank and file chattered their teeth in this uncommonly bitter December air.

The Corporal's attention became attracted by a flight of belated crows flapping along in ragged formation. Above them heavy whitish-gray clouds were commencing to scud furiously across the darkening sky. A regimental clerk appeared at the marquee's flap. He was rubbing ink-stained fingers in an effort to warm them and ended by tucking them under his armpits.

"Maddox! Why in Tunket you loafin' out here? Yer wanted—take a message to Weedon's command."

The Corporal's sharp young features contracted. Weedon? Weedon's brigade was camped about as far as it was possible to go within the new encampment—a generous two miles away. Well, maybe he could warm himself there, the Virginians had been putting the finishing touches on the huts they had built so quickly and according to specification. Old soldiers, they were mighty handy at contriving shelters, didn't stand help-lessly about like the city men of Lachlan McIntosh or Knox's Artillery.

The Corporal began making his way towards a side entrance of the marquee. A faint and querulous outcry drew his attention to an atten-uated V of Canada geese fleeing on rhythmically beating wings before what must certainly be an oncoming storm.

At this familiar discordant music from the sky Tim Maddox's eyes filled, so poignant was the reminder of his home at the mouth of the Pa-tuxent. Why, only a year ago this very Christmas Eve he, Brother John and Billy Stumpp had conducted a mighty successful hunt for just such mighty honkers.

Even inside the marquee, and out of the rising wind, it remained perishingly cold. The chief clerk was still writing, so Maddox seized the opportunity to blow his nose on the dull blue cuff of his stained gray uniform. Those pewter buttons which once had decorated its revers long since had been lost and so did not scratch his nose. Mechanically, the Corporal's stiff red fingers tugged his tunic into a few less wrinkles. He then kicked his feet together, but gently, because the sole of his right shoe was held in precarious security by only two or three oaken pegs and the good Lord knew he didn't want to get his feet full of snow. Of course they had been wet and aching for time out of mind, but still the stout wool of his socks lent a considerable protection.

From beyond a canvas partition separating the orderly room from the rest of the tent rose a deep voice which, somehow, always started a tremor tumbling the length of Tim Maddox's spine.

"You must try to be patient, Wayne. For the moment nothing more can be done than has been done. All this week I have written to every imaginable authority, begging and imploring assistance."

"Then, sir, can we expect no supplies for certain?" Major-General Anthony Wayne's voice was hoarse as the rasping of a grindstone against a sword blade.

"Nothing, I fear, within five days."

"Five days!" The Pennsylvanian exploded. "God in heaven! The army will long since have mutinied and dispersed."

Maddox heard the Commander-in-Chief fetch a slow sigh, indescribably descriptive of fatigue. "You are convinced there is danger of mutiny?"

"As surely as I stand on this spot!" came the immediate reply. "What else can be in the minds of men so betrayed, so victimized by the petty jealousies and greeds of Congress?"

At the far end of the marquee beyond the General's quarters rose angry voices. Maddox recognized them as belonging to various commanding officers. They were lodging complaints and making requisitions which were bound to prove fruitless. The voices grew more strident. One rose above the rest. " 'Fore God we've had no meat in five days, no flour for two! Half of my third platoon wear women's clothes! You don't believe that?" The speaker's accents were shaking with fury. "Then I'll show you. Send in Private Hacker."

Tim Maddox couldn't help peeking around the canvas door in time to behold the shambling entrance of a sunken-eyed, unshaven fellow. He came to an uneasy halt in the midst of a semicircle of red-faced officers. He wore but a single boot; his other foot being clumsily swathed in what looked like a length of lace-edged window curtain. The wrapping was foul, stained with mud and horse manure. Just above his ankle glowed a damp red spot. Private Hacker's breeches hung in tatters, and beneath filthy crossbelts supporting his cartridge box and bayonet was wound a woman's bright red woolen petticoat.

Because he had no sleeves the soldier's arms remained hidden and useless beneath the folds of the petticoat. About his gaunt neck had been twisted an indescribably ragged and worn gray woolen stocking. A woman's dark green calash hat was set on the back of the soldier's head.

"And this, gentlemen," the fierce-eyed Colonel was snapping, "is one of the more warmly dressed of my third platoon." The Colonel, his ear bleeding from an old frostbite, made a derisive gesture. "I give you Private Hacker, sirs, as a Christmas present from our beloved and patriotic Congressmen!"

"What purpose to continue?" A heavy-set major in a patched and bloodstained gray watch cloak turned bitterly aside. "Have we not done all we can? During two long years we have fought the good fight and there remains no strength in us. Tomorrow I resign——"

"And I, too, will send in my commission." The speaker wore the remains of a blue Delaware uniform. "My men are dying of the cold. There is nothing, no straw, no hay, not even fir boughs for them to lie on, let alone blankets."

A hard-pressed commissary officer spread plump hands in despair. "Gentlemen, gentlemen! Would to God I were a magician and could conjure you blankets, uniforms, and provisions out of grass and leaves, but I assure you I am not."

The officers departed sullenly silent or in harsh and bitter complaint. Sulphurous were the curses they laid on Congress and the hopeless inefficiency of the Transport Corps. Mightily depressed, Corporal Maddox returned his attention to the chief clerk. He was barely in time, for that harassed individual was holding out a square of paper sealed with a pale blue wafer.

"For Brigadier-General George Weedon." He coughed. "Urgent; shake your butt getting there, Corporal."

Outside, the wind tore at a man like a harpy's claws, so Maddox halted long enough to tie a battered tricorn onto his head with the bight of a three-yard-long muffler. Right now he wouldn't have taken ten pounds gold for that length of warm green wool.

The sun had almost disappeared but still managed to gild the tops of some hardwood trees towering above the General's marquee. Here and there it sketched bright streaks along the barrels of the guns in a park of artillery arranged along the edge of that great field which would, at a later date, become known as the Grand Parade.

Every few rods Maddox encountered little groups of soldiers stumping along, their heads tilted against the rising wind. Most were lugging armfuls of fagots, but quite a few were engaged in hauling hewn and notched lengths of log towards a row of huts rising among the stark black dogwood trees back of Woodford's Virginia Continentals. Because during the day the snow had become trampled and hard packed their progress was not too painful.

All the same Tim Maddox proceeded gingerly because of his bad shoe. In all directions he discerned knots of soldiers in every manner of garb, sitting on logs, crouched shoulder to shoulder about smoky green wood campfires attempting to cook whatever scraps of food they had been able to discover.

High in the darkening heavens a faint, sibilant singing sound had made itself noticeable. Corporal Maddox recognized the phenomenon at once. Frost—snow, and lots of it, would soon start falling.

The snow beneath his feet commenced to creak—another bad sign. And to think that once, long, comfortable years ago, he, his brothers and sisters had prayed for snow on Christmas Eve!

The wind continued to increase, lashing pitilessly at rows of ribby nags tethered, forlorn and miserable, to the artillery picket lines. Gradually, the beasts were shifting to present their rumps to the impending blizzard. The darker it grew, the more effectively did fires tint the snow a pretty rose red and cast into silhouette the miserable artillerists.

While plodding on across a field tenanted by empty and abandoned baggage wagons the courier came upon three scarecrow figures. They were from Stirling's New York levies. Their capes fluttering like a bird's broken wings, two of them bent over a third who lay motionless and inert across the ruts of mud created by the passage of some heavy caisson.

"Come on, Hans," one of them was pleading. " 'Tain't much further to them fires—not above two hundred yard. Ye can do it, Hans. Then ye'll be nice and warm and maybe, because it's Christmas Eve, they'll give us somethin' to eat."

The other shook the prostrate man's shoulder. "Hans," he cried, "rouse up. You can't lie here like this, ye'll freeze, sure fire. Hans, ain't you and me come all the way from Staten Island? We come all that distance, we can make another— Oh, blazes, it ain't above a hundred yards." But the man lying face downwards in the snow only groaned.

Maddox saw why the soldier, Hans, was unable to rise. The soles of his naked feet had degenerated into a pulpy mass of mud, torn flesh, and sticky blood.

"You'll never get him up," he predicted. "Suppose you fellers take his shoulders and I'll lug his feet."

The New Yorkers looked up, hollow eyes ringed in numb surprise.

"What for you helpin' us? You ain't New York. What outfit are you from anyway?"

"Smallwood's Maryland Cavalry," Maddox announced in conscious pride.

"Shucks! thought all you fancy Nancys had traipsed off south." The larger of the New Yorkers blew his nose with his fingers.

"They were ordered away. I'm a courier at Headquarters."

The smaller New Yorker's lip curled. "Oh, one of them fat cats? Good to know somebody gets something t' eat around here, eh, Job?"

A sharp resentment heated in Maddox's features, but he controlled himself. "Come on, if you want me to help you. I've got a message to deliver."

The weight they lifted was slight, for the man Hans was hardly a man, but a boy roughly Maddox's own age—nineteen. Pretty soon they came up to a sagging tent marked Medical Service. Already it was jam packed, but they slid the semiconscious Hans in on top of a fellow who looked more dead than alive.

"Thanks," was all the two soldiers said, but Maddox didn't expect any more. They were New Yorkers from whom none but a fool would have looked for any politeness.

Pretty soon Corporal Maddox reached the outer cantonments of Anthony Wayne's burly Pennsylvanians and, as he had fully expected, found them in considerably better case. There were enough sturdy German farmers among them to have built huts sufficient to shelter most of their number. In the next company street the courier slowed his pace.

Despite the wind and the penetrating chill, a group of Germans was engaged in dressing a small fir tree with whatever had come to hand. Brass buttons, bits of tarnished gold lace, lengths of soiled pink ribbon were being employed. A big-handed sergeant was, with great care, unraveling a worn-out red stocking. Another was laboriously cutting six pointed stars out of bits of foolscap.

Yes, the Pennsylvanians were mighty lucky; they'd a stone jug warming beside their roaring campfire.

Corporal Maddox would have liked to linger at least until the lice, chilled and dormant in the seams of his clothing, felt impelled to start feeding, but Weedon's troops lay encamped a good mile farther on.

Hands clenched behind him, Major-General Anthony Wayne tramped angrily back and forth over broken leaves, dead grass, and melting snow marking the grimy canvas flooring of the Commander-in-Chief's compartment.

"Your Excellency," he was growling, "there is no longer any purpose in continuing this campaign. Is it not now entirely plain that the Congress has traduced and abandoned us? To disperse at once is our only recourse. Even so hundreds will perish—to delay will cost still more lives. I assure you, sir, our rank and file are utterly dispirited and the officers disgusted. Yesterday alone four regimental surgeons packed up and rode off—no attempt at a by-your-leave. Possibly in the spring, sir, a new army can be assembled, but at present our situation is hopeless—quite hopeless."

The big Pennsylvanian seated himself momentarily on a corner of a map chest. The once-brilliant red revers of his uniform lapels and cuffs looked more than ever faded, worn, and weather-beaten.

General Washington for some instants remained silent, his wide mouth immobile, its lips compressed. At length he said, "All that you say is only too true, old friend, and you never were a faint-heart. To you I will confess that I, too, find myself at my wit's end. How can our people elect such contemptible, self-seeking poltroons and scoundrels to the Congress?"

The Commander-in-Chief's steel-gray eyes lowered themselves until they came to rest on a litter of papers crowding his field desk.

"I have said my say, Your Excellency." Wayne got stiffly to his feet, fixed a look of deep affection upon his chief. "Whatever is your decision I shall abide by it—to the full limit of my ability." Wayne pulled his triple cape tighter about him. "And now a more immediate matter. Pray indulge me if I protest against your refusal to move into Mrs. Hewes's residence. You, sir, constitute the very soul of this army. Without you it would have dispersed long since. Promise at least to sup with me—'tis the eve of Christmas, after all."

The Commander-in-Chief hesitated, half smiled. He felt sorely tempted. Throughout the Continental Service Anthony Wayne had been long renowned for setting an excellent mess even in the midst of the most miserable campaigns.

"I will attempt to indulge you—and myself, Anthony. You may rely upon it. If possible, I will appear by eight of this evening, otherwise, pray do not wait upon my arrival."

Wayne drew himself up, bowed. "May I wish you a Merry Christmas, sir? Would to God there were some hope of fulfillment!"

"There will be other Christmases," the General reminded, but the words fell heavily from his lips as, with a tired gesture, he turned back to that mound of documents awaiting his attention.

He heard Wayne lift the canvas barrier, heard the rhythmic *slap—slap!* of the guard's hands on his piece as he presented arms. As seldom before, the General felt very alone. Light penetrating the canvas was feeble indeed—nearly as dim as the prospects of this half-born Republic.

Mechanically, the General's chilled knuckles rubbed at eyes grown hot and weary from sleeplessness. Practically speaking, what hope remained to an army in a like situation? Even lion-hearts like Nat Greene and Tony Wayne were convinced that the end had come. The weight of massive bullion epaulettes dragged at George Washington's shoulders and his big body sagged on a camp stool until the silvery clamor of wild geese in the sky attracted his attention.

The Potomac must be full of them by now. Christmas Eve! Slaves in the quarters behind his long white mansion would be making merry, crying "Christmas gift!" war or no war. He slumped still more on his stool, absently watched the gray mist of his breath go drifting across the tent. How long since he had ridden his beloved acres? Years. Years. Years.

Christmas at Mount Vernon was a wonderful season—it meant the presence of family friends and neighbors; good wines, fires, candles and lovely women in dazzling silks and brocades.

Grimly, the General surveyed his surroundings. Yonder, only half seen in the gloom, stood a battered chest containing a few clothes, his field desk, and a mud-splashed gray riding cape flung across his folding camp bed. Why must this go on and on? Secretly loving America at the bottom of his heart, Lord Howe undoubtedly would grant the most lenient of terms.

Suddenly the Commander-in-Chief sat erect, selected a sheet of foolscap, and commenced to write.

> In Camp at Valley Forge
> December ye 24, 1777.

To the President of Congress

Sir:

> Conscious of the Fruitlessness of further Contest with the Enemy and aware that my Army has been Abandoned to starvation and neglect by the various State Authorities and by the Congress itself, I have, sir, the Honour herewith to tender my resigna——

The quill ceased its busy scratching. A distant clamor was making itself heard. The General stiffened, listening intently. So Wayne *had* been well informed—already a mutiny was breaking out.

Hastily closing the clasps on his long gray watch cloak, General Washington donned a rabbit's fur cap he favored in cold weather and strode into the anteroom.

"The Sergeant of the Guard and two soldiers will accompany me; no more."

Gray cloak billowing to his long stride, the General strode across the anteroom and, fearful of what awaited in the wind-filled twilight, set off in that direction from which the uproar was arising so rapidly that the three enlisted men at his heels were forced to adopt a sort of dog-trot to keep up.

A keen northeast wind smote him, groped beneath his cloak and uniform like a cold hand equipped with chill fingers. Soon it would be wholly dark, but very pale yellow streaks in the west still marked the last of the daylight. Christmas Eve had indeed commenced.

The tumult had died away; it sounded however as if it had originated somewhere among Major-General Henry Knox's artillery regiments. The Commander-in-Chief halted a moment, listening. As he did so he felt the first gentle impact of falling snowflakes.

"God help us," he muttered. "More snow." More snow, and already this year of 1777 had proved to be the bitterest, snowiest fall and winter within living memory!

Probably children in the streets of Philadelphia were laughing to see the myriad soft white flakes come fluttering, tumbling down to spell good coasting for new Christmas sleds. But to the Valley Forge encampment snow meant blocked roads, ever increasing misery around the campfires, more sick in the hospitals and less hope of supplies.

"Aye, Mark, when it starts dry and fine like this 'tis going to snow hard." The Sergeant of the Guard began cursing softly, and turned up his greasy collar against the chill blasts.

Head bowed against the snowy wind, General Washington made his way towards the nearest ring of campfires and noted that some of the batteries had rigged tarpaulins horizontally between gun carriages and caissons, thus improvising tents under which they huddled. A card game was in progress in one with the players employing bits of biscuit for stakes. A gust of laughter arose when a player's chilled fingers accidentally faced a card and so lost him a big piece of crust.

This, then, was the clamor he had feared. Smiling thinly, the General continued his tour. If mutiny impended, he meant to prepare against it, and at once.

Nearing the outer line of defenses, the tall, erect figure heard, of all things, someone singing, singing an old English Christmas carol. The caroler proved to be a surprisingly aged soldier wearing the tatters of a faded brown uniform; accompanying him was a corporal in a very unsoldierly Quaker hat and some gentleman's long-abandoned dress coat. The garment was of vivid canary-yellow brocade and glowed as if burnished by the campfire's light.

This squad must have something special cooking in the pot, for, unobservant of their visitors, they all kept an eye on it. Vaguely, the General wondered what their prize could be. A moment later he passed, abandoned on the fresh fallen snow, the skins and heads of a pair of striped house cats.

Someone recognized him, immediately sang out, "Here's the General! Three cheers for the Commander-in-Chief. Huzzah! Huzzah!"

The first light layer of snowflakes fell from their clothes as they struggled into a line and stood to attention.

A sergeant, his rag-clad feet flopping and spraying the snow up to his knees, strode forward, saluted awkwardly. "Sorry, sir, I—I can't turn out my platoon no better. Comes another year, sir, we'll turn out fit to make the Royal Tyrant's own guards look like ragpickers."

"Bravely spoken, Sergeant, and I am sure you will. I am profoundly regretful," Washington said in his big clear Southern voice, "that on this holy eve, you and your platoon enjoy so few of the necessities." He tried to sound encouraging. "You may pass the word that I have made the firmest of representations to the Congress."

"Don't concern yourself over us, Gen'ral," a weak voice hailed from the farther corner of the campfire. "We made out before, sir, and by God we'll make out this time, too. Won't we, lads?"

From the bed of a rickety farm wagon appeared two or three tousled heads. Feebly, they joined in the cheering.

"The sick?" General Washington inquired.

"No, sir," the sergeant said uncomfortably. "It's only they ain't got no coats nor shirts so they're layin' together to keep warm." The Sergeant swayed a little.

"When did you last taste meat?" demanded the Commander-in-Chief; his brows, jutting in the falling snow, were catching a few fine flakes.

"Oh, not so long ago, sir."

"Answer me exactly, Sergeant."

"Why, sir, 'twere five, no, six days ago."

The snow fell thicker, and the wind commenced to rattle and toss the bare limbs of a hickory grove behind the caissons.

The General moved on. Sometimes he found the troops crouched like misshapen gnomes about the fires; they never even raised their heads. Their hats and backs gradually were becoming whitened. They looked, on occasion, like stumps in a burnt-over field.

A miserable company of Poor's command had built a roaring bonfire because their huts stood barely commenced.

Unrecognized here, General Washington circulated quietly. He noticed to one side a young man, a corporal by the green worsted knot on his shoulder holding a cowhide knapsack on his knees and, of all things, attempting to write by the dancing firelight.

"May I obtrude on your privacy enough to inquire what prompts you to write on this cold and miserable evening?"

The boy, recognizing an officer, but not his identity, got up, his face pallid and worried-looking. "Why, why, sir, this being the eve of Christmas, I was thinking of home—and my parents."

"Your name and grade?"

"Corporal Richard Wheeler, sir, of Poor's New York Brigade."

"Your letter. I wish to inspect it."

The Corporal blinked eyes red and swollen from long exposure to acrid wood smoke. "Why, why, sir! I swear 'tis only a letter to my mother."

In response to the silent demand presented by the General's outstretched hand Corporal Wheeler surrendered his rumpled bit of paper.

The General turned his back towards the flames in order to read:

December 24, 1777.

Respected Madam,

This is to convey my Christmas love and duty to all at Home. I would not have you Credit certain unpatriotick Rumors concerning the true Situation of this Army. You need have no concern for we are very Comfortable, we are indeed living on the Fat of the Land——

The General swallowed hard and stared into the flying snow a moment before returning the letter. Then, to Corporal Wheeler's amazement this strange officer very gravely saluted him before stalking off into the wind-filled dark.

The next troops in position along the outer perimeter of defenses proved to be Glover's Massachusetts brigade, a curious organization composed largely of fishermen and sailors which had proved itself useful under a hundred difficult circumstances. This particular half company was enjoying the music of a fiddle and the antics of a pair of gap-toothed and unshaven soldiers ridiculously attired in female garments. To a clapped accompaniment they were kicking up their heels in an old country dance. Subconsciously, the General wondered why this half company seemed extra gay. He beckoned a private, who by the half light also failed to recognize him.

"Why all this merriment? You would appear to have small cause for gaiety."

"Why, sir, have you forgot? This is Christmas Eve." The speaker winked, stepped closer. "Besides, us boys have stumbled on a bit of luck—monstrous good luck."

"Good luck?"

The bearded soldier slid an arm from under the woman's green shawl protecting his shoulders. "D'you mark yonder alder copse—and what's in it?"

The General shielded his eyes against hard-driven snowflakes, barely made out a large dark blur and a small one. "A horse, is it not, and a man on guard?"

"Aye, that's what they are, my friend. Just that."

"What is afoot?"

"Yonder stands a snot-nosed artillery-ist with a fixed bayonet."

The General raised his coat collar against the fine particles beginning to sift in.

"But why is he there, soldier?"

"Like us, he's waiting for yonder old crowbait to fall." The speaker gave a great booming laugh and waved his arms. "So long as the nag stands, he belongs to dear General Knox's artillery, but once he falls and can't rise, he's ours, and then, my friend, we eat, by God! Ain't that cause for cheer?

"Hah! Did you mark how he swayed just then? Your pardon!" The speaker dashed off through the whirling snow.

Like winter wolves ringing a crippled moose, an irregular circle of hollow-eyed infantrymen moved to surround that little alder thicket in which stood the poor furry beast. So gaunt that every rib showed, the horse held its snow-powdered head so low that its loose nether lip almost brushed the ground. It began swaying more noticeably and heaving long, shuddering sighs.

Cursing, hurling obscenities at the gathering crowd, the lone artillery-man kept tramping back and forth, trying to keep warm. Why in hell wouldn't the miserable creature collapse? Satan alone knew where this wretched beast had found strength enough to wander thus far from its picket line. By this time what little there was to eat at his unit must have been consumed, which meant for him another long night on an empty belly.

On second thought, the sentry told himself he wouldn't go right back to his battery. He'd linger here and maybe share in the meat, for all it was certain to prove as tough and stringy as an old boot.

Once more the tall figure and his three followers moved on. The wind now was really roaring, and snow flying in fine particles like spume over the bow of a ship laboring through a storm. The Sergeant lengthened his stride, saluted anxiously.

"Begging the General's pardon, what with this storm worsening we're like to lose our way."

"Very well, but I will have a look at Learned's command on our route back to Headquarters."

The Rhode Islanders recognized their commander at once and ran to form a ragged double line in his honor, yelling all the while, "Long live Liberty!" "Long live the United States!" "Three cheers for the Commander-in-Chief!"

A lieutenant commanding the nearest platoon hurried up and saluted stiffly with his sword.

"Your Excellency, we—er—possess a trifle of Medford rum. We would deem ourselves mighty honored an you would give us your opinion of its worth. After all, sir, 'tis Christmas tomorrow." He beckoned forward a soldier who offered a steaming earthenware cup.

There was only a gallon jug among above two hundred rag-clad and blanket-wrapped Rhode Islanders. If each were lucky he might get a tea-spoonful of the fiery spirit.

"Your health—fellow soldiers!" The General barely wet his lips, but made a great pretense of swallowing.

"Next Christmas," called a stumpy little soldier, " 'twill *us* be eatin' roast goose in Philadelphia and the Lobster-backs settin' on their butts out in the cold."

"Perhaps. But have you not suffered enough?" the Commander inquired.

"It's been no bed of roses, sir," the Lieutenant said, "but having come this far we may as well go the rest of the distance. With you to lead us, we *can't* lose!"

The General was repassing Glover's position when there arose a wild yell, followed by delighted shouts of "Merry Christmas! Merry Christmas!"

"That poor skate must have fallen at last," grunted one of the bodyguard. "Ain't they the lucky dogs?"

During the General's absence some holly branches and a larger amount of mistletoe had appeared and were being tied in place by Sergeant Toulmin. Fires had been built up at either end of the Headquarters marquee, and about them a motley assortment of junior officers, some of them French, stood warming their hands. Every now and then they shook themselves, dog-like, to rid their coats and cloaks of the whirling snow.

General Washington paused briefly, a thin smile curving his wide mouth.

"A good evening to you, Gentlemen. Pray seek your quarters and find what cheer you can. May God relieve your sufferings, if the Congress will not. A Merry Christmas to you all!"

Snow-powdered cape asway, the big Virginian turned, re-entered his compartment. His aide, darkly handsome young Major Alexander Hamilton, was working in obvious impatience between a pair of stump candles that drew brief flashes from his always well-polished buttons.

"Sir," he said, "General Wayne's compliments. He is dispatching a mount for your convenience at half after seven. He counts on you for supper."

Washington removed his cape and hung it carefully on its peg. "You will go in my place, Major," he announced. "I shall be too occupied with correspondence to take advantage of General Wayne's hospitality—much as I should enjoy it."

The young West Indian hesitated, his bold black eyes half closed. What was up? In arranging documents on the Commander-in-Chief's desk he had come across that incompleted letter to the President of Congress. General Washington's features, however, were enigmatic—and weary, oh, so weary.

"Do you wish to finish this—er communication, sir?"

"Thank you. I will attend to it."

"There is nothing more, sir?"

"No, no, Major. Go and amuse yourself. You have earned the right."

Major Hamilton saluted and stepped outside, but lingered undecided until he was aware of a sudden flare of light beating through the canvas, a glow such as might be caused by a burning document.

DEAR MADAM:
WE KNOW THAT YOU WILL WANT TO CONTRIBUTE ...

PHYLLIS McGINLEY

Christmas is coming,
The geese are getting fat.
Please to put a penny in an old man's hat.
If you haven't got a penny, a ha'penny will do.
If you haven't got a ha'penny, God help you!

Please to put a nickel,
    Please to put a dime.
How petitions trickle
    In at Christmas time!
Come and Save a Scholar.
    Bring the heathen hope.
Just enclose a dollar
    Within the envelope.
Send along a tenner,
    Anyhow a five,
And let the Friends of Poetry inaugurate their drive.

Share your weekly ration
    With miners up in Nome.
Give a small donation
    To build a Starlings' Home.
Please to send a shillin'
    For lawyers in the lurch.

Drop a pretty bill in
   The offering at church.
Remember all the orphans,
   Recall the boys at camps,
And decorate your letters with illuminated stamps.

The Common Colds Committee
   Implores you to assist.
They're canvassing the city,
   They've got you on their list.
Demonstrate your mettle
   For half a hundred causes.
Fill the yawning kettle
   Of the corner Santa Clauses.
Give for holy Charity
   Wherever she appears.
And don't forget the Firemen and the Southern Mountaineers.

Christmas is coming,
The mail is getting fat.
Please to put a penny in every proffered hat.
If you haven't got a penny, a ha'pence let it be.
If you haven't got a ha'pence left, you're just like me.

OFFICE PARTY

PHYLLIS McGINLEY

This holy night in open forum
   Miss McIntosh, who handles Files,
Has lost one shoe and her decorum.
   Stately, the frozen chairman smiles

On Media, desperately vocal.
   Credit, though they have lost their hopes
Of edging toward an early Local,
   Finger their bonus envelopes.

The glassy boys, the bursting girls
   Of Copy, start a Conga clatter
To a swung carol. Limply curls
   The final sandwich on the platter

Till hark! a herald Messenger
   (Room 414) lifts loudly up
His quavering tenor. Salesmen stir
   Libation for his Lily cup.

"Noel," he pipes, "Noel, Noel."
   Some wag beats tempo with a ruler.
And the plump blonde from Personnel
   Is sick behind the water cooler.

LADY SELECTING HER CHRISTMAS CARDS

PHYLLIS McGINLEY

Fastidiously, with gloved and careful fingers,
   Through the marked samples she pursues her search.
Which shall it be: the snowscape's wintry languors
   Complete with church,

An urban skyline, children sweetly pretty
   Sledding downhill, the chaste, ubiquitous wreath,
Schooner or candle or the simple Scottie
   With verse underneath?

Perhaps it might be better to emblazon
   With words alone the stiff, punctilious square.
(Oh, not Victorian, certainly. This season
   One meets it everywhere.)

She has a duty proper to the weather—
   A Birth she must announce, a rumor to spread,
Wherefore the very spheres once sang together
   And a star shone overhead.

Here are the Tidings which the shepherds panted
   One to another, kneeling by their flocks.
And they will bear her name (engraved, not printed),
   Twelve-fifty for the box.

Shakespeare's Christmas Gift to Queen Bess in 1596

Anna B. McMahan

The numberless diamond-shaped window panes of the Mermaid Tavern are twinkling like so many stars in the chill December air of London. It is the last meeting of the Mermaid Club for the year 1596, and not a member is absent. As they drop in by twos and threes and gather in groups about the room, it is plain that expectation is on tip-toe. . . . Some are young, handsome, fastidious in person and dress; others are bohemian in costume, speech, and action; all wear knee breeches, and nearly all have pointed beards. He of the harsh fighting face, of the fine eye and coarse lip and the shaggy hair, whom they call Ben, although one of the youngest is yet plainly one of the leaders both for wit and for wisdom.

That grave and handsome gentleman whose lordly bearing and princely dress mark his high rank is another favourite. He has written charming poems, has fought gallantly on many fields, has voyaged widely on many seas, has founded colonies in distant America, is a favourite of the Queen. But in this Mermaid Club his chief glory is that he is its founder and leader, the one whose magnetism and personal charm have summoned and cemented in friendship all these varied elements.

At last the all-important matter of the yearly Christmas play at court has been settled; the Master of the Revels has chosen from the rich stores of his manuscripts *The Midsummer Night's Dream,* graciously adding that "for wit and mirth it is like to please her Majesty exceedingly. . . ."

For now the successful candidate is one of the youngest and best beloved of this jolly coterie, and their pride in him is shown by the eager-

ness with which they await his coming to read to them the changes in the manuscript of his play since its former presentation. Ah! hear the burst of applause that greets his late arrival—a high-browed, sandy-haired man of thirty-two, lithe in figure, of middle height, with a smile of great sweetness, yet sad withal. On his face, one may read the lines of recent sorrow, and all know that he has returned but recently to London from the mournful errand which took him to his Stratford home—the burial of his dearly beloved and only son, Hamnet. The plaudits for the author of the most successful play of the season—*Romeo and Juliet* ... —were little heeded by the grief-stricken father as he urged his horse over the rough roads of the four days' journey, arriving just too late for a parting word from dying lips. But private sorrows are not for those who are called to public duties; a writer must trim his pen not to his own mood, but to the mood of the hour. And Queen Elizabeth, old in years, but ever young in her love of fun and frolic and flattery, must be made to forget the heaviness of time and the infirmities of age. If she may no longer take part in outdoor sports—the hunting, the hawking, the bear-baiting—she still may command processions, fetes, masques, and stage-plays. It pleases her now to see this wonderful fairy piece, of which she has heard so much since, two years ago, it graced the nuptials of the Earl of Derby. Does she not remember also that pretty impromptu verse of the author when acting the part of King in another man's play, two years ago at Greenwich? Did she not twice drop her glove near his feet in crossing the stage? ... And how happily had he responded to the challenge! True to the character as well as to the metre of his part, he had picked up the glove, presenting it to its owner with the words:—"And though now bent on this high embassy, Yet stoope we to take up our cousin's glove."

It is Christmas night. Lords, ladies, and ambassadors have been summoned to Whitehall Palace to witness the play for which author, actors, and artists of many kinds have been working so industriously during the past few weeks. The Banqueting Hall, with a temporary stage at one end, has been converted into a fine auditorium.

Facing the stage, and beneath her canopy of state, sits Queen Elizabeth, in ruff and farthingale, her hair loaded with crowns and powdered with diamonds, while her sharp smile and keen glance take note of every incident. Nearest her person and evidently the chief favourite of the moment, is the man who has long been considered the Adonis of the Court. He is now also its hero, having but recently returned from the wars in Spain, where his gallantry and promptitude at Cadiz have won new glories for Her Majesty. In five short years more, his head will come to the block by decree of this same Majesty; but this no one can foresee and all voices now unite in praises for the brave and generous Essex.

Another conspicuous favourite is a blue-eyed, pink-cheeked young fellow of twenty-three, whose scarcely perceptible beard and moustache, and curly auburn hair falling over his shoulders and halfway to his waist, would suggest femininity except for his martial manner and tall figure. His resplendent attire is notable even in this gorgeously arrayed company. His white satin doublet has a broad collar, edged with lace and embroidered with silver thread; the white trunks and knee breeches are laced with gold; the sword belt, embroidered in red and gold, is decorated at intervals with white silk bows; purple garters, embroidered in silver thread, fasten the white stockings below the knee. As one of the handsomest of Elizabeth's courtiers, and also one of the most distinguished for birth, wealth, and wit, he would be a striking figure at any time; but tonight he has the added distinction of being the special friend and munificent patron of the author of the play that they have come to witness. To him had been dedicated the author's first appeal to the reading public—a poem called "Venus and Adonis," published some three years since; also, a certain "sugared sonnet," privately circulated, protesting—

> For to no other pass my verses tend
> Than of your graces and your gifts to tell.

And through the patronage of this man—the gracious Earl of Southampton—the actor-author was first brought to the Queen's notice, finally leading to the present distinction at her hands.

But now the stage compels attention. The silk curtains are withdrawn, disclosing a setting of such elaboration and illusion as never before has been witnessed by sixteenth-century eyes. Never before has the frugal Elizabeth consented to such an expenditure for costumes, properties, lights, and music. In vain the audience awaits the coming of the author; he is behind the scenes, an anxious and watchful partner with the machinist in securing the proper working of these new mechanical appliances, and the smoothness of the scene shifting. The Queen is a connoisseur in these matters, and there must be no bungling. . . .

The Christmas play is over, but not over the Christmas fun. Lords and ladies are but human, and have devised a "stately dance," in which they themselves participate until nearly sunrise, the Queen herself joining at times, and never so happy as when assured of her "wondrous majesty and grace."

Merry Christmas

HERMAN MELVILLE

Chapter 22, Moby-Dick

At length, towards noon, upon the final dismissal of the ship's riggers, and after the *Pequod* had been hauled out from the wharf, and after the ever-thoughtful Charity had come off in a whaleboat, with her last gift—a night-cap for Stubb, the second mate, her brother-in-law, and a spare Bible for the steward—after all this, the two captains, Peleg and Bildad, issued from the cabin, and turning to the chief mate, Peleg said:

'Now, Mr. Starbuck, are you sure everything is right? Captain Ahab is all ready—just spoke to him—nothing more to be got from shore, eh? Well, call all hands, then. Muster 'em aft here—blast 'em!'

'No need of profane words, however great the hurry, Peleg,' said Bildad, 'but away with thee, friend Starbuck, and do our bidding.'

How now! Here upon the very point of starting for the voyage, Captain Peleg and Captain Bildad were going it with a high hand on the quarter-deck, just as if they were to be joint-commanders at sea, as well as to all appearances in port. And, as for Captain Ahab, no sign of him was yet to be seen; only, they said he was in the cabin. But then, the idea was, that his presence was by no means necessary in getting the ship under weigh, and steering her well out to sea. Indeed, as that was not at all his proper business, but the pilot's; and as he was not yet completely recovered—so they said—therefore, Captain Ahab stayed below. And all this seemed natural enough; especially as in the merchant service many captains never show themselves on deck for a considerable time after heaving up the anchor, but remain over the cabin table, having a farewell merry-making with their shore friends, before they quit the ship for good with the pilot.

But there was not much chance to think over the matter, for Captain Peleg was now all alive. He seemed to do most of the talking and commanding, and not Bildad.

'Aft here, ye sons of bachelors,' he cried, as the sailors lingered at the main-mast. 'Mr. Starbuck, drive 'em aft.'

'Strike the tent there!'—was the next order. As I hinted before, this whalebone marquee was never pitched except in port; and on board the *Pequod,* for thirty years, the order to strike the tent was well known to be the next thing to heaving up the anchor.

'Man the capstan! Blood and thunder!—jump!'—was the next command, and the crew sprang for the handspikes.

Now, in getting under weigh, the station generally occupied by the pilot is the forward part of the ship. And here Bildad, who, with Peleg, be it known, in addition to his other offices, was one of the licensed pilots of the port—he being suspected to have got himself made a pilot in order to save the Nantucket pilot-fee to all the ships he was concerned in, for he never piloted any other craft—Bildad, I say, might now be seen actively engaged in looking over the bows for the approaching anchor, and at intervals singing what seemed a dismal stave of psalmody, to cheer the hands at the windlass, who roared forth some sort of a chorus about the girls in Booble Alley, with hearty good will. Nevertheless, not three days previous, Bildad had told them that no profane songs would be allowed on board the *Pequod,* particularly in getting under weigh; and Charity, his sister, had placed a small choice copy of Watts in each seaman's berth.

Meantime, overseeing the other part of the ship, Captain Peleg ripped and swore astern in the most frightful manner. I almost thought he would sink the ship before the anchor could be got up; involuntarily I paused on my handspike, and told Queequeg to do the same, thinking of the perils we both ran, in starting on the voyage with such a devil for a pilot. I was comforting myself, however, with the thought that in pious Bildad might be found some salvation, spite of his seven hundred and seventy-seventh lay; when I felt a sudden sharp poke in my rear, and turning round, was horrified at the apparition of Captain Peleg in the act of withdrawing his leg from my immediate vicinity. That was my first kick.

'Is that the way they heave in the marchant service?' he roared. 'Spring, thou sheep-head; spring, and break thy back bone! Why don't ye spring, I say, all of ye—spring! Quohag! spring, thou chap with the red whiskers;

spring there, Scotch-cap; spring, thou green pants. Spring, I say, all of ye, and spring your eyes out!' And so saying, he moved along the windlass, here and there using his leg very freely, while imperturbable Bildad kept leading off with his psalmody. Thinks I, Captain Peleg must have been drinking something to-day.

At last the anchor was up, the sails were set, and off we glided. It was a short, cold Christmas; and as the short northern day merged into night, we found ourselves almost broad upon the wintry ocean, whose freezing spray cased us in ice, as in polished armor. The long rows of teeth on the bulwarks glistened in the moonlight; and like the white ivory tusks of some huge elephant, vast curving icicles depended from the bows.

Lank Bildad, as pilot, headed the first watch, and ever and anon, as the old craft deep dived into the green seas, and sent the shivering frost all over her, and the winds howled, and the cordage rang, his steady notes were heard,—

> 'Sweet fields beyond the swelling flood,
>   Stand dressed in living green.
> So to the Jews old Canaan stood,
>   While Jordan rolled between.'

Never did those sweet words sound more sweetly to me than then. They were full of hope and fruition. Spite of this frigid winter night in the boisterous Atlantic, spite of my wet feet and wetter jacket, there was yet, it then seemed to me, many a pleasant haven in store; and meads and glades so eternally vernal, that the grass shot up by the spring, untrodden, unwilted, remains at midsummer.

At last we gained such an offing, that the two pilots were needed no longer. The stout sail-boat that had accompanied us began ranging alongside.

It was curious and not unpleasing, how Peleg and Bildad were affected at this juncture, especially Captain Bildad. For loath to depart, yet; very loath to leave, for good, a ship bound on so long and perilous a voyage—beyond both stormy Capes; a ship in which some thousands of his hard-earned dollars were invested; a ship, in which an old shipmate sailed as captain; a man almost as old as he, once more starting to encounter all the terrors of the pitiless jaw; loath to say good-bye to a thing so every way brimful of every interest to him,—poor old Bildad lingered long; paced the deck with anxious strides; ran down into the cabin to speak another farewell word there; again came on deck, and looked to windward; looked towards the wide and endless waters, only bounded by the far-off unseen Eastern Continents; looked towards the land; looked aloft;

looked right and left; looked everywhere and nowhere; and at last, mechanically coiling a rope upon its pin, convulsively grasped stout Peleg by the hand, and holding up a lantern, for a moment stood gazing heroically in his face, as much as to say, 'Nevertheless, friend Peleg, I can stand it; yes, I can.'

As for Peleg himself, he took it more like a philosopher; but for all his philosophy, there was a tear twinkling in his eye, when the lantern came too near. And he, too, did not a little run from cabin to deck—now a word below, and now a word with Starbuck, the chief mate.

But, at last, he turned to his comrade, with a final sort of look about him,—'Captain Bildad—come, old shipmate, we must go. Back the main-yard there! Boat ahoy! Stand by to come close alongside, now! Careful, careful!—come, Bildad, boy—say your last. Luck to ye, Starbuck—luck to ye, Mr. Stubb—luck to ye, Mr. Flask—good-bye, and good luck to ye all—and this day three years I'll have a hot supper smoking for ye in old Nantucket. Hurrah and away!'

'God bless ye, and have ye in His holy keeping, men,' murmured old Bildad, almost incoherently. 'I hope ye'll have fine weather now, so that Captain Ahab may soon be moving among ye—a pleasant sun is all he needs, and ye'll have plenty of them in the tropic voyage ye go. Be careful in the hunt, ye mates. Don't stave the boats needlessly, ye harpooneers; good white cedar plank is raised full three per cent. within the year. Don't forget your prayers, either. Mr. Starbuck, mind that cooper don't waste the spare staves. Oh! the sail-needles are in the green locker! Don't whale it too much a'Lord's days, men; but don't miss a fair chance either, that's rejecting Heaven's good gifts. Have an eye to the molasses tierce, Mr. Stubb; it was a little leaky, I thought. If ye touch at the islands, Mr. Flask, beware of fornication. Good-bye, good-bye! Don't keep that cheese too long down in the hold, Mr. Starbuck; it'll spoil. Be careful with the butter—twenty cents the pound it was, and mind ye, if—'

'Come, come, Captain Bildad; stop palavering—away!' and with that, Peleg hurried him over the side, and both dropt into the boat.

Ship and boat diverged; the cold, damp night breeze blew between; a screaming gull flew overhead; the two hulls wildly rolled; we gave three heavy-hearted cheers, and blindly plunged like fate into the lone Atlantic.

CHRISTMAS STORY

H. L. MENCKEN

Despite all the snorting against them in works of divinity, it has always been my experience that infidels—or freethinkers, as they usually prefer to call themselves—are a generally estimable class of men, with strong overtones of the benevolent and even of the sentimental. This was certainly true, for example, of Leopold Bortsch, *Totsäufer** for the Scharnhorst Brewery, in Baltimore, forty-five years ago, whose story I have told, alas only piecemeal, in various previous communications to the press. If you want a bird's-eye view of his character, you can do no better than turn to the famous specifications for an ideal bishop in I Timothy III, 2–6. So far as I know, no bishop now in practice on earth meets those specifications precisely, and more than one whom I could mention falls short of them by miles, but Leopold qualified under at least eleven of the sixteen counts, and under some of them he really shone.

He was extremely liberal (at least with the brewery's money), he had only one wife (a natural blonde weighing a hundred and eighty-five pounds) and treated her with great humanity, he was (I quote the text) "no striker . . . not a brawler," and he was preëminently "vigilant, sober, of good behavior, given to hospitality, apt to teach." Not once in the days I knew and admired him, *c.* 1900, did he ever show anything remotely resembling a bellicose and rowdy spirit, not even against the pri-

---

* A *Totsäufer* (literally, dead-drinker) is a brewery's customers' man. One of his most important duties is to carry on in a wild and inconsolable manner at the funerals of saloonkeepers.

meval Prohibitionists of the age, the Lutheran pastors who so often plastered him from the pulpit, or the saloonkeepers who refused to lay in Scharnhorst beer. He was a sincere friend to the orphans, the aged, all blind and one-legged men, ruined girls, opium fiends, Chinamen, oyster dredgers, ex-convicts, the more respectable sort of colored people, and all the other oppressed and unfortunate classes of the time, and he slipped them, first and last, many a substantial piece of money.

Nor was he the only Baltimore infidel of those days who thus shamed the churchly. Indeed, the name of one of his buddies, Fred Ammermeyer, jumps into my memory at once. Fred and Leopold, I gathered, had serious dogmatic differences, for there are as many variations in doctrine between infidels as between Christians, but the essential benignity of both men kept them on amicable terms, and they often coöperated in good works. The only noticeable difference between them was that Fred usually tried to sneak a little propaganda into his operations—a dodge that the more scrupulous Leopold was careful to avoid. Thus, when a call went out for Bibles for the paupers lodged in Bayview, the Baltimore almshouse, Fred responded under an assumed name with a gross that had to be scrapped at once, for he had marked all the more antinomian passages with a red, indelible pencil—for example, Proverbs VII, 18–19; John VII, 7; I Timothy V, 23; and the account of David's dealing with Uriah in II Samuel XI. Again, he once hired Charlie Metcalfe, a small-time candy manufacturer, to prepare a special pack of chocolate drops for orphans and ruined girls, with a deceptive portrait of Admiral Dewey on the cover and a print of Bob Ingersoll's harangue over his brother's remains at the bottom of each box. Fred had this subversive exequium reprinted many times, and distributed at least two hundred and fifty thousand copies in Baltimore between 1895 and 1900. There were some Sunday-school scholars who received, by one device or another, at least a dozen. As for the clergy of the town, he sent each and every one of them a copy of Paine's "Age of Reason" three or four times a year—always disguised as a special-delivery or registered letter marked "Urgent." Finally, he employed seedy rabble rousers to mount soap boxes at downtown street corners on Saturday nights and there bombard the assembled loafers, peddlers, and cops with speeches which began seductively as excoriations of the Interests and then proceeded inch by inch to horrifying proofs that there was no hell.

But in the masterpiece of Fred Ammermeyer's benevolent career there was no such attempt at direct missionarying; indeed, his main idea when he conceived it was to hold up to scorn and contumely, by the force of mere contrast, the crude missionarying of his theological opponents. This idea seized him one evening when he dropped into the Central Police Station to pass the time of day with an old friend, a police lieutenant who was then the only known freethinker on the Baltimore force. Christmas was approaching and the lieutenant was in an unhappy and rebellious frame of mind—not because he objected to its orgies as such, or because he sought to deny Christians its beautiful consolations, but simply and solely because he always had the job of keeping order at the annual free dinner given by the massed missions of the town to the derelicts of the waterfront and that duty compelled him to listen politely to a long string of pious exhortations, many of them from persons he knew to be whited sepulchres.

"Why in hell," he observed impatiently, "do all them goddam hypocrites keep the poor bums waiting for two, three hours while they get off their goddam whimwham? Here is a hall full of men who ain't had nothing to speak of to eat for maybe three, four days, and yet they have to set there smelling the turkey and the coffee while ten, fifteen Sunday-school superintendents and W.C.T.U. sisters sing hymns to them and holler against booze. I tell you, Mr. Ammermeyer, it ain't human. More than once I have saw a whole row of them poor bums pass out in faints, and had to send them away in the wagon. And then, when the chow is circulated at last, and they begin fighting for the turkey bones, they ain't hardly got the stuff down before the superintendents and the sisters begin calling on them to stand up and confess whatever skulduggery they have done in the past, whether they really done it or not, *with us cops standing all around.* And every man Jack of them knows that if they don't lay it on plenty thick there won't be no encore of the giblets and stuffing, and two times out of three there ain't no encore anyhow, for them psalm singers are the stingiest outfit outside hell and never give a starving bum enough solid feed to last him until Christmas Monday. And not a damned drop to drink! Nothing but coffee—and without no milk! I tell you, Mr. Ammermeyer, it makes a man's blood boil."

Fred's duly boiled, and to immediate effect. By noon the next day he had rented the largest hall on the waterfront and sent word to the newspapers that arrangements for a Christmas party for bums to end all Christmas parties for bums were under way. His plan for it was extremely simple. The first obligation of hospitality, he announced somewhat prissily, was to find out precisely what one's guests wanted, and the second was to give it to them with a free and even reckless hand. As for what his proposed guests wanted, he had no shade of doubt, for he was a man of worldly experience and he had also, of course, the advice of his friend the lieutenant, a recognized expert in the psychology of the abandoned.

First and foremost, they wanted as much malt liquor as they would buy themselves if they had the means to buy it. Second, they wanted a dinner that went on in rhythmic waves, all day and all night, until the hungriest and hollowest bum was reduced to breathing with not more than one cylinder of one lung. Third, they wanted not a mere sufficiency but a riotous superfluity of the best five-cent cigars on sale on the Baltimore wharves. Fourth, they wanted continuous entertainment, both theatrical and musical, of a sort in consonance with their natural tastes and their station in life. Fifth and last, they wanted complete freedom from evangelical harassment of whatever sort, before, during, and after the secular ceremonies.

On this last point, Fred laid special stress, and every city editor in Baltimore had to hear him expound it in person. I was one of those city editors, and I well recall his great earnestness, amounting almost to moral indignation. It was an unendurable outrage, he argued, to invite a poor man to a free meal and then make him wait for it while he was battered with criticism of his ways, however well intended. And it was an even greater outrage to call upon him to stand up in public and confess to all the false steps of what may have been a long and much troubled life. Fred was determined, he said, to give a party that would be devoid of all the blemishes of the similar parties staged by the Salvation Army, the mission helpers, and other such nefarious outfits. If it cost him his last cent, he would give the bums of Baltimore massive and unforgettable proof that philanthropy was by no means a monopoly of gospel sharks—that its highest development, in truth, was to be found among freethinkers.

It might have cost him his last cent if he had gone it alone, for he was by no means a man of wealth, but his announcement had hardly got out before he was swamped with offers of help. Leopold Bortsch pledged twenty-five barrels of Scharnhorst beer and every other *Totsäufer* in Baltimore rushed up to match him. The Baltimore agents of the Pennsylvania two-fer factories fought for the privilege of contributing the cigars. The poultry dealers of Lexington, Fells Point, and Cross Street markets threw in barrel after barrel of dressed turkeys, some of them in very fair condition. The members of the boss bakers' association, not a few of them freethinkers themselves, promised all the bread, none more than two days old, that all the bums of the Chesapeake littoral could eat, and the public-relations counsel of the Celery Trust, the Cranberry Trust, the Sauerkraut Trust, and a dozen other such cartels and combinations leaped at the chance to serve.

If Fred had to fork up cash for any part of the chow, it must have been for the pepper and salt alone. Even the ketchup was contributed by social-minded members of the Maryland canners' association, and with it they threw in a dozen cases of dill pickles, chowchow, mustard, and mincemeat. But the rent of the hall had to be paid, and not only paid but paid in advance, for the owner thereof was a Methodist deacon, and there were many other expenses of considerable size—for example, for the entertainment, the music, the waiters and bartenders, and the mistletoe and immortelles which decorated the hall. Fred, if he had desired, might have got the free services of whole herds of amateur musicians and elocutionists, but he swept them aside disdainfully, for he was determined to give his guests a strictly professional show. The fact that a burlesque company starved out in the Deep South was currently stranded in Baltimore helped him here, for its members were glad to take an engagement at an inside rate, but the musicians' union, as usual, refused to let art or philanthropy shake its principles, and Fred had to pay six of its members the then prevailing scale of four dollars for their first eight hours of work and fifty cents an hour for overtime. He got, of course, some contributions in cash from rich freethinkers, but when the smoke cleared away at last and he totted up his books, he found that the party had set him back more than a hundred and seventy-five dollars.

Admission to the party was by card only, and the guests were selected with a critical and bilious eye by the police lieutenant. No bum who had ever been known to do any honest work—even such light work as sweeping out a saloon—was on the list. By Fred's express and oft-repeated command it was made up wholly of men completely lost to human decency, in whose favor nothing whatsoever could be said. The doors opened at 11 a.m. of Christmas Day, and the first canto of the dinner began instantly. There were none of the usual preliminaries—no opening prayer, no singing of a hymn, no remarks by Fred himself, not even a fanfare by the band. The bums simply shuffled and shoved their way to the tables and simultaneously the waiters and sommeliers poured in with the chow and the malt. For half an hour no sound was heard save the rattle of crockery, the chomp-chomp of mastication, and the grateful grunts and "Oh boy!"s of the assembled underprivileged.

Then the cigars were passed round (not one but half a dozen to every man), the band cut loose with the tonic chord of G major, and the burlesque company plunged into Act I, Sc. 1 of "Krausmeyer's Alley." There were in those days, as old-timers will recall, no less than five standard versions of this classic, ranging in refinement all the way from one so tony that it might have been put on at the Union Theological Seminary down to one so rowdy that it was fit only for audiences of policemen, bums, newspaper reporters, and medical students. This last was called the

Cincinnati version, because Cincinnati was then the only great American city whose mores tolerated it. Fred gave instructions that it was to be played *à outrance* and *con fuoco,* with no salvo of slapsticks, however brutal, omitted, and no *double entendre,* however daring. Let the boys have it, he instructed the chief comedian, Larry Snodgrass, straight in the eye and direct from the wood. They were poor men and full of sorrow, and he wanted to give them, on at least one red-letter day, a horse doctor's dose of the kind of humor they really liked.

In that remote era the girls of the company could add but little to the exhilarating grossness of the performance, for the strip tease was not yet invented and even the shimmy was still only nascent, but they did the best they could with the muscle dancing launched by Little Egypt at the Chicago World's Fair, and that best was not to be sneezed at, for they were all in hearty sympathy with Fred's agenda, and furthermore, they cherished the usual hope of stage folk that Charles Frohman or Abe Erlanger might be in the audience. Fred had demanded that they all appear in red tights, but there were not enough red tights in hand to outfit more than half of them, so Larry Snodgrass conceived the bold idea of sending on the rest with bare legs. It was a revolutionary indelicacy, and for a startled moment or two the police lieutenant wondered whether he was not bound by his Hippocratic oath to raid the show, but when he saw the whole audience leap up and break into cheers, his dubieties vanished, and five minutes later he was roaring himself when Larry and the other comedians began paddling the girls' cabooses with slapsticks.

I have seen many a magnificent performance of "Krausmeyer's Alley," in my time, including a Byzantine version called "Krausmeyer's Dispensary," staged by the students at the Johns Hopkins Medical School, but never have I seen a better one. Larry and his colleagues simply gave their all. Wherever, on ordinary occasions, there would have been a laugh, they evoked a roar, and where there would have been roars they produced something akin to asphyxia and apoplexy. Even the members of the musicians' union were forced more than once to lay down their fiddles and cornets and bust into laughter. In fact, they enjoyed the show so vastly that when the comedians retired for breath and the girls came out to sing "Sweet Rosie O'Grady" or "I've Been Workin' on the Railroad," the accompaniment was full of all the outlaw *glissandi* and *sforzandi* that we now associate with jazz.

The show continued at high tempo until 2 p.m., when Fred shut it down to give his guests a chance to eat the second canto of their dinner. It was a duplicate of the first in every detail, with second and third helpings of turkey, sauerkraut, mashed potatoes, and celery for everyone who called for them, and a pitcher of beer in front of each guest. The boys ground away at it for an hour, and then lit fresh cigars and leaned back comfortably for the second part of the show. It was still basically "Krausmeyer's Alley," but it was a "Krausmeyer's Alley" adorned and bedizened with reminiscences of every other burlesque-show curtain raiser and afterpiece in the repertory. It went on and on for four solid hours, with Larry and his pals bending themselves to their utmost exertions, and the girls shaking their legs in almost frantic abandon. At the end of an hour the members of the musicians' union demanded a cut-in on the beer and got it, and immediately afterward the sommeliers began passing pitchers to the performers on the stage. Meanwhile, the pitchers on the tables of the guests were kept replenished, cigars were passed round at short intervals, and the waiters came in with pretzels, potato chips, celery, radishes, and chipped beef to stay the stomachs of those accustomed to the free-lunch way of life.

At 7 p.m. precisely, Fred gave the signal for a hiatus in the entertainment, and the waiters rushed in with the third canto of the dinner. The supply of roast turkey, though it had been enormous, was beginning to show signs of wear by this time, but Fred had in reserve twenty hams and forty pork shoulders, the contribution of George Wienefeldter, president of the Wienefeldter Bros. & Schmidt Sanitary Packing Co., Inc. Also, he had a mine of reserve sauerkraut hidden down under the stage, and soon it was in free and copious circulation and the guests were taking heroic hacks at it. This time they finished in three-quarters of an hour, but Fred filled the time until 8 p.m. by ordering a seventh-inning stretch and by having the police lieutenant go to the stage and assure all hands that any bona-fide participant found on the streets, at the conclusion of the exercises, with his transmission jammed would not be clubbed and jugged, as was the Baltimore custom at the time, but returned to the hall to sleep it off on the floor. This announcement made a favorable impression, and the brethren settled down for the resumption of the show in a very pleasant mood. Larry and his associates were pretty well fagged out by now, for the sort of acting demanded by the burlesque profession is very fatiguing, but you'd never have guessed it by watching them work.

At ten the show stopped again, and there began what Fred described as a *Bierabend,* that is, a beer evening. Extra pitchers were put on every table, more cigars were handed about, and the waiters spread a substantial lunch of rye bread, rat-trap cheese, ham, bologna, potato salad, liver pudding, and *Blutwurst.* Fred announced from the stage that the performers needed a rest and would not be called upon again until twelve o'clock when a midnight show would begin, but that in the interval any guest or guests with a tendency to song might step up and show his or their stuff. No less than a dozen volunteers at once went forward, but

Fred had the happy thought of beginning with a quartet, and so all save the first four were asked to wait. The four laid their heads together, the band played the vamp of "Sweet Adeline," and they were off. It was not such singing as one hears from the Harvard Glee Club or the Bach Choir at Bethlehem, Pennsylvania, but it was at least as good as the barbershop stuff that hillbillies now emit over the radio. The other guests applauded politely, and the quartet, operating briskly under malt and hop power, proceeded to "Don't You Hear Dem Bells?" and "Aunt Dinah's Quilting Party." Then the four singers had a nose-to-nose palaver and the first tenor proceeded somewhat shakily to a conference with Otto Strauss, the leader of the orchestra.

From where I sat, at the back of the hall, beside Fred, I could see Otto shake his head, but the tenor persisted in whatever he was saying, and after a moment Otto shrugged resignedly and the members of the quartet again took their stances. Fred leaned forward eagerly, curious to hear what their next selection would be. He found out at once. It was "Are You Ready for the Judgment Day?," the prime favorite of the period in all the sailors' bethels, helping-up missions, Salvation Army bum traps, and other such joints along the waterfront. Fred's horror and amazement and sense of insult were so vast that he was completely speechless, and all I heard out of him while the singing went on was a series of sepulchral groans. The man was plainly suffering cruelly, but what could I do? What, indeed, could anyone do? For the quartet had barely got halfway through the first stanza of the composition before the whole audience joined in. And it joined in with even heartier enthusiasm when the boys on the stage proceeded to "Showers of Blessings," the No. 2 favorite of all seasoned mission stiffs, and then to "Throw Out the Lifeline," and then to "Where Shall We Spend Eternity?," and then to "Wash Me, and I Shall Be Whiter Than Snow."

Halfway along in this orgy of hymnody, the police lieutenant took Fred by the arm and led him out into the cold, stinging, corpse-reviving air of a Baltimore winter night. The bums, at this stage, were beating time on the tables with their beer glasses and tears were trickling down their noses. Otto and his band knew none of the hymns, so their accompaniment became sketchier and sketchier, and presently they shut down altogether. By this time the members of the quartet began to be winded, and soon there was a halt. In the ensuing silence there arose a quavering, boozy, sclerotic voice from the floor. "Friends," it began, "I just want to tell you what these good people have done for me—how their prayers have saved a sinner who seemed past all redemption. Friends, I had a good mother, and I was brought up under the influence of the Word. But in my young manhood my sainted mother was called to heaven, my poor father took to rum and opium, and I was led by the devil into the hands of wicked men—yes, and wicked women, too. Oh, what a shameful story I have to tell! It would shock you to hear it, even if I told you only half of it. I let myself be . . ."

I waited for no more, but slunk into the night. Fred and the police lieutenant had both vanished, and I didn't see Fred again for a week. But the next day I encountered the lieutenant on the street, and he hailed me sadly. "Well," he said, "what could you expect from them bums? It was the force of habit, that's what it was. They have been eating mission handouts so long they can't help it. Whenever they smell coffee, they begin to confess. Think of all that good food wasted! And all that beer! And all them cigars!"

A HINT FOR NEXT CHRISTMAS

A. A. MILNE

O bviously there should be a standard value for a certain type of Christmas present. One may give what one will to one's family or particular friends; that is all right. But in a Christmas house-party there is a pleasant interchange of parcels, of which the string and the brown paper and the kindly thought are the really important ingredients, and the gift inside is nothing more than an excuse for those things. It is embarrassing for you if Jones has apologized for his brown paper with a hundred cigars and you have only excused yourself with twenty-five cigarettes; perhaps still more embarrassing if it is you who have lost so heavily on the exchange. An understanding that the contents were to be worth five shillings exactly would avoid this embarrassment.

And now I am reminded of the ingenuity of a friend of mine, William by name, who arrived at a large country house for Christmas without any present in his bag. He had expected neither to give nor to receive anything but to his horror he discovered on the 24th that everybody was preparing a Christmas present for him, and that it was taken for granted that he would require a little privacy and brown paper on Christmas Eve for the purpose of addressing his own offerings to others. He had wild thoughts of telegraphing to London for something to be sent down, and spoke to other members of the house-party in order to discover what sort of presents would be suitable.

"What are you giving our host?" he asked one of them.

"Mary and I are giving him a book," said John, referring to his wife.

William then approached the youngest son of the house, and discovered that he and his next brother Dick were sharing in this, that, and the other. When he had heard this, William retired to his room and thought profoundly.

He was the first down to breakfast on Christmas morning. All the places at the table were piled high with presents. He looked at John's place. The top parcel said, "To John and Mary from Charles." William took out his fountain-pen and added a couple of words to the inscription. It then read, "To John and Mary from Charles and William," and in William's opinion looked just as effective as before. He moved on to the next place. "To Angela from Father," said the top parcel. "And William," wrote William. At his hostess' place he hesitated for a moment. The first present there was for "Darling Mother, from her loving children." It did not seem that an "and William" was quite suitable. But his hostess was not to be deprived of William's kindly thought; twenty seconds later the handkerchiefs "from John and Mary and William" expressed all the nice things he was feeling for her. He passed on to the next place . . .

It is of course impossible to thank every donor of a joint gift; one simply thanks the first person whose eyes one happens to catch. Sometimes William's eye was caught, sometimes not. But he was spared all embarrassment; and I can recommend his solution of the problem with perfect confidence to those who may be in a similar predicament next Christmas.

ON THE MORNING OF CHRIST'S NATIVITY

JOHN MILTON

I

This is the month, and this the happy morn,
Wherein the Son of Heaven's eternal King,
Of wedded Maid and Virgin Mother born,
Our great redemption from above did bring;
For so the holy sages once did sing,
   That he our deadly forfeit should release,
And with his Father work us a perpetual peace.

II

That glorious form, that light unsufferable,
And that far-beaming blaze of majesty,
Wherewith he wont at Heaven's high council-table
To sit the midst of Trinal Unity,
He laid aside; and here with us to be,
   Forsook the courts of everlasting day,
And chose with us a darksome house of mortal clay.

III

Say, Heavenly Muse, shall not thy sacred vein
Afford a present to the infant God?
Hast thou no verse, no hymn, or solemn strain,
To welcome him to this his new abode,
Now while the Heaven, by the sun's team untrod,
   Hath took no print of the approaching light,
And all the spangled host keep watch in squadrons bright?

IV

See how from far upon the eastern road
The star-led wizards haste with odors sweet!
O run, prevent them with thy humble ode,
And lay it lowly at his blessed feet;
Have thou the honor first thy Lord to greet,
   And join thy voice unto the angel choir,
From out his secret altar touched with hallowed fire.

THE HYMN

I

It was the winter wild
While the Heaven-born child
   All meanly wrapped in the rude manger lies;
Nature in awe to him
Had doffed her gaudy trim,
   With her great Master so to sympathize;
It was no season then for her
To wanton with the sun, her lusty paramour.

II

Only with speeches fair
She woos the gentle air
   To hide her guilty front with innocent snow,
And on her naked shame,
Pollute with sinful blame,
   The saintly veil of maiden white to throw,
Confounded, that her Maker's eyes
Should look so near upon her foul deformities.

III

But he her fears to cease,
Sent down the meek-eyed Peace;
   She, crowned with olive green, came softly sliding
Down through the turning sphere,
His ready harbinger,
   With turtle wing the amorous clouds dividing,
And waving wide her myrtle wand,
She strikes a universal peace through sea and land.

No war or battle's sound
Was heard the world around:
   The idle spear and shield were high uphung;
The hooked chariot stood
Unstained with hostile blood;
   The trumpet spake not to the armed throng;
And kings sat still with awful eye,
As if they surely knew their sovran Lord was by.

But peaceful was the night
Wherein the Prince of Light
   His reign of peace upon the earth began:
The winds with wonder whist,
Smoothly the waters kissed,
   Whispering new joys to the mild ocëan,
Who now hath quite forgot to rave,
While birds of calm sit brooding on the charmed wave.

The stars with deep amaze
Stand fixed in steadfast gaze,
   Bending one way their precious influence,
And will not take their flight
For all the morning light,
   Or Lucifer that often warned them thence;
But in their glimmering orbs did glow,
Until their Lord himself bespake, and bid them go.

And though the shady gloom
Had given day her room,
   The sun himself withheld his wonted speed,
And hid his head for shame,
As his inferior flame
   The new-enlightened world no more should need;
He saw a greater sun appear
Than his bright throne or burning axletree could bear.

The shepherds on the lawn,
Or ere the point of dawn,
   Sat simply chatting in a rustic row;
Full little thought they than
That the mighty Pan
   Was kindly come to live with them below;
Perhaps their loves, or else their sheep,
Was all that did their silly thoughts so busy keep.

IX

When such music sweet
Their hearts and ears did greet,
   As never was by mortal finger strook,
Divinely warbled voice
Answering the stringed noise,
   As all their souls in blissful rapture took;
The air, such pleasure loth to lose,
With thousand echoes still prolongs each heavenly close.

X

Nature that heard such sound
Beneath the hollow round
   Of Cynthia's seat, the airy region thrilling,
Now was almost won
To think her part was done,
   And that her reign had here its last fulfilling;
She knew such harmony alone
Could hold all Heaven and Earth in happier union.

XI

At last surrounds their sight
A globe of circular light,
   That with long beams the shame-faced Night arrayed;
The helmed Cherubim
And sworded Seraphim
   Are seen in glittering ranks with wings displayed,
Harping in loud and solemn choir,
With unexpressive notes to Heaven's new-born Heir.

XII

Such music (as 'tis said)
Before was never made,
    But when of old the sons of morning sung,
While the Creator great
His constellations set,
    And the well-balanced world on hinges hung,
And cast the dark foundations deep,
And bid the weltering waves their oozy channel keep.

XIII

Ring out, ye crystal spheres,
Once bless our human ears
    (If ye have power to touch our senses so),
And let your silver chime
Move in melodious time,
    And let the bass of Heaven's deep organ blow;
And with your ninefold harmony
Make up full consort to the angelic symphony.

XIV

For if such holy song
Enwrap our fancy long,
    Time will run back and fetch the age of gold,
And speckled Vanity
Will sicken soon and die,
    And leprous Sin will melt from earthly mold,
And Hell itself will pass away,
And leave her dolorous mansions to the peering day.

XV

Yea, Truth and Justice then
Will down return to men,
    Orbed in a rainbow; and, like glories wearing,
Mercy will sit between,
Throned in celestial sheen,
    With radiant feet the tissued clouds down steering;
And Heaven, as at some festival,
Will open wide the gates of her high palace hall.

But wisest Fate says no,
This must not yet be so;
   The Babe lies yet in smiling infancy,
That on the bitter cross
Must redeem our loss,
   So both himself and us to glorify;
Yet first to those ychained in sleep,
The wakeful trump of doom must thunder through the deep,

With such a horrid clang
As on Mount Sinai rang
   While the red fire and smoldering clouds outbrake:
The aged Earth aghast
With terror of that blast,
   Shall from the surface to the center shake,
When at the world's last session
The dreadful Judge in middle air shall spread his throne.

And then at last our bliss
Full and perfect is,
   But now begins; for from this happy day
The old Dragon under ground,
In straiter limits bound,
   Not half so far casts his usurped sway,
And, wroth to see his kingdom fail,
Swinges the scaly horror of his folded tail.

The oracles are dumb,
No voice or hideous hum
   Runs through the arched roof in words deceiving.
Apollo from his shrine
Can no more divine,
   With hollow shriek the steep of Delphos leaving.
No nightly trance or breathed spell
Inspires the pale-eyed priest from the prophetic cell.

The lonely mountains o'er,
And the resounding shore,
   A voice of weeping heard, and loud lament;
From haunted spring and dale,
Edged with poplar pale,
   The parting Genius is with sighing sent;
With flower-inwoven tresses torn
The nymphs in twilight shade of tangled thickets mourn.

In consecrated earth,
And on the holy hearth,
   The Lars and Lemures moan with midnight plaint;
In urns and altars round,
A drear and dying sound
   Affrights the flamens at their service quaint;
And the chill marble seems to sweat,
While each peculiar power forgoes his wonted seat.

Peor and Baalim
Forsake their temples dim,
   With that twice-battered god of Palestine;
And mooned Ashtaroth,
Heaven's queen and mother both,
   Now sits not girt with tapers' holy shine;
The Libyc Hammon shrinks his horn,
In vain the Tyrian maids their wounded Thammuz mourn.

And sullen Moloch, fled,
Hath left in shadows dread
   His burning idol all of blackest hue;
In vain with cymbals' ring
They call the grisly king,
   In dismal dance about the furnace blue;
The brutish gods of Nile as fast,
Isis and Orus, and the dog Anubis, haste.

Nor is Osiris seen
In Memphian grove or green,
   Trampling the unshowered grass with lowings loud;
Nor can he be at rest
Within his sacred chest,
   Nought but profoundest Hell can be his shroud;
In vain with timbreled anthems dark
The sable-stoled sorcerers bear his worshiped ark.

He feels from Juda's land
The dreaded Infant's hand,
   The rays of Bethlehem blind his dusky eyn;
Nor all the gods beside
Longer dare abide,
   Not Typhon huge ending in snaky twine:
Our Babe, to show his Godhead true,
Can in his swaddling bands control the damned crew.

So when the sun in bed,
Curtained with cloudy red,
   Pillows his chin upon an orient wave,
The flocking shadows pale
Troop to the infernal jail;
   Each fettered ghost slips to his several grave,
And the yellow-skirted fays
Fly after the night-steeds, leaving their moon-loved maze.

But see, the Virgin blest
Hath laid her Babe to rest.
   Time is our tedious song should here have ending;
Heaven's youngest-teemed star
Hath fixed her polished car,
   Her sleeping Lord with handmaid lamp attending;
And all about the courtly stable
Bright-harnessed angels sit in order serviceable.

December 1629

A VISIT FROM ST. NICHOLAS

CLEMENT C. MOORE

'Twas the night before Christmas, when all through the house
Not a creature was stirring, not even a mouse;
The stockings were hung by the chimney with care,
In hopes that St. Nicholas soon would be there.
The children were nestled all snug in their beds,
While visions of sugar-plums danced through their heads;
And mamma in her kerchief, and I in my cap,
Had just settled our brains for a long winter's nap,
When out on the lawn there arose such a clatter,
I sprang from my bed to see what was the matter.
Away to the window I flew like a flash,
Tore open the shutters and threw up the sash.
The moon on the breast of the new-fallen snow
Gave the lustre of mid-day to objects below;
When, what to my wondering eyes should appear,
But a miniature sleigh and eight tiny reindeer,
With a little old driver, so lively and quick,
I knew in a moment it must be St. Nick.
More rapid than eagles his coursers they came,
And he whistled, and shouted, and called them by name:
"Now Dasher! now, Dancer! now, Prancer! and Vixen!
On, Comet! on, Cupid! on, Donder and Blitzen!
To the top of the porch! to the top of the wall!
Now dash away! dash away! dash away all!"
As dry leaves that before the wild hurricane fly,

When they meet with an obstacle, mount to the sky,
So up to the house-top the coursers they flew,
With the sleighful of toys, and St. Nicholas too.
And then in a twinkling, I heard on the roof
The prancing and pawing of each little hoof.
As I drew in my head, and was turning around,
Down the chimney St. Nicholas came with a bound.
He was dressed all in fur from his head to his foot.
And his clothes were all tarnished with ashes and soot:
A bundle of toys he had flung on his back,
And he looked like a peddlar just opening his pack.
His eyes, how they twinkled! his dimples, how merry!
His cheeks were like roses, his nose like a cherry!
His droll little mouth was drawn up like a bow,
And the beard on his chin was as white as the snow;
The stump of a pipe he held tight in his teeth,
And the smoke, it encircled his head like a wreath.
He had a broad face, and a little round belly
That shook, when he laughed, like a bowl full of jelly.
He was chubby and plump—a right jolly old elf—
And I laughed, when I saw him, in spite of myself;
A wink of his eye, and a twist of his head,
Soon gave me to know I had nothing to dread.
He spoke not a word, but went straight to his work,
And filled all the stockings; then turned with a jerk,
And laying his finger aside of his nose,
And giving a nod, up the chimney he rose.
He sprang to his sleigh, to the team gave a whistle,
And away they all flew, like the down of a thistle,
But I heard him exclaim, e're he drove out of sight,
"Happy Christmas to all, and to all a good-night!"

1823

THE CHRISTMAS TOBACCO

CHRISTOPHER MORLEY

According to an Eastern legend, tobacco used to be grown in the fields outside Bethlehem

From the golden aisles of riot,
From the frantic jostling press,
To a side street's frosty quiet
Homo walked, with bitterness.
All the color, bustle, glamor,
Seemed to him but empty clamor.

In the great stores' teeming spaces,
In the throng of Christmas Eve,
He saw worried, weary faces—
Told himself, "I disbelieve!
Merry Christmas, Day of Days—
Hypocrite commercial phrase!"

Did he have some private reason
Thus so savagely to brood?
Grimly, in the cheerful season
There he walked in cynic mood,
Roaming aimless, without plan,
Lonely, a disheartened man.

Christmas trees, banked high and fragrant
Breathed a whiff of balsam sweet,
But the misanthropic vagrant
Strode ungladdened down the street.
"Holly?" cried a corner grocer—
Homo drew his surtout closer.

Dusk was starred, the purple-vaulted—
People hurried home from work.
Where he saw cigars he halted
By a wooden, turbaned Turk,
Shamed, with empty hands, to see
All had parcels, saving he.

Queer the shop, it seemed, he entered,
Stocked with candy, pipes and toys;
Smiling stood the dealer, centred
In a group of bright-cheeked boys.
Urchins lingered, slowly choosing
Clockwork apes they thought amusing.

Ancient 'bacconist, queer fellow—
Oriental kind of chap—
In complexion rather yellow,
Bearded almost to his lap,
Showing, youthful trade to please,
Tinsel stars for Christmas trees.

Homo waited, rather peevish,
Wearied of the old man's jokes;
Feeling nowise Christmas Eve-ish,
Said, "See here, I want some smokes.
Not these rubbish toys and stars—
Christ's sake, give me some cigars!

"What is this? A kind of toy-shop,
Or a home for nicotine?
Lord, another Yuletide joy-shop?
Bunk!—The Christmas stuff, I mean.
Who reads fables any longer?—
Too mild. Have you nothing stronger?"

Children ran. The old man, turning,
Showed a dark and foreign eye.
Homo, with annoyance burning,
Felt ashamed, he knew not why.
"As you ask, I can't refuse you;
Something special I will choose you."

On a rearward shelf he fumbled,
Drawing out a parcel rich
Wrapped with eastern fabric, jumbled
O'er with patterned silken stitch.
Opened it. "Yes, here's a weed
That's exactly what you need."

Queer cigars, thus recommended!
Brittle, black, and very dry—
But, as he had once offended,
Homo drew his purse to buy.
"You can have just one of these,
And—I'll take no money, please."

Through the smoke-blued air, all hazy,
Homo stared upon the face,
Thinking, "Why the old man's crazy."
Tossed a coin, and left the place.
Shut the door. Above, afar,
In the evening, one great star.

Curious and most amazing
(Homo thought) to see that sky—
Never had he seen such blazing,
Such a gold lamp on high.
That cigar, too, what a flavor!
What a richly pungent savor!

Strangely, too, the air seemed milder,
And, along that humble street
Christmas costume was much wilder
Than he had been wont to meet.
Fancy dress, this part of town?
Very odd, that eastern gown!

By a little park he tarried—
Faint the clang of distant cars;
All the sky was lucent, clarid,
Pallid with a foam of stars.
Soft he heard the church chimes ring
"Hark, the Herald Angels Sing."

What could be those strange shapes moving
Silhouetted in the square?
Lo! he rubbed his eyes, reproving
Sense that so betrayed him there.
What was that tall shambling beast . . . ?
And those turbans of the East?

Down before a shabby dwelling
Knelt the shadow; two; a third;
Strangely clad, tall figures telling
Something in a foreign word.
Lights gleamed; voices came from far—
Then he threw down his cigar.

Crossed the park, his senses whirring,
Toward the house where they had been:
There, beside the curbstone, purring,
Stood a shining limousine.
Asked the chauffeur, standing near:
"Say, what's this—a circus here?"

"Well, it might be! Can you beat it?
That's the car of Doctor Brown,
And I'm saying you don't meet it
Often in this part of town.
What's the trouble? Oh," (with scorn)
"Just some baby being born."

"But," said Homo, "Now the fact is
There were three——" "Say, friend, you're right!
Never in the Doctor's practice
Did I see it like to-night.
Two docs to consult. It's queer,
Three wise guys like that, down here!"

Homo looked upon the lowly
Little home, one pane alight.
Thinking, then he answered slowly:
"Hope they both come through all right.
That's religion, in the end—
Wish you Merry Christmas, friend!"

THE TREE THAT DIDN'T GET TRIMMED

CHRISTOPHER MORLEY

If you walk through a grove of balsam trees you will notice that the young trees are silent; they are listening. But the old tall ones—especially the firs—are whispering. They are telling the story of The Tree That Didn't Get Trimmed. It sounds like a painful story, and the murmur of the old trees as they tell it is rather solemn; but it is an encouraging story for young saplings to hear. On warm autumn days when your trunk is tickled by ants and insects climbing, and the resin is hot and gummy in your knots, and the whole glade smells sweet, drowsy, and sad, and the hardwood trees are boasting of the gay colours they are beginning to show, many a young evergreen has been cheered by it.

All young fir trees, as you know by that story of Hans Andersen's—if you've forgotten it, why not read it again?—dream of being a Christmas Tree some day. They dream about it as young girls dream of being a bride, or young poets of having a volume of verse published. With the vision of that brightness and gayety before them they patiently endure the sharp sting of the ax, the long hours pressed together on a freight car. But every December there are more trees cut down than are needed for Christmas. And that is the story that no one—not even Hans Andersen—has thought to put down.

The tree in this story should never have been cut. He wouldn't have been, but it was getting dark in the Vermont woods, and the man with the ax said to himself, "Just one more." Cutting young trees with a sharp, beautifully balanced ax is fascinating; you go on and on; there's a sort of cruel pleasure in it. The blade goes through the soft wood with one whistling stroke and the boughs sink down with a soft swish.

He was a fine, well-grown youngster, but too tall for his age; his branches were rather scraggly. If he'd been left there he would have been an unusually big tree some day; but now he was in the awkward age and didn't have the tapering shape and the thick, even foliage that people like on Christmas trees. Worse still, instead of running up to a straight, clean spire, his top was a bit lopsided, with a fork in it.

But he didn't know this as he stood with many others, leaning against the side wall of the greengrocer's shop. In those cold December days he was very happy, thinking of the pleasures to come. He had heard of the delights of Christmas Eve: the stealthy setting-up of the tree, the tinsel balls and coloured toys and stars, the peppermint canes and birds with spun-glass tails. Even that old anxiety of Christmas trees—burning candles—did not worry him, for he had been told that nowadays people use strings of tiny electric bulbs which cannot set one on fire. So he looked forward to the festival with a confident heart.

"I shall be very grand," he said. "I hope there will be children to admire me. It must be a great moment when the children hang their stockings on you!" He even felt sorry for the first trees that were chosen and taken away. It would be best, he considered, not to be bought until Christmas Eve. Then, in the shining darkness someone would pick him out, put him carefully along the running board of a car, and away they would go. The tire-chains would clack and jingle merrily on the snowy road. He imagined a big house with fire glowing on a hearth; the hushed rustle of wrapping paper and parcels being unpacked. Someone would say, "Oh, what a beautiful tree!" How erect and stiff he would brace himself in his iron tripod stand.

But day after day went by, one by one the other trees were taken, and he began to grow troubled. For everyone who looked at him seemed to have an unkind word. "Too tall," said one lady. "No, this one wouldn't do, the branches are too skimpy," said another. "If I chop off the top," said the greengrocer, "it wouldn't be so bad?" The tree shuddered, but the customer had already passed on to look at others. Some of his branches ached where the grocer had bent them upward to make his shape more attractive.

Across the street was a Ten Cent Store. Its bright windows were full of scarlet odds and ends; when the doors opened he could see people crowded along the aisles, cheerfully jostling one another with bumpy packages. A buzz of talk, a shuffle of feet, a constant ringing of cash drawers came noisily out of that doorway. He could see flashes of marvellous colour, ornaments for luckier trees. Every evening, as the time drew nearer, the pavements were more thronged. The handsomer trees, not so tall as he but more bushy and shapely, were ranked in front of

him; as they were taken away he could see the gayety only too well. Then he was shown to a lady who wanted a tree very cheap. "You can have this one for a dollar," said the grocer. This was only one-third of what the grocer had asked for him at first, but even so the lady refused him and went across the street to buy a little artificial tree at the toy store. The man pushed him back carelessly, and he toppled over and fell alongside the wall. No one bothered to pick him up. He was almost glad, for now his pride would be spared.

Now it was Christmas Eve. It was a foggy evening with a drizzling rain; the alley alongside the store was thick with trampled slush. As he lay there among broken boxes and fallen scraps of holly strange thoughts came to him. In the still northern forest already his wounded stump was buried in forgetful snow. He remembered the wintry sparkle of the woods, the big trees with crusts and clumps of silver on their broad boughs, the keen singing of the lonely wind. He remembered the strong, warm feeling of his roots reaching down into the safe earth. That is a good feeling; it means to a tree just what it means to you to stretch your toes down toward the bottom of a well-tucked bed. And he had given up all this to lie here, disdained and forgotten, in a littered alley. The splash of feet, the chime of bells, the cry of cars went past him. He trembled a little with self-pity and vexation. "No toys and stockings for me," he thought sadly, and shed some of his needles.

Late that night, after all the shopping was over, the grocer came out to clear away what was left. The boxes, the broken wreaths, the empty barrels, and our tree with one or two others that hadn't been sold, all were thrown through the side door into the cellar. The door was locked and he lay there in the dark. One of his branches, doubled under him in the fall, ached so he thought it must be broken. "So this is Christmas," he said to himself.

All that day it was very still in the cellar. There was an occasional creak as one of the bruised trees tried to stretch itself. Feet went along the pavement overhead, and there was a booming of church bells, but everything had a slow, disappointed sound. Christmas is always a little sad, after such busy preparations. The unwanted trees lay on the stone floor, watching the furnace light flicker on a hatchet that had been left there.

The day after Christmas a man came in who wanted some green boughs to decorate a cemetery. The grocer took the hatchet, and seized the trees without ceremony. They were too disheartened to care. Chop, chop, chop, went the blade, and the sweet-smelling branches were carried away. The naked trunks were thrown into a corner.

And now our tree, what was left of him, had plenty of time to think. He no longer could feel anything, for trees feel with their branches, but they think with their trunks. What did he think about as he grew dry and stiff? He thought that it had been silly of him to imagine such a fine, gay career for himself, and he was sorry for other young trees, still growing in the fresh hilly country, who were enjoying the same fantastic dreams.

Now perhaps you don't know what happens to the trunks of leftover Christmas trees. You could never guess. Farmers come in from the suburbs and buy them at five cents each for bean-poles and grape arbours. So perhaps (here begins the encouraging part of this story) they are really happier, in the end, than the trees that get trimmed for Santa Claus. They go back into the fresh moist earth of spring, and when the sun grows hot the quick tendrils of the vines climb up them and presently they are decorated with the red blossoms of the bean or the little blue globes of the grape, just as pretty as any Christmas trinkets.

So one day the naked, dusty fir-poles were taken out of the cellar, and thrown into a truck with many others, and made a rattling journey out into the land. The farmer unloaded them in his yard and was stacking them up by the barn when his wife came out to watch him.

"There!" she said. "That's just what I want, a nice long pole with a fork in it. Jim, put that one over there to hold up the clothesline." It was the first time that anyone had praised our tree, and his dried-up heart swelled with a tingle of forgotten sap. They put him near one end of the clothesline, with his stump close to a flower bed. The fork that had been despised for a Christmas star was just the thing to hold up a clothesline. It was washday, and soon the farmer's wife began bringing out wet garments to swing and freshen in the clean bright air. And the very first thing that hung near the top of the Christmas pole was a cluster of children's stockings.

That isn't quite the end of the story, as the old fir trees whisper it in the breeze. The Tree That Didn't Get Trimmed was so cheerful watching the stockings, and other gay little clothes that plumped out in the wind just as though waiting to be spanked, that he didn't notice what was going on—or going up—below him. A vine had caught hold of his trunk and was steadily twisting upward. And one morning, when the farmer's wife came out intending to shift him, she stopped and exclaimed. "Why, I mustn't move this pole," she said. "The morning glory has run right up it." So it had, and our bare pole was blue and crimson with colour.

Something nice, the old firs believe, always happens to the trees that don't get trimmed. They even believe that some day one of the Christmas-tree bean-poles will be the starting-point for another Magic Beanstalk, as in the fairy tale of the boy who climbed up the bean-tree and killed the giant. When that happens, fairy tales will begin all over again.

THE CHRISTMAS THAT ALMOST WASN'T

OGDEN NASH

Of happy times and places
I've heard the minstrels sing,
But I wish I'd lived in Lullapat
When Oldwin was the king.

It lay beyond the Seven Seas,
Beyond the mountain heights,
Beyond the smoke of autumn,
Beyond the northern lights.

An olden land, a golden land,
A land of honest mirth,
With a jolly king whose rollicking
Could not reduce his girth.

Good Oldwin, King of Lullapat,
Although not absolutely fat,
Might be described as circular;
Delicious dishes did he dip in
Which left him rounded like a pippin;
His shape was pippindercular;
With rosy cheeks a-plumply rumpling,
He was a royal apple dumpling.

King Oldwin had a quality
Of heartiness and jollity,
Of innocent frivolity,
That made the people chortle;
And Lullapat was rumorous
With tales about him numerous,
So very, very humorous
His name became immortal.
And citizens of other nations
Envied the happy Lullapatians.

Oldwin's admirers were a host,
But one admirer loved him most:
A boy as yet unknown to fame—
A shepherd, Nicholas Knock by name.
Of loyal lads Nick was the loyalest,
A most enthusiastic royalist,
And as he watched his woolly flock
This was the song of Nicky Knock:
"I love my king like anything,
He's such a *Christmas-y* kind of king!"

His subjects cheered with might and main
The twentieth year of Oldwin's reign;
Indeed, their cheers were more than plenty
To echo through another twenty.
The ancient chronicle I quote
Says, "Cheers arose as from one throat."
That's not an accurate catalogue,
For in that throat there was a frog,
Or toad, who, though of Oldwin's blood,
Was a snake in the grass, a worm in the bud;
Toad evil-minded, evil-starred—
King Oldwin's nephew, Evilard.

This was the nastiest of nephews,
A loathly piece of human refuse.
His notion of a pleasant frolic
Was giving little babies colic;
He liked to sprinkle picnic rugs
With creepy, crawly, stinging bugs.
Before a royal ball, I hear,

The floor with sticky sweets he'd smear.
He'd offer a lady fair a chair,
And when she sat, it wasn't there.
This monster toiled from sun to sun
At spoiling other people's fun;
His skull inside was dark and caverny,
And as for heart, he didn't have any.

Life seemed as bright as a coquette's mirror,
Crowds caroled, "Tra-la!" and "Tirra-lirra!"
But Evilard scowled at their tirra-lirracy,
And stealthily hatched a dark conspiracy.
Nights found him slinking hither and hence
In search of fellow malcontents.
He sought the crone cadaverous,
The miser pale with avarice,
The troublemaker rancorous,
The poison tongue cantankerous,
The spiteful and the devious,
The cruel and mischevious;
He cast his net, he spun his web,
Nor ever did his hatred ebb—
But as he skulked around the palace
Each merry face increased his malice.

For weeks he fumed and grumbled at
The dearth of rogues in Lullapat;
But, when at last his pack assembled,
This callous villain almost trembled—
So odious they were, and scurvy,
With consciences all topsy-turvy.

He led them through a secret tunnel
Like venom oozing through a funnel
To where King Oldwin, crown on lap,
Enjoyed his after-luncheon nap.
I hope that he enjoyed his luncheon,
For when he woke, 'twas in a dungeon.

Evilard turned the rusty key
And to his henchmen then spoke he:
"I plan to spend the coming year

Tormenting of my uncle dear;
I'll furnish for his special use
Not foaming ale, but sauerkraut juice;
To titillate his royal throat
Not roast of beef, but stew of stoat;
To lend a savor to the dish,
Instead of jelly, jellyfish;
And cakes and pies all hugger-mugger
Baked with salt, instead of sugar.
The hoarsest minstrels in the land
Outside his cell each night shall stand;
Their task, from dusk to dawn, to troll:
'King Oldwin was a merry old soul. . . .'

"With scrawny fare and broken rest
I'll put his jollity to the test;
And soon the word will creep abroad
That Oldwin's goodness was a fraud;
And stripped of pomp and luxury
Good Oldwin is as mean as me.
This task I to myself assign,
This pleasure must be *mine,* all *mine;*
And while I'm absent from the helm,
I name you viceroys o'er the realm;
I trust I need not tell you twice,
Viceroys, with accent on the *vice.*
Don't fumble with the Gordian knot
Of what to do, to whom, with what;
The Gordian knot is quickly scissorable—
Go, and make *everybody* miserable!"

Three old misers with razor lips;
Three old hags with razor hips;
Three old pettifoggers, sniffling, snuffling;
Three old gossips, hackling, huffling;
Three old busybodies, prying, poking;
Three old jailers, coughing, croaking—
This was the gruesome, grimsome guard
That ruled the land under Evilard
And decided to outlaw Christmas.

The three old misers hate girls and boys;
The three old hags hate fun and noise;
The three old pettifoggers love peace ill;
The three old gossips have no good will;
The three old busybodies can't find time
For a kindly word or a Christmas rhyme;
And the jailers jeer, as they clank the keys,
"No room at the inn? Step this way, please!"
That's what they thought of Christmas.

The three old misers, like three old mules,
Declare that the Three Wise Men were fools;
The three old hags do not believe
That the angels sang on Christmas Eve;
And the three old pettifoggers can't approve
Of a court where the only law is Love;
And the three old gossips raise their brows
And sneer at the cradle among the cows—
And the jailers mock at Christmas.

And the three old misers, they pursed their lips,
And the three old hags put hands on hips,
And the three old pettifoggers passed a law,
And the three old gossips put jaw to jaw,
And the three old busybodies squawked like grackles
And the three old jailers shook their shackles.
And in every town, the watchmen cried
This proclamation far and wide:
THERE SHALL BE NO MORE CHRISTMAS.

They bellowed the news through golden cities
And fields where milkmaids sang their ditties;
It spread to farmers on their farms
And firemen answering alarms,
And merchants numbering their bales,
And fishermen with shining sails,
And topers roistering in taverns
And bandits deep in murky caverns:
THERE SHALL BE NO MORE CHRISTMAS.

The man who cries, "Good Christmas Day!"
Shall have his giblets cut away;

Whoever trims a Christmas tree
Suspended by the thumbs shall be,
And he who sings a jolly carol
Shall be rolled on spikes inside a barrel....
So spoke the rulers, and grimly smiled
Thus to destroy one tiny Child,
The Christ Child and His Christmas.

The helpless citizens bit their nails;
The milkmaids dropped their foaming pails;
The farmers leaped as if stung by adders,
And firemen tumbled off their ladders;
Merchants spilled ink upon their books;
And fishermen caught their thumbs on hooks;
The topers called for whey and curds;
The bandits shuddered at the words:
THERE SHALL BE NO MORE CHRISTMAS.

And now a babbling murmur rose,
Expanding as the whirlwind grows.
One question scurried like a mouse
From room to room, from house to house;
One puzzle like a rocket broke
And hung above the land like smoke;
One frown contorted every forehead
Confronted by the problem horrid—
Who is to tell the children?

Ever the panic grows more rife;
Husband glances away from wife;
No one will undertake the mission—
Not even the parson or physician!
And the murderer would rather swing
Than soil his mouth with the monstrous thing!
And presently life is buried below
Flakes of silence like falling snow—
No one will tell the children.

But what was least said was soonest amended,
For Nature herself was outraged and offended,
And now spread the dirge of dole and despair
To the beasts of the field and the birds of the air.

All was awry in a widdershins world
While tyranny triumphed and freedom was furled.

No one knew when to work,
Nor yet when to play,
For the sun shone by night—
And the moon shone by day!
The mice, they had kittens;
The cats, they had puppies;
The lions had lambs;
And the whales, they had guppies!
The ink, it turned white;
The milk, it turned black;
The pig sang *Tweet-tweet,*
And the cow went *Quack-quack.*
The royal red roses
Made people to stare,
With their heads in the earth
And their roots in the air!

The flour was unground
Into wheat at the mill,
For the river turned round
And flowed back up the hill.
The spots on the leopard
Went rolling away—
And were captured for marbles
By urchins at play.
Great fires in the towns
Grew worser and worser;
Flames put out the firemen,
Instead of vice versa.
From headland to mainland,
From mainland to isthmus,
The wide world rebelled
'Gainst a world with no Christmas.

Now, Nicholas Knock was firm as a rock
Though only going on eight,
And he heard the word, from a passing bird,
Of Lullapat's dreadful fate.

He heard the word, from a passing bird,
Of the doomful days to be—
Of Christmas banned throughout the land.
Said Nicholas: "We shall see."

Nicholas Knock, he heard the clock—
It was striking twenty-three;
"O Tickety-Tock," said Nicholas Knock,
"I believe you strike for me!
The grownups wail, and their cheeks are pale,
And their talk is timid and sick;
A kettle of fish is not what I wish,
But I reckon it's up to Nick.

"This slinky man and his slimy clan
An odious law impose;
And I hereby vow: Somewhere, somehow,
I'll tweak each sniveling nose.
Let usurpers growl and their henchmen howl,
I do not care a tuppence;
I'll restore our Yule and upset their rule,
And give them a fit comeuppance!"

Nick knew for a fact it was time to act,
So he lost no time in pondering;
The adventurous lad was quickly clad
For leagues of weary wandering.
He had boots that were spiked—the kind he liked—
And a pair of leather breeches;
His jacket of sheep with pockets deep,
To carry his jam sand*wiches*.

The adventurous lad, he rapidly bade
Farewell to his loving parents:
"I'd rather remain, but my duty is plain,
So I crave your kind forbearance.
My duty was plain as a weathervane
When I heard the twenty-third chime;
If no one but Nick can do the trick,
I hope I'm the Nick of time."

Nicholas spoke boldly, Nicholas spoke proudly,
Nicholas, unfortunately, spoke a little loudly.
Croaking bird, forgotten, pretended to be flying—
Swooping ever closer, listening and spying;
Snatched at every morsel rebelsome and reckless;
Strung them all together, words into a necklace;
Showed himself a croaker, not an honest chirper;
Flapped away, and tattled to the dark usurper.

Came a hurricane then of alarms and excursions,
Of death-dealing weapons, in various versions,
Of horsemen and footmen and bugles and drums,
And cries of *Who goes?* and cries of *Who comes?*
And soon a small army moved off double-quick
With Evilard's orders to capture young Nick.

But Nicholas Knock was knowing and nimble,
He had more common sense than would fit in a thimble,
And Nicholas Knock had a Nicholas knack
Of seeing what happened in back of his back.
So when Evilard's minions came squirming like eels
All they caught of our Nick was a glimpse of his heels.

There was never a map of the way he must wend;
All he knew was that Christmas was his to defend.
Through the meadow he scudded and on through the forest,
So fast that the rabbits and deer were embarrassed;
And yet he could see, when he lifted an eye,
The detestable croaker patrolling the sky.
Again he looked up, and what should he see
But a tiny green cottage high up in a tree?
Next a ladder appeared, it was silken and thin—
And a sweet little voice called, "Climb up and come in!"
The croaker sank lower, the air filled with peril;
Nick scurried aloft like a regular squirrel.

A pretty little hand caught Nick's big hand
And drew him through the door—
And there he stood, in a pretty little room
With pine needles on the floor,
And holding his hand was a pretty little girl
As dainty as a posy,

And she sat him in a chair beside the fire
Till he felt all safe and cozy.

"You may call me Nell, because Nell's my name,
I'll help you in your plight;
I'm the seventeenth child of a seventeenth child,
And I'm blessed with seventeenth sight.
You must chisel out a path over Crookshank Peak,
And the Foolkill River cross;
Then, asleep in a cave under Greengold Hill,
You will find King Wenceslaus.

"As still as stone sits Wenceslaus,
A hero long unheeded,
And drearily dreams the years away
Until his sword is needed.
But he will wake at your rueful news
As the flame wakes from the ember,
And a Christmas greeting he'll give those rogues
That they will long remember.

"But before you can reach King Wenceslaus
You must foil that croaking snooper,
Else he will betray you, step by step,
To every enemy trooper.
That croaking, poking snooper—
That gloomful, doomful snooper—
That evil-omened, greedy-abdomened,
Underhand, overhead snooper."

She led him to an oaken chest
Piled high with curious raiment,
She clad him anew from head to foot,
And took a smile for payment.
Oh, what a sight was Nicky Knock,
With hat of gaudy tatters,
His jacket full of yellow stains,
His breeches, purple splatters!

There coruscated as he walked
One blue, one scarlet legging;
In truth, young Nick had quite the look
Of a rainbow gone a-begging.

"This scarecrow garb, dear Nick," said Nell,
"Will settle that nosy-poker,
For you're not a common scarecrow now,
But a genuine scare-croaker."

Down climbed the boy, and fiercely down
Came swooping the croaking snooper,
One look at Nick—that did the trick—
It collapsed in a deadly stupor.

"Bless you, Nell!" cried Nicholas Knock,
"The croaker is only poppycock.
There's a peak to scale and a river to cross,
And I'm off to waken King Wenceslaus,
But before I depart I doff my hat
To the fairest maiden in Lullapat."
She threw him a kiss, which he caught one-handed,
So sweet that his fingers for hours were candied.

The three old misers quickly heard
Of the fate that befell their precious bird;
The three old hags, they swallowed pins,
And the three old pettifoggers stroked their chins;
The three old gossips raised a pother;
The three old busybodies blamed each other;
But the three old jailers rubbed their hands,
And danced their devilish sarabands—
And then let loose the bloodhounds.

Between the boulders and through the thicket
Raced Nicholas Knock, as spry as a cricket,
Scaled Crookshank Peak without a rope
And scrambled down the opposite slope.
Sudden he heard a dreadful sound,
The horrid howl of a monstrous hound.
He heard it louder, he heard it clearer,
The faster he ran, he heard it nearer.
So instead of fleeing, down he sits,
Saying, "Nick, my boy, you must use your wits.

"There isn't much time for cogitation,
Or logical ratiocination;

No help in addition or subtraction;
This is the moment for rapid action!
Though I'm not too bright, I am not too dense,
I've been called a fellow with great horse-sense. . . .
That's it," cried Nick—"horse-sense, of course!"
So he summoned it up, and rode off on the horse.

He is over the Foolkill in one mighty bound,
And far, far away dies the voice of the hound;
It is only the rush of the wind that he hears
Instead of the hiss of arrows and spears.
He is over the river and galloping still,
Nor slackens his pace till he glimpses a hill.
A hill? 'Twas a mountain of splendor untold,
Its flanks a gay dazzle of green and of gold!
A manifest magical, miracle mountain,
Cooling its toes in Saint Agnes' Fountain.

His heart now takes wing—hear it sing like a linnet!—
He slips from the saddle and pauses a minute
To water the horse, and his forehead to lave,
Then advances on foot in search of the cave.

He breaks through the brake, and he brushes through brush,
Till something within him cries, *Nicholas, hush!*
He catches his breath as he spies with a thrill
A great iron door in the side of the hill.
Two grim men-at-arms are on guard at the door;
Bolt upright they sleep, and like bulldogs they snore.

Says Nick, "It's a ticklish, Nicholas job,
To open a door lacking keyhole or knob,
But the Tickety-Tock had a message for me,
I'm Nicholas Knock, and it struck twenty-three."
So he knocks on the door with a Nicholas knuckle,
Knocking a mickle and knocking a muckle.
At his twenty-third knock, the door opens wide—
And soft as a sunbeam he tiptoes inside.

Nicholas walked into a world of green,
A cavern dusty with the dust of years;
Green shadows wavered o'er the sleepy scene,
Green candles glowed in golden chandeliers,

And kingly straight upon a throne of gold
Slept Wenceslaus behind his beard of iron;
Heroic was his face, and very old.
But wrinkles could not mask the inner lion.

Circled around him stood his faithful knights
As still as statues in their ancient trance.
The candles flickered; little emerald lights
Twinkled on many a trusty sword and lance.

King Wenceslaus to slumber is a thrall
After a life of valiant chivalry;
Silent and patient, he awaits the call
To strike a final blow at tyranny.

Although Nick's sturdy muscles turn to straw,
He threads his way 'twixt battle-ax and sword,
Down on his knees he falls in reverent awe
And boldly cries, "The time has come, my Lord!"

Life first flows back into the mighty hands,
And like a child he rubs a sleepy eye;
Then, like a lion of a king, demands;
"Who is it wakens Wenceslaus, and why?"

Nicholas stuttered and Nicholas spluttered,
A loon would have laughed at the gabble he uttered;
But Wenceslaus gathered him onto his lap,
And soon had the tale from the tired young chap.
Then he called to his page, "Bring us meat, bring us wine!"
And seated young Nick on a pine log to dine,
Who consumed, being empty as ghosts in a garret,
A pigeon washed down with a smidgin of claret.

At this same moment, Evilard
Was watching Oldwin sup
On mustard pills and porcupine quills,
Which he cheerfully gobbled up.
No longer round, his tenscore pound
Had dwindled to eighty-eight;
Yet all the while he still could smile—
And Evilard writhed with hate.

"I've been too kind," the monster whined,
"This torment is a fiasco;
Tomorrow we'll try some thistle pie,
With vinegar and Tabasco.
Such noxious food will alter your mood
For playing the jolly hero,
And I'll be blest if you stand the test
When your weight is down to zero. . . .

"And remember, Uncle," added this abominable sinner,
"The year there is no Christmas, there is no Christmas dinner.
I do believe by New Year's Eve you will be somewhat thinner."

Now Greengold Hill's a-quiver
With pangs that will not cease,
As if a pent-up river
Were raging for release.
The walls are ripped asunder
When Wenceslaus strides by,
For in his voice is thunder,
And lightning in his eye.
A shout of hope and glory comes roaring from his men,
And Christmas's crusaders are on the march again.

The trumpets bite like ginger;
And like a tidal wave
The hosts of the avenger
Come bursting from the cave.

The king upon his charger
A giant now appears,
Looming larger, ever larger
As the field of battle nears.
The rumor seeps through Lullapat, from mountaintop to plain,
That Wenceslaus is coming, with Christmas in his train.

Beside him rode our Nicky,
Even closer than the page,
Looking less than span-and-spicky,
And older than his age.

He had been a daring rover;
He had done what he'd begun;
But he wished the day were over
And the fight for Christmas won.
It worried him that on the word of someone under ten
King Wenceslaus the Warrior was on the march again.

The three old misers clutch their gold;
The three old hags are too scared to scold;
The three old pettifoggers fume and fuss,
And plan to bring suit against Wenceslaus;
The three old gossips cluck and quack;
The three old busybodies start to pack;
And the three old jailers, with simpering muzzles,
Pretend that their chains are Chinese puzzles;
They cease to jeer at Christmas.

And Evilard, foul Evilard,
What has become of Evilard?

The cowardly tyrant quakes and quails,
He gnaws his knuckles and gnaws his nails,
And savagely bites a spiteful thumb,
Glaring at Oldwin with hatred glum;
And as a final malicious joke,
Throws him a salad of poison oak;
Then stealthily sneaks upstairs to bed
And pulls the covers over his head.

Each conspirator cowers and rails at his doom,
The powers of evil are sunken in gloom,
For the bugles of Wenceslaus deafen their ears,
And the landscape is gleaming with halberds and spears,
With helmet and hauberk and crossbow and pike,
Oh, never had Lullapat gazed on the like!
The powers of evil are broken and battered,
The drawbridge is crossed, the portcullis is shattered.
On, on, the crusaders relentlessly sweep;
Like a cyclone they circle the innermost keep,
And Wenceslaus calls, for his heart is too tender,
"Do you choose to die fighting, or will you surrender?"

The rascals perk up at the sound of his voice,
Not the brashest had hoped he would give them a choice!
Since he hasn't condemned them to hang from a tree,
He must be a fool, and they'll get off scot-free;
So with hypocrite smiles they descend from the keep,
Werewolves, masquerading as innocent sheep.

Now Nicholas Knock unlocked the lock
That confined his royal master,
And Nicholas Knock received a shock,
Though prepared for any disaster.
He remembered Oldwin round and hale
As the harvest golden-hue moon,
And now beheld him silvery-pale
And slivery as the new moon.
But Oldwin simply said, "Thank you, son,
Have you such a thing as a cinnamon bun?"

Came now the matter of what to do
With Evilard and his dismal crew.
King Oldwin asked, like a jolly old goose,
"Why not spank them and set them loose?"
Wenceslaus pondered and stroked his beard:
"These venomous toads are still to be feared.
If they had their due they would surely swing.
But I know of a boiling sulphur spring;
Let them steep in that for a year and a day
Till their bile and spleen are stewed away."
The criminals gave a piglike scream,
And were hustled away to be cleansed in steam.

Time flew so fast it was hard to believe,
But the calendar showed it was Christmas Eve.
The Lullapatians in hurrying ranks
Thronged the churches to offer thanks,
Then lord and lady, peasant and vassal,
Were bid to feast in Oldwin's castle.

Of all the dainties at Oldwin's feast
Cinnamon buns are by far the least.
There's the head of a boar,
With apples galore,

And hare meat and bear meat,
Well-done meat and rare meat,
Pudding plum, pudding hasty,
And venison pasty,
And salmon, and sturgeon, and sirloins, and roasts,
And pheasant and peacock in colorful hosts,
And muffins and stuffing and turkey and grouse,
And a gravy tureen as big as a house;
And for those who must drink to continue to feed
There are barrels of wine and metheglin and mead.
What jellies and cakes and sherbets and ices!
Enough for a vast alimentary crisis!
But though all disappeared to the last little cake,
No one complained of the tiniest ache.

A proud young fellow was Nicholas Knock;
He sat on Oldwin's right;
On his other side was dainty Nell
In a gown of green and white.
Said Wenceslaus, "This very same Nell
Who sped you through wood and water,
The Nell who demolished the croaking bird,
Is my great-great-great-granddaughter."

Said Oldwin, "Nick, it's thanks to you
My kingdom still endures,
And since today you saved my crown,
Someday it shall be yours.
I hope to linger many a year
Upon this goodly scene;
But when I depart, you shall be king,
And Nell shall be your queen.

"Yours shall be everlasting fame,
A part of the Yuletide jolly,
And Lullapatians will bless your name
Whenever they hang the holly;
And wherever they hang their stockings up,
On mainland or isle or isthmus,
They will say a prayer for Nicholas Knock,
The hero who saved their Christmas!"

Nick arose to reply, but his wits were gone,
The words he sought turned into a yawn,
And he fell asleep as his story ends,
Murmuring, "MERRY CHRISTMAS, FRIENDS!"

OUR CRAFTY LITTLE CHRISTMAS

JOHN NEARY

A few years ago, suddenly disgusted with ourselves for annually letting Christmas wobble on stage and sort of happen *to* us, we decided to grab this unpredictable comedy of terrors by the tinsel and do something about it. We would, we determined, de-junk Christmas, strip it down from its rich and costly diet of foods and gifts, and by so doing try to get more of ourselves into it.

We started with the tree. The spectacle of thousands of lovely firs and pines chopped off above the roots and set out for sale like so many shivering orphans, destined to adorn garbage trucks a few days afterward, horrified us. Our three boys groaned at the prospect of not having "a real tree," but we went to a nursery anyway, not far from our home, and bought one we could plant in the ground after Christmas.

Our tree was scarcely three feet high and had sprouted perhaps 20 spindly branches in all. With lights, it would look like the skeleton of some tropical electric eel, but we thought it had lots of promise, jutting so bravely from that ice-glazed burlap sack as I strained to lift it into the car. Although this little inverted popsicle cost $20, it would be worth it, my wife and I reassured each other. It would last and last, a living touchstone that we all could one day stand beneath and be reminded of the special joys of this Christmas.

The other accouterments of this Christmas were going to come from the heart, from our own imaginations, and not from our usual frantic burst of last-minute spendthrift shopping. The gifts we got that way never seemed to do much for the people we gave them to and honking through the traffic, body surfing through the crowds in the stores to get them had done a lot to depress us and our budget.

This year there would be planning and thought in gift-selecting. No more desperation choices: gilded turtles with thermometers set in their shells were out from now on, as were carved ivory seashells containing cunning little pagodas, and birdhouses, bird feeders, bird whistles. No more antique railroad watches for people who really wanted Accutrons, or fancy pipe-tampers for men who had got along for years using old match stubs. I was determined to lose my reputation as purveyor of Christmas atrocities.

Our kids, on the other hand, required some convincing. They had somehow developed a hardened and chronic distrust and distaste for their parents' efforts at self-made divertissement. Their reactions to our earlier haphazard experiments in that direction had ranged from outrage to mocking indulgence to acute embarrassment. I suspect, in fact, that they sometimes felt these undertakings were even shameful; on the family walks that we took they hiked well ahead of us lest their friends spot us all out on foot and think—oh, horror!—that we were *poor*. So, just as they automatically preferred television to living-room slide shows, or movies to walks on the beach, or motels to camping, or flying to driving, or hopping on store-bought bikes to even considering assembling a custom chopper out of the myriad parts that clutter our garage, so did they view with gimlet suspicion any notion that we might somehow craft our own Christmas and succeed.

But, since we wanted to change that outlook, wean them away from the hype of commercialism, try to introduce them to the fun of making do and, not least of all, awaken them to accompanying economies—all were strong motives behind our attempt at a new kind of Christmas in the first place—we insisted they join in. At first perplexed and then, to our great relief, intrigued at the challenge, they set to scheming up their gift lists within the limits my wife Joan set for them: presents had to be either handmade or not cost more than a dollar.

The proprietor of the recording studio in Tin Pan Alley was surprised, skeptical and then amused at the cassette of tape I wanted him to dub onto two discs for me: exactly 11 minutes and 23 seconds of my oldest son, 9-year-old Magruder, trumpeting versions of seasonal favorites like "Good King Wenceslas," "God Rest Ye, Merry Gentlemen," "Mr. Tambourine Man" and "Blowin' in the Wind." I didn't know if his grandparents would actually be transported into some special Christmasy joy at hearing those records, but I did know that Magruder would not be quite the same trumpet student after hearing himself on the very same kind of 12-inch vinyl disc that Louis Armstrong lived on. And giving him a major role in the production of Christmas, I hoped, would build a stronger belief in its legerdemain than any hocus-pocus about Santa would afford. Along with the homemade record we made a homemade picture album of family visits, the photos by my wife Joan and an accompanying text which we all collaborated on.

Christmas Eve, I measured the plump and icy little burlap ball of the tree and started building a box to hold it in our living room. At first the rootball would not fit into it, but at last the burlap thawed enough to be forced down inside. It kept right on thawing, sending a tiny flood of muddy water out onto the waxed hardwood floor. I wistfully recalled the ease of setting up the metal Christmas tree stand we had in the basement,

as I wrapped the box in plastic. Summoning back my resolve, I camou-
flaged the mess with what I hoped was an artfully arranged bedsheet.

By close to midnight, my new spirit fully returned when Joan set out
to cool the few dozen chocolate chip cookies, a couple of mince pies and
two loaves of bread she'd baked. The house had a good rich Christmasy
smell to it. The kids had hauled the ornaments up from the basement to
festoon the tree, and we sat down for a drink and admired it. Trees, however adorned—with angel-hair or drenched in tinsel, or simply and really
naked—had always looked to me just like trees. But this one had a win-
some, earnest ragamuffin quality to it; it looked as if it was *trying*. The
boys, however, were so visibly unimpressed that I was disheartened.

My thoughts on whether we'd done the right thing with the new tree
were abruptly broken by the doorbell. A magazine-artist neighbor was
stopping by for a nightcap—and he had brought with him the framed
original of a work of his that I had long admired. But my joy was
strongly mixed with acute embarrassment; I had nothing appropriately
magnificent to give in return. My cupboard stockpile of unopened sherry,
laid up against the routine retaliations I might have to make in the annual suburban surprise Xmas gift game, seemed woefully inadequate in
comparison with this genuinely thoughtful present. We thanked him
and said we had not quite finished wrapping all of our gifts yet—we
would drop over tomorrow with his.

But what could it possibly be? Then I remembered that a coffee table I
had made had once caught his eye and that out in the garage I had
stashed the makings of another almost like it; a thick slab of driftwood
pine we had found at the beach. Already roughly polished by the sandy
wind and surf, all it needed was four legs and it would become a handsome living room table. Making that table would mean hewing the legs
out of a two-by-four with a hatchet, and hand-augering four wide, deep
holes in the slab with a brace and expansion bit, a job I knew would be
blisteringly exhausting. Having my wife back the car over my foot was
about the only thing I could think of that I would like to happen less
than making that table on Christmas Eve. I finished at 3 a.m.

The new, thought-out and planned-through Christmas dawned
through ragged eyes what felt like five minutes later, the boys banging
on the bedroom door to tell us we had slept long enough. Each of us got
to open just one present before breakfast, a rule we had imposed to pro-
long the suspense, and this year it seemed particularly appropriate since
we were exchanging so few gifts. The operation is always a charade—*they*
know what they're getting having cased every closet and shelf in the
house for several weeks, and *we* know that they know—but this year it

was even flatter than usual. We took turns opening our gifts as the others watched: a popgun for Magruder, a scale-model med school skeleton for Chris, a chemistry set for Ben. Then we quickly ate and got right back at the pile of unopened gifts: a picture book for Joan, who also got title to the tree itself; a belt for me; a walkie-talkie apiece for Chris and Ben; jaunty boots for Magruder.

But something obviously was missing for the boys—perhaps the glittery sparkle of that 10-speed bike I knew Ben wanted, or the air rifle I knew was on Magruder's mind, or something whacky, like the cricket farm that Chris was hoping for. Santa Claus had delivered more ho-hums than ho-ho-hos. Still, everybody had tried: Magruder had given his mother a handmade necklace of skull and crossbones; from Ben she got a new can opener and she got a bouquet of plastic flowers from Chris, who gave me a magnetic tack hammer to go with my big gift, a new electric drill. We could definitely say we had got Christmas under control. But the doubt about whether it was *better* seemed almost palpable.

Later in the day, I got a chance not only to use my new drill but to be a hero. In the tumult of Christmas Eve, Houdini, our escape-artist hamster, had made another getaway and vanished completely. An assemblage of tail-twitching cats at a spot along the living room wall, plus some answering chirps when I tapped there after dinner on Christmas Day, indicated he had fallen from the second-floor eaves down into the framing within the wall. Boring three holes, then cutting a triangular, hamster-shaped chunk out of the wall, I tempted Houdini with bits of apple in a can held over the opening. In a moment we could hear—and feel—the ravenous hamster clambering out for his first meal in 24 hours.

But the rescue turned out to be just about the only event of that Christmas that really went well. Our carefully conceived albums and other handicrafts evoked scarcely more joyous reaction than had the gilded turtle years before. And while the table I built briefly held a place of honor in my friend's living room, it was soon demoted to the yard, where it was used, infrequently, as a cumbersome step stool.

All of our self-conscious attention to the staging of Christmas had only succeeded in almost killing the magic of the holiday. A few days after Christmas, we got a devastating glimpse of another way to do it and do it right, when we visited a relative who most emphatically was not seeking any new-fangled yule. Her relationship is, formally, distant: She is my brother-in-law's mother-in-law, to be painfully exact. But in reality, she is a sort of fairy godmother to us all. Watching the kids' eyes in the glow of the hundreds of candles adorning her magnificent, ceiling-high tree, and as they opened the lavish presents she had given them, and as they asked for seconds of turkey and cranberry sauce, it was clear how *they* stood on the issue of our attempted new-style Christmas versus the old.

A few months later, our little tree died. That event, stretching embarrassingly over weeks of watching it turn slowly brown, almost decided the issue for us grown-ups, too.

When the next Christmas arrived, after a year of catching the lawn mower on that shriveled stump in the front yard, bringing with it a horde of visiting relatives, our holiday swung shamelessly back to where we had been before our experiment: cut tree, beneath it a trove of gifts; turkey; the works. It was a success, but paradoxically, it left us feeling that it had been only a *routine* success; anybody can make that kind of Christmas work, something told us. The challenge of our experimental Christmas had turned out to be harder to kill than the little tree had been.

So last year, with hardly any discussion, we decided to try again. This time the nursery gave us explicit, printed directions for how to plant a tree in the winter solstice and the result was a nearly grave-sized hole in the front yard covered with plastic against the frost and with a sack of peat moss standing by. With no prompting from us, the boys, astonishingly enough, made most of their gifts—although a good many of the presents beneath the little tree were far from austere. After all, this *was* Christmas.

That tree did live. Of course, as Chris pointed out, and loudly, we only had it in the house about two hours on Christmas Day. But, then, we reminded him, this year we can decorate the tree that is flourishing in the front yard for as long as we want. Or maybe we'll get another one. We haven't got around to deciding that yet. No sense in over-planning.

THE CHRISTMAS FOOTBALL MATCH

OSWESTRY *OBSERVER*

I n South Cardiganshire early in the century it seems that the population, rich and poor, male and female, of opposing parishes, turned out on Christmas Day and indulged in the game of football with such vigour that it became little short of a serious fight. The parishioners of Celland and Pencarreg were particularly bitter in their conflicts; men threw off their coats and waistcoats, and women their gowns, and sometimes their petticoats. At Llanwennog, an extensive parish below Lampeter, the inhabitants for football purposes were divided into the Bros and Blaenaus. My informant, a man over eighty, now an inmate of Lampeter Workhouse, gives the following particulars: In North Wales the ball was called the Bel Troed, and was made with a bladder covered with a Cwd Tarw. In South Wales it was called the Bel Ddu, and was usually made by the shoemaker of the parish, who appeared on the ground on Christmas Day with the ball under his arm, and, said my informant, he took good care not to give it up until he got his money for making it. The Bros, it should be stated, occupied the high ground of the parish. They were nick-named "Paddy Bros" from a tradition that they were descendants from Irish people who settled on the hills in days long gone by. The Blaenaus occupied the lowlands, and, it may be presumed, were pure-bred Brythons. The more devout of the Bros and Blaenaus joined in the service at the parish church on Christmas morning. At any rate, the match did not begin until about midday, when the service was finished. Then the whole of the Bros and Blaenaus, rich and poor, male and female, assembled on the turnpike road which divided the highlands from the lowlands. The ball having been redeemed from the crydd, it was thrown high in the air by a strong man, and when it fell Bros and Blaenaus scrambled for its possession, and a quarter of an hour frequently elapsed before the ball was got out from the struggling heap of human beings. Then if the Bros, by hook or by crook, could succeed in taking the ball up the mountain to their hamlet of Rhyddlan they won the day; while the Blaenaus were successful if they got the ball to their end of the parish at New Court. The whole parish was the field of operations, and sometimes it would be dark before either party scored a victory. In the meantime many kicks would be given and taken, so that on the following day some of the competitors would be unable to walk, and sometimes a kick on the shins would lead the two men concerned to abandon the game until they had decided which was the better pugilist. There do not appear to have been any rules for the regulation of the game; and the art of football playing in the olden time seems to have been to reach the goal. When once the goal was reached, the victory was celebrated by loud hurrahs and the firing of guns, and was not disturbed until the following Christmas Day. Victory on Christmas Day, added the old man, was so highly esteemed by the whole country-side that a Bro or a Blaenau would as soon lose a cow from his cowhouse, as the football from his portion of the parish.

1887

CELEBRATION IN CHEROKEE FLATS

GORDON PARKS

from THE LEARNING TREE

Merry Christmas! Merry Christmas!" Newt shouted, rousing all the Wingers from their sleep. He had risen early, made a crackling fire and put on the coffeepot, knowing his father would be less grouchy if his insides were warmed up. By the time everyone was in the front room, bright sunlight was bouncing off the snow through the windows onto the tinsel and colored balls decorating the tree.

And as usual Prissy, with an overpoliteness that irked Newt, handed out the gifts, wearing a new middy blouse over her flannel nightgown as she switched about.

After Newt unwrapped his gifts he noted that they were more practical than ever before. He felt that the overalls, stocking cap, socks, book satchel and dictionary (this last from his mother) reflected his growing up. Proudly, he accepted them in this sense, letting go completely the tin soldier and wind-up car period in which he had found so much joy several Christmases before.

After thanking everyone for his presents, he began thumbing the dictionary (this pleased Sarah mightily) for the word *Papilionidae*. To his great surprise he couldn't find it. But he found *Papilionaceous,* and though he didn't understand one of the explanations for it, he immediately decided to learn the phrasing by heart and spring it on Rodney Cavanaugh when they met again. He jumped up, dashed to his room, grabbed pencil and paper and hurried back to the front room. From the book he scribbled: "Papilionaceous—having an irregular zygomorphic corolla somewhat resembling a butterfly." He copied the words over and over, filling the whole page with the new knowledge. Then he propped himself up on the couch and began memorizing it.

Pete sat on the floor rubbing up a pair of already shiny spurs. Prissy, preening before the mirror, tied and retied the handsome bow on her middy blouse. Jack sat admiring his new rough-grain pipe, and Sarah rocked back and forth fingering and praising the sewing kit that Newt, Prissy and Pete had chipped in to buy her.

"Pete," Newt said suddenly, his head still in the book, "did you or Prissy ever hear the word zy-go—gom, no, zy-go-morp-hic in high school?"

"Not me," Pete said.

"Not me," Prissy said.

Sarah looked up puzzled. "What do you want to know about the word, son?"

"Just what it means."

"What you think that dictionary's for, lunkhead?" Prissy spouted out.

"That's no way to talk, Prissy," Sarah said. "Git over there and help him find the word and what it means."

"Yessem," Prissy answered, twisting the bow. "Oh, I just look sooo de-vine in this here lo-va-ly middy, so lo-va-ly." She flounced over to Newt. "Now, deah brotha, what is the word that you would have thou sista help you with?"

A common four-letter word beginning with s popped into Newt's mind, but his mother's eyes were on him and he answered, "Zy-go-morp-hic."

"Why are you worryin' about a word that you don't know anything about?" Prissy questioned facetiously.

"Prissy," Sarah said, "I'm listenin' to you."

"Yessem. Let's see—w, x, y, z—zy-go-matic bone, arch—oh, here it is. It's zy-go-mor-phic, not zy-go-morp-hic, nut."

"Well, what's the diff'rence, phic or hic. Just 'bout the same," Newt said.

"Oh my," Sarah said impatiently, "just tell him what it means and quit fussin'."

Prissy's cheeks dimpled to a mischievous grin. "It means," she said, "mon-o-sym-metric." She cocked her head at Newt. "That satisfy you, deah brotha?"

Newt was silent, temporarily defeated.

"Prissy, you're bein' smart," Sarah said. "Now, I—"

"No I'm not, Momma. That's all it really says." She took the book to Sarah. "See, look for yourself."

Sarah pushed the book away to a seeing distance. "Well, it must be more to it than that," she said. "Pete, come see if you can't help straighten this thing out."

Pete reluctantly dropped his spurs and moved over to his mother. He took the book and, without speaking, read from zygoma to zymurgy. "Newt," he said finally, "this thing's got me fuddled, but I think mostly it's about bones—cheekbones. It says here to see sym-metrical."

"Zi-go this and zi-go that," Jack growled. "I declare, I wish Prissy'd git out in that kitchen and make some zi-go biscuits. I'm hungry."

"Why ah'd be glad to, Poppa deah," Prissy said, switching across the room.

Jack looked up at her. "That blouse is gonna git you into a mess if you don't watch out, gal," he muttered.

Pete laughed. So did Sarah and Newt. And they were all delighted to let the "zygomorphic" matter drop.

Arcella arrived shortly after breakfast, and when Newt opened the door for her she thrust a package into his hands, pecked him on the cheek and wished him a merry Christmas.

"Merry Christmas to you too," Newt said. "Come on in."

"Can't stay long. Oh, hello, Mr. and Mrs. Winger."

"Hello, Arcella—merry Christmas," they both answered.

"Same to you and to you, Prissy and Pete. I hope all of you have a nice Christmas."

"Very very very," Prissy cooed.

They stood awkwardly for a moment, then Newt motioned Arcella into the front room. "Santa Claus left somethin'—"

"Something," Arcella corrected.

"Sorry—he left something here for you under the tree." He picked up a small, gaily wrapped parcel from the floor and handed it to her. Then he pecked her on the cheek and said, "Merry Christmas, sweetheart."

Prissy started to join them, but Sarah motioned her back. "You just keep out'a there, girl. That's Newt's little party." Prissy shrugged her shoulders and went back to the breakfast dishes.

Arcella and Newt sat in the middle of the floor unwrapping their gifts, and Newt got his open first. It was a book of short stories by Edgar Allan Poe, Newt's favorite author. He flipped the first white page and grinned, for there was an inscription, "A merry merry Christmas to the sweetest person I have ever known. Love, Arcella. December, 1925."

"Thanks. Thanks very much," he said. Then he waited shyly as she opened hers.

"Oh, Newt!" she cried, "it's beautiful, just beautiful." She held the locket out to him, turning her back. "Fasten it. Fasten it. I can't wait to see it on."

Clumsily his fingers pulled the chain with the heart-shaped locket around her neck, and after some trouble he secured the clasp. "There," he said, feeling a warmth all the way to his toes.

Then they were both up before the mirror. "Oh, Newt," she repeated, "it's exactly what I wanted." She kissed him on the lips this time, and he leaned forward for another. There was a quick, breathless embrace, then another kiss, followed by hasty thoughtless chatter. "Got up early this mornin'."

"So did I."

"Then I called everybody and we gave out presents."

"Just about the same over at our place, only not as many people."

"There's five of us here."

"Only three of us. Mother, father and I."

"Well, that's the way it is. Some families are bigger'n others."

"Bigger than. Not bigger'n," she chuckled.

"Momma gave me a dictionary. There's lots of good words in it."

"So now you can stop talking like the rest of that gang of yours."

"They're not so bad."

"If they were as bad as their speech, they would all be in jail, Newt Winger."

"All of them ain—aren't as lucky as I am."

"And what do you mean by that statement?"

"I got you."

Arcella shook her head in playful disgust. " 'I got you,' " she mocked.

"I got you—I have you—I have got you. It all means the same. You're my girl—and that makes me real lucky."

She looked at him for a long nice moment, without saying a word. And he looked back at her, not saying a word. They both felt the need for an early spring, a warm, soft, kiss-luscious spring—each aware of the heat in the other's longing.

"I must go now, Newt."

"See you Saturday for the picture show."

"I hope so."

Arcella bid everyone merry Christmas once more and left. And Newt turned again to the inscription, kissed it and placed the book on top of the dictionary. He stood for a moment in the center of the room. "Momma," he called out, "when I get some more books can I have a shelf in my room like Rodney's?"

"I think that would be fine, son. I'm sure Pete and your poppa will help you make a fine one."

Christmas at Spit's School for Boys wasn't much different from any other day. A few of the exceptionally well-behaved boys were granted trips home for the holidays. The others received a pork chop dinner and a small bag of peppermint candies.

Marcus ate alone in the dimness of his cell. The card from Newt, Beansy, Jappy, Earl and Skunk was propped on the table beside his cot. He glanced at the scribbled names in the weak light, and his mind recalled their faces as they had looked when they stood against him on the road near the river. He thought it was Newt who had betrayed him. Then the face of Jake Kiner mixed with the others, and Kirky's and Judge Cavanaugh's. He began boiling within, and suddenly he took a vicious swipe at the card and it fluttered to the floor. It would be May—with no mishaps—before he could return to Cherokee Flats, and his mind wandered to the river, the open plains and the rolling hills . . .

He had just settled back on the cot when Crapper hollered, "You got some visitors, Savage! Git up and try lookin' happy."

"Screw you," Marcus growled sullenly.

"Fool with me and you don't see nobody," Crapper warned.

"I don't give a goddam. Ain't nobody I want to see nohow."

But by now the visitors were coming down the corridor.

"Right this way, Rev'rend," Crapper said. He spoke with an exaggerated politeness that forced a grunt of disgust from Marcus. The cell door swung open and through it came Reverend Broadnap, Maggie Pullens—carrying a bag of fruit and candy—and Deacon Henry Fuller. Reverend Broadnap stepped over and touched Marcus on the shoulder. Marcus stiffened. He wanted to tell them all to go, but he held his tongue.

"We come to pray for you and to wish you a merry Christmas, son." He didn't answer, and Broadnap turned to the others and said, "Let's pray."

They knelt on the floor. Marcus' fingernails dug into the palms of his hands and his teeth ground together in an angry embarrassment. He kept his eyes low and straight ahead, as if ignoring their presence.

"Oh Almighty God," Broadnap began, "we come to you on bended knee prayin' for the soul of this young sinner." Marcus' muscles flexed and his gaze shot defiantly to the tops of their heads, then to Crapper, who stood in the doorway with an evil grin on his face. "Wash his black sins away in these white snows of your holy Christmas. Lighten the troubles he has brought to his young dark days. Bring peace to his tormented soul and help him to someday leave this place a cleaner and better young man. Oh God, show him the light. Show—"

"Shut up! Shut up!" Marcus shouted, "and git the hell out'a here!" He was on his feet now. "I don't want'a hear none of your Uncle Tom prayin' over me!" The three people rose, shocked beyond belief.

"You don't know what you're sayin', boy," Broadnap half whispered, trying to quiet him down, reaching again toward his shoulder.

"I know much 'bout what I'm sayin' as you do," he shot back, pulling away.

Maggie put the bag of fruit on his bed. Broadnap took out a Sunday school card with the picture of Christ on it and placed it on the table. "Read the scripture here on the back, son," he said, "and pray to the Savior. He'll hear you."

Marcus snatched the card, tore it in half and threw it at the preacher. "You and your white God git the hell out'a here!" he shouted. "I don't want no part of you soul savers—bendin' down, like Paw says you do, kissin' the feet of a poor white trash God." Tears were in his eyes now. "Look at Crapper there! He's white! Whyn't you git down and start moanin' and groanin' to him, so he can kick the crap out'a you like he does all us 'nigga' boys. Yeh, that's what he calls us—nigga! nigga! nigga! Tell 'em, Crapper. Tell 'em what you gonna do to me when they leave! Tell 'em."

"Son—"

"Don't son me. Just git goin'! So Crapper can tease me 'bout you niggas comin' here to pray over me!"

Broadnap, Maggie and Henry Fuller filed out, their heads shaking. Crapper slammed the door shut and followed them down the corridor. Marcus sat very still awhile, then suddenly he began to feel a deep sense of guilt, deeper than any he had ever felt in his whole life. He was bewildered. These people had come all that way to help him and he had hurt them, said things he didn't realize he could say. But what he'd said was more for Crapper than for them, he realized. If Crapper hadn't stood in the door with that silly grin on his face, things might have been different. But it was too late now. The harm was done. Yet, somehow, he felt he had got a point across to Crapper. He didn't know just what. Maybe he was really defending those people against somebody like Crapper, who had once told him, "All niggas are stupid and crazy." In a way he was telling him that they weren't, that he was on to his kind and their "lily-white God" that his paw damned when he got drunk.

He glanced up. Crapper was back. Marcus said nothing.

"Merry Christmas—nigga," Crapper said disdainfully, and turned back down the corridor.

Marcus was silent. His head fell back in the shadows and he closed his eyes, trying to form the image of a God with black skin, thick lips and coarse hair like his—but he couldn't. The image on the torn card at the foot of his bed had been implanted much too long before. It was difficult to erase that image now, or even substitute another one for it.

THE CHRISTMAS BIRD COUNT

Tsi-lick! goes the Henslow's

GEORGE PLIMPTON

I should admit at the outset that my credentials as a birdwatcher are slightly sketchy. True, birdwatching *is* a hobby, and if pressed I tell people that I truly enjoy it: on picnics I pack along a pair of binoculars and the Peterson field guide. But I am not very good at it. Identification of even a mildly rare bird or a confusing fall warbler is a heavy, painstaking business, with considerable riffling through the Peterson, and then a numbing of spirit since I am never really *sure*. As a birder I have often thought of myself as rather like a tone-deaf person with just a lesson or two in his background who enjoys playing the flute—it's probably mildly pleasurable, but the results are uncertain.

Pressure to better myself as a birder has been consistently exacted on me by my younger brother and sister, who are both good birdwatchers and can hardly wait for fall and the possibility of being confused by warblers during the migration.

Sometimes, when we are all going somewhere in a car, they involve me in a birding quiz which utilizes the Peterson guide. My sister will say, opening the book at random, "All right, the two of you, see if you can guess this one."

She summarizes: "4¾ to 5¼ inches in length. O.K.? The bird is short-tailed and flat-headed with a big pale bill; finely streaked below. The head is olive-colored and striped, and the wings are reddish. Its flight is low and jerky with a twisting motion of the tail . . ."

"Got it," snaps my brother. "A cinch."

My sister looks at me.

"Well, it's not a brant goose," I say.

"That's very perceptive," she says.

"What's its call?" I ask, indulging in a holding action since I've never been able to remember or indeed hear in my inner ear the dreamy *tseeeee-tsaaays* or the syrupy *zzzchuwunks* that pepper Peterson's descriptions.

My sister reads directly from the book. "This bird 'perches atop a weed, from which it utters one of the poorest vocal efforts of any bird; throwing back its head, it ejects a hiccoughing *tsi-lick*. As if to practice this "song" so that it might not always remain at the bottom of the list, it often hiccoughs, all night long.' "

"You're making that up," I say in astonishment. "That doesn't sound like Peterson at all."

"An absolute cinch," says my brother. "You *must* know."

I decide to take a guess. "A red-eyed vireo."

Both of them groan.

"What is it, Oakes?" my sister asks.

"Henslow's sparrow."

"Of course," she says smugly.

Despite such shortcomings, I was invited last winter to participate in the National Audubon Society's seventy-third annual Christmas Bird Count. I accepted with alacrity, if only in the hope of improving my birdwatching ability, and perhaps, at the least, so I could do better in the Peterson contest with my brother and sister.

For the uninitiated, the Christmas Bird Count was originated in 1900 by the editor of *Bird-Lore* magazine, Frank M. Chapman, who wished to organize a substitute for a traditional Christmas time wildlife slaughter known as the "side hunt," in which the gentry would "choose sides" and spend a day in the woods and fields blazing at everything that moved to increase their team's total toward the grand accounting at the end of the day.

Chapman's first Christmas count involved twenty-seven people and twenty-five localities. The largest list of birds spotted came from Pacific Grove, California (36 species), and Chapman himself reported the second largest (18 species) from Englewood, New Jersey. Those pioneer bird counters could not have been particularly proficient since the 1972 count near Pacific Grove was 179, and the New Jersey count nearest to Englewood was 72.

From its modest beginnings, the Audubon Christmas Bird Count has mushroomed over seven decades—until last year, during the two-week Christmas period, some 20,000 observers were involved. The participating teams (each has one day of search time allowed and is confined to an area with a fifteen-mile diameter) numbered over 1,000.

I thought I might join two counts—selecting one in the more temperate climate which would be competing for the greatest number of species (presumably over 200) and then perhaps one at the other extreme, such as the 1970 Nome, Alaska, count where a total of only *three* species was turned up.

Over the past few years the competition for the highest count has been between three areas in California (San Diego, Santa Barbara, and Point Reyes, where in 1971 a huge army of 193 observers was mustered); Cocoa Beach, Florida, where the redoubtable Allan Cruickshank is the field marshal; and Freeport, Texas, a relatively new count organized sixteen years ago by ornithologist Victor Emanuel, who worked at the job until, in 1971, Freeport set the Christmas Bird Count record of 226 species, an astounding total considering the limitations of the fifteen-mile circle of land and water.

The Freeport count was the one I decided to join. Emanuel was described to me as being young, eager, and perhaps best known in bird-watching circles for his observations of the Eskimo curlew on Galveston Island in 1959. I told him nothing of my birding inadequacies. A week before Christmas I flew to Houston and drove down to the Freeport area, arriving in the late evening at an A-frame beach house on the Gulf of Mexico (appropriately called "The Royal Tern") just in time to hear Emanuel give a peptalk to his team. His group was young—many of them in their twenties, quite a few beards among them—and an overall mood of intense dedication prevailed, as if a guerrilla operation were afoot.

Emanuel's pep rally essentially sounded as follows: "All right, let's try to get *both* cormorants, the double-crested and the olivaceous. Get close. Compare. It's the only way. The green heron is a problem bird, and so is the yellow-crowned night heron. And the least bittern, a tremendous problem! We've only had it once. Flush him out. He lurks in the cattail areas. Leap up and down. Clap your hands. That sort of behavior will get him up. Ross' goose? I'm concerned. We only had four last year. Look in the sky every once in a while for the ibis soaring. Search among the green-winged teal for the cinnamon." He ran his finger down the list through the ducks. "An oldsquaw would be very nice. The hooded merganser is a problem. Hawks! Cooper's and sharp-shinned—not easy at *all*. You people in the woods, make a special effort. Look at all the buteos for the Harlan's. The caracara is a big problem, especially if they're held down by the rain; but they might be flying around. Rails? We're relying on you people in the marsh buggy for the rails, and the purple gallinule as well. As for shorebirds, last year we did not do well at all."

"We did our best," someone called out from the shadows.

"Emanuel's right. We missed the marbled godwit," a bearded man said from the corner.

Emanuel continued as if he hadn't heard: "We have a barn owl staked out. Keep an eye out for the screech owl. We have often missed him. There ought to be some groove-billed anis around. Can't miss *them*. They have weird, comical calls and they look, when they move around, like they're going to fall apart. Check every flicker for the red-shafted. Say's phoebe might be around. Check the ditches. Bewick's wren, a *big* problem bird." He tapped his list. "Now," he said. "I'm very worried about the warblers. Last year we were lucky with vireos; we got five different species, and we got seventeen out of the possible twenty warblers. The cold weather is going to drive the insect-eaters like warblers farther south. So I am not at all sanguine about the vireos and warblers. I'd be surprised if we get more than ten. Check every myrtle warbler for the bright-yellow throat that's going to mean Audubon's." He paused. "Now, meadowlarks," he said. "Keep your ears open for the western meadowlark's song. It's quite different from the eastern's, and it's the only way to distinguish between the two species."

Someone interrupted from the back of the room. "Do you realize that the eastern has learned to *imitate* the western?"

Shouts and cries of "Shut up, Ben!" The man next to me whispered that it was Ben Feltner, a great birding rival of Emanuel's, the first man to spot the famous Galveston Island Eskimo curlew, then thought to be extinct.

Emanuel continued unperturbed. "The sparrow that'll give us the most problem is probably the lark. Search the edges of the brush. It's been missed, and it's very upsetting to miss. Henslow's is another." My heart jumped. My sister's voice, reading from Peterson, sang in my head. "It's better than a groove-billed ani to find a Henslow's," Emanuel was saying—"a *devil* of a bird. Watch for those reddish wings."

What a moment, I thought, to make an impression—to call out to that roomful of experts, "And don't forget that twisting tail in flight, and that soft hiccough, the *tsi-lick* that marks the Henslow's." I stirred, but said nothing.

"Longspurs," Emanuel was continuing. "This might be a year for longspurs with the cold snap bringing them in." He folded the list. "Well, that's the end. Good luck to all of you. Don't forget to look behind you. Too many birdwatchers forget to do that—to see what it is that they've stirred up while walking through. My own prognosis is that if we bird well and hard, we'll beat 200 tomorrow, and possibly even get up to 220, but it will take some doing."

A few hands clapped sharply in the back of the room, and someone offered up an exhortatory cry: "Down with Cocoa Beach!"

"I've got them psyched up," Emanuel said to me as people got up from the floor and began to stir around. "They have to be. It's not only Cocoa Beach I'm worried about, but San Diego. It's all very nerve-racking."

"I can sense that," I said truthfully. "I feel as though I've been spying on a professional football team's locker room before the Big Game."

"No one's going to get much sleep," Emanuel said.

"Absolutely not."

The next day, on the run, I kept notes. Victor Emanuel kept me with him as a partner. (Most teams covering the twelve areas of the Freeport count worked as pairs or trios.) Emanuel's personal plan was to hit as many areas as he could to see how his teams were working. My notes, somewhat helter-skelter, read as follows:

> Eight cars crowded with birdwatchers are moving slowly down a cart track, bouncing in the ruts, and then the line turns into a field bordering a large pond. It is barely light. Rhode Island Reds are crowing from a nearby barn. From the farmer's bedroom window the cars moving slowly in a row through the dawn half-light must suggest a sinister procession of some sort—a Mafia burial ceremony.
>
> The horizon toward the Gulf sparkles with the constellation of lights that mark the superstructures of the oil refineries, illuminating the tall steamlike plumes of smoke. Electric pylons are everywhere. Quite incongruous to think that this highly visible industrial tangle can contain such a rich variety of birdlife. I mention it to Emanuel. He has just whispered to me that the year before a least grebe had turned up in this area. At my comment I could see his face wince in the dim light and he snorted. He tells me that only a fraction of the wildlife John James Audubon observed when he visited the Texas coast remained. But, still it is a birder's paradise. Why is that so?
>
> "Trees," he said, "large and thick enough to contain and hold the eastern birds; and yet the area is far enough south to get southern and western birds. The cover is so good that the area gets more warblers in its count than Corpus Christi does, which is much farther to the south. Furthermore, there is

great diversity—cattle grazing land, the beaches, swampland, ditches, and the Gulf. Since the count started in 1957, the same basic 136 species have turned up every year—which gives you some idea of the huge diversity of the regular bird population.

I am tagging along having a good time. I am in awe of Emanuel. Just a flash of wing, or the mildest of sounds, and he has himself an identification. He is so intense that I rarely ask questions. But he shows me things. I have gazed upon the groove-billed ani. True, the bird does fly as if it were about to come apart at the seams. A black wing fluttering down here, a foot there. I have done nothing on my own. Early in the dawn I saw a woodcock flutter across the road, but I was too intimidated to say anything about it. I know the woodcock from New England. Then, at the pond where we were peering at the barely discernible shapes of the ducks beginning to stir out on the slate-black water, the experts rattling them off (gadwall, canvasback, pintail, et al.), someone said, "Oh, did anyone spot the woodcocks coming across the road from the pasture?" And I said "Yes!" like an explosion. "Absolutely!"

Emanuel caught the despairing eagerness in my voice. He has a nice gift for hyperbole. "That's a terrific bird," he said to me. "Well done!"

We got in Emanuel's car and headed for another area he wanted to bird. I asked him about the Eskimo curlew. He said he hadn't been the first to see the one that had caused all the excitement. On March 22, 1959, two Houston birders—Dudley Deaver and Ben Feltner, the fellow I saw at the peptalk the evening before, wearing the blue jay insignia on his field jacket—had been birding on Galveston Island looking for their first whimbrel, or Hudsonian curlew. In a flock of long-billed curlews they noticed a smallish curlew which they assumed was the whimbrel. But there was something odd about it. It had a very buffy look, and most noticeable was a bill much thinner and shorter than the whimbrel's. With considerable excitement they realized they might be looking at a bird which had last been collected in the United States near Norfolk, Nebraska, on April 17, 1915, and which had been categorized as "probably extinct." The only uncertainty lay in Ludlow Griscom's description in Peterson's field guide that the leg color of the Eskimo curlew was dark green. The legs of the curlew they were looking at on Galveston Island were slaty gray.

Two weeks later they took Emanuel out to see what *he* thought. They discovered the little curlew several miles from where Deaver and Feltner had made the original sighting. "You can imagine how exciting that was," Emanuel told me. "Damn, it was like seeing a dinosaur."

Emanuel was also bothered by the leg color, but some research disclosed that not all reports described the Eskimo curlew's legs as dark green. A number of authorities put them down as a "dull slate color" or "grayish blue."

The curlew returned to Galveston for four years in a row. A number of Texas birders got a chance to look at it—on one occasion from about 100 feet away through a 30-power telescope, powerful enough to fill the eyepiece with the bird. All of the experts were convinced. It was a time, Emanuel told me, that he thinks back on a lot.

We met a birder named Dave Smith, who had come in from Wheeling, West Virginia, because he felt his home turf was so limited. Emanuel said, "Hell, I thought you'd come out here for the glory of the Freeport count."

"No," Smith said. "There's not enough swamps in Wheeling."

I asked Emanuel what he considers the qualities of a great birder, and he began talking about Jim Tucker. "He is a superb birder. He found us the red-necked grebe at the Texas City dike. He is a vegetarian. He never sleeps. He's got terrific, keen hearing, and since hearing a bird counts just as much as seeing one, that's a grand asset. He eats a cracker and keeps going. He stays out on a bird count day until 11 p.m. and he's critical of people who aren't out at midnight at the start, so they can spot, say, a sanderling in the moonlight on the beach, or catch the calls of a migrant bird overhead. One of his most extraordinary feats was to lead a party that spotted 229 species in a single day in Texas, a new national record.

"Now his partner is Roland Wauer. He has the great gift of being able to pick up birds through his binoculars rather than scanning with his eyes. You can imagine what an advantage that is, being able to scan for birds through the binoculars. He'll look down a ravine with his glasses and he'll say, 'Oh, wow, there ought to be a gray vireo in here somewhere,' and he'll *find* it. That's quite a team, those two."

At lunch, which we were having in a restaurant near the beach (not as much roughing-it as I expected), a balding gentleman assigned to count on the beaches came rushing up behind Victor Emanuel, who was bending over a cup of soup at the counter, and cried out: "Oregon junco!"

Emanuel started at the sharp explosion of sound behind him. Then, when he had spun around on his stool, he seemed skeptical.

"But it had pinkish sides," the gentleman said proudly. "It didn't look at *all* like the slate-colored junco. There were a lot of *those* around, maybe 50 or 60, but this fellow was a single junco playing around in the ruts of the road just off the beach."

Emanuel said, "Sometimes the slate-coloreds have pinkish sides."

"Oh," said the balding man. He looked crestfallen.

"No harm in reporting it at the tabulation dinner tonight. The jury will decide."

"I'll think about it," said the man. "I wouldn't want to be taken for a fool."

Emanuel has just given me a lesson on how to tell the difference between Sprague's pipit and the water pipit. Both have the habit of rising vertically out of the gorselike shrubbery of the hummocky country hereabouts, fluttering quite high, as if to look to the horizon to see if anything's of interest, then dropping back quite abruptly to the place where they started from. It's the method of descent that is different. The Sprague's closes its wings at the apogee of its climb and falls like a stone until it is just above the ground, where it brakes abruptly and banks into a bush. The water pipit, on the other hand, drops from the top of its flight in bouncy stages, like a ball tumbling down steep stairs.

"That's a great thing to know," I said. "I'm not sure it's a piece of knowledge I can do very much with. I mean it's not a distinction of daily usage."

Just then, a pipit sprang up in front of us, fluttering up, and then dropped sharply back to earth.

"Sprague's," I said.

"Absolutely brilliant," said Emanuel. "You see, you never know."

Emanuel had to take an hour out of birdwatching to be honored at a chamber of commerce meeting. A punch was served and chocolate-chip cookies. A number of birders were there, looking uncomfortable, minds on their lists and anxious to move on.

An official of the chamber rapped for silence. He had an American flag in his lapel. He said in a clear, sincere municipal voice that the community was proud to have the great Freeport bird count in its area. Texas was number *one,* as everyone was aware, but the nearest municipality, Houston, had been letting everybody down with the Houston Oilers, and the Houston Astros, and the Houston Rockets, who were not displaying the Texas winning spirit worth a damn. It was refreshing to know that at least the bird count team was number one. He called out, "We've got to be number one in something!"

He looked (rather desperately, I thought) at Emanuel, who nodded vaguely and said they had a very good chance to be.

"Well, go and *bust* them," the official said, with a gesture that slopped some of the fruit punch out of his glass. "What we might do," he went on, "is put some sort of statue around here to show that this area is number one in birds. A big, tall stone, or maybe a *brass* bird." The muscles of his face subsided in reflection. The buzz of conversation rose around the room.

With the official greeting over, a number of the townspeople came up to offer suggestions. I heard one person saying to a member of the count team, "I just promise you—there was a falcon, a big tall falcon, sitting on a branch behind the bank. Sure'n shootin' you rush over and he's there to be spotted. Big tall fellah." The birdwatchers listened politely. Emanuel nudged me and said that it was often worthwhile. The Freeport count, he said, had always relied on the "hummingbird lady" who had a feeding station to which three kinds of hummingbirds had come the previous year. She didn't know enough to distinguish one from another, but the birds came to her, and they'd had a count team in her garden which came back with the ruby-throated, the buff-bellied, and the rufous. Of course, that had been a warm Christmas. Still, a team was assigned the "hummingbird lady," and they'd be making their report at the tabulation dinner.

A somewhat brassy female reporter came up to David Marrack, a British-born birdwatcher, and asked: "I am hearing that the warblers—is that the right word—are off. Is that bad news for your bird-hunters . . . I mean *watchers?*"

Marrack replied: "The cold has destroyed the insects. *Quod*—no warblers."

"I beg your pardon."

He inspected her. "It's too bloody *cold,*" he announced clearly.

We are running through cottonwood thickets looking for Harris'
sparrow—the biggest of the sparrows, which summers in the subarctic
forests (Emanuel tells me) and winters in the central plains, west to
north Texas. With the cold weather, a specimen should be in the vicinity, most likely in amongst the white-crowned sparrows. Every once in a
while in our search we step around the whitened bones of a cow skeleton—drowned, I suppose, by the flooding of the creek that flows by just
beyond the trees.

In midafternoon Emanuel spots a bird in the top of a tree. He begins
swaying back and forth in his excitement. "Oh my." Without taking his
eyes from his binoculars, he motions me forward.

"A Harris' sparrow?" I ask.

"It's better," he whispers. "Much better. It's a rose-breasted grosbeak.
No one else will get this. Oh terrific. It's only been seen once before on
the count." We stared at the bird. I could see the wash of pink at its
throat. When it flew, the sun made it blaze, and then oddly, a barn owl
floated out of the trees behind it.

An hour later. What has happened has eclipsed the excitement of the
rose-breasted grosbeak. The two of us had not been seeing much, winding down after the long day, and I was trailing along behind Emanuel,
idly speculating about what sort of a bird he most closely resembled. It is
not an uncommon speculation. William Faulkner once said he would
like to be a buzzard because nothing hates him or envies him or wants
him and he could eat anything. I myself have always opted for hadedah
ibis, a large African wading bird that springs into the air when flushed
from a riverbed with a haunting loud bellow, which gives it its name,
and defecates wildly into the water below. It is not so much the latter
habit that I envy as the *habitat* of the bird, to be able to perch on the
smooth bark of the acacia and overlook the swift water of the river and
see what comes down to it, that great variety of life, and what happens.

I had no intention of pressing Emanuel on such a fancy, but my own
speculation, watching him peer this way and that through the shrubbery,
furtive and yet sleek, is that he might pass . . . well, as a brown thrasher.

Just then, he froze in front of me, staring at a spot twenty or thirty feet

in front of him. His bird glasses came up. "Oh my," I heard him whisper. "Wait until I tell Ben."

"Is it Harris' sparrow?" I asked.

"My God, no, look . . . It's the magnolia warbler. Oh, Ben is going to die, absolutely die! Don't you see? It's a first for the count." He was almost breathless with excitement.

I spotted the warbler through my glasses. Beside me Emanuel kept up a running whispering commentary. "My first thought was that it was a myrtle warbler. Then I saw yellow underneath, and I knew we had something good. White eye-ring, very delicate yellow pip over the beak. No doubt. Oh, wow! It will *kill* Ben. Green back. Two wing bars, one short, one long. White in tail. Very prominent. Very beautiful."

He took out a pad of paper and began writing down a description of the warbler, which was now fluttering about in a bush in front of us.

"He's feeding well. The magnolia is very common in migration, but it's never lingered like this. It's such a joy to find a warbler in winter."

Just then the bird flew. "Ah!" cried Emanuel happily. "The white flash in the tail. That's the absolute clincher." He turned, his eyes shining with excitement.

"Oh, yes," I said. I struggled for something else to say. "That's the damnedest thing I ever saw," I said.

Wow! This was all beginning to go to my head. The sun was starting to go down. I found that I had been absolutely exhausted by Emanuel's enthusiasm.

The tabulation dinner was held at a roadside cafe called Jack's Restaurant in the town of Angleton, which is about halfway between Freeport and Houston. Almost all of the bird count teams (55 people altogether) were there. We sat at long tables arranged in rows along three sides of a brightly lighted banquet room with red-and-green Christmas crepe pinned up between the light fixtures. The place was taut with expectation. Some of the birders gossiped about what they had seen; others affected a smug air of superiority and mystery, containing themselves until the tabulation. I overheard Emanuel saying to Ben Feltner, "I got a bird's never been on the Freeport list."

"You're kidding," said Ben.

Emanuel grinned enormously. "You'll jump out of your seat."

"What is it?"

"I won't tell you. It's a warbler."

Ben stared at him. "Come on."

"You'll have to wait," Emanuel said.

After the dinner Emanuel began the proceedings with a short speech. He announced that the panel that would rule on questionable sightings would consist of himself, Ben Feltner, and Jim Tucker. He said that it was important to maintain the integrity of the Freeport count, and that the panel would strive for a high degree of accuracy. It was important that the judgments be made right away, that very evening, so that those birdwatchers who had accidentals or rare sightings to offer should be prepared to substantiate them. He hoped no one would be *defensive* about his birds; it was a necessary procedure.

Emanuel's master list was divided into three categories—the regular species (birds seen on practically every Freeport count); the essential species (birds seen on most counts but which were present in low numbers and required hard work to locate, and are the keys to a successful high count); and finally the bonus birds, which are rare and not to be expected at all.

Emanuel rattled his list, looked down at it, and began—calling out the name of a bird and looking around the room for someone to raise a hand in acknowledgment that the bird had been seen. Some of the acknowledgments produced cries of delight—and often the team responsible, sitting together at the table, slapped each other's hands like the delighted gestures of ballplayers running back to the bench after a touchdown. Sometimes, though, a missed bird, especially if it was an "essential" species, brought cries of woe.

"Horned grebe?" Emanuel looked around. No hands were up. Dismay. "Ross' goose? Black duck? Goldeneye?" Gloom.

But then Dennis Shepler heightened spirits considerably by putting his hand up for the cinnamon teal. "Three males, two females," he said. Shouts of approbation.

"Bald eagle?"

A hand went up. Pandemonium! The bird described was a single adult, soaring over the lake. Emanuel cried out, "Wonderful, marvelous." Spirits were lifted; some good-natured badinage began—the eagle team being joshed for sighting "a crated bird." "They brought it with them!" someone shouted happily.

The tabulation went on. No hummingbirds had been seen at the "hummingbird lady's" feeder. Horrified cries. Emanuel shook his head. He paused before going on, as if someone would surely recollect that small buzz of color and announce it. He waited, then disconsolately went on. A caracara had been seen. Abruptly the mood shifted again. Shouts of delight. One of the team responsible said they had watched the caracara catch a shrike and eat it. More shouts of glee. I wondered moodily if the shrike would be remembered in the count.

"Peregrine falcon?" Two had been seen, but no pigeon hawks were acknowledged. Groans. The marsh buggy team got a solid round of handclapping for having flushed up a yellow rail.

The climax of emotion came with the approach of the count to the plateau of 200. When a few hands went up for the parula warbler, the 200th bird identified, the entire room rose amidst a storm of clapping and cheering.

At 203 the master list was done, and it was time for the birdwatchers to stand up and offer bonus species. The room quieted down. The 204th species was a pyrrhuloxia, a bird I had never even heard of. The birder, who was an expert from New Jersey, stood and described the specimen in a soft and very difficult stutter, everyone at the tables leaning forward in sympathy with his effort to get his description out. He talked about the bird's yellow bill and its loose crest and how he'd seen it in the salt cedars. One heavily bearded birder astounded everyone by announcing *four* bonus birds—my old pal the Henslow's sparrow, a fish crow, an eastern wood pewee, and the Philadelphia vireo. Each was described; he said he had flushed the sparrow out of dry grass. He didn't mention the hiccoughing song. A Swainson's hawk was 209. Then Emanuel himself rose and announced his two prizes, the rose-breasted grosbeak and the magnolia warbler, grinning in triumph at Ben Feltner as he described the latter. Feltner's eyebrows went up. He pulled at his beard. It was difficult to tell how he was taking it. Emanuel said that I had been along with him and was there for verification; I gave a slight nod at Feltner and looked very arch. There was a tumult of applause when Emanuel sat down.

The 215th, and last, bird offered was a Harlan's hawk. The birdwatcher was quizzed quite sharply by the panel. The hawk was in the light phase, he said, and the sun shone through the tail, which was completely pale except for a black marking toward the end. No, he hadn't seen the back of the bird. It was paler than a red-tailed. The panel looked skeptical; Emanuel tapped a spoon against his front teeth.

Emanuel's panel then disappeared to discuss not only the bonus birds but questionable sightings from the master list. They came back and Emanuel announced that seven birds had not been allowed. He did not say which seven—that might have embarrassed some people who may simply have been overzealous.

The balding man from the beach had his Oregon junco accepted. I grinned at him, and he came over. "Good news, eh?" he said. "Well, *I* was confident. I know the Oregon junco very well; I've trapped them, and banded them, and maybe the jury took that into consideration. There're not many people around who know the Oregon junco like I do, no*sir!*"

Afterwards Emanuel told me the sort of process the panel had gone through. "Well, we knocked out the olivaceous cormorant from the master list; we'll have to assume it was a double-crested. The spotter didn't mention the white border along the pouch, which is an essential field mark, and besides, it's very difficult to distinguish the olivaceous unless you get a size comparison with the double-crested. So we let it go. We dropped the gray-cheeked thrush because the observer who saw it hasn't had that much experience and his description wasn't right. It's *not* uniform brown with a grayish tail. And it's extremely rare in winter. We also dropped the yellow-throated vireo because the observer didn't emphasize the vireo's slower and skulkier movements. He probably saw a pine warbler. Then from the bonus birds we voted out the Philadelphia vireo, and also the sighting of the wood pewee because it's easily confused with the eastern phoebe. As for that fish crow, well, heavens, his voice is unmistakable, that nasal *cah,* and that essential was never mentioned. The Harlan's hawk just didn't sound right either; it could have been a red-tailed."

He went through the list, ticking off the disallowed birds with obvious sorrow. Some of the votes of the panel had not been unanimous, and every rejection lowered the chances of winning the bird count championship. "Let's see," he said. "That's 208 birds. I'm scared," he said. "We'll have to keep our fingers crossed."

A few days later, Emanuel called me in New York to tell me how Freeport had fared in competition with other high-count areas. He recapitulated that the areas that bothered him competitively were the three major California counts. To his delight he had found that the cold weather had hurt these California counts as much as it had Freeport's and that San Diego and Santa Barbara were tied with only 195 species.

That left Cocoa Beach, Florida, to be worried about. Two years before, Cocoa Beach had beaten out Freeport by just one species, 205 to 204. Emanuel decided he was going to wait until after the count period ended (January 1st) before calling Allan Cruickshank, his counterpart, to find out what their total was. In the meantime he was going off to Mexico to take his mind off the competition by doing some birding down there. His special loves are hawks, and there are two hawks in Mexico he would just about fall down and die to see—the orange-breasted falcon, which hangs around ruins (he told me), and the black-collared or chestnut hawk.

In mid-January he wrote me a letter in which he said that the Mexico trip had been an astounding success. He had not seen his two hawks, but his letter was lively with accounts of sightings of flocks of military macaws, "a veritable din of squawking as a magnificent flock came pouring over the side of the mountain."

He wrote that on his return he had gone back down to Freeport on December 31st with a friend from Tennessee "to show him some birds." While there he decided to drop in on the "hummingbird lady" to find out what had happened on count day. She was sitting with her mother in the parlor watching the Dallas Cowboys on television. "Well," she said, "*certainly* two kinds of hummingbirds had turned up that day." Emanuel's eyes widened. The hummingbirds came to the feeder every morning at 8:00 a.m. ("You could almost set your clock by them"), and that day was no exception. She had seen them a number of times. The trouble was that the ladies from the count team hadn't arrived until midafternoon, when the birds had left the feeder for the last time. Emanuel gave a whoop at this, making the mother, who was idly watching the Cowboys standing around during a timeout, start in her seat, and he forthwith boosted the Freeport count to 209.

It turned out to be a fortuitous visit—since a January 7th call to Cruickshank produced the information that the Cocoa Beach count was also 209. Thus the two leading bird count areas in the country were matched in an unprecedented tie.

I wrote Emanuel a short letter of congratulations. I told him that I was proud to have been on a championship team, even if their triumph had to be shared. I didn't tell him that I myself had had a birdwatcher's triumph of sorts recently. I had found myself seated next to a lady at dinner who had begun talking about birds quite without my prompting (the dining room had framed Audubon prints on the wall, perhaps that was why), and she said that the trouble with people who enjoyed birdwatching was that so many of them were unbearably *pretentious*. "Now take those disgusting people who take so much stock in that ritual of the Christmas Bird Count . . ."

"What a coincidence," I said. "I was on the Freeport count."

She was very arch.

"Oh?"

Something stirred in my memory. "I'll bet you can't guess what we turned up," I said. "Perched on a weed, its head thrown back, and uttering the feeblest of hiccoughing noises, a sort of *tsi-lick*. Are those enough hints for you?" She looked at me with a gaze of distaste. "Flattish head, as I recall," I went on, "with a tail that twists in flight. Why that's *Henslow's sparrow*," I said quickly, in case she knew enough to interrupt me.

I hitched my chair forward. "How are you on pipits?" I asked. "Would you care to hear a rather nice field characteristic that'll straighten them out for you. Let's start with Sprague's," I said in a strong voice that turned heads at the table . . .

A CHRISTMAS STORY

KATHERINE ANNE PORTER

An episode in the short life of the author's niece, who died at the age of five-and-a-half years

When she was five years old, my niece asked me again why we celebrated Christmas. She had asked when she was three and when she was four, and each time had listened with a shining, believing face, learning the songs and gazing enchanted at the pictures which I displayed as proof of my stories. Nothing could have been more successful, so I began once more confidently to recite in effect the following:

The feast in the beginning was meant to celebrate with joy the birth of a Child, an event of such importance to this world that angels sang from the skies in human language to announce it and even, if we may believe the old painters, came down with garlands in their hands and danced on the broken roof of the cattle shed where He was born.

"Poor baby," she said, disregarding the angels, "didn't His papa and mama have a house?"

They weren't quite so poor as all that, I went on, slightly dashed, for last year the angels had been the center of interest. His papa and mama were able to pay taxes at least, but they had to leave home and go to Bethlehem to pay them, and they could have afforded a room at the inn, but the town was crowded because everybody came to pay taxes at the same time. They were quite lucky to find a manger full of clean straw to sleep in. When the baby was born, a goodhearted servant girl named

Bertha came to help the mother. Bertha had no arms, but in that moment she unexpectedly grew a fine new pair of arms and hands, and the first thing she did with them was to wrap the baby in swaddling clothes. We then sang together the song about Bertha the armless servant. Thinking I saw a practical question dawning in a pure blue eye, I hurried on to the part about how all the animals—cows, calves, donkeys, sheep——

"And pigs?"

Pigs perhaps even had knelt in a ring around the baby and breathed upon Him to keep Him warm through His first hours in this world. A new star appeared and moved in a straight course toward Bethlehem for many nights to guide three kings who came from far countries to place important gifts in the straw beside Him: gold, frankincense and myrrh.

"What beautiful clothes," said the little girl, looking at the picture of Charles the Seventh of France kneeling before a meek blond girl and a charming baby.

It was the way some people used to dress. The Child's mother, Mary, and His father, Joseph, a carpenter, were such unworldly simple souls they never once thought of taking any honor to themselves nor of turning the gifts to their own benefit.

"What became of the gifts?" asked the little girl.

Nobody knows, nobody seems to have paid much attention to them, they were never heard of again after that night. So far as we know, those were the only presents anyone ever gave to the Child while He lived. But He was not unhappy. Once He caused a cherry tree in full fruit to bend down one of its branches so His mother could more easily pick cherries. We then sang about the cherry tree until we came to the words *Then up spake old Joseph, so rude and unkind.*

"Why was he unkind?"

I thought perhaps he was just in a cross mood.

"What was he cross about?"

Dear me, what should I say now? After all, this was not *my* daughter, whatever would her mother answer to this? I asked her in turn what she was cross about when she was cross? She couldn't remember ever having been cross but was willing to let the subject pass. We moved on to *The Withy Tree,* which tells how the Child once cast a bridge of sunbeams over a stream and crossed upon it, and played a trick on little John the Baptist, who followed Him, by removing the beams and letting John fall in the water. The Child's mother switched Him smartly for this with a branch of withy, and the Child shed loud tears and wished bad luck upon the whole race of withies for ever.

"What's a withy?" asked the little girl. I looked it up in the dictionary and discovered it meant osiers, or willows.

"Just a willow like ours?" she asked, rejecting this intrusion of the commonplace. Yes, but once, when His father was struggling with a heavy piece of timber almost beyond his strength, the Child ran and touched it with one finger and the timber rose and fell properly into place. At night His mother cradled Him and sang long slow songs about a lonely tree waiting for Him in a far place; and the Child, moved by her tears, spoke long before it was time for Him to speak and His first words were, "Don't be sad, for you shall be Queen of Heaven." And there she was in an old picture, with the airy jeweled crown being set upon her golden hair.

I thought how nearly all of these tender medieval songs and legends about this Child were concerned with trees, wood, timbers, beams, cross-pieces; and even the pagan north transformed its great druidic tree festooned with human entrails into a blithe festival tree hung with gifts for the Child, and some savage old man of the woods became a rollicking saint with a big belly. But I had never talked about Santa Claus, because myself I had not liked him from the first, and did not even then approve of the boisterous way he had almost crowded out the Child from His own birthday feast.

"I like the part about the sunbeam bridge the best," said the little girl, and then she told me she had a dollar of her own and would I take her to buy a Christmas present for her mother.

We wandered from shop to shop, and I admired the way the little girl, surrounded by tons of seductive, specially manufactured holiday merchandise for children, kept her attention fixed resolutely on objects appropriate to the grown-up world. She considered seriously in turn a silver tea service, one thousand dollars; an embroidered handkerchief with lace on it; five dollars; a dressing-table mirror framed in porcelain flowers, eighty-five dollars; a preposterously showy crystal flask of perfume, one hundred twenty dollars; a gadget for curling the eyelashes, seventy-five cents; a large plaque of colored glass jewelry, thirty dollars; a cigarette case of some fraudulent material, two dollars and fifty cents. She weakened, but only for a moment, before a mechanical monkey with real fur who did calisthenics on a crossbar if you wound him up, one dollar and ninety-eight cents.

The prices of these objects did not influence their relative value to her and bore no connection whatever to the dollar she carried in her hand. Our shopping had also no connection with the birthday of the Child or the legends and pictures. Her air of reserve toward the long series of blear-eyed, shapeless old men wearing red flannel blouses and false, white-wool whiskers said all too plainly that they in no way fulfilled her notions of Christmas merriment. She shook hands with all of them politely, could not be persuaded to ask for anything from them and seemed not to question the obvious spectacle of thousands of persons everywhere buying presents instead of waiting for one of the army of Santa Clauses to bring them, as they all so profusely promised.

Christmas is what we make it and this is what we have so cynically made of it: not the feast of the Child in the straw-filled crib, nor even the homely winter bounty of the old pagan with the reindeer, but a great glittering commercial fair, gay enough with music and food and extravagance of feeling and behavior and expense, more and more on the order of the ancient Saturnalia. I have nothing against Saturnalia, it belongs to this season of the year: but how do we get so confused about the true meaning of even our simplest-appearing pastimes?

Meanwhile, for our money we found a present for the little girl's mother. It turned out to be a small green pottery shell with a colored bird perched on the rim which the little girl took for an ash tray, which it may as well have been.

"We'll wrap it up and hang it on the tree and *say* it came from Santa Claus," she said, trustfully making of me a fellow conspirator.

"You don't believe in Santa Claus any more?" I asked carefully, for we had taken her infant credulity for granted. I had already seen in her face that morning a skeptical view of my sentimental legends, she was plainly trying to sort out one thing from another in them; and I was turning over in my mind the notion of beginning again with her on other grounds, of making an attempt to draw, however faintly, some boundary lines between fact and fancy, which is not so difficult; but also further to show where truth and poetry were, if not the same being, at least twins who could wear each other's clothes. But that couldn't be done in a day nor with pedantic intention. I was perfectly prepared for the first half of her answer, but the second took me by surprise.

"No, I don't," she said, with the freedom of her natural candor, "but please don't tell my mother, for she still does."

For herself, then, she rejected the gigantic hoax which a whole powerful society had organized and was sustaining at the vastest pains and expense, and she was yet to find the grain of truth lying lost in the gaudy debris around her, but there remained her immediate human situation, and that she could deal with, or so she believed: her mother believed in Santa Claus, or she would not have said so. The little girl did not believe in what her mother had told her, she did not want her mother to know she did not believe, yet her mother's illusions must not be disturbed. In that moment of decision her infancy was gone forever, it had vanished there before my eyes.

Very thoughtfully I took the hand of my budding little diplomat, whom we had so lovingly, unconsciously prepared for her career, which no doubt would be quite a successful one; and we walked along in the bright sweet-smelling Christmas dusk, myself for once completely silenced.

THE TAILOR OF GLOUCESTER

BEATRIX POTTER

"I'll be at charges for a looking-glass; and entertain a score or two of tailors."
Richard III

In the time of swords and periwigs and full-skirted coats with flowered lappets—when gentlemen wore ruffles, and gold-laced waistcoats of paduasoy and taffeta—there lived a tailor in Gloucester.

He sat in the window of a little shop in Westgate Street, cross-legged on a table, from morning till dark.

All day long while the light lasted he sewed and snippeted, piecing out his satin and pompadour, and lutestring; stuffs had strange names, and were very expensive in the days of the Tailor of Gloucester.

But although he sewed fine silk for his neighbours, he himself was very, very poor—a little old man in spectacles, with a pinched face, old crooked fingers, and a suit of thread-bare clothes.

He cut his coats without waste, according to his embroidered cloth; there were very small ends and snippets that lay about upon the table— "Too narrow breadths for nought—except waistcoats for mice," said the tailor.

One bitter cold day near Christmas-time the tailor began to make a coat—a coat of cherry-coloured corded silk embroidered with pansies and roses, and a cream-coloured satin waistcoat—trimmed with gauze and green worsted chenille—for the Mayor of Gloucester.

The tailor worked and worked, and he talked to himself. He measured the silk, and turned it round and round, and trimmed it into shape with his shears; the table was all littered with cherry-coloured snippets.

"No breadth at all, and cut on the cross; it is no breadth at all; tippets for mice and ribbons for mobs! for mice!" said the Tailor of Gloucester.

When the snow-flakes came down against the small leaded window-panes and shut out the light, the tailor had done his day's work; all the silk and satin lay cut out upon the table.

There were twelve pieces for the coat and four pieces for the waistcoat; and there were pocket flaps and cuffs, and buttons all in order. For the lining of the coat there was fine yellow taffeta; and for the button-holes of the waistcoat, there was cherry-coloured twist. And everything was ready to sew together in the morning, all measured and sufficient—except that there was wanting just one single skein of cherry-coloured twisted silk.

The tailor came out of his shop at dark, for he did not sleep there at nights; he fastened the window and locked the door, and took away the key. No one lived there at night but little brown mice, and they run in and out without any keys!

For behind the wooden wainscots of all the old houses in Gloucester, there are little mouse staircases and secret trap-doors; and the mice run from house to house through those long narrow passages; they can run all over the town without going into the streets.

But the tailor came out of his shop, and shuffled home through the snow. He lived quite near by in College Court, next the doorway to College Green; and although it was not a big house, the tailor was so poor he only rented the kitchen.

He lived alone with his cat; it was called Simpkin.

Now all day long while the tailor was out at work, Simpkin kept house by himself; and he also was fond of the mice, though he gave them no satin for coats!

"Miaw?" said the cat when the tailor opened the door. "Miaw?"

The tailor replied—"Simpkin, we shall make our fortune, but I am worn to a ravelling. Take this groat (which is our last fourpence) and Simpkin, take a china pipkin; buy a penn'orth of bread, a penn'orth of milk and a penn'orth of sausages. And oh, Simpkin, with the last penny of our fourpence buy me one penn'orth of cherry-coloured silk. But do not lose the last penny of the fourpence, Simpkin, or I am undone and worn to a thread-paper, for I have NO MORE TWIST."

Then Simpkin again said, "Miaw?" and took the groat and the pipkin, and went out into the dark.

The tailor was very tired and beginning to be ill. He sat down by the hearth and talked to himself about that wonderful coat.

"I shall make my fortune—to be cut bias—the Mayor of Gloucester is to be married on Christmas Day in the morning, and he hath ordered a coat and an embroidered waistcoat—to be lined with yellow taffeta—and the taffeta sufficeth; there is no more left over in snippets than will serve to make tippets for mice——"

Then the tailor started; for suddenly, interrupting him, from the dresser at the other side of the kitchen came a number of little noises—

Tip tap, tip tap, tip tap tip!

"Now what can that be?" said the Tailor of Gloucester, jumping up from his chair. The dresser was covered with crockery and pipkins, willow pattern plates, and tea-cups and mugs.

The tailor crossed the kitchen, and stood quite still beside the dresser, listening, and peering through his spectacles. Again from under a tea-cup, came those funny little noises—

Tip tap, tip tap, tip tap tip!

"This is very peculiar," said the Tailor of Gloucester; and he lifted up the tea-cup which was upside down.

Out stepped a little live lady mouse, and made a curtsey to the tailor! Then she hopped away down off the dresser, and under the wainscot.

The tailor sat down again by the fire, warming his poor cold hands, and mumbling to himself——

"The waistcoat is cut out from peach-coloured satin—tambour stitch and rose-buds in beautiful floss silk. Was I wise to entrust my last four-pence to Simpkin? One-and-twenty button-holes of cherry-coloured twist!"

Tip tap, tip tap, tip tap tip!

"This is passing extraordinary!" said the Tailor of Gloucester, and turned over another tea-cup, which was upside down.

Out stepped a little gentleman mouse, and made a bow to the tailor!

And then from all over the dresser came a chorus of little tappings, all sounding together, and answering one another, like watch-beetles in an old worm-eaten window-shutter—

Tip tap, tip tap, tip tap tip!

And out from under tea-cups and from under bowls and basins, stepped other and more little mice who hopped away down off the dresser and under the wainscot.

The tailor sat down, close over the fire, lamenting—"One-and-twenty button-holes of cherry-coloured silk! To be finished by noon of Saturday: and this is Tuesday evening. Was it right to let loose those mice, undoubtedly the property of Simpkin? Alack, I am undone, for I have no more twist!"

The little mice came out again, and listened to the tailor; they took notice of the pattern of that wonderful coat. They whispered to one another about the taffeta lining, and about little mouse tippets.

And then all at once they all ran away together down the passage behind the wainscot, squeaking and calling to one another, as they ran from house to house; and not one mouse was left in the tailor's kitchen when Simpkin came back with the pipkin of milk!

Simpkin opened the door and bounced in, with an angry "G-r-r-miaw!" like a cat that is vexed: for he hated the snow, and there was snow in his ears, and snow in his collar at the back of his neck. He put down the loaf and the sausages upon the dresser, and sniffed.

"Simpkin," said the tailor, "where is my twist?"

But Simpkin set down the pipkin of milk upon the dresser, and looked suspiciously at the tea-cups. He wanted his supper of little fat mouse!

"Simpkin," said the tailor, "where is my TWIST?"

But Simpkin hid a little parcel privately in the tea-pot, and spit and growled at the tailor; and if Simpkin had been able to talk, he would have asked: "Where is my MOUSE?"

"Alack, I am undone!" said the Tailor of Gloucester, and went sadly to bed.

All that night long Simpkin hunted and searched through the kitchen, peeping into cupboards and under the wainscot, and into the tea-pot where he had hidden that twist; but still he found never a mouse!

Whenever the tailor muttered and talked in his sleep, Simpkin said "Miaw-ger-r-w-s-s-ch!" and made strange horrid noises, as cats do at night.

For the poor old tailor was very ill with a fever, tossing and turning in his four-post bed; and still in his dreams he mumbled—"No more twist! no more twist!"

All that day he was ill, and the next day, and the next; and what should become of the cherry-coloured coat? In the tailor's shop in Westgate Street the embroidered silk and satin lay cut out upon the table— one-and-twenty button-holes—and who should come to sew them, when the window was barred, and the door was fast locked?

But that does not hinder the little brown mice; they run in and out without any keys through all the old houses in Gloucester!

Out of doors the market folks went trudging through the snow to buy their geese and turkeys, and to bake their Christmas pies; but there would be no Christmas dinner for Simpkin and the poor old Tailor of Gloucester.

The tailor lay ill for three days and nights; and then it was Christmas Eve, and very late at night. The moon climbed up over the roofs and chimneys, and looked down over the gateway into College Court. There were no lights in the windows, nor any sound in the houses; all the city of Gloucester was fast asleep under the snow.

And still Simpkin wanted his mice, and he mewed as he stood beside the four-post bed.

But it is in the old story that all the beasts can talk, in the night between Christmas Eve and Christmas Day in the morning (though there are very few folk that can hear them, or know what it is that they say).

When the Cathedral clock struck twelve there was an answer—like an echo of the chimes—and Simpkin heard it, and came out of the tailor's door, and wandered about in the snow.

From all the roofs and gables and old wooden houses in Gloucester came a thousand merry voices singing the old Christmas rhymes—all the old songs that ever I heard of, and some that I don't know, like Whittington's bells.

First and loudest the cocks cried out: "Dame, get up, and bake your pies!"

"Oh, dilly, dilly, dilly!" sighed Simpkin.

And now in a garret there were lights and sounds of dancing, and cats came from over the way.

"Hey, diddle, diddle, the cat and the fiddle! All the cats in Gloucester—except me," said Simpkin.

Under the wooden eaves the starlings and sparrows sang of Christmas pies; the jack-daws woke up in the Cathedral tower; and although it was the middle of the night the throstles and robins sang; the air was quite full of little twittering tunes.

But it was all rather provoking to poor hungry Simpkin!

Particularly he was vexed with some little shrill voices from behind a wooden lattice. I think that they were bats, because they always have very small voices—especially in a black frost, when they talk in their sleep, like the Tailor of Gloucester.

They said something mysterious that sounded like—

> "Buz, quoth the blue fly; hum, quoth the bee;
> Buz and hum they cry, and so do we!"

and Simpkin went away shaking his ears as if he had a bee in his bonnet.

From the tailor's shop in Westgate came a glow of light; and when Simpkin crept up to peep in at the window it was full of candles. There was a snippeting of scissors, and snappeting of thread; and little mouse voices sang loudly and gaily—

> "Four-and-twenty tailors
> Went to catch a snail,

The best man amongst them
Durst not touch her tail;
She put out her horns
Like a little kyloe cow,
Run, tailors, run! or she'll have you all e'en now!"

Then without a pause the little mouse voices went on again—

"Sieve my lady's oatmeal,
Grind my lady's flour,
Put it in a chestnut,
Let it stand an hour——"

"Mew! Mew!" interrupted Simpkin, and he scratched at the door. But the key was under the tailor's pillow, he could not get in.

The little mice only laughed, and tried another tune—

"Three little mice sat down to spin,
Pussy passed by and she peeped in.
What are you at, my fine little men?
Making coats for gentlemen.
Shall I come in and cut off your threads?
Oh, no, Miss Pussy, you'd bite off our heads!"

"Mew! Mew!" cried Simpkin. "Hey diddle dinketty?" answered the little mice—

"Hey diddle dinketty, poppetty pet!
The merchants of London they wear scarlet;
Silk in the collar, and gold in the hem,
So merrily march the merchantmen!"

They clicked their thimbles to mark the time, but none of the songs pleased Simpkin; he sniffed and mewed at the door of the shop.

"And then I bought
A pipkin and a popkin,
A slipkin and a slopkin,
All for one farthing——

and upon the kitchen dresser!" added the rude little mice.

"Mew! scratch! scratch!" scuffled Simpkin on the window-sill; while the little mice inside sprang to their feet, and all began to shout at once in little twittering voices: "No more twist! No more twist!" And they barred up the window shutters and shut out Simpkin.

But still through the nicks in the shutters he could hear the click of thimbles, and little mouse voices singing—

"No more twist! No more twist!"

Simpkin came away from the shop and went home, considering in his mind. He found the poor old tailor without fever, sleeping peacefully.

Then Simpkin went on tip-toe and took a little parcel of silk out of the tea-pot, and looked at it in the moonlight; and he felt quite ashamed of his badness compared with those good little mice!

When the tailor awoke in the morning, the first thing which he saw upon the patchwork quilt, was a skein of cherry-coloured twisted silk, and beside his bed stood the repentant Simpkin!

"Alack, I am worn to a ravelling," said the Tailor of Gloucester, "but I have my twist!"

The sun was shining on the snow when the tailor got up and dressed, and came out into the street with Simpkin running before him.

The starlings whistled on the chimney stacks, and the throstles and robins sang—but they sang their own little noises, not the words they had sung in the night.

"Alack," said the tailor, "I have my twist; but no more strength—nor time—than will serve to make me one single button-hole; for this is Christmas Day in the Morning! The Mayor of Gloucester shall be married by noon—and where is his cherry-coloured coat?"

He unlocked the door of the little shop in Westgate Street, and Simpkin ran in, like a cat that expects something.

But there was no one there! Not even one little brown mouse!

The boards were swept clean; the little ends of thread and the little silk snippets were all tidied away, and gone from off the floor.

But upon the table—oh joy! the tailor gave a shout—there, where he had left plain cuttings of silk—there lay the most beautifullest coat and embroidered satin waistcoat that ever were worn by a Mayor of Gloucester.

There were roses and pansies upon the facings of the coat; and the waistcoat was worked with poppies and corn-flowers.

Everything was finished except just one single cherry-coloured button-hole, and where that button-hole was wanting there was pinned a scrap of paper with these words—in little teeny weeny writing—

And from then began the luck of the Tailor of Gloucester; he grew quite stout, and he grew quite rich.

He made the most wonderful waistcoats for all the rich merchants of Gloucester, and for all the fine gentlemen of the country round.

Never were seen such ruffles, or such embroidered cuffs and lappets! But his button-holes were the greatest triumph of it all.

The stitches of those button-holes were so neat—*so* neat—I wonder how they could be stitched by an old man in spectacles, with crooked old fingers, and a tailor's thimble.

The stitches of those button-holes were so small—*so* small—they looked as if they had been made by little mice!

THE KID HANGS UP HIS STOCKING

JACOB RIIS

The clock in the West Side Boys' Lodging-house ticked out the seconds of Christmas eve as slowly and methodically as if six fat turkeys were not sizzling in the basement kitchen against the morrow's spread, and as if two-score boys were not racking their brains to guess what kind of pies would go with them. Out on the avenue the shopkeepers were barring doors and windows, and shouting "Merry Christmas!" to one another across the street as they hurried to get home. The drays ran over the pavement with muffled sounds; winter had set in with a heavy snow-storm. In the big hall the monotonous click of checkers on the board kept step with the clock. The smothered exclamations of the boys at some unexpected, bold stroke, and the scratching of a little fellow's pencil on a slate, trying to figure out how long it was yet till the big dinner, were the only sounds that broke the quiet of the room. The superintendent dozed behind his desk.

A door at the end of the hall creaked, and a head with a shock of weather-beaten hair was stuck cautiously through the opening.

"Tom!" it said in a stage-whisper. "Hi, Tom! Come up an' git on ter de lay of de Kid."

A bigger boy in a jumper, who had been lounging on two chairs by the group of checker players, sat up and looked toward the door. Something in the energetic toss of the head there aroused his instant curiosity, and he started across the room. After a brief whispered conference the door closed upon the two, and silence fell once more on the hall.

They had been gone but a little while when they came back in haste. The big boy shut the door softly behind him and set his back against it.

"Fellers," he said, "what d'ye t'ink? I'm blamed if de Kid ain't gone an' hung up his sock fer Chris'mas!"

The checkers dropped, and the pencil ceased scratching on the slate, in breathless suspense.

"Come up an' see," said Tom, briefly, and led the way.

The whole band followed on tiptoe. At the foot of the stairs their leader halted.

"Yer don't make no noise," he said, with a menacing gesture. "You, Savoy!"—to one in a patched shirt and with a mischievous twinkle—"you don't come none o' yer monkey-shines. If you scare de Kid you'll get it in de neck, see!"

With this admonition they stole upstairs. In the last cot of the double tier of bunks a boy much smaller than the rest slept, snugly tucked in the blankets. A tangled curl of yellow hair strayed over his baby face. Hitched to the bedpost was a poor, worn little stocking, arranged with much care so that Santa Claus should have as little trouble in filling it as possible. The edge of a hole in the knee had been drawn together and tied with a string to prevent anything falling out. The boys looked on in amazed silence. Even Savoy was dumb.

Little Willie, or, as he was affectionately dubbed by the boys, "the Kid," was a waif who had drifted in among them some months before. Except that his mother was in the hospital, nothing was known about him, which was regular and according to the rule of the house. Not as much was known about most of its patrons; few of them knew more themselves, or cared to remember. Santa Claus had never been anything to them but a fake to make the colored supplements sell. The revelation of the Kid's simple faith struck them with a kind of awe. They sneaked quietly downstairs.

"Fellers," said Tom, when they were all together again in the big room—by virtue of his length, which had given him the nickname of "Stretch," he was the speaker on all important occasions—"ye seen it yerself. Santy Claus is a-comin' to this here joint to-night. I wouldn't 'a' believed it. I ain't never had no dealin's wid de ole guy. He kinder forgot I was around, I guess. But de Kid says he is a-comin' to-night, an' what de Kid says goes."

Then he looked round expectantly. Two of the boys, "Gimpy" and Lem, were conferring aside in an undertone. Presently Gimpy, who limped, as his name indicated, spoke up.

"Lem says, says he——"

"Gimpy, you chump! you'll address de chairman," interrupted Tom, with severe dignity, "or you'll get yer jaw broke, if yer leg *is* short, see!"

"Cut it out, Stretch," was Gimpy's irreverent answer. "This here ain't no regular meetin', an' we ain't goin' to have none o' yer rot. Lem, he says, says he, let's break de bank an' fill de Kid's sock. He won't know but it wuz ole Santy done it."

A yell of approval greeted the suggestion. The chairman, bound to exercise the functions of office in season and out of season, while they lasted, thumped the table.

"It is regular motioned an' carried," he announced, "that we break de bank fer de Kid's Chris'mas. Come on, boys!"

The bank was run by the house, with the superintendent as paying teller. He had to be consulted, particularly as it was past banking hours; but the affair having been succinctly put before him by a committee, of which Lem and Gimpy and Stretch were the talking members, he readily consented to a reopening of business for a scrutiny of the various accounts which represented the boys' earnings at selling papers and blacking boots, minus the cost of their keep and of sundry surreptitious flings at "craps" in secret corners. The inquiry developed an available surplus of three dollars and fifty cents. Savoy alone had no account; the run of craps had recently gone heavily against him. But in consideration of the season, the house voted a credit of twenty-five cents to him. The announcement was received with cheers. There was an immediate rush for the store, which was delayed only a few minutes by the necessity of Gimpy and Lem stopping on the stairs to "thump" one another as the expression of their entire satisfaction.

The procession that returned to the lodging-house later on, after wearing out the patience of several belated storekeepers, might have been the very Santa's supply-train itself. It signalized its advent by a variety of discordant noises, which were smothered on the stairs by Stretch, with much personal violence, lest they wake the Kid out of season. With boots in hand and bated breath, the midnight band stole up to the dormitory and looked in. All was safe. The Kid was dreaming, and smiled in his sleep. The report roused a passing suspicion that he was faking, and Savarese was for pinching his toe to find out. As this would inevitably result in disclosure, Savarese and his proposal were scornfully sat upon. Gimpy supplied the popular explanation.

"He's a-dreamin' that Santy Claus has come," he said, carefully working a base-ball bat past the tender spot in the stocking.

"Hully Gee!" commented Shorty, balancing a drum with care on the end of it, "I'm thinkin' he ain't far out. Look's ef de hull shop'd come along."

It did when it was all in place. A trumpet and a gun that had made vain and perilous efforts to join the bat in the stocking leaned against the bed in expectant attitudes. A picture-book with a pink Bengal tiger and a green bear on the cover peeped over the pillow, and the bedposts and rail were festooned with candy and marbles in bags. An express-wagon with a high seat was stabled in the gangway. It carried a load of fir branches that left no doubt from whose livery it hailed. The last touch was supplied by Savoy in the shape of a monkey on a yellow stick, that was not in the official bill of lading.

"I swiped it fer de Kid," he said briefly in explanation.

When it was all done the boys turned in, but not to sleep. It was long past midnight before the deep and regular breathing from the beds proclaimed that the last had succumbed.

The early dawn was tinging the frosty window panes with red when from the Kid's cot there came a shriek that roused the house with a start of very genuine surprise.

"Hello!" shouted Stretch, sitting up with a jerk and rubbing his eyes. "Yes, sir! in a minute. Hello, Kid, what to——"

The Kid was standing barefooted in the passageway, with a base-ball bat in one hand and a trumpet and a pair of drumsticks in the other, viewing with shining eyes the wagon and its cargo, the gun and all the rest. From every cot necks were stretched, and grinning faces watched the show. In the excess of his joy the Kid let out a blast on the trumpet that fairly shook the building. As if it were a signal, the boys jumped out of bed and danced a breakdown about him in their shirt-tails, even Gimpy joining in.

"Holy Moses!" said Stretch, looking down, "if Santy Claus ain't been here an' forgot his hull kit, I'm blamed!"

KARMA

EDWIN ARLINGTON ROBINSON

Christmas was in the air and all was well
With him, but for a few confusing flaws
In divers of God's images. Because
A friend of his would neither buy nor sell,
Was he to answer for the axe that fell?
He pondered; and the reason for it was,
Partly, a slowly freezing Santa Claus
Upon the corner, with his beard and bell.

Acknowledging an improvident surprise,
He magnified a fancy that he wished
The friend whom he had wrecked were here again.
Not sure of that, he found a compromise;
And from the fulness of his heart he fished
A dime for Jesus who had died for men.

CHRISTMAS

ELEANOR ROOSEVELT

The times are so serious that even children should be made to understand that there are vital differences in people's beliefs which lead to differences in behavior.

This little story, I hope, will appeal enough to children so they will read it and as they grow older, they may understand that the love, and peace and gentleness typified by the Christ Child, leads us to a way of life for which we must all strive.

St. Nicholas's Eve 1940 was cold and the snow was falling. On the hearth in Marta's home there was a fire burning, and she had been hugging that fire all day, asking her mother to tell her stories, telling them afterwards to her doll.

This was not like St. Nicholas's Eve of last year. Then her father had come home. Seven-year-old Marta asked her mother to tell her the story over and over again, so her mother, whose fingers were never idle now that she was alone and had to feed and clothe herself and Marta, sat and knit long woolen stockings and talked of the past which would never come again, and of St. Nicholas's Eve 1939.

The war was going on in Europe in 1939, but Jon was only mobilized. He was just guarding the border, and was allowed to come home for the holiday. Marta's mother said:

"On Monday I got the letter and on Tuesday, St. Nicholas's Eve, he came. I got up early in the morning and started cleaning the house. I wanted everything to shine while your father was home. Soon I called you, and when you were dressed and had had your breakfast, you took your place in the window watching for him to come. Every time you saw a speck way down the road, you would call out to me, but I had time to get much of the holiday cooking prepared and the house in good order before you finally cried: 'Here he is,' and a cart stopped by our gate. You threw open the door and ran down the path. I saw him pick you up in his arms, but he was in such a hurry that he carried you right on in with him and met me as I was running half-way down the path."

Her mother always sighed and Marta wondered why her eyes looked so bright, then she would go on and tell of Jon's coming into the house and insisting on saying: *"Vroolijk Kerstfeest,"* meaning "Merry Christmas," all over again to her and to Marta, just as though he had not greeted them both outside.

Marta's mother had been busy making cakes, *"bankletters"* and *"speculaas,"* just a few since that year none of the family or friends could come to spend St. Nicholas's Eve with them, for no one could spend money to travel in such anxious times. She and Marta had saved and saved to get the food for the feast, and now that was in the larder waiting to be cooked.

They both felt sorry that the two grandmothers and the two grandfathers could not come that year, for Jon and big Marta had lived near enough to their parents so that they could often spend the holidays together. Little Marta loved to think about her grandfathers. One grandfather could tell her so much about the animals and the birds and make them seem just like people, and her mother's father could tell her stories, long, long stories, about things that happened in cities, about processions and having seen the Queen, and so many wonderful things that she could dream about after the visit was over.

Besides, it meant that both her grandmothers helped her mother, and that gave her mother more time to go out with her, so it really was a disappointment when the grandparents could not be with them for this St. Nicholas's Eve. Little Marta did not know it, but to her father's parents it was more than a disappointment. They had wanted so much to see their son again. Like all mothers, his mother feared the worst where her own boy was concerned. Perhaps she had had a premonition of what the future held, but, as with all peasants, the hard facts of life are there to be counted, and the money saved for the trip would keep food in the larder if the winter was going to be as hard as everything indicated, so they did not travel.

Marta's mother had told her that perhaps St. Nicholas, on his white horse with his black servant, Peter, would not bring any presents that year to fill her wooden shoes, but Marta would not believe it. Her first question to her father was: "Will St. Nicholas forget us?"

"No, little Marta," said her father. "The good Saint, who loves little children, will come tonight if you go to bed like a good girl and go quickly to sleep."

Marta put her little shoes down by the big fireplace, and her mother took her into the bedroom and tucked her away behind the curtains which shielded her bunk along the wall on the cold winter night.

Then there had been a long quiet time when Jon and Marta's mother sat together and talked a little, Jon telling what life was like for the army on the frontier and then lapsing into that complete silence which can only come to two people who are very fond of each other. After a while Jon opened up his knapsack and took out the things he had managed to bring to fill those little wooden shoes, and the package which held the last present from her husband that Marta's mother was ever to receive. With it was the usual rhyme:

> To a busy little housewife
> From one who thinks of her through strife,
> To keep her safe from all alarm
> And never let her come to harm,
> Is all he dreams of night and day
> And now forever "Peace" would say.

Needless to say, she guessed the giver before they went to bed.

On Christmas morning Marta woke and ran to look for her wooden shoes. "St. Nicholas has been here," she cried, "and he's given me many sweets, a doll, and bright red mittens just like the stockings Mother made me as a Christmas gift." Then the whole family went skating on the river and there were many other little girls with their fathers and mothers. Everyone glided about and the babies were pushed or dragged in their little sleds. The boys and girls chased one another, sometimes long lines took hands and, after skating away, gathered in a circle, going faster and faster until they broke up because they could not hold on any longer.

Then at last they went home to dinner. On the table a fat chicken and a good soup.

At first they ate silently and then as the edge of their hunger wore off, they began to talk.

"Marta," said her father, "have you learned to read in school yet? Can you count how many days there are in a month?"

"Oh, yes," replied Marta, "and Mother makes me mark off every day that you are gone, and when we are together we always say: 'I wonder if Father remembers what we are doing now,' and we try to do just the things we do when you are home so you can really know just where we are and can almost see us all the time."

Her father smiled rather sadly and then her mother said:

"Jon, perhaps it is good for us all that we have to be apart for a while, because we appreciate so much more this chance of being together. There is no time for cross words when you know how few minutes there are left. It should make us all realize what it would be like if we lived with the thought of how quickly life runs away before us. But you are so busy, Jon, you do not have time to think about us much in the army, do you?"

A curious look came into his eyes and Jon thought for a moment with anguish of what he might have to do some day to other homes and other children, or what might happen to his, and then he pulled himself together and you could almost hear him say: "This at least is going to be a happy memory," and turning to Marta, he began to tease her about her fair hair, which stuck out in two little pigtails from the cap which she wore on her head. Seizing one of them he said:

"I can drive you just like an old horse. I will pull this pigtail and you will turn this way. I will pull the other one and you go that way."

Peals of laughter came from Marta, and before they knew it, the meal was over and the dishes washed and she had demanded that they play a make-believe game with her new doll, where she was a grown-up mother and they had come to see her child.

Such a jolly, happy time, and then as the dusk fell, Marta's father put on his uniform again, kissed her mother, took Marta in his arms, and hugged her tightly, saying: "Take good care of Moeder until I come back."

Then he was gone and they were alone again. The year seemed to travel heavily. First letters came from Jon, and then one day a telegram, and her mother cried and told Marta that her father would never come back, but her mother never stopped working, for now there was no one to look after them except God and He was far away in His heaven. Marta talked to Him sometimes because Mother said He was everyone's Father, but it never seemed quite true. Marta could believe, however, that the Christ Child in the Virgin's arms in the painting in the church was a real child and she often talked to Him.

Strange things Marta told the Christ Child. She confided in Him that she never had liked that uniform which her father went away in. It must have had something to do with his staying away. He had never gone away in the clothes he wore every day and not come back. She liked him best in his everyday clothes, not his Sunday ones, which made him look rather stiff, but his nice comfortable, baggy trousers and blouse. She was never afraid of him then, and he had a nice homey smell; something of the cows and horses came into the house with him, and like a good little country girl Marta liked that smell. She told the Christ Child that her mother had no time to play with her any more. She had to work all the time, she looked different, and sometimes tears fell on her work and she could not answer Marta's questions.

There was no school any more for her to go to and on the road she met children who talked a strange language and they made fun of her and said now this country was theirs. It was all very hard to understand and she wondered if the Christ Child really did know what was happening to little children down here on earth. Sometimes there was nothing to eat in the house, and then both she and her mother went hungry to bed and she woke in the morning to find her mother gone and it would be considerably later before her mother returned with something for breakfast.

Thinking of all these things as her mother told the story again, on this St. Nicholas's Eve 1940, Marta took off her wooden shoes and put them down beside the open fire. Sadly her mother said: "St. Nicholas will not come tonight," and he did not. Marta had an idea of her own, however, which she thought about until Christmas Eve came. Then she said to her mother: "There is one candle in the cupboard left from last year's feast. May I light it in the house so the light will shine out for the Christ Child to see His way? Perhaps He will come to us since St. Nicholas forgot us."

Marta's mother shook her head, but smiled, and Marta took out the candle and carefully placed it in a copper candlestick which had always held a lighted candle on Christmas Eve.

Marta wanted to see how far the light would shine out into the night, so she slipped into her wooden shoes again, put her shawl over her head, opened the door, and slipped out into the night. The wind was blowing around her and she could hardly stand up. She took two or three steps and looked back at the window. She could see the twinkling flame of the candle, and while she stood watching it, she was conscious of a tall figure in a dark cloak standing beside her.

Just at first she hoped the tall figure might be her father, but he would not have stood there watching her without coming out into the candle-light and picking her up and running into the house to greet her mother. She was not exactly afraid of this stranger, for she was a brave little girl, but she felt a sense of chill creeping through her, for there was something awe-inspiring and rather repellent about this personage who simply stood in the gloom watching her.

Finally he spoke:

"What are you doing here, little girl?"

Very much in awe, Marta responded: "I came out to make sure that the Christ Child's candle would shine out to guide His footsteps to our house."

"You must not believe in any such legend," remonstrated the tall, dark man. "There is no Christ Child. That is a story which is told for the weak. It is ridiculous to believe that a little child could lead the people of the world, a foolish idea claiming strength through love and sacrifice. You must grow up and acknowledge only one superior, he who dominates the rest of the world through fear and strength."

This was not very convincing to Marta. No one could tell her that what she had believed in since babyhood was not true. Why, she talked to the Christ Child herself. But she had been taught to be respectful and to listen to her elders and so silence reigned while she wondered who this man was who said such strange and curious things. Was he a bad man? Did he have something to do with her father's going away and not coming back? Or with her mother's worrying so much and working so hard? What was he doing near her house anyway? What was a bad man like? She had never known one.

He had done her no harm—at least, no bodily harm—and yet down inside her something was hurt. Things could be taken away from people. They had had to give up many of their chickens and cows because the government wanted them. That had been hard because they loved their animals and they had cared for them and it meant also that they would have little to eat and much less money when they lost them, but that was different from the way this man made her feel. He was taking away a hope, a hope that someone could do more even than her mother could do, could perhaps make true the dream, that story she told herself every night, both awake and asleep, of the day when her father would come home, the day when hand in hand they would walk down the road again together. When he would put her on his shoulder and they would go skating on the canal. Somehow this man hurt that dream and it was worse than not having St. Nicholas come. It seemed to pull down a curtain over the world.

Marta was beginning to feel very cold and very much afraid, but all her life she had been told to be polite to her elders and ask for permission to do anything she wished to do. She said: "I am hoping the Christ Child will come. May I go in now and will you not come into my house?"

The man seemed to hesitate a minute, but perhaps he decided it would be interesting to see the inside of such a humble home where there was so much simple faith. In any case, he wanted to impress upon this child and upon her mother that foolish legends were not the right preparation for living in a world where he, the power, dominated, so he followed Marta into the house without knocking. Marta's mother, who had been sitting by the fire knitting when Marta went out, was still there, yes, but in her arms was a baby and around the baby a curious light shone and Marta knew that the Christ Child had come. The man in the door did not know, he thought it was an ordinary room with an ordinary baby in a woman's arms.

Striding in, he said: "Madam, you have taught this child a foolish legend. Why is this child burning a candle in the hope that the Christ Child will come?"

The woman answered in a very low voice: "To those of us who suffer, that is a hope we may cherish. Under your power, there is fear, and you have created a strength before which people tremble. But on Christmas Eve strange things happen and new powers are sometimes born."

Marta was not interested any more in the tall figure in the cloak. The Christ Child was there in her mother's lap. She could tell Him all her troubles and He would understand why she prayed above everything else for the return of her father. St. Nicholas would never again leave them without the Christmas dinner and she could have the new doll, and the sweets which she longed to taste again. Perhaps if only she went to sleep like a good little girl, there would be a miracle and her father would be there. Off she trotted to the second room, slipped off her shoes, and climbed behind the curtain.

Marta could not go to sleep at once, because though there was no sound from the other room, she still could not free herself from the thought of that menacing figure. She wondered if he was responsible for the tears of the little girl up the road whose father had not come home last year and who had not been visited either by St. Nicholas.

Then before her eyes she suddenly saw a vision of the Christ Child. He was smiling and seemed to say that the little girl up the road had her father this year and that all was well with her. Marta was happy, fathers are so very nice. Perhaps if she prayed again to the Christ Child, when she woke up He would have her father there too, and so she said first the prayer she had always been taught to say and then just for herself she added: "Dear Christ Child, I know you will understand that though God is the Father of all of us, He is very, very far away and the fathers we have down here are so much closer. Please bring mine back so that we can have the cows, the pigs and the chickens again and all we want to eat and the tears will not be in my mother's eyes." The murmur of her prayer died away as she fell asleep.

A long time the power stood and watched Marta's mother, and finally there came over him a wave of strange feeling. Would anyone ever turn eyes on him as lovingly as this woman's eyes turned on that baby? Bowing low before her, he said: "Madam, I offer you ease and comfort, fine raiment, delicious food. Will you come with me where these things are supplied, but where you cannot keep to your beliefs?"

Marta's mother shook her head and looked down at the baby lying in her lap. She said: "Where you are, there is power and hate and fear among people, one of another. Here there are none of the things which you offer, but there is the Christ Child. The Christ Child taught love. He drove the money-changers out of the temple, to be sure, but that was because He hated the system which they represented. He loved His family, the poor, the sinners, and He tried to bring out in each one the love for Him and for each other which would mean a Christlike spirit in the world. I will stay here with my child, who could trust the legend and therefore brought with her into this house the Christ Child spirit which makes us live forever. You will go out into the night again, the cold night, to die as all must die who are not born again through Him at Christmas time."

The man turned and went out, and as he opened the door, he seemed to be engulfed in the dark and troubled world without. The snow was falling and the wind was howling, the sky was gloomy overhead. All that he looked upon was fierce and evil. These evil forces of nature were ruling also in men's hearts and they brought sorrow and misery to many human beings. Greed, personal ambition, and fear all were strong in the world fed by constant hate. In the howling of the wind he heard these evil spirits about him, and they seemed to run wild, unleashed with no control.

This has happened, of course, many times in the world before, but must it go on happening forever? Suddenly he turned to look back at the house from which he had come. Still from the window shone the little child's candle and within he could see framed the figure of the mother and the Baby. Perhaps that was a symbol of the one salvation there was in the world, the heart of faith, the one hope of peace. The hope he had taken away from Marta for the moment shone out increasingly into the terrible world even though it was only the little Christ Child's candle.

With a shrug of his shoulders, he turned away to return to the luxury of power. He was able to make people suffer. He was able to make people do his will, but his strength was shaken and it always will be. The light in the window must be the dream which holds us all until we ultimately win back to the things for which Jon died and for which Marta and her mother were living.

MR. K*A*P*L*A*N
AND THE MAGI

LEO ROSTEN

When Mr. Parkhill saw that Miss Mitnick, Mr. Bloom, and Mr. Hyman Kaplan were absent, and that a strange excitement pervaded the beginners' grade, he realized that it was indeed the last night before the holidays and that Christmas was only a few days off. Each Christmas the classes in the American Night Preparatory School for Adults gave presents to their respective teachers. Mr. Parkhill, a veteran of many sentimental Yuletides, had come to know the procedure. That night, before the class session had begun, there must have been a hurried collection; a Gift Committee of three had been chosen; at this moment the Committee was probably in Mickey Goldstein's Arcade, bargaining feverishly, arguing about the appropriateness of a pair of pajamas or the color of a dozen linen handkerchiefs, debating whether Mr. Parkhill would prefer a pair of fleece-lined slippers to a set of mother-of-pearl cuff links.

"We shall concentrate on—er—spelling drill tonight," Mr. Parkhill announced.

The students smiled wisely, glanced at the three empty seats, exchanged knowing nods, and prepared for spelling drill. Miss Rochelle Goldberg giggled, then looked ashamed as Mrs. Rodriguez shot her a glare of reproval.

Mr. Parkhill always chose a spelling drill for the night before the Christmas vacation: it kept all the students busy simultaneously; it dampened the excitement of the occasion; above all, it kept him from the necessity of resorting to elaborate pedagogical efforts in order to hide his own embarrassment.

Mr. Parkhill called off the first words. Pens and pencils scratched, smiles died away, eyes grew serious, preoccupied, as the beginners' grade assaulted the spelling of "Banana . . . Romance . . . Groaning." Mr. Parkhill sighed. The class seemed incomplete without its star student, Miss Mitnick, and barren without its most remarkable one, Mr. Hyman Kaplan. Mr. Kaplan's most recent linguistic triumph had been a fervent speech extolling the D'Oyly Carte Company's performance of an operetta by two English gentlemen referred to as "Goldberg and Solomon."

"Charming . . . Horses . . . Float," Mr. Parkhill called off.

Mr. Parkhill's mind was not really on "Charming . . . Horses . . . Float." He could not help thinking of the momentous event which would take place that night. After the recess the students would come in with flushed faces and shining eyes. The Committee would be with them, and one member of the Committee, carrying an elaborately bound Christmas package, would be surrounded by several of the largest students in the class, who would try to hide the parcel from Mr. Parkhill's eyes. The class would come to order with uncommon rapidity. Then, just as Mr. Parkhill resumed the lesson, one member of the Committee would rise, apologize nervously for interrupting, place the package on Mr. Parkhill's desk, utter a few half-swallowed words, and rush back to his or her seat. Mr. Parkhill would say a few halting phrases of gratitude and surprise, everyone would smile and fidget uneasily, and the lesson would drag on, somehow, to the final and distant bell.

"*Ac*cept . . . *Ex*cept . . . Cucumber."

And as the students filed out after the final bell, they would cry "Merry Christmas, Happy New Year!" in joyous voices. The Committee would crowd around Mr. Parkhill with tremendous smiles to say that if the present wasn't *just right* in size or color (if it was something to wear) or in design (if it was something to use), Mr. Parkhill could exchange it. He didn't *have* to abide by the Committee's choice. He could exchange the present for *any*thing. They would have arranged all that carefully with Mr. Mickey Goldstein himself.

That was the ritual, fixed and unchanging, of the last night of school before Christmas.

"Nervous . . . Goose . . . Violets."

The hand on the clock crawled around to eight. Mr. Parkhill could not keep his eyes off the three seats, so eloquent in their vacancy, which Miss Mitnick, Mr. Bloom, and Mr. Kaplan ordinarily graced with their presences. He could almost see these three in the last throes of decision in Mickey Goldstein's Arcade, harassed by the competitive attractions of gloves, neckties, an electric clock, a cane, spats, a "lifetime" fountain pen. Mr. Parkhill grew cold as he thought of a fountain pen. Three times already he had been presented with "lifetime" fountain pens, twice with "lifetime" pencils to match. Mr. Parkhill had exchanged these gifts: he had a fountain pen. Once he had chosen a woollen vest instead; once a pair of mittens and a watch chain. Mr. Parkhill hoped it wouldn't be a fountain pen. Or a smoking jacket. He had never been able to understand how the Committee in '32 had decided upon a smoking jacket. Mr. Parkhill did not smoke. He had exchanged it for fur-lined gloves.

Just as Mr. Parkhill called off "Sardine . . . *Ex*quisite . . . Palace" the recess bell rang. The heads of the students bobbed up as if propelled by a single spring. There was a rush to the door, Mr. Sam Pinsky well in the lead. Then, from the corridor, their voices rose. Mr. Parkhill began to print "Banana" on the blackboard, so that the students could correct their own papers after recess. He tried not to listen, but the voices in the corridor were like the chatter of a flock of sparrows.

"Hollo, Mitnick!"

"Bloom, Bloom, vat is it?"

'So vat did you gat, Keplen? Tell!"

Mr. Parkhill could hear Miss Mitnick's shy "We bought—" interrupted by Mr. Kaplan's stern cry, "Mitnick! Don' say! Plizz, faller-students! Come *don* mit de voices! Titcher vill awreddy hearink, you hollerink so lod! Still! Order! Plizz!" There was no question about it: Mr. Kaplan was born to command.

"Did you bought a Tscheaffer's Fontain Pan Sat, guarantee for de whole life, like *I* said?" one voice came through the door. A Sheaffer Fountain Pen Set, Guaranteed. That was Mrs. Moskowitz. Poor Mrs. Moskowitz, she showed so little imagination, even in her homework. "Moskovitz! Mein Gott!" the stentorian whisper of Mr. Kaplan soared through the air. "Vy you don' open op de door Titcher should *positivel* hear? Ha! Let's goink to odder and fromm de hall!"

The voices of the beginners' grade died away as they moved to the "odder and" of the corridor, like the chorus of "Aïda" vanishing into Egyptian wings.

Mr. Parkhill printed "Charming" and "Horses" on the board. For a moment he thought he heard Mrs. Moskowitz's voice repeating stubbornly, "Did—you—bought—a—Tsheaffer—Fontain—Pan—Sat—*Guarantee?*"

Mr. Parkhill began to say to himself, "Thank you, all of you. It's *just* what I wanted," again and again. One Christmas he hadn't said "It's just what I wanted" and poor Mrs. Oppenheimer, chairman of the Committee that year, had been hounded by the students' recriminations for a month.

It seemed an eternity before the recess bell rang again. The class came in *en masse,* and hastened to the seats from which they would view the impending spectacle. The air hummed with silence.

Mr. Parkhill was printing "Cucumber." He did not turn his face from the board as he said, "Er—please begin correcting your own spelling. I have printed most of the words on the board."

There was a low and heated whispering. "Stend op, Mitnick!" he heard Mr. Kaplan hiss. "You should stend op *too!*"

"The *whole* Committee," Mr. Bloom whispered. "Stand op!"

Apparently Miss Mitnick, a gazelle choked with embarrassment, did not have the fortitude to "stend op" with her colleagues.

"A fine raprezantitif *you'll* gonna make!" Mr. Kaplan hissed scornfully. "Isn't for *mine* sek I'm eskink, Mitnick. Plizz *stend op!*"

There was a confused, half-muted murmur, and the anguished voice of Miss Mitnick saying, "I *can't.*" Mr. Parkhill printed "Violets" on the board. Then there was a tense silence. And then the voice of Mr. Kaplan rose, firmly, clearly, with a decision and dignity which left no doubt as to its purpose.

"Podden me, Mr. Pockheel!"

It had come.

"Er—yes?" Mr. Parkhill turned to face the class.

Messrs. Bloom and Kaplan were standing side by side in front of Miss Mitnick's chair, holding between them a large, long package, wrapped in cellophane and tied with huge red ribbons. A pair of small hands touched the bottom of the box, listlessly. The owner of the hands, seated in the front row, was hidden by the box.

"De hends is Mitnick," Mr. Kaplan said apologetically.

Mr. Parkhill gazed at the tableau. It was touching.

"Er—yes?" he said again feebly, as if he had forgotten his lines and was repeating his cue.

"Hau Kay!" Mr. Kaplan whispered to his confreres. The hands disappeared behind the package. Mr. Kaplan and Mr. Bloom strode to the platform with the box. Mr. Kaplan was beaming, his smile rapturous, exalted. They placed the package on Mr. Parkhill's desk, Mr. Bloom dropped back a few paces, and Mr. Kaplan said, "Mr. Pockheel! Is mine beeg honor, becawss I'm Chairman fromm de Buyink an' Deliverink to You a Prazent Committee, to givink to you dis fine peckitch."

Mr. Parkhill was about to stammer, "Oh, thank you," when Mr. Kaplan added hastily, "Also I'll sayink a few voids."

Mr. Kaplan took an envelope out of his pocket. He whispered loudly, "Mitnick, *you still got time to comm op mit de Committee,*" but Miss Mitnick only blushed furiously and lowered her eyes. Mr. Kaplan sighed, straightened the envelope, smiled proudly at Mr. Parkhill, and read.

"Dear Titcher—dat's de beginnink. Ve stendink on de adge fromm a beeg holiday." He cleared his throat. "Ufcawss is all kinds holidays in U.S.A. Holidays for politic, for religious, an' *plain* holidays. In Fabrary, ve got Judge Vashington's boitday, a *fine* holiday. Also Abram Lincohen's. In May ve got Memorable Day, for dad soldiers. In July comms, net-cheral, Fort July. Also ve have Labor Day, Denksgivink, for de Peelgrims, an' for de feenish fromm de Voild Var, *Armistress* Day."

Mr. Parkhill played with a piece of chalk nervously.

"But arond dis time year ve have a *difference* kind holiday, a spacial, movvellous time. Dat's called—Chrissmas."

Mr. Parkhill put the chalk down.

"All hover de voild," Mr. Kaplan mused, "is pipple celebraking dis vunderful time. Becawss for som pipple is Chrissmas like for *odder* pipple is Passover. Or Chanukah, batter. De most fine, de most beauriful, de most *secret* holiday fromm de whole bunch!"

(" 'Sacred,' Mr. Kaplan, 'sacred,' " Mr. Parkhill thought, ever the ped-agogue.)

"Ven ve valkink don de stritt an' is snow on de floor an' all kinds tar-rible cold!" Mr. Kaplan's hand leaped up dramatically, like a flame. "Ven ve see in de vindows trees mit rad an' grin laktric lights boinink! Ven is de time for tellink de fancy-tales abot Sandy Claws commink fromm Naut Pole on rain-enimals, an' climbink don de jiminies mit *stockings* for all de leetle kits! Ven ve hearink abot de beauriful toughts of de Tree Vise Guys who vere follerink a star fromm de dasert! Ven pipple sayink, 'Oh, Mary Chrissmas! Oh, Heppy Noo Yiss! Oh, bast regotts!' Den ve *all* got a varm fillink in de heart for all humanity vhich should be brodders!"

Mr. Feigenbaum nodded philosophically at this profound thought; Mr. Kaplan, pleased, nodded back.

"*You* got de fillink, Mr. Pockheel. *I* got de fillink, dat's no qvastion abot! Bloom, Pinsky, Caravello, Schneiderman, even Mitnick"—Mr. Kaplan was punishing Miss Mitnick tenfold for her perfidy—"got de fil-link! An' vat is it?" There was a momentous pause. "De Chrissmas Spir-its!"

(" 'Spir*it*,' Mr. Kaplan, 'spir*it*,' " the voice of Mr. Parkhill's con-science said.)

"Now I'll givink de prazent," Mr. Kaplan announced subtly. Mr. Bloom shifted his weight. "Becawss you a foist-class titcher, Mr. Pock-heel, an' learn abot gremmer an' spallink an' de hoddest pots pernoncia-tion—ve know is a planty hod jop mit soch students—so ve fill you should havink a sample fromm our—fromm our—" Mr. Kaplan turned the envelope over hastily—"aha! Fromm our santimental!"

Mr. Parkhill stared at the long package and the huge red ribbons.

"Fromm de cless, to our lovely Mr. Pockheel!"

Mr. Parkhill started. "Er—?" he asked involuntarily.

"Fromm de cless, to our lovely Mr. Pockheel!" Mr. Kaplan repeated with pride.

(" 'Beloved,' Mr. Kaplan, 'beloved.' ")

A hush had fallen over the room. Mr. Kaplan, his eyes bright with joy, waited for Mr. Parkhill to take up the ritual. Mr. Parkhill tried to say, "Thank you, Mr. Kaplan," but the phrase seemed meaningless, so big, so ungainly, that it could not get through his throat. Without a word Mr. Parkhill began to open the package. He slid the big red ribbons off. He broke the tissue paper inside. For some reason his vision was blurred and it took him a moment to identify the present. It was a smoking jacket. It was black and gold, and a dragon with a green tongue was embroidered on the breast pocket.

"Horyantal style," Mr. Kaplan whispered delicately.

Mr. Parkhill nodded. The air trembled with the tension. Miss Mitnick looked as if she were ready to cry. Mr. Bloom peered intently over Mr. Kaplan's shoulder. Mrs. Moskowitz sat entranced, sighing with behemothian gasps. She looked as if she were at her daughter's wedding.

"Thank you," Mr. Parkhill stammered at last. "Thank you, all of you."

Mr. Bloom said, "Hold it op everyone should see."

Mr. Kaplan turned on Mr. Bloom with an icy look. "*I'm* de chairman!" he hissed.

"I—er—I can't tell you how much I appreciate your kindness," Mr. Parkhill said without lifting his eyes.

Mr. Kaplan smiled. "So now you'll plizz hold op de prazent. Plizz."

Mr. Parkhill took the smoking jacket out of the box and held it up for all to see. There were gasps—"Oh!"s and "Ah!"s and Mr. Kaplan's own ecstatic "My! Is beauriful!" The green tongue on the dragon seemed alive.

"Maybe ve made a mistake," Mr. Kaplan said hastily. "Maybe you don't smoke—dat's how *Mitnick* tought." The scorn dripped. "But I said, 'Ufcawss is Titcher smokink! Not in de cless, netcheral. At home! At least a *pipe!*' "

"No, no, you didn't make a mistake. It's—it's *just* what I wanted!"

The great smile on Mr. Kaplan's face became dazzling. "Hooray! Vear in de bast fromm helt" he cried impetuously. "Mary Chrissmas! Heppy Noo Yiss! You should have a *hondert* more!"

This was the signal for a chorus of acclaim. "Mary Chrissmas!" "Wear in best of health!" "Happy New Year!" Miss Schneiderman burst into applause, followed by Mr. Scymzak and Mr. Weinstein. Miss Caravello, carried away by all the excitement, uttered some felicitations in rapid Italian. Mrs. Moskowitz sighed once more and said, "Soch a *sweet* ceremonia." Miss Mitnick smiled feebly, blushing, and twisted her handkerchief.

The ceremony was over. Mr. Parkhill began to put the smoking jacket back into the box with fumbling hands. Mr. Bloom marched back to his seat. But Mr. Kaplan stepped a little closer to the desk. The smile had congealed on Mr. Kaplan's face. It was poignant and profoundly earnest.

"Er—thank you, Mr. Kaplan," Mr. Parkhill said gently.

Mr. Kaplan shuffled his feet, looking at the floor. For the first time since Mr. Parkhill had known him. Mr. Kaplan seemed to be embarrassed. Then, just as he turned to rush back to his seat, Mr. Kaplan whispered, so softly that no ears but Mr. Parkhill's heard it, "Maybe de spitch I rad vas too *formmal*. But avery void I said—it came fromm *below mine heart!*"

Mr Parkhill felt that, for all his weird, unorthodox English, Mr. Kaplan had spoken with the tongues of the Magi.

I Am Christmas

JAMES RYMAN

Now have good day, now have good day!
I am Cristmas, and now I go my way.

Here have I dwelled with more and lass
From Halowtide till Candelmas,
And now must I from you hens pass;
  Now have good day!

I take my leve of king and knight,
And erl, baròn, and lady bright;
To wilderness I must me dight;
  Now have good day!

And at the good lord of this hall
I take my leve, and of gestes all;
Me think I here Lent doth call;
  Now have good day!

And at every worthy officère,
Marshall, panter, and butlère,
I take my leve as for this yere;
  Now have good day!

Another yere I trust I shall
Make mery in this hall,
If rest and peace in England fall;
  Now have good day!

But oftentimes I have herd say
That he is loth to part away
That often biddeth 'Have good day!';
  Now have good day!

Now fare ye well, all in fere,
Now fare ye well for all this yere;
Yet for my sake make ye good chere;
  Now have good day!

NOW IS THE TIME OF CHRISTMAS

JAMES RYMAN

Make we mery, both more and lass,
For now is the time of Cristymas.

Let no man cum into this hall,
Grome, page, nor yet marshàll,
But that some sport he bring withall,
  For now is the time of Cristmas.

If that he say he can not sing,
Some other sport then let him bring
That it may please at this festing,
  For now is the time of Cristmas.

If he say he can nought do,
Then for my love ask him no mo,
But to the stokkes then let him go,
  For now is the time of Cristmas.

Reginald's Christmas Revel

SAKI

They say (said Reginald) that there's nothing sadder than victory except defeat. If you've ever stayed with dull people during what is alleged to be the festive season, you can probably revise that saying. I shall never forget putting in a Christmas at the Babwolds'. Mrs. Babwold is some relation of my father's—a sort of to-be-left-till-called-for cousin—and that was considered sufficient reason for my having to accept her invitation at about the sixth time of asking; though why the sins of the father should be visited by the children—you won't find any notepaper in that drawer; that's where I keep old menus and first-night programmes.

Mrs. Babwold wears a rather solemn personality, and has never been known to smile, even when saying disagreeable things to her friends or making out the Stores list. She takes her pleasures sadly. A state elephant at a Durbar gives one a very similar impression. Her husband gardens in all weathers. When a man goes out in the pouring rain to brush caterpillars off rose trees, I generally imagine his life indoors leaves something to be desired; anyway, it must be very unsettling for the caterpillars.

Of course there were other people there. There was a Major Somebody who had shot things in Lapland, or somewhere of that sort; I forget what they were, but it wasn't for want of reminding. We had them cold with every meal almost, and he was continually giving us details of what they measured from tip to tip, as though he thought we were going to make them warm under-things for the winter. I used to listen to him with a rapt attention that I thought rather suited me, and then one day I quite modestly gave the dimensions of an okapi I had shot in the Lincolnshire fens. The Major turned a beautiful Tyrian scarlet (I remember thinking at the time that I should like my bathroom hung in that colour), and I think that at that moment he almost found it in his heart to dislike me. Mrs. Babwold put on a first-aid-to-the-injured expression, and asked him why he didn't publish a book of his sporting reminiscences; it would be *so* interesting. She didn't remember till afterwards that he had given her two fat volumes on the subject, with his portrait and autograph as a frontispiece and an appendix on the habits of the Arctic mussel.

It was in the evening that we cast aside the cares and distractions of the day and really lived. Cards were thought to be too frivolous and empty a way of passing the time, so most of them played what they called a book game. You went out into the hall—to get an inspiration, I suppose—then you came in again with a muffler tied round your neck and looked silly, and the others were supposed to guess that you were *Wee MacGreegor*. I held out against the inanity as long as I decently could, but at last, in a lapse of good-nature, I consented to masquerade as a book, only I warned them that it would take some time to carry out. They waited for the best part of forty minutes while I went and played wineglass skittles with the page-boy in the pantry; you play it with a champagne cork, you know, and the one who knocks down the most glasses without breaking them wins. I won, with four unbroken out of seven; I think William suffered from over-anxiousness. They were rather mad in the drawing-room at my not having come back, and they weren't a bit pacified when I told them afterwards that I was *At the end of the passage*.

"I never did like Kipling," was Mrs. Babwold's comment, when the situation dawned upon her. "I couldn't see anything clever in *Earthworms out of Tuscany*—or is that by Darwin?"

Of course these games are very educational, but, personally, I prefer bridge.

On Christmas evening we were supposed to be specially festive in the Old English fashion. The hall was horribly draughty, but it seemed to be the proper place to revel in, and it was decorated with Japanese fans and Chinese lanterns, which gave it a very Old English effect. A young lady with a confidential voice favoured us with a long recitation about a little girl who died or did something equally hackneyed, and then the Major gave us a graphic account of a struggle he had with a wounded bear. I privately wished that the bears would win sometimes on these occasions; at least they wouldn't go vapouring about it afterwards. Before we had time to recover our spirits, we were indulged with some thought-reading by a young man whom one knew instinctively had a good mother and an indifferent tailor—the sort of young man who talks unflaggingly through the thickest soup, and smooths his hair dubiously as though he thought it might hit back. The thought-reading was rather a success; he announced that the hostess was thinking about poetry, and she admitted that her mind was dwelling on one of Austin's odes. Which was near enough. I fancy she had been really wondering whether a scrag-end of mutton and some cold plum-pudding would do for the kitchen dinner next day. As a crowning dissipation, they all sat down to play progressive halma, with milk-chocolate for prizes. I've been carefully brought up, and I don't like to play games of skill for milk-chocolate, so I invented a headache and retired from the scene. I had been preceded a few minutes earlier by Miss Langshan-Smith, a rather formidable lady, who always got up at some uncomfortable hour in the morning, and gave you the impression that she had been in communication with most of the European Governments before breakfast. There was a paper pinned on her door with a signed request that she might be called particularly early on the morrow. Such an opportunity does not come twice in a lifetime. I covered up everything except the signature with another notice, to the effect that before these words should meet the eye she would have ended a misspent life, was sorry for the trouble she was giving, and would like a military funeral. A few minutes later I violently exploded an air-filled paper bag on the landing, and gave a stage moan that could have been heard in the cellars. Then I pursued my original intention and went to bed. The noise those people made in forcing open the good lady's door was positively indecorous; she resisted gallantly, but I believe they searched her for bullets for about a quarter of an hour, as if she had been a historic battlefield.

I hate travelling on Boxing Day, but one must occasionally do things that one dislikes.

A BROOKLYN CHRISTMAS

BETTY SMITH

from A TREE GROWS IN BROOKLYN

Christmas was a charmed time in Brooklyn. It was in the air, long before it came. The first hint of it was Mr. Morton going around the schools teaching Christmas carols, but the first sure sign was the store windows.

You have to be a child to know how wonderful is a store window filled with dolls and sleds and other toys. And this wonder came free to Francie. It was nearly as good as actually having the toys to be permitted to look at them through the glass window.

Oh, what a thrill there was for Francie when she turned a street corner and saw another store all fixed up for Christmas! Ah, the clean shining window with cotton batting sprinkled with star dust for a carpet! There were flaxen-haired dolls and others which Francie liked better who had hair the color of good coffee with lots of cream in it. Their faces were perfectly tinted and they wore clothes the like of which Francie had never seen on earth. The dolls stood upright in flimsy cardboard boxes. They stood with the help of a bit of tape passed around the neck and ankles and through holes at the back of the box. Oh, the deep blue eyes framed by thick lashes that stared straight into a little girl's heart and the perfect miniature hands extended, appealingly asking, "Please, won't *you* be my mama?" And Francie had never had a doll except a two-inch one that cost a nickel.

And the sleds! (Or, as the Williamsburg children called them, the sleighs.) There was a child's dream of heaven come true! A new sled with a flower someone had dreamed up painted on it—a deep blue flower with bright green leaves—the ebony-black painted runners, the smooth steering bar made of hard wood and gleaming varnish over all! And the names painted on them! "Rosebud!" "Magnolia!" "Snow King!" "The Flyer!" Thought Francie, "If I could only have one of those, I'd never ask God for another thing as long as I live."

There were roller skates made of shining nickel with straps of good brown leather and silvered nervous wheels, tensed for rolling, needing but a breath to start them turning, as they lay crossed one over the other, sprinkled with mica snow on a bed of cloud-like cotton.

There were other marvelous things. Francie couldn't take them all in. Her head spun and she was dizzy with the impact of all the seeing and all the making up of stories about the toys in the shop windows.

The spruce trees began coming into the neighborhood the week before Christmas. Their branches were corded to hold back the glory of their spreading and probably to make shipping easier. Vendors rented space on the curb before a store and stretched a rope from pole to pole and leaned the trees against it. All day they walked up and down this one-sided avenue of aromatic leaning trees, blowing on stiff ungloved fingers and looking with bleak hope at those people who paused. A few ordered a tree set aside for the day; others stopped to price, inspect and conjecture. But most came just to touch the boughs and surreptitiously pinch a fingerful of spruce needles together to release the fragrance. And the air was cold and still, and full of the pine smell and the smell of tangerines which appeared in the stores only at Christmas time and the mean street was truly wonderful for a little while.

There was a cruel custom in the neighborhood. It was about the trees still unsold when midnight of Christmas Eve approached. There was a saying that if you waited until then, you wouldn't have to buy a tree; that "they'd chuck 'em at you." This was literally true.

At midnight on the Eve of our dear Saviour's birth, the kids gathered where there were unsold trees. The man threw each tree in turn, starting with the biggest. Kids volunteered to stand up against the throwing. If a boy didn't fall down under the impact, the tree was his. If he fell, he forfeited his chance at winning a tree. Only the roughest boys and some of the young men elected to be hit by the big trees. The others waited shrewdly until a tree came up that they could stand against. The little kids waited for the tiny, foot-high trees and shrieked in delight when they won one.

On the Christmas Eve when Francie was ten and Neeley nine, mama consented to let them go down and have their first try for a tree. Francie had picked out her tree earlier in the day. She had stood near it all afternoon and evening praying that no one would buy it. To her joy, it was still there at midnight. It was the biggest tree in the neighborhood and its price was so high that no one could afford to buy it. It was ten feet high. Its branches were bound with new white rope and it came to a sure pure point at the top.

The man took this tree out first. Before Francie could speak up, a neighborhood bully, a boy of eighteen known as Punky Perkins, stepped forward and ordered the man to chuck the tree at him. The man hated the way Punky was so confident. He looked around and asked:

"Anybody else wanna take a chance on it?"

Francie stepped forward. "Me, Mister."

A spurt of derisive laughter came from the tree man. The kids snickered. A few adults who had gathered to watch the fun, guffawed.

"Aw g'wan. You're too little," the tree man objected.

"Me and my brother—we're not too little together."

She pulled Neeley forward. The man looked at them—a thin girl of ten with starveling hollows in her cheeks but with the chin still baby-round. He looked at the little boy with his fair hair and round blue eyes—Neeley Nolan, all innocence and trust.

"Two ain't fair," yelped Punky.

"Shut your lousy trap," advised the man who held all power in that hour. "These here kids is got nerve. Stand back, the rest of yous. These kids is goin' to have a show at this tree."

The others made a wavering lane. Francie and Neeley stood at one end of it and the big man with the big tree at the other. It was a human funnel with Francie and her brother making the small end of it. The man flexed his great arms to throw the great tree. He noticed how tiny the children looked at the end of the short lane. For the split part of a moment, the tree thrower went through a kind of Gethsemane.

"Oh, Jesus Christ," his soul agonized, "why don't I just give 'em the tree, say Merry Christmas and let 'em go? What's the tree to me? I can't sell it no more this year and it won't keep till next year." The kids watched him solemnly as he stood there in his moment of thought. "But then," he rationalized, "if I did that, all the others would expect to get 'em handed to 'em. And next year nobody a-tall would buy a tree off of me. They'd all wait to get 'em handed to 'em on a silver plate. I ain't a big enough man to give this tree away for nothin'. No, I ain't big enough. I ain't big enough to do a thing like that. I gotta think of myself and my own kids." He finally came to his conclusion. "Oh, what the hell! Them two kids is gotta live in this world. They *got* to get used to it. They got to learn to give and to take punishment. And by Jesus, it ain't give but *take, take, take* all the time in this God-damned world." As he threw the tree with all his strength, his heart wailed out, "It's a God-damned, rotten, lousy world!"

Francie saw the tree leave his hands. There was a split bit of being when time and space had no meaning. The whole world stood still as something dark and monstrous came through the air. The tree came towards her blotting out all memory of her ever having lived. There was nothing—nothing but pungent darkness and something that grew and grew as it rushed at her. She staggered as the tree hit them. Neeley went to his knees but she pulled him up fiercely before he could go down. There was a mighty swishing sound as the tree settled. Everything was dark, green and prickly. Then she felt a sharp pain at the side of her head where the trunk of the tree had hit her. She felt Neeley trembling.

When some of the older boys pulled the tree away, they found Francie and her brother standing upright, hand in hand. Blood was coming from scratches on Neeley's face. He looked more like a baby than ever with his bewildered blue eyes and the fairness of his skin made more noticeable because of the clear red blood. But they were smiling. Had they not won the biggest tree in the neighborhood? Some of the boys hollered "Horray!" A few adults clapped. The tree man eulogized them by screaming,

"And now get the hell out of here with your tree, you lousy bastards."

Francie had heard swearing since she had heard words. Obscenity and profanity had no meaning as such among those people. They were emotional expressions of inarticulate people with small vocabularies; they made a kind of dialect. The phrases could mean many things according to the expression and tone used in saying them. So now, when Francie heard themselves called lousy bastards, she smiled tremulously at the kind man. She knew that he was really saying, "Goodbye—God bless you."

TREE-SHAKING DAY

LILLIAN SMITH

from MEMORY OF A LARGE CHRISTMAS

Christmas began when pecans started falling. The early November rains loosened the nuts from their outer shells and sent them plopping like machine gun bullets on the roof of the veranda. In the night, you'd listen and you'd know IT would soon be here.

It was *not* Thanksgiving. We skipped that day. At school, there were exercises, yes, and we dressed up like New England Pilgrims and play-acted Priscilla and Miles Standish and made like we had just landed on Plymouth Rock. But the truth is, the only Plymouth Rocks we saw in our minds were the black and white hens scratching round at the hen house. In those days, the Pilgrims and Thanksgiving did not dent the imaginations of little Southerners, some of whose parents wouldn't concede they had a thing to be thankful for, anyway. It was football that elevated the day into a festival—but that was later than these memories.

We eased over the national holiday without one tummy ache. Turkey? that was Christmas. Pumpkin pie? not for us. Sweet potato pie was Deep South dessert in the fall. We had it once or twice a week. Now and then, Mother varied it with sweet potato pone—rather nice if you don't try it often: raw sweet potato was grated, mixed with cane syrup, milk, eggs and spices and slowly baked, then served with thick unbeaten cream; plain, earthy, caloric and good. But not Christmasy.

Pecans were. Everybody in town had at least one tree. Some had a dozen. No matter. Pecans were prestige. They fitted Christmas.

And so you lay there, listening to the drip drip of rain and plop plop of

nuts, feeling something good is going to happen, something good and it won't be long now. And you'd better sneak out early in the morning before your five brothers and three sisters and get you a few pecans and hide them. Strange how those nuts made squirrels out of us. Nothing was more plentiful and yet we hid piles of them all over the place. Of course, when there are nine of you and the cousins, you get in the habit of hiding things.

Our father chose the auspicious Monday to shake the trees. (Our weekly school holiday was Monday.) The shaking occurred after breakfast. He would stay long enough from the mill to get us well organized. You organized nine kids and the cousins when Big Grandma was around; if you didn't, she would take over—and there'd be a riot.

I cannot remember a nonconforming breakfast on tree-shaking day, but on ordinary days breakfast could be highly unpredictable. One never knew where rebellion would break out.

Our father customarily arose at five o'clock, drank a cup of coffee, walked to the mill, got things going there; got the logging train off to the woods, the mules off to the turpentine farm, got things going at the planing mill, the dry kiln, the shingle mill and the big mill, got things going at the commissary, going at the office, going at the ice plant, going at the Supply Store which he owned half interest in, and at the light plant and water works which he owned three-quarters interest in. Then, with everything going, he walked home to have breakfast with his children.

We were all in the dining room when he came back. A fire was sputtering in the fireplace if the day was cold, the bay window was fluttering with windy white curtains and sunshine and the nervous cage of the canary who was being stalked by one of the cats. The big long table was spread with a white Irish damask cloth—one of Mother's few self-indulgences. There were platters at each end of mullet roe (crisply fried), or perhaps, smothered steak; there were three bowls of grits, and four plates of thin light biscuits and two dishes of homemade butter and three pitchers of cane syrup scattered in between.

We each had our place. The two oldest sat on either side of our mother; the two youngest sat in high chairs on either side of our father; the others sat according to age in between. You took your turn sitting by Big Granny. You sat under duress, for not only was she wide, she had a habit of reaching over to your plate with her fork when both your hands were busy and spearing the morsel you had saved for last. On the walnut-paneled wall, behind the picture (lambs huddling in terrible snow storm) was a small shelf on which lay the Bible and a thin peach-sprout switch. The Bible was read every morning. The thin switch was used to quell whatever disorder was popping up among the younger ones.

We sat down. Our father read briefly from the Bible, closed it, rested his hand on it for a moment as though it gave him strength (and I think it did), then put it back on the shelf. He returned to the table, looked round at his nine, smiled, studied a face now and then as though it was new, beamed at Mother, then encouragingly asked for our verses. Each of us then said what we had gleaned from the Bible. The youngest always said, *Jesus wept.* The next one always said, *God is love.* The others were on their own. Verses began with the oldest and came down like a babbling stream to the youngest.

It was usually routine. But there were sudden uprisings. One morning, the six-year-old, when his turn came, calmly shouted "Jesus wept!" Silence. A scream from the youngest, "He tant have Thesus wept, he tant it's mine he tant he tant—" A scream from the four-year-old, "He tant have my Dod is love neider he tant he tant he tant—"

"Sssh . . . nobody's going to take your Jesus wept or your G—" He turned to the deviationist. "Why, son," he asked gravely, "did you say your little sister's verse?"

"I'm tired," said son. Father looked at Mother. Mother looked at the tired one who flashed his softest smile on her. When Father was not present it worked. No response now. He looked at Big Granny who could be fetched by it, too, but B.G. had seized the opportunity to spear a big piece of roe from an unguarded plate. Six-Year-Old swallowed hard, "I'm plumb wore out," he quavered.

Dissent more often came from the higher echelons. There was the summer when Age Fifteen decided it was time for subversion. He came close to bringing off a successful *coup* by the simple and highly effective device of teaching the *Song of Solomon* to one and all, even the littlest. He trained with cruel disregard of all the things we wanted to dream about or run and do. His sense of timing was superb; his dominance over us was complete, for we adored Age Fifteen whose imagination never went to sleep, we would have loved to move into his mythic mind and live there forever with him. So we chanted our lines, as he ordered, and rechanted—quick, quick, he'd say, no wait, be ready, hook on now; and finally, we were zipping along like a chain reaction and he announced we were ready.

The morning came. He led off with "How beautiful are thy feet with shoes, O prince's daughter . . . thy navel is like a round goblet which wanteth not liquor . . . thy two breasts are like two young roes that are twins . . . thy neck . . ." Each picked up his split-second cue and carried on, and it was climaxed by the two-year-old who piped out gaily, "Tay me wif flagons, tomfort me wif apples for I am thick of love."

And there was the time when one of the sisters—eleven years old that year—craving economy of effort and a smidge of excitement, specialized in the Begats. Each morning this pigtailed plump daughter sang out to the dining room her story of begetting: "Enos lived ninety years and begat Cainan . . . And Cainan lived seventy years and begat Mahalaleel . . . and Mahalaleel lived sixty-five years and begat Jared"—etc.

The parents could play it cool when they wanted to. For three mornings, they quietly ignored the giggles of the eight and the cousins, as Eleven-Year-Old begatted. But Eleven was too proud of her memory and her acrobatic skill with Semitic names and she loved the spotlight. The next morning she hung on to Genesis and begat and begat and begat. Her audience was hysterical. Then the two youngest, giggling wildly about what they could not comprehend, seized the chance to steal a biscuit before the Blessing and promptly choked on their dual pleasures and our father, beating alternately on two little wheezy backs, yelled (a measure reserved for near-disaster) Stop it, you!

Age Eleven, a thinskinned if loquacious show-off, blushed and began to cry silently. And Big Granny who had been having a ball spearing food off the platters along with the littlest ones put a sausage on the conquered one's plate and told her to hush and eat, eating would make anything all right and WHAT DID THE POOR CHILD DO THAT WAS SO WRONG she shouted from *her* soapbox, seizing this chance to heckle her son-in-law.

Our father looked at Mother. And Mother swiftly said, "Papa, please say the Blessing—the other verses can wait until tomorrow."

But on tree-shaking day we were meek. We said proper verses, we bowed our heads for the Blessing, we ate quickly, did not kick each other or yap at Big Grandma.

The moment we were excused from the table we ran to the linen closet for old sheets and spread them under the trees as our father directed. We got the baskets without being told. We were gloriously good. Even the little ones listened when Papa told them not to cry if the nuts hit their heads—anyway, they didn't need to get under the tree, did they? Of course, they needed to get under the tree but they said yessuh and waved him goodby as he walked down the tiled walk which led to the street which led to his office.

The one chosen to shake the tree first was usually the eldest. But now and then, an ambitious underling snatched the honor away by bringing in wood for all twelve fireplaces without being told to or washing and polishing Mother's brougham and offering to drive her out to Cousin Lizzie's; or maybe, he cleaned (with his sisters' help) all twenty-two lamp chimneys. (The town's young electric light plant was still pretty unstable; one never knew what to count on; but my father took care of that, too, by arranging a signal of two quick blinks and one delayed one, which was the communal code for *light your oil lamps quick!* Even on its placid evenings, the light plant turned "the juice" off at nine-thirty.)

Whoever won by fair or foul means the title of shaker of the tree did a pull-up to the first limb, hefted himself to catch the falling nuts, begging the shaker to shake her some and everybody was begging for more nuts on his side of the tree, for his turn shaking, for another basket—

This was how Christmas began for us. . . .

THE BURNING BABE

ROBERT SOUTHWELL

As I in hoary Winter's night stood shiveringe in the snow,
Surpris'd I was with sodayne heat, which made my hart to glowe;
And liftinge upp a fearefull eye to vewe what fire was nere,
A pretty Babe all burninge bright did in the ayre appeare,
Who scorched with excessive heate, such floodes of teares did shedd,
As though His floodes should quench His flames which with His teares
    were fedd;
Alas! quoth He, but newly borne, in fiery heates I frye,
Yet none approach to warme their hartes or feele my fire but I!
My faultles brest the fornace is, the fuell woundinge thornes,
Love is the fire, and sighes the smoke, the ashes shame and scornes;
The fuell Justice layeth on, and Mercy blowes the coales,
The mettall in this fornace wrought are men's defiled soules,
For which, as nowe on fire I am, to worke them to their good,
So will I melt into a bath to wash them in My bloode:
With this He vanisht out of sight, and swiftly shroncke awaye,
And straight I callèd into mynde that it was Christmas-daye.

CHRISTMAS AT SEA

ROBERT LOUIS STEVENSON

The sheets were frozen hard, and they cut the naked hand;
The decks were like a slide, where a seaman scarce could stand;
The wind was a nor'-wester, blowing squally off the sea;
And cliffs and spouting breakers were the only things a-lee.

They heard the surf a-roaring before the break of day;
But 'twas only with the peep of light we saw how ill we lay.
We tumbled every hand on deck instanter, with a shout,
And we gave her the maintops'l, and stood by to go about.

All day we tacked and tacked between the South Head and the North;
All day we hauled the frozen sheets, and got no further forth;
All day as cold as charity, in bitter pain and dread,
For very life and nature we tacked from head to head.

We gave the South a wider berth, for there the tide-race roared;
But every tack we made we brought the North Head close aboard.
So's we saw the cliff and houses and the breakers running high,
And the coastguard in his garden, with his glass against his eye.

The frost was on the village roofs as white as ocean foam;
The good red fires were burning bright in every longshore home;
The windows sparkled clear, and the chimneys volleyed out;
And I vow we sniffed the victuals as the vessel went about.

The bells upon the church were rung with a mighty jovial cheer;
For it's just that I should tell you how (of all days in the year)
This day of our adversity was blessèd Christmas morn,
And the house above the coastguard's was the house where I was born.

O well I saw the pleasant room, the pleasant faces there,
My mother's silver spectacles, my father's silver hair;
And well I saw the firelight, like a flight of homely elves,
Go dancing round the china plates that stand upon the shelves.

And well I knew the talk they had, the talk that was of me,
Of the shadow on the household and the son that went to sea;
And O the wicked fool I seemed, in every kind of way,
To be here and hauling frozen ropes on blessèd Christmas Day.

They lit the high sea-light, and the dark began to fall.
"All hands to loose topgallant sails," I heard the captain call.
"By the Lord, she'll never stand it," our first mate, Jackson, cried.
. . . "It's the one way or the other, Mr. Jackson," he replied.

She staggered to her bearings, but the sails were new and good,
And the ship smelt up to windward just as though she understood;
As the winter's day was ending, in the entry of the night,
We cleared the weary headland, and passed below the light.

And they heaved a mighty breath, every soul on board but me,
As they saw her nose again pointing handsome out to sea;
But all that I could think of, in the darkness and the cold,
Was just that I was leaving home and my folks were growing old.

1888

* 415 *

THE CHRISTMAS WRECK

FRANK STOCKTON

W ell, sir," said old Silas, as he gave a preliminary puff to the pipe he had just lighted, and so satisfied himself that the draught was all right, "the wind's a comin', an' so's Christmas. But it's no use bein' in a hurry fur either of 'em, for sometimes they come afore you want 'em, anyway."

Silas was sitting in the stern of a small sailing-boat which he owned, and in which he sometimes took the Sandport visitors out for a sail; and at other times applied to its more legitimate, but less profitable use, that of fishing. That afternoon he had taken young Mr. Nugent for a brief excursion on that portion of the Atlantic Ocean which sends its breakers up on the beach of Sandport. But he had found it difficult, nay, impossible just now, to bring him back, for the wind had gradually died away until there was not a breath of it left. Mr. Nugent, to whom nautical experiences were as new as the very nautical suit of blue flannel which he wore, rather liked the calm; it was such a relief to the monotony of rolling waves. He took out a cigar and lighted it, and then he remarked:

"I can easily imagine how a wind might come before you sailors might want it, but I don't see how Christmas could come too soon."

"It come wunst on me when things couldn't a looked more onready fur it," said Silas.

"How was that?" asked Mr. Nugent, settling himself a little more comfortably on the hard thwart. "If it's a story, let's have it. This is a good time to spin a yarn."

"Very well," said old Silas. "I'll spin her."

The bare-legged boy, whose duty it was to stay forward and mind the jib, came aft as soon as he smelt a story, and took a nautical position which was duly studied by Mr. Nugent, on a bag of ballast in the bottom of the boat.

"It's nigh on to fifteen year ago," said Silas, "that I was on the barque, 'Mary Auguster,' bound for Sydney, New South Wales, with a cargo of canned goods. We was somewhere about longitood a hundred an' seventy, latitood nothin', an' it was the twenty-second o' December, when we was ketched by a reg'lar typhoon which blew straight along, end on, fur a day an' a half. It blew away the storm sails; it blew away every yard, spar, shroud, an' every strand o' riggin', an' snapped the masts off, close to the deck; it blew away all the boats; it blew away the cook's caboose, an' every thing else on deck; it blew off the hatches, an' sent 'em spinnin' in the air, about a mile to leeward; an' afore it got through, it washed away the cap'n an' all the crew 'cept me an' two others. These was Tom Simmons, the second mate, an' Andy Boyle, a chap from the Andirondack Mountins, who'd never been to sea afore. As he was a landsman he ought, by rights, to a been swep' off by the wind an' water, consid'rin' that the cap'n an' sixteen good seamen had gone a'ready. But he had hands eleven inches long, an' that give him a grip which no typhoon could git the better of. Andy had let out that his father was a miller up there in York State, an' a story had got round among the crew that his gran'father an' great gran'father was millers too; an' the way the fam'ly got such big hands come from their habit of scoopin' up a extry quart or two of meal or flour for themselves when they was levelin' off their customers' measures. He was a good-natered feller, though, an' never got riled when I'd tell him to clap his flour-scoops onter a halyard.

"We was all soaked, an' washed, an' beat, an' battered. We held on some way or other till the wind blowed itself out, an' then we got on our legs an' began to look about us to see how things stood. The sea had washed into the open hatches till the vessel was more'n half full of water, an' that had sunk her so deep that she must 'a looked like a canal boat loaded with gravel. We hadn't had a thing to eat or drink durin' that whole blow, an' we was pretty ravenous. We found a keg of water which was all right, and a box of biscuit, which was what you might call soft tack, for they was soaked through and through with sea-water. We eat a lot of them so, fur we couldn't wait, an' the rest we spread on the deck to dry, fur the sun was now shinin' hot enough to bake bread. We couldn't go below much, fur there was a pretty good swell on the sea, and things was floatin' about so's to make it dangerous. But we fished out a piece of canvas, which we rigged up agin the stump of the mainmast so that we could have somethin' that we could sit down an' grumble under. What struck us all the hardest was that the barque was loaded with a whole cargo of jolly things to eat, which was just as good as ever they was, fur the water couldn't git through the tin cans in which they was all put up; an' here we was with nothin' to live on but them salted biscuit. There was no way of gittin' at any of the ship's stores, or any of the fancy prog, fur everythin' was stowed away tight under six or seven feet of water, an' pretty nigh all the room that was left between decks was filled up with extry spars, lumber, boxes, an' other floatin' stuff. All was shiftin', an' bumpin', an' bangin' every time the vessel rolled.

"As I said afore, Tom was second mate, an' I was bosen. Says I to Tom, 'the thing we've got to do is to put up some kind of a spar with a rag on it for a distress flag, so that we'll lose no time bein' took off.' 'There's no use a slavin' at anythin' like that,' says Tom, 'fur we've been blowed off the track of traders, an' the more we work the hungrier we'll git, an' the sooner will them biscuit be gone.'

"Now when I heerd Tom say this I sot still, and began to consider. Being second mate, Tom was, by rights, in command of this craft; but it was easy enough to see that if he commanded there'd never be nothin' for Andy an' me to do. All the grit he had in him he'd used up in holdin' on durin' that typhoon. What he wanted to do now was to make himself comfortable till the time come for him to go to Davy Jones's Locker; an' thinkin', most likely, that Davy couldn't make it any hotter fur him than it was on that deck, still in latitood nothin' at all, fur we'd been blowed along the line pretty nigh due West. So I calls to Andy, who was busy turnin' over the biscuits on the deck. 'Andy,' says I, when he had got under the canvas, 'we's goin' to have a 'lection fur skipper. Tom here is about played out. He's one candydate, an' I'm another. Now, who do you vote fur? An', mind yer eye, youngster, that you don't make no mistake.' 'I vote fur you,' says Andy. 'Carried unanermous!' says I. 'An' I want you to take notice that I'm cap'n of what's left of the "Mary Auguster," an' you two has got to keep your minds on that, an' obey orders.' If Davy Jones was to do all that Tom be Simmons said when he heard this, the old chap would kept busier than he ever was yit. But I let him growl his growl out, knowin' he'd come round all right, fur there wasn't no help fur it, consid'rin' Andy an' me was two to his one. Pretty soon we all went to work, an' got up a spar from below which we rigged to the stump of the foremast, with Andy's shirt atop of it.

"Them sea-soaked, sun-dried biscuit was pretty mean prog, as you might think, but we eat so many of 'em that afternoon an' 'cordingly drank so much water that I was obliged to put us all on short rations the next day. 'This is the day before Christmas,' says Andy Boyle, 'an' to-night will be Christmas Eve, an' it's pretty tough fur us to be sittin' here with not even so much hard tack as we want, an' all the time thinkin' that the hold of this ship is packed full of the gayest kind of good things to eat.' 'Shut up about Christmas!' says Tom Simmons. 'Them two youngsters of mine, up in Bangor, is havin' their toes and noses pretty nigh froze, I 'spect, but they'll hang up their stockin's all the same to-night, never thinkin' that their dad's bein' cooked alive on a empty stom-ach.' 'Of course they wouldn't hang 'em up,' says I, 'if they knowed what a fix you was in, but they don't know it, an' what's the use of grumblin' at 'em for bein' a little jolly.' 'Well,' says Andy, 'they couldn't be more jollier than I'd be if I could git at some of them fancy fixin's down in the hold. I worked well on to a week at 'Frisco puttin' in them boxes, an' the names of the things was on the outside of most of 'em, an' I tell you what it is, mates, it made my mouth water, even then, to read 'em, an' I wasn't hungry nuther, havin' plenty to eat three times a day. There was roast beef, an' roast mutton, an' duck, an' chicken, an' soup, an' peas, an' beans, an' termaters, an' plum-puddin', an' mince-pie——' 'Shut up with your mince-pie!' sung out Tom Simmons. 'Isn't it enough to have to gnaw on these salt chips, without hearin' about mince-pie?' 'An' more'n that,' says Andy, 'there was canned peaches, an' pears, an' plums, an' cherries.'

"Now these things did sound so cool an' good to me on that broilin' deck, that I couldn't stand it, an' I leans over to Andy, an' I says: "Now look a here, if you don't shut up talkin' about them things what's stowed below, an' what we can't git at, nohow, overboard you go!' 'That would make you short-handed,' says Andy, with a grin. 'Which is more'n you could say,' says I, 'if you'd chuck Tom an' me over'—alludin' to his eleven-inch grip. Andy didn't say no more then, but after a while he comes to me as I was lookin' round to see if anything was in sight, an' says he, 'I s'pose you ain't got nuthin' to say agin my divin' into the hold just aft of the foremast, where there seems to be a bit of pretty clear water, an' see if I can't git up something?' 'You kin do it, if you like,' says I, 'but it's at your own risk. You can't take out no insurance at this office.' 'All right then,' says Andy, 'an' if I git stove in by floatin' boxes you an' Tom'll have to eat the rest of them salt crackers.' 'Now, boy,' says I—an' he wasn't much more, bein' only nineteen year old—'you'd better keep out o' that hold. You'll just git yourself smashed. An' as to movin' any of them there heavy boxes, which must be swelled up as tight as if they was part of the ship, you might as well try to pull out one of the "Mary Auguster's" ribs.' 'I'll try it,' says Andy, 'fur to-morrer is

Christmas, an' if I kin help it I ain't goin' to be floatin' atop of a Christmas dinner without eatin' any on it.' I let him go, fur he was a good swimmer and diver, an' I did hope he might root out somethin' or other, fur Christmas is about the worst day in the year fur men to be starvin' on, and that's what we was a comin' to.

"Well, fur about two hours Andy swum, an' dove, an' come up blubberin', an' dodged all sorts of floatin' an' pitchin' stuff, fur the swell was still on; but he couldn't even be so much as sartain that he'd found the canned vittles. To dive down through hatchways, an' among broken bulkheads, to hunt fur any partiklar kind o' boxes under seven feet of sea-water, ain't no easy job; an' though Andy says he got hold of the end of a box that felt to him like the big 'uns he'd noticed as havin' the meat pies in, he couldn't move it no more'n if it had been the stump of the foremast. If we could have pumped the water out of the hold we could have got at any part of the cargo we wanted, but as it was, we couldn't even reach the ship's stores, which, of course, must have been mostly spiled anyway; whereas the canned vittles was just as good as new. The pumps was all smashed, or stopped up, for we tried 'em, but if they hadn't a been we three couldn't never have pumped out that ship on three biscuit a day, and only about two days' rations at that.

"So Andy he come up, so fagged out that it was as much as he could do to get his clothes on, though they wasn't much, an' then he stretched himself out under the canvas an' went to sleep, an' it wasn't long afore he was talkin' about roast turkey an' cranberry sass, an' punkin pie, an' sech stuff, most of which we knowed was under our feet that present minute. Tom Simmons he just b'iled over, an' sung out: 'Roll him out in the sun and let him cook! I can't stand no more of this!' But I wasn't goin' to have Andy treated no sech way as that, fur if it hadn't been fur Tom Simmons' wife an' young uns, Andy'd been worth two of him to anybody who was consid'rin' savin' life. But I give the boy a good punch in the ribs to stop his dreamin', fur I was as hungry as Tom was, and couldn't stand no nonsense about Christmas dinners.

"It was a little arter noon when Andy woke up, an' he went outside to stretch himself. In about a minute he give a yell that made Tom and me jump. 'A sail!' he hollered, 'a sail!' An' you may bet your life, young man, that 'twasn't more'n half a second before us two had scuffled out from under that canvas, an' was standin' by Andy. 'There she is!' he shouted, 'not a mile to win'ard.' I give one look, an' then I sings out: 'Tain't a sail! It's a flag of distress! Can't you see, you land-lubber, that that's the stars and stripes upside down?' 'Why, so it is,' said Andy, with a couple of reefs in the joyfulness of his voice. An' Tom, he began to growl as if somebody had cheated him out of half a year's wages.

"The flag that we saw was on the hull of a steamer that had been driftin' down on us while we was sittin' under our canvas. It was plain to see she'd been caught in the typhoon too, fur there wasn't a mast or a smoke stack on her; but her hull was high enough out of the water to catch what wind there was, while we was so low-sunk that we didn't make no way at all. There was people aboard, and they saw us, an' waved their hats an' arms, an' Andy an' me waved ours, but all we could do was to wait till they drifted nearer, fur we hadn't no boats to go to 'em if we'd a wanted to.

" 'I'd like to know what good that old hulk is to us,' said Tom Sim-

mons. 'She can't take us off.' It did look to me somethin' like the blind leadin' the blind; but Andy he sings out: 'We'd be better off aboard of her, fur she ain't water-logged, an', more'n that, I don't s'pose her stores are all soaked up in salt water.' There was some sense in that, and when the steamer had got to within half a mile of us, we was glad to see a boat put out from her with three men in it. It was a queer boat, very low an' flat, an' not like any ship's boat I ever see. But the two fellers at the oars pulled stiddy, an' pretty soon the boat was 'longside of us, an' the three men on our deck. One of 'em was the first mate of the other wreck, an' when he found out what was the matter with us, he spun his yarn, which was a longer one that ours. His vessel was the 'Water Crescent,' nine hundred tons, from 'Frisco to Melbourne, and they had sailed about six weeks afore we did. They was about two weeks out when some of their machinery broke down, an' when they got it patched up it broke agin, worse than afore, so that they couldn't do nothin' with it. They kep' along under sail for about a month, makin' mighty poor headway till the typhoon struck 'em, an' that cleaned their decks off about as slick as it did ours, but their hatches wasn't blowed off, an' they didn't ship no water wuth mentionin', an' the crew havin' kep' below, none on 'em was lost. But now they was clean out of provisions and water, havin' been short when the break-down happened, fur they had sold all the stores they could spare to a French brig in distress that they overhauled when about a week out. When they sighted us they felt pretty sure they'd git some provisions out of us. But when I told the mate what a fix we was in his jaw dropped till his face was as long as one of Andy's hands. How-somdever he said he'd send the boat back fur as many men as it could bring over, and see if they couldn't get up some of our stores. Even if they was soaked with salt water, they'd be better than nothin'. Part of the cargo of the 'Water Crescent' was tools an' things fur some railway con-tractors out in Australier, an' the mate told the men to bring over some of them irons that might be used to fish out the stores. All their ship's boats had been blowed away, an' the one they had was a kind of shore boat for fresh water, that had been shipped as part of the cargo, an' stowed below. It couldn't stand no kind of a sea, but there wasn't nothin' but a swell on; an' when it come back it had the cap'n in it, an' five men, besides a lot of chains an' tools.

"Them fellers an' us worked pretty nigh the rest of the day, an' we got out a couple of bar'ls of water, which was all right, havin' been tight bunged; an' a lot of sea biscuit, all soaked an' sloppy, but we only got a half bar'l of meat, though three or four of the men stripped an' dove fur more'n an hour. We cut up some of the meat, an' eat it raw, an' the cap'n sent some over to the other wreck, which had drifted past us to leeward, an' would have gone clean away from us if the cap'n hadn't had a line got out an' made us fast to it while we was a workin' at the stores.

"That night the cap'n took us three, as well as the provisions we'd got out, on board his hull, where the 'commodations was consid'able better than they was on the half-sunk 'Mary Auguster.' An' afore we turned in he took me aft, an' had a talk with me as commandin' off'cer of my vessel. 'That wreck o' yourn,' says he, 'has got a vallyble cargo in it, which isn't spiled by bein' under water. Now, if you could get that cargo into port it would put a lot of money in your pocket, fur the owners couldn't git out of payin' you fur takin' charge of it, an' havin' it brung in. Now I'll tell you what I'll do. I'll lie by you, an' I've got carpenters aboard that'll put your pumps in order, an' I'll set my men to work to pump out your vessel. An' then, when she's afloat all right, I'll go to work agin at my vessel, which I didn't s'pose there was any use o' doin'; but whilst I was huntin' round amongst our cargo to-day I found that some of the machinery we carried might be worked up so's to take the place of what is broke in our engin'. We've got a forge aboard an' I believe we can make these pieces of machinery fit, an' git goin' agin. Then I'll tow you into Sydney, an' we'll divide the salvage money. I won't git nothin' for savin' my vessel, coz that's my bizness; but you wasn't cap'n o' yourn, an' took charge of her a purpose to save her, which is another thing.'

"I wasn't at all sure that I didn't take charge of the 'Mary Auguster' to save myself an' not the vessel, but I didn't mention that, an' asked the cap'n how he expected to live all this time. 'Oh, we kin git at your stores easy enough,' says he, 'when the water's pumped out.' 'They'll be mostly spiled,' says I. 'That don't matter,' says he, 'men'll eat anythin', when they can't git nothin' else.' An' with that he left me to think it over.

"I must say, young man, an' you kin b'lieve me if you know anythin' about sech things, that the idee of a pile of money was mighty temptin' to a feller like me, who had a girl at home ready to marry him, and who would like nothin' better'n to have a little house of his own, an' a little vessel of his own, an' give up the other side of the world altogether. But while I was goin' over all this in my mind, an' wonderin' if the cap'n ever could git us into port, along comes Andy Boyle, and sits down beside me. 'It drives me pretty nigh crazy,' says he, 'to think that to-morrer's Christmas, an' we've got to feed on that sloppy stuff we fished out of our stores, an' not much of it nuther, while there's all that roast turkey, an' plum-puddin', an' mince-pie, a floatin' out there just before our eyes, an' we can't have none of it.' 'You hadn't oughter think so much about eatin', Andy,' says I, 'but if I was talkin' about them things I wouldn't leave out canned peaches. By George! Of a hot Christmas like this is goin' to be, I'd be the jolliest Jack on the ocean if I could git at that canned fruit.' 'Well, there's a way,' says Andy, 'that we might git some of 'em. A part of the cargo of this ship is stuff for blastin' rocks; catridges, 'lectric bat'ries, an' that sort of thing; an' there's a man aboard who's goin' out to take charge of 'em. I've been talkin' to this bat'ry man, an' I've made up my mind it'll be easy enough to lower a little catridge down among our cargo, an' blow out a part of it.' 'What ud be the good of it,' says I, 'blowed into chips?' 'It might smash some,' he said, 'but others would be only loosened, an' they'd float up to the top, where we could get 'em, 'specially them as was packed with pies, which must be pretty light.' 'Git out, Andy,' says I, 'with all that stuff!' An' he got out.

"But the idees he'd put into my head didn't git out, an' as I laid on my back on the deck, lookin' up at the stars, they sometimes seemed to put themselves into the shape of little houses, with a little woman cookin' at the kitchin fire, an' a little schooner layin' at anchor just off shore; an' then agin they'd hump themselves up till they looked like a lot of new tin cans with their tops off, an' all kinds of good things to eat inside, 'specially canned peaches—the big white kind—soft an' cool, each one split in half, with a holler in the middle filled with juice. By George, sir, the very thought of a tin can like that made me beat my heels agin the deck. I'd been mighty hungry, an' had eat a lot of salt pork, wet an' raw, an' now the very idee of it, even cooked, turned my stomach. I looked up to the stars agin, an' the little house an' the little schooner was clean gone, an' the whole sky was filled with nothin' but bright new tin cans.

"In the mornin', Andy, he come to me agin. 'Have you made up your mind,' says he, 'about gittin' some of them good things for Christmas dinner?' 'Confound you!' says I, 'you talk as if all we had to do was to go an' git 'em.' 'An' that's what I b'lieve we kin do,' says he, 'with the help of that bat'ry man.' 'Yes,' says I, 'an' blow a lot of the cargo into flinders, an' damage the "Mary Auguster" so's she couldn't never be took into port.' An' then I told him what the cap'n had said to me, an' what I was goin' to do with the money. 'A little catridge,' says Andy, 'would do all we want, an' wouldn't hurt the vessel nuther. Besides that, I don't b'lieve what this cap'n says about tinkerin' up his engin'. Tain't likely he'll ever git her runnin' agin, nor pump out the "Mary Auguster" nuther. If I was you I'd a durned sight ruther have a Christmas dinner in hand than a house an' wife in the bush.' 'I ain't thinkin' o' marryin' a girl in Australier,' says I. An' Andy he grinned, an' said I wouldn't marry nobody if I had to live on spiled vittles till I got her.

"A little after that I went to the cap'n, an' I told him about Andy's idee, but he was down on it. 'It's your vessel, an' not mine,' says he, 'an' if you want to try to git a dinner out of her I'll not stand in your way.

But it's my 'pinion you'll just damage the ship, an' do nothin'.' Howsomdever I talked to the bat'ry man about it, an' he thought it could be done, an' not hurt the ship nuther. The men was all in favor of it, for none of 'em had forgot it was Christmas day. But Tom Simmons, he was agin it strong, for he was thinkin' he'd git some of the money if we got the 'Mary Auguster' into port. He was a selfish-minded man, was Tom, but it was his nater, an' I s'pose he couldn't help it.

"Well, it wasn't long afore I began to feel pretty empty, an' mean, an' if I'd a wanted any of the prog we got out the day afore, I couldn't have found much, for the men had eat it up nearly all in the night. An' so, I just made up my mind without any more foolin', an' me, and Andy Boyle, an' the bat'ry man, with some catridges an' a coil of wire, got into the little shore boat, and pulled over to the 'Mary Auguster.' There we lowered a small catridge down the main hatchway, an' let it rest down among the cargo. Then we rowed back to the steamer, uncoilin' the wire as we went. The bat'ry man clumb up on deck, an' fixed his wire to a 'lectric machine, which he'd got all ready afore we started. Andy and me didn't git out of the boat; we had too much sense for that, with all them hungry fellers waitin' to jump in her; but we just pushed a little off, an' sot waitin', with our mouths a waterin', for him to touch her off. He seemed to be a long time about it, but at last he did it, an' that instant there was a bang on board the 'Mary Auguster' that made my heart jump. Andy an' me pulled fur her like mad, the others a hollerin' arter us, an' we was on deck in no time. The deck was all covered with the water that had been throwed up; but I tell you, sir, that we poked an' fished about, an' Andy stripped an' went down, an' swum all round, an' we couldn't find one floatin' box of canned goods. There was a lot of splinters, but where they come from we didn't know. By this time my dander was up, an' I just pitched around savage. That little catridge wasn't no good, an' I didn't intend to stand any more foolin'. We just rowed back to the other wreck, an' I called to the bat'ry man to come down, an' bring some bigger catridges with him, fur if we was goin' to do anythin' we might as well do it right. So he got down with a package of bigger ones, an' jumped into the boat. The cap'n he called out to us to be keerful, an' Tom Simmons leaned over the rail, an' swored, but I didn't pay no 'tention to nuther of 'em, an' we pulled away.

"When I got aboard the 'Mary Auguster' I says to the bat'ry man: 'We don't want no nonsense this time, an' I want you to put in enough catridges to heave up somethin' that'll do fur a Christmas dinner. I don't know how the cargo is stored, but you kin put one big catridge 'midship, another for'ard, an' another aft, an' one or nuther of 'em oughter fetch up somethin'.' Well, we got the three catridges into place. They was a good deal bigger than the one we first used, an' we j'ined 'em all to one wire, an' then we rowed back, carryin' the long wire with us. When we reached the steamer, me an' Andy was a goin' to stay in the boat as we did afore, but the cap'n sung out that he wouldn't allow the bat'ry to be touched off till we come aboard. 'Ther's got to be fair play,' says he. 'It's your vittles, but it's my side that's doin' the work. After we've blasted her this time you two can go in the boat, an' see what there is to get hold of, but two of my men must go along.' So me an' Andy had to go on deck, an' two big fellers was detailed to go with us in the little boat when the time come; an' then the bat'ry man, he teched her off.

"Well, sir, the pop that followed that tech was somethin' to remember. It shuck the water, it shuck the air, an' it shuck the hull we was on. A reg'lar cloud of smoke, an' flyin' bits of things rose up out of the 'Mary Auguster.' An' when that smoke cleared away, an' the water was all bilin' with the splash of various sized hunks that come rainin' down from the sky, what was left of the 'Mary Auguster' was sprinkled over the sea like a wooden carpet for water birds to walk on.

"Some of the men sung out one thing, an' some another, an' I could hear Tom Simmons swear, but Andy an' me said never a word, but scuttled down into the boat, follered close by the two men who was to go with us. Then we rowed like devils for the lot of stuff that was bobbin' about on the water, out where the 'Mary Auguster' had been. In we went, among the floatin' spars and ship's timbers, I keepin' the things off with an oar, the two men rowin', an' Andy in the bow.

"Suddenly Andy give a yell, an' then he reached himself for'ard with sech a bounce that I thought he'd go overboard. But up he come in a minnit, his two 'leven-inch hands gripped round a box. He sot down in the bottom of the boat with the box on his lap, an' his eyes screwed on some letters that was stamped on one end. 'Pidjin pies!' he sings out. 'Tain't turkeys, nor 'tain't cranberries. But, by the Lord Harry, it's Christmas pies all the same!' After that Andy didn't do no more work, but sot holdin' that box as if it had been his fust baby. But we kep' pushin' on to see what else there was. It's my 'pinion that the biggest part of that bark's cargo was blowed into mince meat, an' the most of the rest of it was so heavy that it sunk. But it wasn't all busted up, an' it didn't all sink. There was a big piece of wreck with a lot of boxes stove into the timbers, and some of these had in 'em beef ready biled an' packed into cans, an' there was other kinds of meat, an' dif'rent sorts of vegetables, an' one box of turtle soup. I looked at every one of 'em as we took 'em in, an' when we got the little boat pretty well loaded I wanted to still keep on searchin', but the men, they said that shore boat ud sink if we took in any more cargo, an' so we put back, I feelin' glummer'n I oughter felt, fur I had begun to be afeared that canned fruit, such as peaches, was heavy, an' li'ble to sink.

"As soon as we had got our boxes aboard, four fresh men put out in the boat, an' after awhile they come back with another load; an' I was mighty keerful to read the names on all the boxes. Some was meat pies, an' some was salmon, an' some was potted herrins, an' some was lobsters. But nary a thing could I see that ever had growed on a tree.

"Well, sir, there was three loads brought in, altogether, an' the Christmas dinner we had on the for'ard deck of that steamer's hull was about the jolliest one that was ever seen of a hot day aboard of a wreck in the Pacific Ocean. The cap'n kept good order, an' when all was ready the tops was jerked off the boxes, and each man grabbed a can an' opened it with his knife. When he had cleaned it out, he tuk another without doin' much questionin' as to the bill of fare. Whether anybody got pidjin pie 'cept Andy, I can't say, but the way we piled in Delmoniker prog would a made people open their eyes as was eatin' their Christmas dinners on shore that day. Some of the things would a been better, cooked a little more, or het up, but we was too fearful hungry to wait for that, an' they was tip-top as they was.

"The cap'n went out afterwards, an' towed in a couple of bar'ls of flour that was only part soaked through, an' he got some other plain prog that would do fur futur use; but none of us give our minds to stuff like this arter the glorious Christmas dinner that we'd quarried out of the 'Mary Auguster.' Every man that wasn't on duty went below, and turned in for a snooze. All 'cept me, an' I didn't feel just altogether satisfied. To be sure I'd had an A 1 dinner, an' though a little mixed, I'd never eat a jollier one on any Christmas that I kin look back at. But, fur all that, there was a hanker inside o' me. I hadn't got all I'd laid out to git, when we teched off the 'Mary Auguster.' The day was blazin' hot, an' a lot of the things I'd eat was pretty peppery. 'Now,' thinks I, 'if there had a been just one can o' peaches sech as I see shinin' in the stars last night,' an' just then, as I was walkin' aft, all by myself, I seed lodged on the stump of the mizzenmast, a box with one corner druv down among the splinters. It was half split open, an' I could see the tin cans shinin' through the crack. I give one jump at it, an' wrenched the side off. On the top of the first can I seed was a picture of a big white peach with green leaves. That box had been blowed up so high that if it had come down anywhere 'cept among them splinters it would a smashed itself to flinders, or killed somebody. So fur as I know, it was the only thing that fell nigh us, an' by George, sir, I got it! When I had finished a can of 'em I hunted up Andy, an' then we went aft, an' eat some more. 'Well,' says Andy, as we was a eatin', 'how d'ye feel now about blowin' up your wife, an' your house, an' that little schooner you was goin' to own?'

" 'Andy,' says I, 'this is the joyfulest Christmas I've had yit, an' if I was to live till twenty hundred I don't b'lieve I'd have no joyfuler, with things comin' in so pat, so don't you throw no shadders.'

" 'Shadders,' says Andy, 'that ain't me. I leave that sort of thing fur Tom Simmons.'

" 'Shadders is cool,' says I, 'an' I kin go to sleep under all he throws.'

"Well sir," continued old Silas, putting his hand on the tiller and turning his face seaward, "if Tom Simmons had kept command of that wreck, we all would a laid there an' waited an' waited till some of us was starved, an' the others got nothin' fur it, fur the cap'n never mended his engin', an' it was more'n a week afore we was took off, an' then it was by a sailin' vessel, which left the hull of the 'Water Crescent' behind her, just as she would a had to leave the 'Mary Auguster' if that jolly old Christmas wreck had a been there.

"An' now sir," said Silas, "d'ye see that stretch o' little ripples over yander, lookin' as if it was a lot o' herrin' turnin' over to dry their sides? Do you know what that is? That's the supper wind. That means coffee, an' hot cakes, an' a bit of br'iled fish, an' pertaters, an' p'raps—if the old woman feels in a partiklar good humor—some canned peaches, big white uns, cut in half, with a holler place in the middle filled with cool, sweet juice."

CHRISTMAS ON THE FRONTIER

JOANNA L. STRATTON

from PIONEER WOMEN

Like the holiday season elsewhere, Christmas on the frontier was a joyous and festive occasion for children and grownups alike. Pioneer families, clinging to their sentimental customs, were determined to celebrate with what little they had. The traditional tree and hand-made decorations added a touch of color to an otherwise stark cabin, and a simple gift was fashioned for each child from whatever materials were at hand.

Special holiday prayers and meals shared with friends and neighbors were often the highlight of the festivities. While the fields outdoors glistened with snow and ice, indoors blazing fires gave each small home a warm, hospitable glow. Long red stockings adorned the hearth, and the aroma of freshly made cakes, cookies and candies filled the house. "Christmas was a glad time for us," Nellie Goss recollected. "We were happy when it came and sorry when gone. In the late fall would come a barrel of canned fruits, preserves, jelly and the cans packed in dried apples, quinces, peaches, pears and cling peaches dried with the pits in them, and the contents were kept from us children and on Xmas eve we would hang up our stockings and in them was placed some of each kind of the dried fruits.

"In the barrel was also packed a pail of sorghum molasses for Mother to make the Xmas taffy, and gingersnaps. Grandma did some hand work out of pretty flannel scraps, that was tucked in the barrel, made little flannel mittens and bound them with wool braid, ear muffs for the

little boys, rag dolls and little quilts, etc., that was real Xmas. And Mother always shared with her neighbors, especially did the little folks enjoy the bread and jam (corn bread usually)."

Like children everywhere, pioneer youngsters anxiously awaited the arrival of Santa Claus. In contrast to the austerity and hardships in their lives, they treasured the few simple gifts tucked into their stockings and eagerly joined in the recitations of holiday poems and prayers and the singing of carols. Mary Rarick Rouse wrote: "We knew the Christmas story well and the boy Jesus whose birthday it was. As for gifts, if we ever had any they were homemade. No toys to buy if we wanted them, and nothing to buy with. Our stocking was always hung up, faith of childhood for Santa, an apple or popcorn ball or wooden doll or rag one, all homemade. We always found something and how happy we were."

Harriet Adams described the special jubilation and excitement she felt as a child in the 1870s:

"The Christmas which made the first lasting impression upon my mind, I think, must have been the one following my seventh birthday. I remember so distinctly the air of expectancy and secrecy which invaded the household. Sister Zu was quite active in fostering the spirit. She was an able entertainer, and furnished the stimulation necessary to make the approach of Christmas a very exciting event. Among our books was a volume of selected poems, some of which were illustrated. Zu often read to us from this, and before that Christmas this invaluable collection must have been consulted again and again, for between its covers, somewhere in the middle, was a fascinating picture of a jolly, white-bearded old man with a sleigh and reindeer, and oh! the undescribable delight of that little group as Zu read, ' 'Twas the night before Christmas, and all through the house not a creature was stirring, not even a mouse.' Then too, the moon and the weather must have fitted in more perfectly to the description, 'The moon on the breast of the new-fallen snow, gave the luster of mid-day to objects below.' For, after dark I would peep out of the window, or out of the door to consider anxiously whether all conditions were favor-able, the glistening expanse of snow deep enough to support that won-drous reindeer-drawn sleigh.

"Then as Christmas Eve approached I was filled with anxious ques-tioning as to how St. Nick could get into our house, to fill our waiting stockings. There was no chimney down which he could slide safely, in fact I finally decided that it was an absolute impossibility for him to fit into the house through any chimney it possessed. My concern on this matter finally reached such a pitch that I took it up with Mother. I told her my fears, and she said he would most certainly be able to leave his gifts, for when no large chimney was provided, the parents would leave the door open a crack at least, so he could push his way in with no diffi-culty whatever. This was a most reasonable solution of the difficulty, and I was fully satisfied, and later events proved that my faith in her explana-tion was justified.

"No Christmas is ever quite complete without a tree and candles, and we little folk saw all the preparation of the tree. We were living but a short distance from the Little Blue River, and on the bluff nearest our home was a scattering growth of cedars. Father took us with him as he carried an axe and selected the tree, which he cut, and big brother helped carry it home. Then Father set it up securely in the center of the living room and found a piece of tin and made the candle holders, and fastened them to the tree. When that much was accomplished, it was time for the little folk to get to bed, for under no consideration would it be good form for any of the children to be awake when Santa would arrive.

"Christmas morning we were awake early, but it was an inviolate rule that the tree could not be seen until after breakfast was eaten. So we hur-ried through a perfunctory meal, then lined up outside the living room door, the least child ready to lead the grand march, while Father and Mother went in to remove the sheet with which it had been necessary to cover the tree to protect it from prying eyes, and to light the candles.

"When the door was opened we marched in and clear around the tree, taking in the beauty of the candles, and the tree festooned with strings of cranberries and popcorn and gay colored ribbons, while we looked for the gifts hidden in the branches and protruding from our stockings. Then there was the most delightful odor of scorching cedar, and Father would keep walking around and around the tree smothering every smoking stem and keeping the candles burning safely, while he and Mother distributed the gifts which Santa Claus had brought.

"I was blissfully happy, and I am sure my little brother George was too. There was nothing lacking to make it a perfect Christmas. I have long since forgotten what toys that magic tree bore, except one thing, and that was a Noah's Ark. To this day when Christmas shopping and I see a Noah's Ark among the other toys, I can picture two small children, a little girl and a smaller, sturdy little boy, side by side as they arranged twigs from the Christmas Cedar into rows or groups of trees and placed amongst them the animals which Noah had saved from extinction.

"In children the sense of comparative values is largely undeveloped, and I doubt very much if children of the present day, with the profusion of toys now attainable, derive any more joy from their expensive array than did we, with the less expensive and simpler ones which Santa Claus gave us."

CRISP NEW BILLS FOR MR. TEAGLE

FRANK SULLIVAN

C oming down in the elevator, Clement Teagle noticed an un-wonted cordiality in Steve, the elevator boy, and Harry, the doorman, but thought nothing of it until he stopped at the bank on the corner to cash a check and noticed the date.

December the twenty-fourth.

"Good gosh," Mr. Teagle thought, "I haven't bought a present for Essie yet."

Then he remembered Steve and Harry.

His eye caught a legend on a Christmas placard on the wall. "It is more blessed to give than to receive," said the placard.

"Oh, yeah?" remarked Mr. Teagle, who, alas, was somewhat of a cynic.

Grumbling, he tore up the check he had started to write, and made out another, for a larger amount.

"Will you please give me new bills?" he asked.

"Indeed I shall," said Mr. Freyer, the teller, cordially.

He counted out one hundred dollars in new bills—crisp new bills—and passed them over to Mr. Teagle.

Then he tore up the check and handed the fragments to Mr. Teagle.

"Don't be alarmed, Mr. Teagle," said Mr. Freyer. "The bank of the Manhattan Company wants you to accept that one hundred dollars as a slight token of its esteem, with its best wishes for a Merry Christmas. You have been a loyal depositor here these many years. You have over-drawn fewer times than most of your fellow-depositors. You never argue about your monthly statements. You never feel insulted when a new teller identifies your signature before cashing your check. You are the kind of depositor who makes banking a joy, and I want to take this opportunity to tell you that we fellows around here, although we are not very demonstrative about that sort of thing, love you very much. A merry Christmas to you."

"You mean the bank is *giving* me this money?" said Mr. Teagle.

"That is the impression I was trying to convey," said Mr. Freyer, with a chuckle.

"Why—uh, thanks, Mr. Freyer. And—and thank the bank. This is—um—quite a surprise."

"Say no more about it, Mr. Teagle. And every Christmas joy to you, sir."

When Mr. Teagle left the bank he was somewhat perturbed, and a little stunned. He went back to the apartment to place the crisp new bills in envelopes for the boys, and as he left the elevator at his floor, Steve handed him an envelope.

"Merry Christmas, Mr. Teagle," said Steve.

"Thanks, Steve," said Mr. Teagle. "I'll—I'll be wishing you one a little later," he added significantly.

"You don't need to, Mr. Teagle," said Steve. "A man like you wishes the whole world a merry Christmas every day, just by living."

"Oh, Steve, damn nice of you to say that, but I'm sure it's not deserved," said Mr. Teagle, modestly struggling with a feeling that Steve spoke no more than the simple truth.

"Well, I guess we won't argue about *that,*" said Steve, gazing affectionately at Mr. Teagle.

"I really believe that lad meant it," thought Mr. Teagle, as he let himself into the apartment. "I really believe he did."

Mr. Teagle opened the envelope Steve had handed him. A crisp new five-dollar bill fell out.

Downstairs in the lobby, a few minutes later, Steve was protesting.

"I tell you it wasn't a mistake, Mr. Teagle. I put the bill in there on purpose. For you."

"Steve, I couldn't take—"

"But you *can* take it, and you *will,* Mr. Teagle. And a very merry Christmas to you."

"Then you accept this, Steve, and a merry Christmas to *you.*"

"Oh, no, Mr. Teagle. Not this year. You have been pretty swell to we fellows all the years you've lived here. Now it's our turn."

"You bet it is," said Harry the doorman, joining them and pressing a crisp new ten-dollar bill into Mr. Teagle's hand. "Merry Christmas, Mr.

Teagle. Buy yourself something foolish with this. I only wish it could be more, but I've had rather a bad year in the market."

"I think the boys on the night-shift have a little surprise for Mr. Teagle, too," said Steve, with a twinkle in his eye.

Just then the superintendent came up.

"Well, well, well," he said jovially. "Who have we got here? Mr. Teagle, it may interest you to hear that I've been having a little chat about you with a certain old gentleman with a long, snowy beard and twinkling little eyes. Know who I mean?"

"Santa Claus?" Mr. Teagle asked.

"None other. And guess what! He asked me if you had been a good boy this year, and I was delighted to be able to tell him you had been, that you hadn't complained about the heat, hadn't run your radio after eleven at night, and hadn't had any late parties. Well, sir, you should have seen old Santa's face. He was tickled to hear it. Said he always knew you were a good boy. And what do you suppose he did?"

"What?" asked Mr. Teagle.

"He asked me to give you this and to tell you to buy yourself something for Christmas with it. Something foolish."

The super pressed a crisp new twenty-dollar bill upon Mr. Teagle.

"Merry Christmas, Mr. Teagle," said the super.

"Merry Christmas, Mr. Teagle," said Steve the elevator boy.

"Merry Christmas, Mr. Teagle," said Harry the doorman.

"Merry Christmas," said Mr. Teagle, in a voice you could scarcely hear. Remembering that he had to buy a present for Essie, he walked out, with the air of a bewildered gazelle. He was in a very, very puzzled state of mind as he walked down East Fifty-first Street, an agitation which did not subside when the proprietor of a cigar-store on Third Avenue rushed out, pressed a box of cigars on him, cried, "Merry Christmas, stranger!" and rushed back into his shop without another word.

To rush out of your store and give a box of cigars to a perfect stranger! And those boys at the apartment house! *And* the super!

Mr. Teagle thought of the many times he had grumbled at being kept waiting a few minutes for the elevator or for a taxi. He felt ashamed. "By George," Mr. Teagle thought, "maybe Dickens was right."

Mr. Teagle approached the business of choosing a present for his wife in a far less carping spirit than was his Christmas wont.

"I'll get Essie something that'll knock her eye out," he thought. "She's a good old girl and she deserves a lot of credit for living with a grouch like me all these years. The best is none too good for her."

Suiting the action to the word, Mr. Teagle turned in at Cartier's and asked to see some square-cut emeralds. He selected one that could have done duty on a traffic light.

"I'm afraid I haven't the cash on me," he told the clerk. "I'll give you a check, and you can call the bank and verify—"

"That will not be necessary, sir," said the clerk, with a radiant smile. "You are Mr. Clement Teagle, I believe. In that case, Cartier wishes you to accept this trinket with the Christmas greetings of the firm. We are only sorry that you did not see fit to choose a diamond stomacher. Cartier will feel honored that one of its emeralds is adorning the finger of the wife of a man like Clement Teagle, a man four-square, a man who is a credit—All right, all right, all *right*, Mr. Teagle! Not another word, please. Cartier is adamant. You take this emerald or we may grow ugly about it. And don't lose it, sir, or I venture to say your good wife will give you Hail Columbia. Good day, sir, and God rest ye."

Mr. Teagle found himself on the street. He accosted the first passer-by.

"Excuse me, stranger, but would you mind pinching me?"

"Certainly not, certainly not," said the stranger, cheerily. "There. Feel better?"

"Yes. Thank you very much," said Mr. Teagle.

"Here, buy yourself something for Christmas," said the stranger, pressing Mr. Teagle's hand. Mr. Teagle looked in the hand and found himself the possessor of a crisp new fifty-dollar bill.

At Fifth Avenue and Fifty-seventh Street, a Park & Tilford attendant rushed out and draped a huge basket, bedecked with ribbons and holly, on Mr. Teagle's arm.

"Everything drinkable for the Yuletide dinner, with love and kisses from Park & Tilford," whispered the clerk jovially. "Tell your wife to be sure and put the champagne in ice early, so it will be nice and cold."

"Oh, come on, come on," protested the butcher at Madison Avenue and Sixty-first Street. "Don't tell me you're too loaded down to carry a simple little turkey home, with the affectionate Christmas wishes of Shaffer's Market."

Mr. Shaffer laughed the rich laugh of the contented butcher.

"Don't take me too seriously when I say simple little turkey," he said. "That bird you got would make Roosevelt's Christmas turkey look like a humming bird. An undernourished humming bird. Pay for it? Certainly you won't pay for it! What do you take me for? It's Christmas. And you are Clement Teagle."

"Am I?" said Mr. Teagle, humbly.

Long before he reached home, Mr. Teagle had had such a plethora of gifts pressed upon him by friendly strangers that there was nothing to do but load them into a taxicab. And Mr. Teagle was not quite as surprised as he might have been earlier in the day when the driver refused to accept any money, but grinned and said: "Let's just charge this trip to good old St. Nick."

"Why, Clem!" said Mrs. Teagle, when, with the aid of the entire house staff, Mr. Teagle had deposited his gifts in the dining room. "Why, Clem, I already *bought* a turkey! Clem, you've been drinking."

"I have *not!*" Mr. Teagle shouted.

"Well, don't get on your high horse," said Mrs. Teagle. "It's Christmas Eve. I don't mind. Only—you know your stomach. And you do look funny."

"I may look funny, but I have not been drinking," Mr. Teagle insisted. "Look! H-h-h-h-h-h."

His breath was as the new-mown hay.

"See what I got you for Christmas, Essie." Mrs. Teagle opened the jewel-case and the emerald gleamed up at her. It was a moment before she could speak.

"No, Clem," she said. "You work too hard for your money. I don't deserve this. I won't take it from you. You've been too good to me as it is. I don't want any Christmas present from you, dear. I want to *give* you one—and oh, by the way, Clem, before I forget it, the funniest thing happened this afternoon. The income-tax man was here, the federal income-tax man. Said he just dropped in to wish you a merry Christmas. He left this check for your entire last year's income tax. He said the Government wants to give it back to you as a token of affection and in recognition of your many superb qualities as a citizen and—oh, I can't remember everything he said, but he made quite a flowery speech about you, dear—Why, Clem, what's the matter?"

Mr. Teagle had burst into tears.

"A merry Christmas, Essie," he said, through his sobs, and, in the language of Tiny Tim, " 'God bless us every one.' "

Is There a Santa Claus?

THE SUN

The following article originally appeared on the editorial page of the New York Sun, September 21, 1897, and was reprinted for many years in the December 24 editions of the newspaper

We take pleasure in answering at once and thus prominently the communication below, expressing at the same time our great gratification that its faithful author is numbered among the friends of *The Sun:*

Dear Editor, I am 8 years old.
Some of my little friends say there is no Santa Claus.
Papa says "If you see it in *The Sun* it's so."
Please tell me the truth. Is there a Santa Claus?
                                   Virginia O'Hanlon
                                   115 West Ninety-fifth Street

VIRGINIA, Your little friends are wrong. They have been affected by the skepticism of a skeptical age. They do not believe except they see. They think that nothing can be which is not comprehensible by their little minds. All minds, Virginia, whether they be men's or children's, are little. In this great universe of ours man is a mere insect, an ant, in his intellect, as compared with the boundless world about him, as measured by the intelligence capable of grasping the whole of truth and knowledge.

Yes, Virginia, there is a Santa Claus. He exists as certainly as love and generosity and devotion exist, and you know that they abound and give to your life its highest beauty and joy. Alas! how dreary would be the world if there were no Santa Claus! It would be as dreary as if there were no Virginias. There would be no childlike faith then, no poetry, no romance to make tolerable this existence. We should have no enjoyment, except in sense and sight. The eternal light with which childhood fills the world would be extinguished.

Not believe in Santa Claus! You might as well not believe in fairies! You might get your papa to hire men to watch in all the chimneys on Christmas Eve to catch Santa Claus, but even if they did not see Santa Claus coming down what would that prove? Nobody sees Santa Claus but that is no sign that there is no Santa Claus. The most real things in the world are those that neither children nor men can see. Did you ever see fairies dancing on the lawn? Of course not, but that's no proof that they are not there. Nobody can conceive or imagine all the wonders there are unseen and unseeable in the world.

You tear apart the baby's rattle and see what makes the noise inside, but there is a veil covering the unseen world which not the strongest man, not even the united strength of all the strongest men that ever lived, could tear apart. Only faith, fancy, poetry, love, romance, can push aside that curtain and view and picture the supernal beauty and glory beyond. Is it all real? Ah, Virginia, in all this world there is nothing else real and abiding.

No Santa Claus! Thank God! he lives, and he lives forever. A thousand years from now, Virginia, nay, ten times ten thousand years from now, he will continue to make glad the heart of childhood.

IN MEMORIAM A. H. H.

ALFRED, LORD TENNYSON

From the poem in memory of Tennyson's friend, Arthur Henry Hallam, who died in September 1833

28

The time draws near the birth of Christ.
    The moon is hid; the night is still;
    The Christmas bells from hill to hill
Answer each other in the mist.

Four voices of four hamlets round,
    From far and near, on mead and moor,
    Swell out and fail, as if a door
Were shut between me and the sound;

Each voice four changes on the wind,
    That now dilate, and now decrease,
    Peace and goodwill, goodwill and peace,

Peace and goodwill, to all mankind.

This year I slept and woke with pain,
    I almost wished no more to wake,
    And that my hold on life would break
Before I heard those bells again.

But they my troubled spirit rule,
  For they controlled me when a boy;
  They bring me sorrow touched with joy,
The merry merry bells of Yule.

29

With such compelling cause to grieve
  As daily vexes household peace,
  And chains regret to his decease,
How dare we keep our Christmas Eve;

Which brings no more a welcome guest
  To enrich the threshold of the night
  With showered largess of delight
In dance and song and game and jest?

Yet go, and while the holly boughs
  Entwine the cold baptismal font,
  Make one wreath more for Use and Wont,
That guard the portals of the house;

Old sisters of a day gone by,
  Gray nurses, loving nothing new;
  Why should they miss their yearly due
Before their time? They too will die.

30

With trembling fingers did we weave
  The holly round the Christmas hearth;
  A rainy cloud possessed the earth,
And sadly fell our Christmas Eve.

At our old pastimes in the hall
  We gamboled, making vain pretense
  Of gladness, with an awful sense
Of one mute Shadow watching all.

We paused. The winds were in the beech;
  We heard them sweep the winter land;
  And in a circle hand-in-hand
Sat silent, looking each at each.

Then echo-like our voices rang;
   We sung, though every eye was dim,
   A merry song we sang with him
Last year; impetuously we sang.

We ceased; a gentler feeling crept
   Upon us: surely rest is meet.
   "They rest," we said, "their sleep is sweet,"
And silence followed, and we wept.

Our voices took a higher range;
    Once more we sang: "They do not die
    Nor lose their mortal sympathy,
Nor change to us, although they change;

"Rapt from the fickle and the frail
    With gathered power, yet the same,
    Pierces the keen seraphic flame
From orb to orb, from veil to veil."

Rise, happy morn, rise, holy morn,
    Draw forth the cheerful day from night;
    O Father, touch the east, and light
The light that shone when hope was born.

78

Again at Christmas did we weave
    The holly round the Christmas hearth;
    The silent snow possessed the earth;
And calmly fell our Christmas Eve.

The yule-log sparkled keen with frost,
    No wing of wind the region swept,
    But over all things brooding slept
The quiet sense of something lost.

As in the winters left behind,
    Again our ancient games had place,
    The mimic picture's breathing grace,
And dance and song and hoodman-blind.

Who showed a token of distress?
    No single tear, no mark of pain:
    O sorrow, then can sorrow wane?
O grief, can grief be changed to less?

O last regret, regret can die!
    No—mixed with all this mystic frame,
    Her deep relations are the same,
But with long use her tears are dry.

105

Tonight ungathered let us leave
  This laurel, let this holly stand;
  We live within the stranger's land,
And strangely falls our Christmas Eve.

Our father's dust is left alone
  And silent under other snows;
  There in due time the woodbine blows,
The violet comes, but we are gone.

No more shall wayward grief abuse
  The genial hour with mask and mime;
  For change of place, like growth of time,
Has broke the bond of dying use.

Let cares that petty shadows cast,
  By which our lives are chiefly proved,
  A little spare the night I loved,
And hold it solemn to the past.

But let no footstep beat the floor,
  Nor bowl of wassail mantel warm;
  For who would keep an ancient form
Through which the spirit breathes no more?

Be neither song, nor game, nor feast;
  Nor harp be touched, nor flute be blown;
  No dance, no motion, save alone
What lightens in the lucid East

Of rising worlds by yonder wood.
  Long sleeps the summer in the seed;
  Run out your measured arcs, and lead
The closing cycle rich in good.

106

Ring out, wild bells, to the wild sky,
  The flying cloud, the frosty light;
  The year is dying in the night;
Ring out, wild bells, and let him die.

Ring out the old, ring in the new,
  Ring, happy bells, across the snow;
  The year is going, let him go;
Ring out the false, ring in the true.

Ring out the grief that saps the mind,
  For those that here we see no more;
  Ring out the feud of rich and poor,
Ring in redress to all mankind.

Ring out a slowly dying cause,
  And ancient forms of party strife;
  Ring in the nobler modes of life,
With sweeter manners, purer laws.

Ring out the want, the care, the sin,
  The faithless coldness of the times;
  Ring out, ring out my mournful rimes,
But ring the fuller minstrel in.

Ring out false pride in place and blood,
  The civic slander and the spite;
  Ring in the love of truth and right,
Ring in the common love of good.

Ring out old shapes of foul disease;
  Ring out the narrowing lust of gold;
  Ring out the thousand wars of old,
Ring in the thousand years of peace.

Ring in the valiant man and free,
  The larger heart, the kindlier hand;
  Ring out the darkness of the land,
Ring in the Christ that is to be.

107
It is the day when he was born,
  A bitter day that early sank
  Behind a purple-frosty bank
Of vapor, leaving night forlorn.

The time admits not flowers or leaves
　　To deck the banquet. Fiercely flies
　　The blast of North and East, and ice
Makes daggers at the sharpened eaves,

And bristles all the brakes and thorns
　　To yon hard crescent, as she hangs
　　Above the wood which grides and clangs
Its leafless ribs and iron horns

Together, in the drifts that pass
　　To darken on the rolling brine
　　That breaks the coast. But fetch the wine,
Arrange the board and brim the glass;

Bring in great logs and let them lie,
　　To make a solid core of heat;
　　Be cheerful-minded, talk and treat
Of all things even as he were by;

We keep the day. With festal cheer,
　　With books and music, surely we
　　Will drink to him, whate'er he be,
And sing the songs he loved to hear.

DOCTOR BIRCH AND HIS YOUNG FRIENDS

WILLIAM MAKEPEACE THACKERAY

Epilogue from CHRISTMAS BOOKS OF M. A. TITMARSH

The play is done; the curtain drops,
Slow falling, to the prompter's bell:
A moment yet the actor stops,
And looks around, to say farewell.
It is an irksome word and task;
And when he's laughed and said his say,
He shows, as he removes the mask,
A face that's anything but gay.

One word, ere yet the evening ends,
Let's close it with a parting rhyme,
And pledge a hand to all young friends,
As fits the merry Christmas time.
On life's wide scene you, too, have parts,
That Fate ere long shall bid you play;
Good-night! with honest gentle hearts
A kindly greeting go alway!

Good-night! I'd say the griefs, the joys,
Just hinted in this mimic page,
The triumphs and defeats of boys,
Are but repeated in our age.

I'd say, your woes were not less keen,
Your hopes more vain, than those of men;
Your pangs or pleasures of fifteen,
At forty-five played o'er again.

I'd say, we suffer and we strive
Not less nor more as men than boys;
With grizzled beards at forty-five,
As erst at twelve, in corduroys.
And if, in time of sacred youth,
We learned at home to love and pray,
Pray Heaven, that early love and truth
May never wholly pass away.

And in the world, as in the school,
I'd say, how fate may change and shift;
The prize be sometimes with the fool,
The race not always to the swift.
The strong may yield, the good may fall,
The great man be a vulgar clown,
The knave be lifted over all,
The kind cast pitilessly down.

Who knows the inscrutable design?
Blessed be He who took and gave:
Why should your mother, Charles, not mine,
Be weeping at her darling's grave?
We bow to Heaven that will'd it so,
That darkly rules the fate of all,
That sends the respite or the blow,
That's free to give or to recall.

This crowns his feast with wine and wit:
Who brought him to that mirth and state?
His betters, see, below him sit,
Or hunger hopeless at the gate.
Who bade the mud from Dives's wheel
To spurn the rags of Lazarus?
Come, brother, in that dust we'll kneel,
Confessing Heaven that ruled it thus.

So each shall mourn in life's advance,
Dear hopes, dear friends, untimely killed;
Shall grieve for many a forfeit chance,
A longing passion unfulfilled.
Amen: whatever Fate be sent,—
Pray God the heart may kindly glow,
Although the head with cares be bent,
And whitened with the winter snow.

Come wealth or want, come good or ill,
Let young and old accept their part,
And bow before the Awful Will,
And bear it with an honest heart.
Who misses, or who wins the prize?
Go, lose or conquer as you can:
But if you fail, or if you rise,
Be each, pray God, a gentleman,

A gentleman, or old or young
(Bear kindly with my humble lays):
The sacred chorus first was sung
Upon the first of Christmas-days.
The shepherds heard it overhead—
The joyful angels raised it then:
Glory to Heaven on high, it said,
And peace on earth to gentle men.

My song, save this, is little worth;
I lay the weary pen aside,
And wish you health, and love, and mirth,
As fits the solemn Christmas tide.
As fits the holy Christmas birth,
Be this, good friends, our carol still—
Be peace on earth, be peace on earth,
To men of gentle will.

CONVERSATION ABOUT CHRISTMAS

DYLAN THOMAS

From a BBC talk, 1945

SMALL BOY: Years and years ago, when you were a boy . . .

SELF: When there were wolves in Wales, and birds the colour of red-flannel petticoats whisked past the harp-shaped hills, when we sang and wallowed all night and day in caves that smelt like Sunday afternoons in damp front farmhouse parlours, and chased, with the jawbones of deacons, the English and the bears . . .

SMALL BOY: You are not so old as Mr. Beynon Number Twenty-Two who can remember when there were no motors. Years and years ago, when you were a boy . . .

SELF: Oh, before the motor even, before the wheel, before the duchess-faced horse, when we rode the daft and happy hills bareback . . .

SMALL BOY: You're not so daft as Mrs. Griffiths up the street, who says she puts her ear under the water in the reservoir and listens to the fish talk Welsh. When you were a boy, what was Christmas like?

SELF: It snowed.

SMALL BOY: It snowed last year, too. I made a snowman and my brother knocked it down and I knocked my brother down and then we had tea.

SELF: But that was not the same snow. Our snow was not only shaken in whitewash buckets down the sky. I think it came shawling out of the ground and swam and drifted out of the arms and hands and bodies of the trees; snow grew overnight on the roofs of the houses like a pure and grandfather moss, minutely ivied the walls, and settled on the postman, opening the gate, like a dumb, numb thunderstorm of white, torn Christmas cards.

SMALL BOY: Were there postmen, then, too?

SELF: With sprinkling eyes and wind-cherried noses, on spread, frozen feet they crunched up to the doors and mittened on them manfully. But all that the children could hear was a ringing of bells.

SMALL BOY: You mean that the postman went rat-a-tat-tat and the doors rang?

SELF: The bells that the children could hear were inside them.

SMALL BOY: I only hear thunder sometimes, never bells.

SELF: There were church bells, too.

SMALL BOY: Inside them?

SELF: No, no, no, in the bat-black, snow-white belfries, tugged by bishops and storks. And they rang their tidings over the bandaged town, over the frozen foam of the powder and ice-cream hills, over the crackling sea. It seemed that all the churches boomed, for joy, under my window; and the weathercocks crew for Christmas, on our fence.

SMALL BOY: Get back to the postmen.

SELF: They were just ordinary postmen, fond of walking, and dogs, and Christmas, and the snow. They knocked on the doors with blue knuckles . . .

SMALL BOY: Ours has got a black knocker . . .

SELF: And then they stood on the white welcome mat in the little, drifted porches, and clapped their hands together, and huffed and puffed, making ghosts with their breath, and jogged from foot to foot like small boys wanting to go out.

SMALL BOY: And then the Presents?

SELF: And then the Presents, after the Christmas box. And the cold postman, with a rose on his button-nose, tingled down the teatray-slithered run of the chilly glinting hill. He went in his ice-bound boots like a man on fishmonger's slabs. He wagged his bag like a frozen camel's hump, dizzily turned the corner on one foot, and, by God, he was gone.

SMALL BOY: Get back to the Presents.

SELF: There were the Useful Presents: engulfing mufflers of the old coach days, and mittens made for giant sloths; zebra scarves of a substance like silky gum that could be tug-o'-warred down to the goloshes; blinding tam-o'-shanters like patchwork tea-cosies, and bunny-scutted busbies and balaclavas for victims of head-shrinking tribes; from aunts who always wore wool next to the skin, there were moustached and rasping vests that made you wonder why the aunties had any skin left at all; and once I had a little crocheted nosebag from an aunt now, alas, no longer whinnying with us. And pictureless books in which small boys, though warned, with quotations, not to, *would* skate on Farmer Garge's pond, and did, and drowned; and books that told me everything about the wasp, except why.

SMALL BOY: Get on to the Useless Presents.

SELF: On Christmas Eve I hung at the foot of my bed Bessie Bunter's black stocking, and always, I said, I would stay awake all the moonlit, snowlit night to hear the roof-alighting reindeer and see the hollied boot descend through soot. But soon the sand of the snow drifted into my eyes, and, though I stared towards the fireplace and around the flickering room where the black sack-like stocking hung, I was asleep before the chimney trembled and the room was red and white with Christmas. But in the morning, though no snow melted on the bedroom floor, the stocking bulged and brimmed: press it, it squeaked like a mouse-in-a-box; it smelt of tangerine; a furry arm lolled over, like the arm of a kangaroo out of its mother's belly; squeeze it hard in the middle, and something squelched; squeeze it again—squelch again. Look out of the frost-scribbled window: on the great loneliness of the small hill, a blackbird was silent in the snow.

SMALL BOY: Were there any sweets?

SELF: Of course there were sweets. It was the marshmallows that squelched. Hardboileds, toffee, fudge and allsorts, crunches, cracknels, humbugs, glaciers, and marzipan and butterwelsh for the Welsh. And troops of bright tin soldiers who, if they would not fight, could always run. And Snakes-and-Families and Happy Ladders. And Easy Hobbi-Games for Little Engineers, complete with Instructions. Oh, easy for Leonardo! And a whistle to make the dogs bark to wake up the old man next door to make him beat on the wall with his stick to shake our picture off the wall. And a packet of cigarettes: you put one in your mouth and you stood at the corner of the street and you waited for hours, in vain, for an old lady to scold you for smoking a cigarette and then, with a smirk, you ate it. And, last of all, in the toe of the stocking, sixpence like a silver corn. And then downstairs for breakfast under the balloons!

SMALL BOY: Were there Uncles, like in our house?

SELF: There are always Uncles at Christmas. The same Uncles. And on Christmas mornings, with dog-disturbing whistle and sugar fags, I would scour the swathed town for the news of the little world, and find always a dead bird by the white Bank or by the deserted swings: perhaps a robin, all but one of his fires out, and that fire still burning on his breast. Men and women wading and scooping back from church or chapel, with tap-room noses and wind-smacked cheeks, all albinos, huddled their stiff black jarring feathers against the irreligious snow. Mistletoe hung from the gas in all the front parlours; there was sherry and walnuts and bottled beer and crackers by the dessertspoons; and cats in their fur-abouts watched the fires; and the high-heaped fires crackled and spat, all ready for the chestnuts and the mulling pokers. Some few large men sat in the front parlours, without their collars, Uncles almost certainly, trying their new cigars, holding them out judiciously at arm's-length, returning them to their mouths, coughing, then holding them out again as though waiting for the explosion; and some few small aunts, not wanted in the kitchen, nor anywhere else for that matter, sat on the very edges of their chairs, poised and brittle, afraid to break, like faded cups and saucers. Not many those mornings trod the piling streets: an old man always, fawn-bowlered, yellow-gloved, and, at this time of year, with spats of snow, would take his constitutional to the white bowling-green, and back, as he would take it wet or fine on Christmas Day or Doomsday; sometimes two hale young men, with big pipes blazing, no overcoats, and wind-blown scarves, would trudge, unspeaking, down to the forlorn sea, to work up an appetite, to blow away the fumes, who knows, to walk into the waves until nothing of them was left but the two curling smoke clouds of their inextinguishable briars.

SMALL BOY: Why didn't you go home for Christmas dinner?

SELF: Oh, but I did, I always did. I would be slap-dashing home, the gravy smell of the dinners of others, the bird smell, the brandy, the pudding and mince, weaving up my nostrils, when out of a snow-clogged side-lane would come a boy the spit of myself, with a pink-tipped cigarette and the violet past of a black eye, cocky as a bullfinch, leering all to himself. I hated him on sight and sound, and would be about to put my dog-whistle to my lips and blow him off the face of Christmas when suddenly he, with a violet wink, put *his* whistle to *his* lips and blew so stridently, so high, so exquisitely loud, that gobbling faces, their cheeks bulged with goose, would press against their tinselled windows, the whole length of the white echoing street.

SMALL BOY: What did you have for dinner?

SELF: Turkey, and blazing pudding.

SMALL BOY: Was it nice?

SELF: It was not made on earth.

SMALL BOY: What did you do after dinner?

SELF: The Uncles sat in front of the fire, took off their collars, loosened all buttons, put their large moist hands over their watch-chains, groaned a little, and slept. Mothers, aunts, and sisters scuttled to and fro, bearing tureens. The dog was sick. Auntie Beattie had to have three aspirins, but Auntie Hannah, who liked port, stood in the middle of the snowbound backyard, singing like a big-bosomed thrush. I would blow up balloons to see how big they would blow up to; and, when they burst, which they all did, the Uncles jumped and rumbled. In the rich and heavy afternoon, the Uncles breathing like dolphins and the snow descending, I would sit in the front room, among festoons and Chinese lanterns, and nibble at dates, and try to make a model man-o'-war, following the Instructions for Little Engineers, and produce what might be mistaken for a sea-going tram. And then, at Christmas tea, the recovered Uncles would be jolly over their mince-pies; and the great iced cake loomed in the centre of the table like a marble grave. Auntie Hannah laced her tea with rum, because it was only once a year. And in the evening, there was Music. An uncle played the fiddle, a cousin sang Cherry Ripe, and another uncle sang Drake's Drum. It was very warm in the little house. Auntie Hannah, who had got on to the parsnip wine, sang a song about Rejected Love, and Bleeding Hearts, and Death, and then another in which she said that her Heart was like a Bird's Nest; and then everybody laughed again, and then I went to bed. Looking through my bedroom window, out into the moonlight and the flying, unending, smoke-coloured snow, I could see the lights in the windows of all the other houses on our hill, and hear the music rising from them up the long, steadily falling night. I turned the gas down, I got into bed. I said some words to the close and holy darkness, and then I slept.

SMALL BOY: But it all sounds like an ordinary Christmas.

SELF: It was.

SMALL BOY: But Christmas when you were a boy wasn't any different to Christmas now.

SELF: It was, it was.

SMALL BOY: Why was Christmas different then?

SELF: I mustn't tell you.

SMALL BOY: Why mustn't you tell me? Why is Christmas different for me?

SELF: I mustn't tell you.

SMALL BOY: Why can't Christmas be the same for me as it was for you when you were a boy?

SELF: I mustn't tell you. I mustn't tell you because it is Christmas now.

A WINTER WALK

HENRY DAVID THOREAU

The wind has gently murmured through the blinds, or puffed with feathery softness against the windows, and occasionally sighed like a summer zephyr lifting the leaves along, the livelong night. The meadow mouse has slept in his snug gallery in the sod, the owl has sat in a hollow tree in the depth of the swamp, the rabbit, the squirrel, and the fox have all been housed. The watch-dog has lain quiet on the hearth, and the cattle have stood silent in their stalls. The earth itself has slept, as it were its first, not its last sleep, save when some street sign or woodhouse door has faintly creaked upon its hinge, cheering forlorn nature at her midnight work—the only sound awake 'twixt Venus and Mars—advertising us of a remote inward warmth, a divine cheer and fellowship, where gods are met together, but where it is very bleak for men to stand. But while the earth has slumbered, all the air has been alive with feathery flakes descending, as if some northern Ceres reigned, showering her silvery grain over all the fields.

We sleep, and at length awake to the still reality of a winter morning. The snow lies warm as cotton or down upon the window sill; the broadened sash and frosted panes admit a dim and private light, which enhances the snug cheer within. The stillness of the morning is impressive. The floor creaks under our feet as we move toward the window to look abroad through some clear space over the fields. We see the roofs stand under their snow burden. From the eaves and fences hang stalactites of snow, and in the yard stand stalagmites covering some concealed core. The trees and shrubs rear white arms to the sky on every side; and where were walls and fences, we see fantastic forms stretching in frolic gambols across the dusky landscape, as if Nature had strewn her fresh designs over the fields by night as models for man's art.

Silently we unlatch the door, letting the drift fall in, and step abroad to face the cutting air. Already the stars have lost some of their sparkle, and a dull, leaden mist skirts the horizon. A lurid brazen light in the east proclaims the approach of day, while the western landscape is dim and spectral still, and clothed in a somber Tartarean light, like the shadowy realms. They are Infernal sounds only that you hear—the crowing of cocks, the barking of dogs, the chopping of wood, the lowing of kine, all seem to come from Pluto's barnyard and beyond the Styx—not for any melancholy they suggest, but their twilight bustle is too solemn and mysterious for earth. The recent tracks of the fox or otter, in the yard, remind us that each hour of the night is crowded with events, and the primeval nature is still working and making tracks in the snow. Opening the gate, we tread briskly along the lone country road, crunching the dry and crisped snow under our feet, or aroused by the sharp, clear creak of the wood sled, just starting for the distant market, from the early farmer's door, where it has lain the summer long, dreaming amid the chips and stubble; while far through the drifts and powdered windows we see the farmer's early candle, like a paled star, emitting a lonely beam, as if some severe virtue were at its matins there. And one by one the smokes begin to ascend from the chimneys amid the trees and snows.

> The sluggish smoke curls up from some deep dell,
> The stiffened air exploring in the dawn,
> And making slow acquaintance with the day
> Delaying now upon its heavenward course,
> In wreathèd loiterings dallying with itself,
> With as uncertain purpose and slow deed
> As its half-awakened master by the hearth,
> Whose mind still slumbering and sluggish thoughts
> Have not yet swept into the onward current
> Of the new day—and now it streams afar,
> The while the chopper goes with step direct,
> And mind intent to swing the early axe.
> First in the dusky dawn he sends abroad
> His early scout, his emissary, smoke,
> The earliest, latest pilgrim from the roof,
> To feel the frosty air, inform the day;
> And while he crouches still beside the hearth,
> Nor musters courage to unbar the door,
> It has gone down the glen with the light wind,

And o'er the plain unfurled its venturous wreath,
Draped the treetops, loitered upon the hill,
And warmed the pinions of the early bird;
And now, perchance, high in the crispy air,
Has caught sight of the day o'er the earth's edge,
And greets its master's eye at his low door,
As some refulgent cloud in the upper sky.

MERRY CHRISTMAS

JAMES THURBER

I t didn't surprise me to learn that Americans send out a billion and a half Christmas cards every year. That would have been my guess, give or take a quarter of a billion. Missing by 250 million is coming close nowayears, for what used to be called astronomical figures have now become the figures of earth. I am no longer staggered by the massive, but I can still be shaken by the minor human factors involved in magnificent statistics. A national budget of 71 thousand million is comprehensible to students of our warlike species, but who is to account for the rising sales of vodka in this nation—from 108,000 bottles in 1946 to 32,500,000 bottles in 1956? The complexities of federal debt and personal drinking are beyond my grasp, but I think I understand the Christmas card situation, or crisis.

It disturbed me to estimate that two-fifths of the 1956 Christmas cards, or six hundred million, were received by people the senders barely knew and could count only as the most casual of acquaintances, and that approximately thirty million recipients were persons the senders had met only once, in a bar, on a West Indies cruise, at a doctor's office, or while fighting a grass fire in Westchester. The people I get Christmas cards from every year include a Jugoslav violist I met on the *Leviathan* in 1925, the doorman of a restaurant in Soho, a West Virginia taxi driver who is writing the biography of General Beauregard, the young woman who cured my hiccoughs at Dave Chasen's in 1939 (she twisted the little finger of my left hand and made me say Garbo backward), innumerable people who know what to do about my eye and were kind enough to tell me so in hotel lobbies and between the acts of plays, seven dog owners who told me at Tim's or Bleeck's that they have a dog exactly like the one I draw, and a lovely stranger in one of these saloons who snarled at a proud dog owner: "The only dog that looks like the dog this guy draws is the dog this guy draws."

The fifteen hundred million annual Yuletide greetings are the stamp and sign of the American character. We are a genial race, as neighborly abroad as at home, fond of perpetuating the chance encounter, the golden hour, the unique experience, the prewar vacation. "I think this calls for a drink" has long been one of our national slogans. Strangers take turns ordering rounds because of a shared admiration or disdain, a suddenly discovered mutual friend in Syracuse, the same college fraternity, a similar addiction to barracuda fishing. A great and lasting friendship rarely results, but the wife of each man adds the other's name to her Christmas list. The American woman who has been married ten years or longer, at least the ones I know, sends out about two hundred Christmas cards a year, many of them to persons on the almost forgotten fringe of friendship.

I had the good luck to be present one December afternoon in the living room of a couple I know just as the mail arrived. The wife asked if we minded her glancing at the cards, but she had already read one. "My God!" she exclaimed. "The Spragues are still together! They were this really charming couple we met in Jamaica eight years ago. He had been a flier, I think, and had got banged up, and then he met Marcia—I think her name was Marcia." She glanced at the card again and said, "Yes, Marcia. Well, Philip was on leave in Bermuda and he saw her riding by in a carriage and simply knew she was the girl, although he had never laid eyes on her before in his life, so he ran out into the street and jumped up on the carriage step, and said, 'I'm going to marry you!' Would you believe it, he didn't even tell her his name, and of course he didn't know her from Adam—or Eve, I guess I ought to say—and they were married. They fell in love and got married in Bermuda. Her family was terribly opposed to it, of course, and so was his when they found out about hers, but they went right ahead anyway. It was the most romantic thing I ever heard of in my life. This was four or five years before we met them, and—"

"Why are you so astonished that they are still together?" I asked.

"Because their meeting was a kind of third-act curtain," said my friend's husband. "Boy meets girl, boy gets girl—as simple as that. All that's left is boy loses girl. Who the hell are Bert and Mandy?" he asked, studying a Christmas card.

Another greeting card category consists of those persons who send out photographs of their families every year. In the same mail that brought the greetings from Marcia and Philip, my friend found such a conversation piece. "My God, Lida is enormous!" she exclaimed. I don't know why women want to record each year, for two or three hundred people to see, the ravages wrought upon them, their mates, and their progeny by the artillery of time, but between five and seven per cent of Christmas cards, at a rough estimate, are family groups, and even the most charitable recipient studies them for little signs of dissolution or derangement. Nothing cheers a woman more, I am afraid, than the proof that another woman is letting herself go, or has lost control of her figure, or is clearly driving her husband crazy, or is obviously drinking more than is good for her, or still doesn't know what to wear. Middle-aged husbands in such photographs are often described as looking "young enough to be her son," but they don't always escape so easily, and a couple opening envelopes in the season of mercy and good will sometimes handle a male friend or acquaintance rather sharply. "Good Lord!" the wife will say. "Frank looks like a sex-crazed shotgun slayer, doesn't he?" "Not to me," the husband may reply. "To me he looks more like a Wilkes-Barre dentist who is being sought by the police in connection with the disappearance of a choir singer."

Anyone who undertakes a comparative analysis of a billion and a half Christmas cards is certain to lose his way once in a while, and I now find myself up against more categories than I can handle. Somewhere in that vast tonnage of cardboard, for example, are—I am just guessing now—three hundred million cards from firms, companies, corporations, corner stores, and other tradespeople. In the old days they sent out calendars for the New Year, and skipped Christmas, but I figure they are now responsible for about a fifth of the deluge. Still another category includes inns, bars, restaurants, institutions, councils, committees, leagues, and other organizations. One of my own 1956 cards came from the Art Department of Immaculate Heart College, in Los Angeles, whose point of contact with me has eluded my memory. A certain detective agency used to send me a laconic word every December, but last year, for some disturbing reason, I was struck off the agency's list. I don't know how I got on it in the first place, since I have never employed a private investigator to shadow anybody, but it may be that I was one of the shadowed. The agency's slogan is "When we follow him he stays followed," and its card was invariably addressed to "Mr. James Ferber." This hint of alias added a creepy note to the holidays, and, curiously enough, the sudden silence has had the same effect. A man who is disturbed when he hears from a detective agency, and when he doesn't, may be put down, I suppose, as a natural phenomenon of our nervous era.

I suddenly began wondering, in one of my onsets of panic, what becomes of all these cards. The lady in my house who adds two hundred items to the annual avalanche all by herself calmed my anxiety by telling me that most of them get burned. Later, I found out, to my dismay, that this is not actually true. There are at least nine million little girls who consider Christmas cards too beautiful to burn, and carefully preserve them. One mother told me that her garage contains fifteen large cartons filled with old Christmas cards. This, I am glad to say, is no problem of mine, but there is a major general somewhere who may have to deal with it one of these years if the accumulation becomes a national menace, hampering the movement of troops.

Ninety per cent of women employ the annual greeting as a means of fending off a more frequent correspondence. One woman admitted to me that she holds at least a dozen friends at arm's, or year's, length by turning greeting cards into a kind of annual letter. The most a man will consent to write on a Christmas card is "Hi, boy!" or "Keep pitching," but a wife often manages several hundred words. These words, in most instances, have a way of dwindling with the march of the decades, until they become highly concentrated and even cryptic, such as "Will you ever forget that ox bice cake?" or "George says to tell Jim to look out for the 36." Thus the terrible flux of December mail is made up, in considerable part, of the forgotten and the meaningless. The money spent on all these useless cryptograms would benefit some worthy cause by at least three million dollars.

The sex behind most of the billion and a half Christmas cards is, of course, the female. I should judge that about 75,000,000 cards are received annually by women from former cooks, secretaries, and hairdressers, the formerness of some of them going back as far as 1924. It is not always easy for even the most experienced woman card sender to tell an ex-hairdresser from someone she met on a night of high wind and Bacardi at Cambridge Beaches in Bermuda. The late John McNulty once solved this for my own wife by saying, "All hairdressers are named Dolores." The wonderful McNulty's gift of inspired oversimplification, like his many other gifts, is sorely missed by hundreds of us. McNulty and I, both anti-card men, never exchanged Christmas greetings, except in person or on the phone. There was a time when I drew my own Christmas cards, but I gave it up for good after 1937. In that year I had drawn what purported to be a little girl all agape and enchanted in front of a strangely ornamented Christmas tree. The cards were printed in Paris and mailed to me, two hundred of them, in Italy. We were spending Christmas in Naples. The cards were held up at the border by the Italian authorities, agents of Mussolini who suspected everything, and returned to Paris. "I should think," commented an English friend of mine, "that two hundred copies of any drawing of yours might well give the authorities pause."

One couple, to conclude this survey on an eerie note, had sent out the same engraved Christmas card every year. Last time "From John and Joan" had undergone a little change. Joan had crossed out "John and." Her friends wonder just how many of these cheery greetings the predeceased Joan has left. So passed one husband, with only a pencil stroke to mark his going. Peace on earth, good will to women.

CHRISTMAS AT CLAREMONT

QUEEN VICTORIA'S JOURNAL

Queen Victoria's reign began in 1837 and lasted until 1901. At the time of her accession she was eighteen years old

Claremont, December 24, 1836

I awoke after 7 and got up at 8. After 9 breakfasted, at a little after 10 we left Kensington with dearest Lehzen, Lady Conroy and— Dashy! and reached Claremont at a quarter to 12. Played and sang. At 2 dearest Lehzen, Victoire and I went out, and came home at 20 minutes past 8. No one was stirring about the gipsy encampment except George, which I was sorry for as I was anxious to know how our poor friends were, after this bitterly cold night. Played and sang. Received from dearest, best Lehzen as a Christmas box two lovely little Dresden China figures, two pair of lovely little chased gold buttons, a small lovely button with an angel's head which she used to wear herself, and a pretty music book; from good Louis a beautiful piece of Persian stuff for an album; and from Victoire and Emily Gardiner a small box worked by themselves. Wrote my journal, went down to arrange Mamma's table for her. At 6 we dined. Mr. Edward Byrne and Mr. Conroy stayed here. Mr. Byng is going to stay here a night or two. Very soon after dinner Mamma sent for us into the gallery, where all the things were arranged on different tables. From my dear Mamma I received a beautiful massive gold buckle in the shape of two serpents; a lovely little delicate gold chain with turquoise clasp; a lovely coloured sketch of dearest Aunt Louise by Partridge copied from the picture he brought and so like her; 3 beautiful drawings by Munn, one lovely seaview by Peser and one cattle piece by Cooper (all coloured), 3 prints, a book called Finden's Tableau, Heath's Picturesque Annual, Ireland; both these are very pretty; Friendship's offering and the English Annual for 1837, the Holy Land illustrated beautifully, two handkerchiefs, a very pretty black satin apron trimmed with red velvet, and two almanacks. I am very thankful to my dear Mamma for all these very pretty things. From dear Uncle Leopold a beautiful turquoise ring; from the Queen a fine piece of Indian gold tissue, and from Sir J. Conroy a print. I gave my dear Lehzen a green morocco jewel case, and the Picturesque Annual; Mamma gave her a shawl, a pair of turquoise earrings, an annual, and handkerchiefs. I then took Mamma to the Library where my humble table was arranged; I gave her a bracelet made of my hair, and the Keepsake, and Oriental Annual. I stayed up til eleven!

The Annual Crisis of Love

Loudon Wainwright

There comes a time for me on Christmas when the holiday changes suddenly, when the event—like a fall season—is past its peak of color and excitement and the day begins to sink. The precise moment may vary, but it is most likely to arrive before the turkey is done and when the litter of gift-giving remains. At our house we burn this gaudy trash in the fireplace, and I always feel a certain reluctance at throwing the long strands of red ribbon and the crumpled pieces of shiny wrapping paper into the flames. Somehow the best, often the most personal part of giving curls to ash in the fire, and the gifts themselves—the gloves, games, toys, ties, the what-is-it from Aunt Betty, all placed in piles according to ownership—take on the anonymity of loot. At such moments I am the victim of a curious mixture of disappointment (what made her think I would like that terrible color?) and guilt (just think of all the people who really *need* these things), and I begin to look forward eagerly to the wine. I wish, in short, that Christmas had never come.

But I have weathered too many Christmases to be surprised at the letdown. And I don't really think it can be attributed to the usual complaints about the season. Indeed, there is crass commercialization, the greeting cards are just awful, and the shabby Santa Clauses come out too soon. There is, too, the hysteria of shopping in time with the amplified tinkling of sleighbells, and there is even a limit to the number of times one can tearfully respond to those crutch-propelled twins of Christmas, Tiny Tim and Amahl. But these are all mere nitpicks, and I always hope that—this year—the magic will not pall. Still, it does, and I think the reason for it rests in the fact that Christmas is not so much a holiday as it is an annual crisis of love. We must somewhere suffer its effects.

That it is just such a crisis seems obvious when one considers the sheer emotional baggage of the day. It is a frightfully heavy load, and it increases with the years. Among other things our expectations for our own behavior seem extraordinarily high at this time. We expect ourselves to be cheerful and generous on Christmas even though we may have been getting no practice in these areas for the rest of the year. Under such pressure, it is no surprise to me to hear that reformed drunks have celebrated Christmas by plunging off the wagon and that Yuletide gaiety is sometimes marred by bitter, even violent, family quarrels. With expectations so high, it is almost impossible not to fail, at least a bit.

The most successful Christmases are enjoyed by people three or four years old. They understand what's going on well enough to look forward to something big and juicy, everyone they love is offering them lots of attention and the presents are a grab bag of dazzling surprises. If little things go wrong around them, they don't notice. After those early years it gets tougher: the disappointments of Christmas, disappointments of love, become tangible.

I can remember—or think I can—the year Santa Claus was unfrocked. Out for a walk on a bitter-cold December 24th afternoon, I *saw* him, the sled, the reindeer, the whole outfit in a bunch of clouds near the horizon where the sun was setting. Thrilled by this hallucination of hope, I must have slept badly, for I woke with the door to my bedroom being softly opened. This did not alarm me, because at our place Santa Claus was expected to provide room service with the stockings while he stacked everything else under the tree downstairs. When my parents crept into the room with the stocking, I pretended to be asleep. My disappointment at this sudden understanding of the huge Christmas hoax was very sharp. My father and mother—not Santa Claus—were the frauds.

On a much later occasion I bought a bicycle for one of my sons, who had years earlier survived the Santa Claus crisis. I had found a very good second-hand one in a bike shop and, congratulating myself on a big saving, repainted it. Naturally, the boy was instantly aware that his present had a past, and though he thanked me gamely, it was clear he was astounded that I thought he would ever be interested in good, safe transportation.

"It's just what I wanted" seems to me a hideously ambiguous expression of Christmas gratitude. It covers a multitude of meanings, and it is especially inadequate when it reflects the truth. As a matter of fact, one of the hardest things in the Christmas crisis of love can be giving or getting something that is really wanted. To see a member of my family actually moved by something I have given fills me with a feeling approaching alarm. I want to confess: "Oh, it's not so good. It's not nearly as nice as the thing I should have got you. It doesn't tell you at all how I feel." And my own gratefulness at finding exactly the right thing under the wrappings is laced sometimes with a kind of chagrin. On second thought, that feeling seems to say, why should I have what I want? I should not be loved that much.

Still, I would not suggest changing any of it. Families need the annual Christmas crisis. More than any other time it forces people to expose themselves and their feelings to those who are the very closest. If there is too much tension in it, too bad. At least we come to know each other better. More often than not, the tension is a healthy one, and at the day's end—stuffed, sated, perhaps a little disappointed—we have nonetheless connected.

For the letdown period some will find it easing to read the old story from Luke; others might prefer to go outside and see if that toy airplane will really fly. Creature of the habits of a lifetime, I will do next week as I've always done and lurch through the festivities and duties leading up to the big day. My list of wants this year is small and can readily be tampered with: some Mozart records, some books and, if Santa listens, some longish socks. I've already started shopping for my family and I've discovered a splendid toy I cannot possibly buy. It is a stuffed baby elephant exactly the size of a real baby elephant and it costs $475. I'm sure my daughter will survive not having it—and I hope that the child who does get it will understand that it is being given with love.

THE DISTANT MUSIC
OF THE HOUNDS

E. B. WHITE

from THE SECOND TREE FROM THE CORNER

To perceive Christmas through its wrapping becomes more difficult with every year. There was a little device we noticed in one of the sporting-goods stores—a trumpet that hunters hold to their ears so that they can hear the distant music of the hounds. Something of the sort is needed now to hear the incredibly distant sound of Christmas in these times, through the dark, material woods that surround it. "Silent Night," canned and distributed in thundering repetition in the department stores, has become one of the greatest of all noisemakers, almost like the rattles and whistles of Election Night. We rode down on an escalator the other morning through the silent-nighting of the loudspeakers, and the man just in front of us was singing, "I'm gonna wash this store right outa my hair, I'm gonna wash this store . . ."

The miracle of Christmas is that, like the distant and very musical voice of the hound, it penetrates finally and becomes heard in the heart—over so many years, through so many cheap curtain-raisers. It is not destroyed even by all the arts and craftiness of the destroyers, having an essential simplicity that is everlasting and triumphant, at the end of confusion. We once went out at night with coon-hunters and we were aware that it was not so much the promise of the kill that took the men away from their warm homes and sent them through the cold shadowy woods, it was something more human, more mystical—something even simpler. It was the night, and the excitement of the note of the hound, first heard, then not heard. It was the natural world, seen at its best and most haunting, unlit except by stars, impenetrable except to the knowing and the sympathetic.

Christmas in this year of crisis must compete as never before with the dazzling complexity of man, whose tangential desires and ingenuities have created a world that gives any simple thing the look of obsolescence—as though there were something inherently foolish in what is simple, or natural. The human brain is about to turn certain functions over to an efficient substitute, and we hear of a robot that is now capable of handling the tedious details of psychoanalysis, so that the patient no longer need confide in a living doctor but can take his problems to a machine, which sifts everything and whose "brain" has selective power and the power of imagination. One thing leads to another. The machine that is imaginative will, we don't doubt, be heir to the ills of the imagination; one can already predict that the machine itself may become sick emotionally, from strain and tension, and be compelled at last to consult a medical man, whether of flesh or of steel. We have tended to assume that the machine and the human brain are in conflict. Now the fear is that they are indistinguishable. Man not only is notably busy himself but insists that the other animals follow his example. A new bee has been bred artificially, busier than the old bee.

So this day and this century proceed toward the absolutes of convenience, of complexity, and of speed, only occasionally holding up the little trumpet (as at Christmas time) to be reminded of the simplicities, and to hear the distant music of the hound. Man's inventions, directed always onward and upward, have an odd way of leading back to man himself, as a rabbit track in snow leads eventually to the rabbit. It is one of his more endearing qualities that man should think his tracks lead outward, toward something else, instead of back around the hill to where he has already been; and it is one of his persistent ambitions to leave earth entirely and travel by rocket into space, beyond the pull of gravity, and perhaps try another planet, as a pleasant change. He knows that the atomic age is capable of delivering a new package of energy; what he doesn't know is whether it will prove to be a blessing. This week, many will be reminded that no explosion of atoms generates so hopeful a light as the reflection of a star, seen appreciatively in a pasture pond. It is there we perceive Christmas—and the sheep quiet, and the world waiting.

An Editorial on Christmas Day, 1917

WIPERS TIMES

The World War I trench newspaper was published by British troops in Ypres, Belgium, site of some of the costliest battles of that war

H ere we are, knocking the Xmas number into shape again. It certainly does not seem to be twelve months since we were engaged on the same job, and yet quite a lot seems to have happened in the interval. By the time this number is published we shall have been running for two years and the first volume (containing first 15 numbers) should have made its bow to (let us hope) a kind and uncritical public. This Xmas we are more ambitious, and are making an effort to fill 20 pages, and the success of the venture must depend on how our wild appeals for copy are received by units. Of course it's quite likely that this war business may interfere with our plans and disturb the even tenor of our ways, so that our readers will understand, should the number contain less than the advertised 20 pages, that we have had to drop the pen for the sword, and go and liberate some more French villages, and thus fight the demon of oppression and barbarism, the last remaining relics of bestiality, brutality and Kultur. Should it come to this then indeed is the knell of Germanic despotism sounded, as the Sub-Editor is a holy terror at the end of a sword, and should once it be forced into his hand then Heaven help Hindenburg, as no one else could. However, there seems to be no alternative, and the Publisher has written home for a new pair of spurs and a mess canteen, so that he is evidently considering the necessity of taking an active part in the quarrel at no very distant date. However, one hopes that we may be allowed to have Xmas in peace. We cannot close without giving one and all the old greetings. Here's a Happy Xmas and New Year to you all, and may next Xmas see the whole damned business over. We are laying six to four on.

The Editor.

THE MAGI

WILLIAM BUTLER YEATS

Now as at all times I can see in the mind's eye,
In their stiff, painted clothes, the pale unsatisfied ones
Appear and disappear in the blue depth of the sky
With all their ancient faces like rain-beaten stones,
And all their helms of silver hovering side by side,
And all their eyes still fixed, hoping to find once more,
Being by Calvary's turbulence unsatisfied,
The uncontrollable mystery on the bestial floor.

Elsevier-Dutton Publishing Co., Inc., and Curtis Brown Ltd., London, on behalf of C. R. Milne: "A Hint for Next Christmas," from *If I May* by A. A. Milne. Copyright 1921 by E. P. Dutton & Co., Inc. Copyright renewed 1949 by A. A. Milne.

Harper & Row, Publishers, Inc.: "The Distant Music of the Hounds," from *The Second Tree From the Corner* by E. B. White. Copyright 1949 by E. B. White. This selection appeared originally in *The New Yorker*.

Harper & Row, Publishers, Inc., and Paul Gitlin, Attorney-in-Fact, Estate of Christopher Morley: "The Tree That Didn't Get Trimmed" and "The Christmas Tobacco," from *Essays* by Christopher Morley. Copyright 1919, 1925, 1927 by Christopher Morley. Published by J. B. Lippincott Company.

Harper & Row, Publishers, Inc., and Gordon Parks: Chapter 7 (retitled: "Celebration in Cherokee Flats") from *The Learning Tree,* by Gordon Parks. Copyright © 1963 by Gordon Parks.

Harper & Row, Publishers, Inc.: A selection (retitled: "A Brooklyn Christmas") from *A Tree Grows in Brooklyn,* by Betty Smith. Copyright 1943, 1947 by Betty Smith.

William Heinemann Ltd.: A selection from *Wipers Times,* Introduction, Notes and Glossary by Patrick Beaver.

Holt, Rinehart and Winston, Publishers, and Jonathan Cape Ltd.: "Christmas Trees," from *The Poetry of Robert Frost,* edited by Edward Connery Lathem. Copyright 1916, © 1969 by Holt, Rinehart and Winston. Copyright 1944 by Robert Frost.

Alfred A. Knopf, Inc.: A selection (retitled: "Joy in Freetown") from *The Taste of Country Cooking,* by Edna Lewis. Copyright © 1976 by Edna Lewis. A selection from *Christmas Story,* by H. L. Mencken. Copyright 1944, 1946 by H. L. Mencken. This selection appeared originally in *The New Yorker*.

Alfred A. Knopf, Inc., and Alistair Cooke: A selection from *Christmas Eve,* by Alistair Cooke. Copyright 1952 by Alistair Cooke.

Alfred A. Knopf, Inc., and Virago Limited: "December Night," from *Death Comes for the Archbishop* by Willa Cather. Copyright 1927 by Willa Cather and renewed 1955 by The Executors of the Estate of Willa Cather.

Alfred A. Knopf, Inc., and International Creative Management: "Christmas Is a Sad Season for the Poor," from *The Stories of John Cheever* by John Cheever. Copyright 1949 and renewed 1977 by John Cheever.

Liveright Publishing Corporation and Granada Publishing Limited: "little tree," from *Tulips & Chimneys* by E. E. Cummings. Copyright 1923, 1925, and renewed 1951, 1953 by E. E. Cummings. Copyright © 1973, 1976 by Nancy T. Andrews. Copyright © 1973, 1976 by George James Firmage.

Macmillan Publishing Co., Inc.: "Karma," from *Collected Poems* by Edwin Arlington Robinson. Copyright 1925 by Edwin Arlington Robinson, renewed 1953 by Ruth Nivison and Barbara R. Holt.

Macmillan Publishing Co., Inc., and Macmillan, London & Basingstoke: "The Oxen," from *The Complete Poems of Thomas Hardy,* edited by James Gibson, New York, Macmillan, 1978.

Macmillan Publishing Co., Inc., M. B. Yeats, Anne Yeats, A. P. Watt Ltd., and Macmillan London Limited: "The Magi," from *Collected Poems* by W. B. Yeats. Copyright 1916 by Macmillan Publishing Co., Inc., renewed 1944 by Bertha Georgie Yeats.

Harold Matson Company, Inc.: "Valley Forge: 24 December 1777," by F. Van Wyck Mason. Copyright 1946 by F. Van Wyck Mason.

Scott Meredith Literary Agency, Inc.: "What Was the Star of Bethlehem?" (retitled: "What Was the Christmas Star?"), by Arthur C. Clarke, from *Holiday* magazine, December, 1954. Copyright 1954 by Arthur C. Clarke.

William Morris Agency, Inc.: "An Iowa Christmas" (Chapter One), from *Prairie Christmas* by Paul Engle. Copyright © 1960 by Paul Engle.

John Neary: "Our Crafty Little Christmas," by John Neary, from *Long Island Newsday,* December 24, 1972. Copyright © 1972 by John Neary.

New Directions Publishing Corporation and David Higham Associates Limited: "Conversation about Christmas," from *A Prospect of the Sea* by Dylan Thomas. Copyright 1954 by New Directions Publishing Corporation.

The New York Times Company: "A Christmas Gift of Music, Long Ago," by Hans Fantel, from *The New York Times,* December 21, 1980. Copyright © 1980 by The New York Times Company.

The New Yorker: "Crisp New Bills for Mr. Teagle," by Frank Sullivan, from *The New Yorker,* December 21, 1935. Copyright 1935, © 1963 by The New Yorker Magazine, Inc.